EXPLORING AN ISLAMIC EMPIRE

The Institute of Ismaili Studies
Ismaili Heritage Series, 7
General Editor: Farhad Daftary

Previously published titles:

1. Paul E. Walker, *Abū Yaʿqūb al-Sijistānī: Intellectual Missionary* (1996)
2. Heinz Halm, *The Fatimids and their Traditions of Learning* (1997)
3. Paul E. Walker, *Ḥamīd al-Dīn al-Kirmānī: Ismaili Thought in the Age of al-Ḥākim* (1999)
4. Alice C. Hunsberger, *Nasir Khusraw, The Ruby of Badakhshan: A Portrait of the Persian Poet, Traveller and Philosopher* (2000)
5. Farouk Mitha, *Al-Ghazālī and the Ismailis: A Debate on Reason and Authority in Medieval Islam* (2001)
6. Ali S. Asani, *Ecstasy and Enlightenment: The Ismaili Devotional Literature of South Asia* (2002)

Exploring an Islamic Empire

Fatimid History and its Sources

Paul E. Walker

I.B.Tauris *Publishers*
LONDON • NEW YORK
in association with
The Institute of Ismaili Studies
LONDON

Published in 2002 by I.B.Tauris & Co Ltd
6 Salem Rd, London W2 4BU
175 Fifth Avenue, New York NY 10010
www.ibtauris.com

in association with The Institute of Ismaili Studies
42–44 Grosvenor Gardens, London SW1W 0EB
www.iis.ac.uk

In the United States of America and in Canada distributed by
St Martin's Press, 175 Fifth Avenue, New York NY 10010

ISBN 1 86064 692 1 HB
1 86064 875 4 PB

A full CIP record for this book is available from the British Library
A full CIP record for this book is available from the Library of Congress

Library of Congress catalog card: available

Typeset in ITC New Baskerville by Hepton Books, Oxford
Printed and bound in Great Britain by MPG Books Ltd, Bodmin

The Institute of Ismaili Studies

The Institute of Ismaili Studies was established in 1977 with the object of promoting scholarship and learning on Islam, in the historical as well as contemporary contexts, and a better understanding of its relationship with other societies and faiths.

The Institute's programmes encourage a perspective which is not confined to the theological and religious heritage of Islam, but seek to explore the relationship of religious ideas to broader dimensions of society and culture. The programmes thus encourage an interdisciplinary approach to the materials of Islamic history and thought. Particular attention is also given to issues of modernity that arise as Muslims seek to relate their heritage to the contemporary situation.

Within the Islamic tradition, the Institute's programmes seek to promote research on those areas which have, to date, received relatively little attention from scholars. These include the intellectual and literary expressions of Shiʿism in general, and Ismailism in particular.

In the context of Islamic societies, the Institute's programmes are informed by the full range and diversity of cultures in which Islam is practised today, from the Middle East, South and Central Asia and Africa to the industrialised societies of the West, thus taking into consideration the variety of contexts which shape the ideals, beliefs and practices of the faith.

These objectives are realised through concrete programmes and activities organised and implemented by various departments of the Institute. The Institute also collaborates periodically, on a programme-specific basis, with other institutions of learning in the United Kingdom and abroad.

The Institute's academic publications fall into several distinct and interrelated categories:

1. Occasional papers or essays addressing broad themes of the relationship between religion and society, with special reference to Islam.
2. Monographs exploring specific aspects of Islamic faith and culture, or the contributions of individual Muslim figures or writers.
3. Editions or translations of significant primary or secondary texts.
4. Translations of poetic or literary texts which illustrate the rich heritage of spiritual, devotional and symbolic expressions in Muslim history.
5. Works on Ismaili history and thought, and the relationship of the Ismailis to other traditions, communities and schools of thought in Islam.
6. Proceedings of conferences and seminars sponsored by the Institute.
7. Bibliographical works and catalogues which document manuscripts, printed texts and other source materials.

This book falls into category five listed above.

In facilitating these and other publications, the Institute's sole aim is to encourage original research and analysis of relevant issues. While every effort is made to ensure that the publications are of a high academic standard, there is naturally bound to be a diversity of views, ideas and interpretations. As such, the opinions expressed in these publications are to be understood as belonging to their authors alone.

Ismaili Heritage Series

A major Shi'i Muslim community, the Ismailis have had a long and eventful history. Scattered in many regions of the world, in Asia, Africa, Europe and North America, the Ismailis have elaborated diverse intellectual and literary traditions in different languages. On two occasions they had states of their own, the Fatimid caliphate and the Nizari State of Iran and Syria during the Alamut period. While pursuing particular religio-political aims, the leaders of these Ismaili states also variously encouraged intellectual, scientific, artistic and commercial activities.

Until recently, the Ismailis were studied and judged almost exclusively on the basis of the evidence collected or fabricated by their enemies, including the bulk of the medieval heresiographers and polemicists who were hostile towards the Shi'a in general and the Ismailis among them in particular. These authors in fact treated the Shi'i interpretations of Islam as expressions of heterodoxy or even heresy. As a result, a 'black legend' was gradually developed and put into circulation in the Muslim world to discredit the Ismailis and their interpretation of Islam. The Christian Crusaders and their occidental chroniclers, who remained almost completely ignorant of Islam and its internal divisions, disseminated their own myths of the Ismailis, which came to be accepted in Europe as true descriptions of Ismaili teachings and practices. Modern orientalists, too, have studied the Ismailis on the basis of these hostile sources and fanciful accounts of medieval times. Thus, legends and misconceptions have continued to surround the Ismailis to the present day.

In more recent decades, however, the field of Ismaili studies has been revolutionised due to the recovery and study of genuine Ismaili sources on a large scale – manuscript materials which in different ways survived the destruction of the Fatimid and Nizari Ismaili libraries. These sources, representing diverse literary traditions produced in Arabic, Persian and Indic languages, had hitherto been secretly preserved in private collections in India, Central Asia, Iran, Afghanistan, Syria and the Yemen.

Modern progress in Ismaili studies has already necessitated a complete re-writing of the history of the Ismailis and their contributions to Islamic civilisation. It has now become clear that the Ismailis founded important libraries and institutions of learning such as al-Azhar and the Dar al-ʿIlm in Cairo, while some of their learned *daʿis* or missionaries developed unique intellectual traditions amalgamating their theological doctrine with a diversity of philosophical traditions in complex metaphysical systems. The Ismaili patronage of learning and extension of hospitality to non-Ismaili scholars was maintained even in such difficult times as the Alamut period, when the community was preoccupied with its survival in an extremely hostile milieu.

The Ismaili Heritage Series, published under the auspices of the Department of Academic Research and Publications of The Institute of Ismaili Studies, aims to make available to wide audiences the results of modern scholarship on the Ismailis and their rich intellectual and cultural heritage, as well as certain aspects of their more recent history and achievements.

Contents

Illustrations

11 *Ṭirāz* textile fragment, with single line of Kufic text, Fatimid Egypt 5th/11th century, (private collection, London).
12 Page from the *Khiṭaṭ* of al-Maqrīzī, 966/1558, Egypt or Syria (The Institute of Ismaili Studies Library).

Acknowledgements

This book began in response to my continuing frustration over the lack of attention given to the Fatimids by English language scholars. In a period when studies of Islamic history and thought in general are flourishing, the history of the Fatimids lags behind. One need only compare work on them to that, for example, on the early Abbasids or the Ayyubids and Mamluks. To remedy the situation I decided to write an introduction to the subject and to outline in it the full range of sources and how they might be used to investigate the Fatimids. My aim is to make it easier to enter this field and thereby hopefully attract others to it. Fortunately, the Institute of Ismaili Studies in London was willing to encourage this project and to arrange publication of the result in their Ismaili Heritage Series with I.B. Tauris. I am most grateful to Farhad Daftary, friend, colleague and fellow scholar in this field, who also happens to be Head of the Department of Academic Research and Publications at the Institute. He accepted my general plan for this book without hesitation and he has guided the end product to its successful conclusion.

Once I had produced a first draft of the text, Bruce Craig, Director of the Center for Middle East Documentation at the University of Chicago and editor of *Mamluk Studies Review,* kindly read the whole work carefully and in the process saved me from many slips and errors. At a subsequent stage Sumaiya Hamdani of

George Mason University likewise went through the text from beginning to end and caught a number of mistakes. She also raised numerous challenges to my interpretations, thus forcing me to rethink more critically several key points. In a similar way Marlis Saleh of the University of Chicago who, like Sumaiya Hamdani, is an expert in the field of Fatimid studies, generously took the trouble to review, with a knowledgeable eye, what I had written, finding problems and asking questions that helped improve the final version of the work.

However, any undertaking of this kind depends on years of previous research. Throughout them all the efforts of many individuals, teachers and advisers, friends and fellow travellers, have helped in ways too numerous to recall in specific detail at this late date. I can only hope to thank here those who contributed directly to this particular volume, among them Michael Bates, Jonathan Bloom, Sheila Blair, Leonard Chiarelli, Wilferd Madelung, Ayman Fuʾād Sayyid, Abbas Hamdani, Ismail K. Poonawala, Th. Emil Homerin, Steven Humphreys, Nasser Rabbat and Anne Broadbridge. I must offer in addition a special extra thanks to Michael Bates and Jonathan Bloom for their advice and contributions to the chapter on coins and art. Donald Whitcomb and Tracy L. Hoffman brought the Ascalon inscription to my attention and David Schloen provided me with a photograph of it.

The actual writing of the final text was aided immeasurably by the grant of a fellowship from the National Endowment for the Humanities, which I held in 1999 to 2000.

Paul E. Walker

Abbreviations

AI	*Annales islamologiques*
AnnalesESC	*Annales: Economies, sociétés, civilisations*
BEO	*Bulletin d'études orientales de l'Institut français de Damas*
BIE	*Bulletin de l'Institut d'Égypte*
BIFAO	*Bulletin de l'Institut français d'archéologie orientale*
BSOAS	*Bulletin of the School of Oriental and African Studies*
BRISMES	*British Society for Middle Eastern Studies Bulletin*
CT	*Les Cahiers de Tunisie*
EI2	*The Encyclopaedia of Islam, New Edition*
IJMES	*International Journal of Middle East Studies*
JA	*Journal asiatique*
JAOS	*Journal of the American Oriental Society*
JARCE	*Journal of the American Research Center in Egypt*
JBBRAS	*Journal of the Bombay Branch of the Royal Asiatic Society*
JESHO	*Journal of the Economic and Social History of the Orient*
JNES	*Journal of Near Eastern Studies*
JRAS	*Journal of the Royal Asiatic Society*
JSAI	*Jerusalem Studies in Arabic and Islam*
MCIA	van Berchem, *Matériaux pour un corpus inscriptionum arabicarum*
MIDEO	*Mélanges de l'Institut dominicain d'études orientales*
MIFAO	*Mémoires de l'Institut français d'archéologie orientale du Caire*
NS	*new series*

RCEA	*Répertoire chronologique d'épigraphie arabe*
RSO	*Rivista degli Studi Orientali*
REI	*Revue des études islamiques*
SI	*Studia Islamica*
WO	*Die Welt des Orients*
ZDMG	*Zeitschrift der Deutchen Morgenländischen Gesellschaft*

Introduction

The Fatimids rose to political dominion in North Africa in 296/909 after a long period of clandestine struggle in various regions of the Islamic world and they formally proclaimed their caliphate soon after in 297/910. The new caliph, al-Mahdī, was already the Imam of the Shiʿi Ismailis but, until then, he had not actually ruled a politically defined territory. His triumph, however, represented a true revolution in which he restored the rights of the Prophet's family by bringing back to power a descendant of ʿAlī b. Abī Ṭālib in the line of ʿAlī's wife Fāṭima, the Prophet's own daughter and the mother of his only grandsons. Thereafter al-Mahdī and his successors were thus both imams in the religious sense and also rulers of an empire that grew from its original base in what are now Tunisia, Algeria and Sicily. In 358/969, having by then subdued nearly all of North Africa and the lands of the southern Mediterranean, the Fatimids finally added Egypt, much of Syria and the holy cities of Arabia to their growing empire. In Egypt they founded the city of Cairo as their new headquarters and proceeded, by further conquests, toward the completion of a long-sought goal to supplant the Abbasid caliphate.

Over the next two centuries the fortunes of the Fatimid dynasty both waxed and waned. At one high point in the middle of the eleventh century, they briefly controlled Baghdad, the capital city of their Abbasid rivals. Their decline was also prolonged and slow. When the European Crusaders captured Jerusalem in 493/

1099, they took that city away from these same Fatimids, who had recovered it for themselves once again the previous year. Later still, as the Latin crusader states under Amalric I, King of Jerusalem, became directly involved in Egypt, the government there was still Fatimid. Only in 567/1171, over two hundred and sixty years after the foundation of their state, did Saladin (Ṣalāḥ al-Dīn), the most famous of the Muslim opponents of the Crusaders, who was at that time wazir to the last of the Fatimid imam-caliphs, finally abolish the dynasty. Upon the death of the previous ruler he simply refused to allow a successor to assume the caliphate.

Both for the extent of their government over time and territory and their challenge to Sunni Islam and its Abbasid caliphate – or even for their opposition to the Umayyads of Spain, another enemy – the Fatimids merit careful and extensive consideration in modern scholarship. Their two hundred-year rule over Egypt is by itself enough to warrant such interest. Under them Egypt became independent for the first time in the Islamic period and it remained so until the Ottoman conquest in 923/1517. The history of this dynasty also involves North Africa, Sicily, Syria, the Hijaz and Yemen, and it comprises a religious dimension that functioned outside of its political territory.

As imams of the Ismailis, the Fatimids controlled a network of missions (*daʿwa*s) that reached deep (often, though not always, secretly) into areas inside the domains of their opponents. For his religious followers, the Fatimid ruler, in his capacity as Ismaili imam, was the absolute authority in all matters including most especially any issue of religion and religious doctrine or interpretation. Naturally, this aspect of their government was not recognised by Sunni Muslims either inside or outside the empire and was poorly understood by them, if at all. The Abbasid caliphs did not have the same degree of religious authority. Similarly, non-Ismaili Shiʿa, such as the Twelvers and the Zaydīs, although they better comprehended the Shiʿi theory of the imamate, did not admit to any religious supremacy on the part of the Fatimid imams. None the less, it is impossible to explain this dynasty and its rule adequately without fully grasping the character and importance of its religious ideology, which was, moreover, all but unique in

Islamic history. There are no examples like it in the Sunni world and the Twelver Shiʿa never saw their imam achieve rulership in the political sense. Only a few small Zaydī principalities in out of the way regions had anything resembling a comparable government among the Shiʿa.

All of these issues affect scholarship about the Fatimids. Medieval sources are divided into those that express a Sunni attitude, on the one hand, or an Ismaili affinity, on the other. A few are Shiʿa in sympathy but none the less are not actually Ismaili. The degree of hostility displayed by the non-Ismaili writers varies greatly. Most were then and are now simply ignorant of true Ismaili doctrines. Some, however, objected to the Ismaili understanding of Islam on basic principles rooted so deeply in how they perceived what they wrote that their anti-Ismaili hatred coloured their account of the facts. To a real extent modern scholarship proves that the same divisions continue to exist among those who now write about the Fatimids.

In general, relative to slightly later but comparable periods in the Middle East, the study of the Fatimids has received so much less attention as to border on serious neglect, especially in English language scholarship. This judgement is less true for French and Arabic. The documentation for Fatimid rule and for the societies that lived under it is certainly poorer than for a dynasty like that of the Mamluks. But lack of materials and sources does not entirely explain or justify the apparent disregard by Middle East historians of this two hundred and fifty-year span of the Fatimid caliphate, especially the two centuries during which Cairo and thus Egypt was the capital of the empire. One reason for this oversight surely stems from an aversion to, or perhaps unease and unfamiliarity with, Ismaili Shiʿism and its special doctrinal literature.

These religious issues, however, certainly require an explanation, one that sets out as clearly as possible the peculiar differences that might arise in the investigations of the Fatimids and their rule. In addition, it is essential to understand these matters in the context of time and place. The Shiʿa, for example, were always a minority within Islam and thus in opposition to the dominant trends. They traced their origin to the refusal of the most powerful of the Prophet's Companions to admit that he had designated his cousin ʿAlī as his successor. Failure to recognise ʿAlī's rights was condemned by the Shiʿa, who thus regard themselves as the partisans of ʿAlī. Their enemies were the supporters of any of those who denied ʿAlī, an opposition so basic and fundamental in early Islam as to leave its mark on the respective communities ever after. As the weaker of the contending parties, however, the Shiʿa were frequently persecuted accordingly, forcing them into a silent dissent in which serious political action could be undertaken only with great caution and secrecy.

For ʿAlī himself, who finally achieved the rank of supreme leader of the Muslims as the Commander of the Faithful only after Abū Bakr, ʿUmar and ʿUthmān, the ultimate enemy was the surviving head of ʿUthmān's Umayyad clan, Muʿāwiya. The Umayyads were then, and were to remain, implacably hostile to ʿAlī, to his lineage, and to his Hāshimite clan. That is important because, although the Umayyads were eventually overthrown by the Abbasids, they survived in Spain where much later they continued their opposition to both the more distant Abbasids and the closer, newly emerging Fatimids. The Abbasids, though once eager for the support of ʿAlī's descendants, had, by the late ninth century when the Ismaili *daʿwa* began to spread most rapidly, long since abandoned their pro-Shiʿa policies. They had become equally hostile.

In that era the majority in a given Muslim (Sunni) community, as, for example, in the provincial capital of North Africa, normally consisted of various factions divided in the first instance by schools of legal interpretation. Law in Islam has a fundamental bearing on religious rites and rituals, personal status, and many matters not covered in other, non-Muslim systems. The Shiʿa of that same city, as was common there and elsewhere, hid their religious inclination altogether, to the point that some among them, in order to gain an education, pretended an interest in one of these Sunni schools. Beyond the domain of law, moreover, additional issues of religious difference were subsumed within theological doctrine or what was called more generally the 'principles of faith' (*uṣūl al-dīn*). As with law there were competing schools in this area too. In Qayrawān in the third/ninth century, most citizens were either Mālikī or Ḥanafī with respect to their legal affiliation. These two legal schools traced their origin respectively to the Madinese jurist Mālik b. Anas or to the Iraqi Abū Ḥanīfa and his immediate followers. Most of those who subscribed to either tendency were simply uninterested in theology and the majority refused to engage in speculation about it. Therefore, since theology occupied such a minor role, only those few who actually espoused a deliberate position on an important issue belonged to what might be termed a school in this area. In Qayrawān at the time of the advent of the Fatimids, to be called a Muʿtazila – the one clearly recognisable school of theology – indicated to the majority a theological heresy opposed by the majority. Few Mālikīs were ever, therefore, also Muʿtazila, although still among the Sunnis a number of the Ḥanafīs had espoused this brand of theology. By that time, however, a considerable number of the Shiʿa, some even in Qayrawān, but most in the east, had adopted Muʿtazilī positions.

The Ismaili movement itself developed largely within Shiʿi circles that, in part because of the obvious requirement of secrecy, remain obscure. Still some general features of this early Shiʿism are reasonably clear from surviving evidence. The story is, however, not simple. From the time of ʿAlī b. Abī Ṭālib to the beginning of the Fatimid caliphate – a span of almost two hundred and fifty years – the Shiʿa themselves split up frequently into various sectarian groupings, later just as frequently reformed into a larger cohesive movement. The era of the Imam Jaʿfar al-Ṣādiq (d.148/765) witnessed rare accord across a broad range of the Shiʿa, but the succession to him was fraught with difficulty leading to major separations between the supporters of one son over another. The Ismaili movement commenced in the aftermath of these troubles; what was later to become the Twelver Shiʿa followed one line and the Ismailis another.

What is at stake in the line of succession is the imamate, a doctrine of utmost importance to the Shiʿa but little understood by the Sunnis. In Sunni theory the community itself chooses the supreme leader of the Muslims, a form of election. What actually happened in nearly all cases, however, involved the selection of an heir or successor by the previous ruler. For the Shiʿa it is axiomatic that God would never abandon humans to the folly of their own desires and whims. In fact, in their view, God guided His Prophet to select and designate ʿAlī as his immediate successor; not to admit this point was and is tantamount to rebellion against God Himself. ʿAlī thereafter designated his son Ḥasan who likewise designated his brother Ḥusayn, the latter his son ʿAlī, and so on. Designation precludes election, just as it conveys instead God's choice. The imams, according to the Shiʿa, are divinely appointed. Each is infallible, incapable of sin and error. Religion, true religion, lives in them and through them. Only they know what it is with absolute incontrovertible accuracy. Moreover, they are its only source; hence not to recognise the imams, most especially the living imam of the present, carries with such refusal the threat of perdition and hell.

For the Sunnis this is a doctrine quite foreign to their understanding of Islam. The imamate in their theory exists but on a much less serious plane and the consequences of having elevated an unfit leader can be remedied by his removal from office. An imam is a leader, the leader of Friday congregational prayer, for example, or the founder of a legal school, or even the caliph, as was the case with the Umayyad or Abbasid rulers, all subject in theory to review and recall. But none of these positions commands absolute authority in religious affairs. Nor does replacement require the officeholder necessarily to select his own successor, as is the case with the Shiʿi imam. For the Ismailis there is no other procedure; the community cannot replace the imam under any circumstances at all. Thus, in the view of the Sunnis, the Fatimid caliphs were simply at best equal to the Abbasids in the degree of their religious authority. For Ismailis, however, the Fatimid caliph was the imam of his time. In him and through him Islam is pure; there is no valid religion without him. Moreover, while religious doctrine follows the ruling of previous imams, it does so only until superseded by the judgement of the living imam, if and when it occurs. One consequence is that for the Ismailis Islamic law depends solely on the imam (or on his predecessors, if, in the absence of a new ruling, it remains as it was under them).

Most historians who have written about the Fatimids fail to take note of this doctrine which means that the imam-caliph was not obliged to follow any previously-held notion of Islamic law or any other aspect of the faith. The *daʿwa*, the mission in support of the imamate, was in fact less generically in favour of the Fatimids as a dynasty than of each individual imam, one by one. The *daʿwa* is a call for obedience and loyalty to the imam, the living imam. Lineage is of course essential; the Fatimids always named their prophetic ancestor and honoured the deceased members of their line. Sacred descent was crucial to their legitimacy, but it meant nothing without the living representative of it in every age.

The *daʿwa* also consisted of a vast network of missions each directed by regional authorities commonly called *dāʿīs*. Prior to the commencement of the caliphate, the Ismaili *daʿwa* had spread to most areas of the Islamic world. The centre of all this attention was the imam but, following upon the creation of the caliphate, what was previously purely an Ismaili movement became territorial with responsibility for a populace of considerable size, only a few of whom were Ismailis. While many of the rest lived in those domains simply as citizens by default, many accepted Fatimid rule and, despite religious reservations, actively sought to enter government service. Over the long period of Fatimid rule, there are examples of important officeholders who belonged personally to a complete range of Muslim factions: Mālikīs, Ḥanafīs, Shāfiʿīs and Ḥanbalīs, to name the four Sunni legal schools, Shiʿa of various non-Ismaili groups, even Jews and Christians, all with great responsibility in the state, a condition that presumes their personal political loyalty to it. Thus the imam, whatever his position with respect to his own Ismaili followers, could not risk the outright alienation of his non-Ismaili subjects. Religious policy within the Fatimid empire was, therefore, always a matter of considerable delicacy. Accordingly, the historian's reconstruction of how that policy played out must account for both private sentiments of extravagant devotion or bitter hostility (or somewhere in between) and the public expressions of either one. The imam's *daʿwa* could teach one set of doctrines to initiates sworn by oath to undying secrecy even as, meanwhile, his regime attempted to accommodate a much broader spectrum of the populace with official tolerance and compromise. Needless to say, however, this policy was not always and everywhere as benign as it was at its best.

The historiographical implications of Fatimid religious policy are likewise complicated by the attitudes and points of view expressed both in the sources and by the historians who write about them. Still what made the Fatimids unique was their religious claim to the imamate in the Shiʿi sense of the term. To ignore this dimension of their rule deprives the dynasty of its reason for existence. But it must also be admitted that the issues involved are not easy to investigate. Perhaps the inherent secrecy of the *daʿwa*, a result of long experience of persecution and danger, contributed to the suppression of information that might now help explain it and its activities. Even after the establishment of the very state in which the appeal for Ismaili loyalty was surely well protected and thus safe from harm, the *daʿwa* continued to function largely in seclusion from the public. There were, to be sure, programmes of a more open nature; the preachers of Ismailism did offer their guidance to the citizens when and where they found a suitable opportunity. But, because the *daʿwa* remained committed to the spread of the movement abroad and because the government feared alienating its non-Ismaili subjects, its activities were less obvious than they might otherwise have been. Outside the empire, conditions were now even more dangerous than before because of the political consequences inherent in supporting the Fatimid caliph against either the Abbasids or Umayyads.

The peculiar interaction of religion and state in the case of the Fatimids is, even so, highly significant and a proper understanding of how it functioned is a critical factor in the history of the dynasty. It has not, however, been well covered in previous scholarship. Historians most often treat the Fatimids as if the religious questions are secondary or of little import. Some tend to avoid discussing the dynasty because of the difficulty of adequately investigating such matters. Those most comfortable with Sunni sources and the concomitant view of Islamic history represented in them shy away from the unfamiliar Shiʿism involved here. Ironically, researchers who have a command of Shiʿi theory and are sympathetic to it find the Fatimids an awkward subject because what we can discern of their history depends heavily on later Sunni chroniclers who were blatantly hostile to them on religious grounds.

Another major part of the problem of studying the Fatimids is access to Ismaili sources. Whereas the standard Arabic sources such as, for example, the better known works of Ibn ʿIdhārī, Ibn al-Athīr, and especially al-Maqrīzī, are indispensable, many extremely important sources exist only in the libraries of the Ṭayyibī Ismailis. This literature is almost always sectarian, and much of it is doctrinal rather than historical. Nevertheless, it provides valuable information that cannot be ignored in analysing Fatimid rule. For the subject of religion in the Fatimid state, these sources often supply the only authentic evidence that we have. Yet, these sectarian works fall outside the normal competency of most Islamic historians.

While the religious dimension of Fatimid rule is difficult to explain for the reasons just mentioned, there is also another problem. The Ismailis, even in their own state, never constituted a majority. As a result, their teaching and proselytising institutions hardly ever functioned without due circumspection and caution. The religious policy of the Fatimids, even for such critical issues as succession to the imamate, was thus often shrouded in semi-secrecy. This tendency frequently created confusion among those who observed what was or was not policy and what did or did not happen. It is a confusion reflected in the oldest sources, particularly those not privy to the highest Ismaili authority. Even now, many misconceptions about the nature of Fatimid institutions persist.

There are, however, also valid reasons for the study of the Fatimids and the Fatimid period quite apart from matters of religion. In the Maghrib, for example, the Fatimids came after the Aghlabids and before the Zīrids; the situation in Sicily is similar. In Egypt the Fatimids fall between the Ikhshidids and the Ayyubids. For the history of either the Maghrib or Egypt, what came before and after are a part of the story of those regions. The Fatimids do not of necessity occupy a distinct place in it. In North Africa they founded al-Mahdiyya, an important capital city for several centuries after they had departed; likewise Cairo owes its very existence to them and, in contrast to al-Mahdiyya, Cairo has never ceased to be the centre of Egyptian life. The Fatimid city was, and continues to be, the capital of the country. Long after the Ismailis had disappeared, the inhabitants of Cairo remembered the Fatimids not as Shiʿi imams but as a dynasty of caliphs who had been responsible for building and embellishing their city. Even while the Fatimids ruled, the majority of their subjects were of another *madhhab.* Therefore there is an important difference between the study of Ismailism and of the Fatimids caliphate or of the period of their political empire. While some issues overlap, many others in Fatimid studies have less to do with Ismailism, and some have no connection at all.

Accordingly, historians of the various geographical regions that once belonged to the Fatimid empire not infrequently express much less concern with the Ismailis than with the long term trends – economic and social, for example – in the particular country of their focus. A historian of medieval Egypt needs to know about the Fatimids and also about the Tulunids and Ikhshidids before, and Ayyubids afterward and, even more to the point, know about Egypt and its inhabitants quite apart from the rulers and their governments. It is certainly understandable, therefore, that these historians follow in the first instance their own sources, which in many cases also have a regional focus. For Egypt these are in the main later chroniclers whose own interest is Egypt and not the Ismailis. The special characteristics of the dynasty, as far as they are concerned, are Cairo, its buildings, its political history and more rarely, its institutions – all seen, more often than not, in the context of conditions at the time of the writer, as existed, for example, under the Mamluks for someone writing in that much later period.

Regional interest among later historians likewise tends to divide the Fatimid experience into its initial phase in the Maghrib and Sicily, and a later phase in the east. Each region has its own historians, both medieval and modern. It is also true that many of the best sources of information about the Fatimids are medieval chronicles written substantially after their reign had ended and which cover a much longer time period than this one dynasty. A significant number of them purport to be universal histories that deal with all past human events from the creation to the present. In the latter case, naturally, the Fatimids occupy a relatively minor place.

The empire created by the Fatimids was also not small, especially at the height of its power. And it faced on its many borders competitors with whom it was often at war but also at peace and in friendly contact. Its international political strategy varied over time subject to opportunities that arose. And it was not always driven by religious considerations. Here then is another subject that affects the historiography of the period. Fatimid relations with Umayyad Spain and the Abbasid east were most often hostile, bitterly so, and how persons living and writing in either place saw this dynasty influenced what they said about it. The same is largely true of the observers who came after its demise, many of whom lived or worked in a similar milieu. Lacking the same kind of religious antagonism toward the Fatimids, the Byzantines were not always inimically opposed to them. These two super powers certainly clashed violently often enough in Sicily, southern Italy and northern Syria, but they also frequently accepted from each other treaties of peace and mutual aid. The advent of the Latin Crusaders, themselves not always on friendly terms with the Byzantines, complicated the situation. Once they had arrived in the Levant, the Latin Europeans became yet one more enemy confronting the Fatimid empire. But, whereas Umayyad and Abbasid enmity was endemic and, although it might be dormant in brief periods, never abated for long, the opposition of the Christian powers came and went, subject to choice and circumstances.

The scope of Fatimid hegemony and of its aspirations generated an empire both in reality and in theory. The very first caliph, al-Mahdī, to cite one striking example, dispatched a mission to Constantinople immediately after commencing his reign. His aim was apparently the conversion of Byzantium, or at least, such of its citizens as might be susceptible to such an appeal. Similar ventures went out to the west, the south and the east. In the caliph's mind the four corners of the earth properly belonged within his domain, spiritually if not physically. One interesting measure of what the empire included is shown in the ethnicity of its army. At one period or another it comprised separate regiments composed of Kutāma and Ṣanhāja Berbers, Maṣāmida (another North African tribal group), Slavs (from the north), various sub-Saharan Africans and Sudanese, Turks, Daylamīs, Armenians, Zanjīs (all from the east), contingents from a number of semi-nomadic Arab tribes that lived in Egypt and Palestine, and many others.

There are now hardly any real histories of the Fatimids, separate and by themselves, either medieval or modern. Of those known to have been written long ago, which might have become important sources had they survived, nearly all are no longer extant. One exception is, however, especially noteworthy. That is the ninth/fifteenth-century Mamluk historian al-Maqrīzī's *Ittiʿāẓ al-ḥunafāʾ bi-akhbār al-aʾimma al-fāṭimiyyīn al-khulafāʾ*. It is a large work and is entirely devoted to the Fatimids, both in North Africa and in Egypt and the east. The works of al-Maqrīzī – this and others including his famous topography, the *Khiṭaṭ*, as will become obvious throughout the pages to follow, despite his lack of access to the records of the Ismaili *daʿwa*, and thus his inability to understand that dimension of Fatimid rule – are none the less simply indispensable.

Still, al-Maqrīzī was a historian writing about a dynasty that had disappeared almost two full centuries before he was born. He was thus neither an eyewitness nor a contemporary, but rather a scholar in search of information in much older records. It was from such historical sources that he formed his own narrative, not unlike a modern historian does now. And up to the time of his death in 845/1442, he did just that, assiduously combing through the work of his predecessors for what it might say about the Fatimids. Another like example comes from the same late period. Idrīs ʿImād al-Dīn was head of the Ṭayyibī Ismaili community in Yemen; he died in 872/1468, only twenty-six years after al-Maqrīzī. Yet his history of the Ismaili imams, the *ʿUyūn al-akhbār*, is practically the only one of its kind. Although in his case, in contrast to al-Maqrīzī, his main sources were principally the works of long dead Ismaili writers, like his Mamluk counterpart, he too depended completely on much older materials. In many ways, despite the passing of several additional centuries, the task of the modern historian is the same now as it was for either al-Maqrīzī or Idrīs.

Despite occasional signs of renewed interest in the Fatimids, modern scholarship has accomplished relatively little in comparison to what has been done on the subsequent Ayyubid and Mamluk periods. The role of religious ideology in Fatimid rule thus remains largely an open and unexplored question, although there have been several useful advances particularly in the recovery and examination of sources. Farhad Daftary's *The Ismāʿīlīs* (1990) is an especially valuable general account of this community, and Ismail Poonawala's *Biobibliography* (1977) remains a basic tool for locating Ismaili sources. Heinz Halm's volume on the North African period, *Das Reich des Mahdi* (1991, Eng. tr. 1996) and Ayman Fu'ād Sayyid's *al-Dawla al-fāṭimiyya fī Miṣr* (1992, 2nd ed. 2000) are the best of the recent works devoted strictly to the Fatimids. Halm is reportedly actively engaged in extending his admirable study into the later periods and, unlike Sayyid, he fully appreciates the religious problems of Fatimid rule and its connection to organisations for teaching and *daʿwa*. Sayyid, on the other hand, is the leading expert on the non-Ismaili Arabic sources for the Egyptian phase, many of which he has personally edited or re-edited and re-published.

Fatimid history is thus a subject as vast and as varied as the geography and the peoples it included or touched. The writing of that history is likewise both as wide as the empire and as narrow as the thousands of particular topics that help explain any portion of it. The present book, however, aims not to encompass all, or even a major portion of it, but to offer an introduction to what it contains or might contain and how to explore these possibilities, to begin to suggest what sources exist, and how historians, both in former periods and now, have used them or could use them even yet. To reach that goal it is necessary to propose a framework in which the material and themes of Fatimid history might fit, which thereafter will serve as the focus for analysis and investigation. But the purpose here is to open this field, not to close it. By making it easier to study the Fatimids, hopefully this work will help lead the way along both well-worn and also as yet untried paths.

To accomplish that task, this book consists of two parts followed by a comprehensive bibliography of both sources and modern studies, not merely of works cited in this study, but of the whole range of what has been written to date about the Fatimids. Part I presents an overview of the shape and content of Fatimid history, arranged in three chapters, one each on the main phases of the dynasty. These are, first, North Africa and the Maghrib, 296/909–362/973; second, a century of empire, 362/973–466/1074; and finally, a century of military wazirs, 466/1074–567/1171. Part II contains separate chapters on the various kinds of historical sources that provide what information there is for historical reconstruction and analysis. They are, first, coins and other artefacts (*ṭirāz*, building dedications, art objects, archaeological finds) that supply direct evidence (normally inscriptions) of historical events and processes; second, documents and letters, both originals and copies of them; third, eyewitness and contemporary accounts; fourth, histories, topographies and biographical dictionaries; fifth, *adab* and other kinds of literary writings; and last, a look at the work of those modern scholars who have contributed the most to this subject.

I

The Shape and Content of Fatimid History

I *The Maghrib*

The Rising in the West and its Background

On 20 Rabīʿ II 297/ Friday, 4 January 910,[1] the mosques of the old Aghlabid governorate in North Africa and Sicily rang with the proclamation of a new ruler, one no longer subservient to an eastern caliphal overlord but completely independent, replacing, in fact, not only all former rulers but the earlier forms of Islamic government back to the golden era of the Prophet himself and of his rightful successor ʿAlī b. Abī Ṭālib. The caliph al-Mahdī's victory was in reality a revolution in the true sense. For his Ismaili followers, it constituted a restoration of correct and righteous government, and of God's ordinance; it represented the assumption of power by His real friends, the family of His prophet and their most loyal supporters. Years of hardship and repression at the hands of usurpers were now over; in this one corner of the far west, a lengthy period of secret struggle in many other regions of the Islamic empire had at last achieved a glorious end.[2]

Although al-Mahdī publicly claimed the caliphate in the formal manner just described only at that date, the story of his movement and of his own personal history to that point already constituted many years of adventure full of dangerous escapes, house arrest and a long flight from the east to the distant Maghribi city of Sijilmāsa. Those most immediately responsible for his victory, moreover, had themselves spent as much as two decades or more in service to the same cause. Al-Mahdī's caliphate began with his triumphant entry into Raqqāda, an administrative suburb of Qayrawān, which was the capital of the Maghrib at that time, but his nominal rule had begun tenth months earlier with the military conquest of the same cities by his agent, the famous Abū ʿAbdallāh, who was known locally simply as al-Shīʿī. Backed by an army of Kutāma Berber warriors that he had converted, taught, and organised, he finally succeeded in bringing the Aghlabids to a stunningly complete defeat and destruction in the early Spring of 296/909. Like his master al-Mahdī, Abū ʿAbdallāh's career as a missionary and revolutionary has its own intrinsic interest. He had then spent eighteen years working with the Kutāma Berbers, although his own personal origins were found in the Iraqi city of Kufa where, even earlier, he was first recruited to the cause.

Thus, despite these overt acts which represent the establishment of the Fatimid state and indicate the rule of the new imam-caliphs over the territories they inherited, a history of their reign must commence years prior to them. As Ismaili imams these Fatimid caliphs were by their own claim already the rightful holders of this office. Certainly for their followers, the change implied in their ascension to the caliphate counted less than succession to the imamate. In these terms al-Mahdī, though not under that name, had been fully vested with his office over ten years before when he succeeded the previous leader of the Ismailis. That event occurred in the town of Salamiyya in north central Syria in about 286/899 – the exact date is not known. Therefore, in one quite real sense, the history of the Fatimids must begin back at that moment. Al-Mahdī was to be the founder of the state but it was his imamate that was to become a political empire as well; the one was in part a consequence of the other.

Like most revolutions, however, the story is not quite so simple. It is possible, among other factors, to trace the Ismailis further back, to the leadership of al-Mahdī's predecessors in Salamiyya and even before in other towns of the east. Abū ʿAbdallāh's career as an agent propagating the cause among the Berbers began in 280/893; and he had first signed on two years before that. Thus, by the advent of al-Mahdī's imamate, he had already been in the mountains of eastern Algeria six years. But, while all of the early history of the Ismailis is relevant, there are special reasons to single out the accession in this case as the starting point of the later caliphate. As will become evident, the sources available to the modern historian for the founding of the Fatimid state are unusually rich in comparison to other phases of this rule. For the period prior to al-Mahdī's imamate, by contrast, matters are quite obscure.[3]

Except for the mission of Abū ʿAbdallāh and those in the movement with whom he worked directly, those events in the east prior to al-Mahdī and just after, although important, even vital in coming to understand subsequent activities, are known now from two sets of information that are often in conflict. The sources for this early history derive, in the first instance, from reports and other accounts preserved by Abbasid authorities who were in part responsible for extracting it from local informants. Still, there is always an added caution in regard to this information. The agents in the east, whose aim was the overthrow of the existing government, operated under dangerous conditions; the Ismaili movement worked, moreover, for both political and religious change and many adherents appear in the eastern, that is, Abbasid, records under false or assumed names. Because the same material was later also used for extremely hostile polemics against the Fatimids and other Ismaili movements such as the Qarmatians, what is accurate and what is merely slanderous is difficult to determine. Nevertheless, much of the information given, once separated from the exaggerated rhetoric of such hostility, is likely valid.

The other body of information comes from the records collected and preserved by the Fatimids themselves. In general this latter material should have a higher claim to accuracy, except in that it, too, represents only one of several viewpoints.[4]

A central issue is the claim by the future al-Mahdī, near the beginning of his rise to the leadership of the movement, that he was, in fact, the imam and that he would henceforth actively seek to establish a political state based on that fact. The best information about prior doctrine among the adherents of the Ismaili movement was that their leader – that is, the head of the cause, who then directed it from Salamiyya – was merely an agent for the absent Imam-in-Concealment, Muḥammad b. Ismāʿīl b. Jaʿfar al-Ṣādiq. The term *Ismāʿīlī* – although the word itself was not necessarily used by those groups the modern historians, looking back later, would deem Ismailis – meant at that time the upholders of this Ismāʿīl's succession to the imamate in accord with the designation of his father Jaʿfar. How then could the future al-Mahdī insist that he was now the imam, and what had happened to the older teaching that Muḥammad b. Ismāʿīl would himself return to the world as the *mahdī*?

There is no real way to resolve this dilemma to the satisfaction and agreement of all. What is clear is that many of the agents of the old movement refused to accept the change. Quite a few thus rebelled against the new imam. Generally known as Qarmatians, the followers of the dissenting view thereafter went their separate way, often in open conflict with the Fatimids, a term that now defines more succinctly only the movement behind al-Mahdī and his rise to eventual political dominion. In any case Fatimid accounts of the pre-history of the dynasty naturally support al-Mahdī's position in opposition to what remained of the opposing claims put forth by the Qarmatians.

Some agents switched loyalties and eventually rejoined the Fatimids. The most intriguing case is that of Ḥamdan Qarmaṭ/Abū ʿAlī.[5] In the eastern Abbasid accounts he has the former name and, along with his brother-in-law ʿAbdān, is said to have rejected al-Mahdī's claim. Upon the latter's murder, however, Ḥamdan Qarmaṭ disappeared, only to resurface in Egypt under the second name. This man is especially important because it was he who recruited Abū ʿAbdallāh and the latter's brother Abu'l-ʿAbbās. And except for the period of his uncertainty and apparent rebellion, he directed their activities, as he likely did for many other operatives in the movement as a whole.

The career of Abū ʿAbdallāh represents one of the better documented phases of the pre-state Ismaili movement. The details of his trip to Kutāma territory and his proselytising there are well known.[6] Likewise, when the new imam was forced to flee from Salamiyya because of the premature rising of the sons of Zakaruya, known respectively as the Man with the She-camel and the Man with the Mole, who, although ostensibly his supporters, none the less threatened him personally and might have exposed him, the details of his subsequent journey, first to Egypt and then to Sijilmāsa, exist in a variety of accounts. Chief among the latter is a personal memoir by al-Mahdī's own manservant Jaʿfar as related many years later and only then written down for posterity.[7]

With the imam under house arrest two months away in Sijilmāsa, Abū ʿAbdallāh's military campaign intensified accordingly. Patient years of work with the Kutāma provided the Ismaili movement not only with a large core of devoted followers that included scholars and teachers, but also the army necessary for the final conquest. The movement in the east at that time was by no means dead but it had weakened. Yemen, for example, once another promising territory for the establishment of a Fatimid state, no longer seemed likely. Thus many of those who remained loyal eagerly anticipated Abū ʿAbdallāh's victory. He, however, proceeded with extreme caution. The Aghlabids could, until worn down, raise and field forces that were better trained and armed. Abū ʿAbdallāh simply stayed out of their way; his refuge was Īkjān, a backcountry, rural settlement of his own choosing, located in mountains controlled by the Kutāma. But, as the Aghlabids began to fall apart, the Ismaili army closed in, finally achieving a total rout of the enemy.

Abū ʿAbdallāh thereafter began to improvise a new government, appointing a local Shiʿi scholar as qadi of the major city, Qayrawān, and several of his trusted commanders as regional governors. He then summoned his own brother, who was waiting not far away in Tripoli, to come and take charge in conjunction with his long-time associate the Berber leader, Abū Zākī, as interim rulers while he marched west to rescue the imam. As with the story of both the imam's journey to Sijilmāsa and Abū ʿAbdallāh's prior career, the initial events in the creation of the new rule are covered well in surviving Fatimid records.[8] More information exists as well in accounts written by local scholars who, quite hostile to the new power and wishing to remember the Fatimid revolution as an abomination, preserved their records for an opposite reason.[9]

In sum, it must be admitted that the advent of the Fatimids, and even the pre-history of the movement behind the imams who were to rule as caliphs, is reasonably well attested by a fairly impressive set of sources, not all of which are Ismaili in provenance. Al-Mahdī's imamate, including his policies and decisions, beginning already in 286/993 are far less obscure than those of any of his predecessors. Similarly the mission and activities of Abū ʿAbdallāh can be reconstructed in detail and this judgement applies as well to his brother and others in the movement. In part this material, which is so strikingly rich in comparison with other phases of Fatimid history, is due to the interest of the later Fatimid historians, who were responsible for saving and transmitting the information or the accounts in which it occurs.

Moreover, later North African sources, although eventually all anti-Fatimid in tone and intent, nevertheless preserve much valuable information. For those opposed to the Ismaili state, who include principally authors belonging to the Mālikī legal school, the coming of Shiʿism represented the triumph of heresy. As Fatimid influence declined in the Maghrib during the fifth/eleventh century, the Mālikīs also wreaked a horrible revenge on the remaining Ismaili communities there. All that had to be justified by a counter claim of early repression of their own when the dynasty began. Yet in relationship to later eras when the material of history and histories was either lost, as is often the case, or never composed, for this very earliest phase it is abundant. But, if hostility explains the interest of the anti-Fatimid historians, what is the reason for the apparent richness of Ismaili literature about the establishment of the Fatimid empire and the lack of it later?

Ruling North Africa and Sicily

With al-Mahdī's arrival and the proclamation of his rule, the various elements of the far flung movement that had put him in power rejoiced and came together in the new capital. Abū ʿAbdallāh had discovered that there were a number of Shiʿa among the local scholarly elite of Qayrawān. He quickly convinced them all to enlist as did more than a few of the Ḥanafīs, all converted thus to the Ismaili cause and to its appeal on behalf of al-Mahdī. The Kutāma were, of course, already a part of the movement, including significantly several important figures among them who contributed an expertise in law and religious learning and who served thereafter as judges and administrators.

Given that no one connected with the Ismaili organisation had until then actually served in an administrative role, governing the Maghrib might have appeared an impossible task. Al-Mahdī therefore readily drew on the talent he could find already there. He assigned leaders of the Kutāma many positions of responsibility, particularly of governing individual towns and staffing the army. One critically important post, that of qadi of Qayrawān, had already been delegated to a local Shiʿi expert. Others of this small group were similarly employed. On the whole, however, al-Mahdī tended to prefer to replace the departed Aghlabids with officials who were either active in a similar capacity under the old regime or had administrative experience of the same kind. Many of those who came forward to support him or to participate in the new government became Ismailis in the true sense – some even later serving as missionaries abroad – but not all made such a serious adjustment, preferring instead to recognise the Fatimids as rulers in the same way they had previously understood the Abbasids.

At the time there was euphoria and general enthusiasm over the movement's success. Abū ʿAlī (Ḥamdan Qarmaṭ) was finally permitted to travel from Egypt, where he was then serving, to Raqqāda, the imam's new headquarters. But almost as quickly as the old missionaries converged or new ones joined up, they were sent out again to a long list of destinations both near and far. Victory in this one isolated and remote corner of the greater world was clearly only a step, and quite a preliminary one, on the road to supplanting the enemies of righteousness everywhere. North Africa was soon covered with missionaries; others went to Spain, to Constantinople, and to the cities of the east as far as India.

Nevertheless, despite widespread enthusiasm and acceptance, there were serious problems in many places. Al-Mahdī may have hoped for a smooth transition to empire, but it did not come without a heavy price. And a major part of his difficulty came from within. In general the ensuing troubles were engendered by exaggerated expectations. For the decades leading up to its triumph, the agents of Ismaili doctrine had preached a messianic concept often embellished – perhaps even over-embellished – with the miraculous. Even discounting these hopes for the advent of a messiah, a *mahdī*, who would usher in an earthly paradise, a promise not dispelled by the choice of a throne name that itself pointed to messianic expectations, various of the forces behind al-Mahdī's success wanted their own rewards. The Kutāma in particular anticipated far more than they could be given. They saw the victory as theirs and themselves as the ones to inherit Aghlabid power and prerogatives.

Abū ʿAbdallāh and his brother likewise felt entitled to a share of rule. Al-Mahdī, however, had not come to the Maghrib to stay, nor to create a Berber kingdom or even a North African regional state. He aimed at the full restoration of the greater Islamic empire, east, west, north and south. His style of rule was imperial since his purpose was much larger than the conversion of the Kutāma or the conquest of Ifrīqiya and Sicily. Perhaps then a clash between the caliph and Abū ʿAbdallāh and his most intimate Berber followers was inevitable. Yet, tragically, al-Mahdī found himself confronted by a conspiracy that included Abū Zākī and Abū Mūsā, two of the highest ranking Kutāma leaders and the two brothers, Abu'l-ʿAbbās and Abū ʿAbdallāh, and he ordered their execution barely a year after his glorious entry into Raqqāda. Oddly, Fatimid historiography later tended to put the main blame for this disaster on the head of Abu'l-ʿAbbās. Such an explanation, while probably the officially approved account of the matter, like the whole incident itself, continues to be puzzling.[10]

Although al-Mahdī survived this crisis and managed in the process to retain the loyalty of the majority of the Kutāma, signs of their disaffection continued to appear. In one telling incident, a portion of the Berbers adopted another messianic figure, a native Berber, as their *mahdī*, a kind of counter-*mahdī*. Beyond these examples of overt troubles, the Kutāma often proved contentious and, although irreplaceable in the army, they were unreliable as administrators and garrison troops in areas where they were distinctly alien.

The Maghrib that al-Mahdī now had to govern was never a unified province. The Kutāma constituted a tribal grouping and in their own territory they held sway more in the rural areas than in the cities and towns. The major settled districts dominated by sizeable cities or in proximity to them were controlled by an Arab elite. But towns at some distance from Qayrawān, especially when separated by mountainous terrain, hardly felt the control of the capital. No ruler could easily maintain total dominance over all of the Maghrib without the willing co-operation of many elements of the local population: various Berber tribes and confederations, religious parties, remnants of the older elite and various Arab clans, each with their own aspirations. All too often, the situation required force. During al-Mahdī's reign he frequently had to send an army westward to re-establish his authority. But just as frequently, once the main army departed, local factions re-emerged; the Berber princes of this or that area threw out or massacred the limited garrison left behind. Even in those cases where the pre-existing regional clan leaders agreed to rule as deputies of the Fatimids, they tended to act in their own interest rather than accept the control of a distant capital.

Moreover, despite the presence of some Shiʿa, even prior to Abū ʿAbdallāh's mission there, and his own sterling record of conversions, the region persisted in its majority attachment to Sunni Islam. Many of the urban population, most notably the scholarly classes, belonged to the Mālikī legal school which, prior to the Fatimids, often fought with the local Ḥanafīs. The latter school had been supported by the Aghlabids. Unlike the situation in the east where the Umayyads had disappeared completely, in the west they continued to rule in Spain. Since the Aghlabids governed on behalf of the Abbasids, their opponents tended to support the Umayyads, who continued to be the sworn enemies of the Abbasid dynasty that had replaced it everywhere but in Spain.

With the establishment of the Fatimid state, the Mālikīs found themselves all but totally cut off. The new regime early on imposed a strict public policy requiring Shiʿi law and ritual. As but one example, the supererogatory prayers commonly said during Ramaḍān were outlawed if said with an imam in a mosque. The

Shiʿa regard this practice an unacceptable innovation; but the Mālikīs believe it is required by law. It would be quite some time before such differences could be accommodated and the earliest years were the hardest. Many of the local Mālikīs simply left for Spain where they subsequently served the Umayyads. Most significantly, even when much later the Fatimids, following a later policy of religious tolerance, appointed Mālikī judges to key positions such as the chief judge of Qayrawān or of Egypt, Mālikī hostility never ceased.

The Umayyads, who were quite naturally opposed to the Fatimids, if for no other reason than the ancient conflict between Muʿāwiya and ʿAlī, thus had plenty of help against their new enemy. For their part the Fatimids, who had come to power on the strength of the Kutāma confederation, faced not only the religious opponents among the local Arabs but a long-standing antagonism endemic in rival Berber groups also aided and abetted by religious differences. Large sections of the Berbers were already Kharijite, that is adherents of a religious movement that had as its very foundation rejection of ʿAlī's right to rule, a position even more inimical, if possible, to the Fatimids than that of the Umayyads.

In the face of well established and long entrenched local opposition, al-Mahdī wisely decided early to move his capital away from Raqqāda, which was near enough to Qayrawān to constitute a suburb of the bigger city. His choice fell on a small peninsula jutting out from the east coast of Tunisia and there he created a fortified enclave quite well protected by a formidable land wall and yet with ready access to the sea. The new city was called Mahdiyya after its founder. Later the Fatimid caliph al-Manṣūr followed the same pattern of constructing a new capital for himself – one that in being totally new would not be threatened by disloyal elements among previous inhabitants. He thus built yet another city, but less peripherally located, which was called Manṣūriyya, again after its founder. Much later still one more city was built by the Fatimids, that one in Egypt. It, too, was named initially after the caliph who created it, al-Qāhira al-Muʿizziyya, 'The City of al-Muʿizz's Victory'.

In later Fatimid legend al-Mahdī's foresight in moving to the coast and his use there of the easily and almost naturally fortified al-Mahdiyya was given the character of a miracle. Indeed the rebellion of the Kharijite Abū Yazīd Makhlad b. Kaydād came so close to destroying the Ismaili state that the rebel's failure to capture al-Mahdiyya and the subsequent reversal of his fortunes soon afterward, leading eventually to Fatimid victory over him, appeared to the faithful as preordained.

More readily forgotten was how seriously the government had miscalculated the opposition, particularly religious opposition, among large segments of the North African population. Attempting to impose Shiʿism on either the Sunnis, who were generally Mālikī and thus tended to be pro-Umayyad, or the Berber tribes, such as the major confederation of the Zanāta, who were staunchly Kharijite, Fatimid religious policy, although understandable, was risky. Ismaili judges insisted on Shiʿi rites and Shiʿi law, thereby excluding and antagonising those opposed to it. Given the inherent difficulty of managing all the conflicting factors, and most especially having closely observed the manner in which they themselves had overthrown the Aghlabids, the Fatimids should have predicted or, at the least, responded more quickly and surely to the rising of Abū Yazīd and his Kharijite-inspired tribesmen.[11]

Like many other revolts among the Berbers, this one had a long period of incubation in the early career of its instigator. Nevertheless, the trouble ultimately fell upon the authorities with unusual swiftness. Once Tahart, the main city of Kharijite resistance, had been cleansed of its opposition 'imam', Abū Yazīd himself, after working there, returned in seeming obscurity to the extreme south of Tunisia, his home base. Following several run-ins with the Fatimids, he eventually formed an association with Zanāta Berber clans willing to take up his cause. Their military progress thereafter moved along the same course as the Kutāma rebellion under Abū ʿAbdallāh, except that what took the latter six years to accomplish, the Kharijites managed in six months. All at once they swooped down upon the cities of the central Maghrib, capturing Tunis in the earlier autumn of 332/944 and Qayrawān in the month after. Al-Mahdiyya, despite its fortifications, was not entirely safe. Abū Yazīd set up camp in front of it, forcing what amounted to a siege throughout the winter, spring and summer of 333/945. He suffered his first real defeat, and was thus stopped, only at the beginning of that autumn. But Fatimid forces were in serious disarray nearly everywhere; the government had clearly not reacted as vigorously as the situation required.

True to his Kharijite beliefs, Abū Yazīd first observed carefully a rigid ascetic demeanour. He adopted as his riding mount a donkey – thus earning his nickname the 'Master of the Donkey' (*ṣāḥib al-ḥimār*) – and was accorded high respect for his piety. He and his Kharijite followers were, for the Sunni populace, heretics like the Fatimids, although of a radically different kind. Nevertheless initially, out of hostility to their Ismaili rulers, they sided with the rebels. On their part, however, the Kharijites regarded both the Shiʿa and the Sunnis as apostate Muslims and thus without rights in Islamic law. As the rebellion wore on this unpleasant consequence for the Sunnis became increasingly obvious. When Abū Yazīd temporarily abandoned his ascetic lifestyle, disaffection with the whole enterprise was one result and, except for the original hard core of Zanāta clans, his support began to dissolve.

About the same time the Fatimids saw a dramatic change of their own. The caliph, al-Qāʾim, though few had actually seen him for some time, was said to have announced that his son Ismāʿīl would succeed. That event occurred in the late spring of 334/946. The important city of Sousse was then under a dangerous siege by the still resilient forces of Abū Yazīd. Not long afterward, however, al-Qāʾim died. Keeping that fact secret the new imam, acting as if he were merely the son of the caliph, took to the field with his armies, whereupon he began a long relentless campaign to chase the 'Dajjāl' (the Deceiver), as Fatimid sources invariably call Abū Yazīd, from the face of the earth. But it was not until Muḥarram 336/August 947 that he finally succeeded. Only then did he proclaim his own elevation to the imamate, appropriately adopting the throne name al-Manṣūr (the Victor).

The consequences of this revolt were many. The Fatimids learned from it how insecure their rule over the Maghrib would always be without a continual display of overwhelming force and that a milder policy with respect to their non-Shiʿi subjects would better serve their long range purpose. From that point onward they preferred, when possible, to co-opt rather than to confront the opposition. In general, later Fatimid caliphs avoided religious conflicts with the non-Ismaili inhabitants of their domains.

External Affairs

There can be no doubt that, once his state had come into being, al-Mahdī was fully resolved to return east as quickly as possible. It is highly likely that the conquest of Egypt had been envisioned as far back as his sojourn there en route, as it turned out, to Sijilmāsa. There are, for example, hints that when at last his North African forces were to approach Egypt from the west, he had once expected his followers in Yemen to field an army for exactly such a purpose. By then, however, although his own son and heir, the future al-Qāʾim, twice marched into Egypt with Fatimid troops from the Maghrib ready to occupy the country (in 302–03/914–15 and in 308–09/921), the Ismaili movement in Yemen, beset with severe internal dissension, could offer no help. However, the growing strength of the Qarmatian Ismailis on several occasions enabled them to threaten Abbasid Baghdad with their own military forces. Were it not for the antagonisms engendered at the beginning of al-Mahdī's imamate over questions of doctrine, a unified combination of Ismaili might surely had a real prospect of overthrowing their enemy in the east.

These factors clearly affected al-Mahdī's aspirations both for the long term and the short. In most regions of the Islamic world, there were already pockets of Ismailis,though often acting in secret. Still, from the agents abroad who were loyal to the Fatimid imams, the new caliphal power could expect support and a steady donation of funds. They never gave up hope that the rift would heal and that the eastern Qarmatian Ismailis would rejoin the fold. Nevertheless, such an accommodation seldom happened; when, under the leadership of the fourth imam, al-Muʿizz, Egypt eventually fell, the Qarmatians bitterly opposed the move and to prove it almost forced the invading Fatimid army out of the Nile valley.

But some of the easterners did change and re-pledge their allegiance. In regard to the earliest missionaries in areas like central Iran, Iraq and Khurāsān, most evidence suggests that they rejected al-Mahdī's claim to be the imam. In the next generation, however, there was one brilliant exception; that was the well-known Neoplatonist thinker, Abū Yaʿqūb al-Sijistānī, who came to uphold the rights of the Fatimids after previously denying them.[12]

It is, however, a mistake to assume that the Ismaili movement looked only eastward. True, the east continued to represent the centre of the Islamic realm and it was therefore a necessary goal. In contrast, the west and north, regions controlled by the Umayyads of Spain and the Byzantines of Anatolia respectively, constituted more of a menacing rear. None the less, it is curious that almost from the very moment of his ascension as caliph, al-Mahdī sent his agents to Spain (and, of course, many areas of the Maghrib far to the west of Tunisia) as well as, most interestingly of all, to Constantinople. Evidently he anticipated the success of his appeal in all directions, not solely in the east.

Fatimid interest in its northern domains stemmed, in part, from having inherited Aghlabid territory in Sicily and southern Italy. Over much of the third/ninth century Muslim armies steadily acquired control over Sicily and then portions of Italy. The Fatimids continued this trend. One motive was the spread of Islam; but another, of equal importance, was to gain riches in the form of booty from raiding Christian areas ever northward of those conquered previously. The historical sources for both the Aghlabids and the early Fatimids frequently report the arrival in North Africa of a squadron of ships full of gold, precious objects and slaves recently taken from the north. While it would be impossible to calculate accurately how much wealth entered the Maghrib in this fashion, it was obviously a significant factor in sustaining the local economy at a level that would not have been attainable without it. When finally the balance of power in Italy shifted, and Christian resistance began to reverse this trend, a major source of financial support slipped steadily away, leaving an increasingly weakened government in Ifrīqiya as one consequence of the change.

Fatimid policy encouraged the raiding and yet also often attempted to deal with the Byzantines by treaty and the exchange of ambassadors. As the caliphs well knew, the Byzantines were rulers over parts of Italy and held a claim to Sicily in addition to portions of northern Syria, an area of long-term interest for the Ismaili movement (it was the birthplace of al-Mahdī himself). The Umayyads of Spain were another matter. There the enmity could hardly be the subject of a treaty. The Umayyads attempted to interfere with or to confront the Fatimids wherever possible, and the Fatimids did likewise, including reciprocal raiding by sea on each other's home territory. In many cases, including the rebellion of Abū Yazīd, but several others as well, where some prince or local power in the Maghrib expressed opposition to the Fatimids, Spain provided support for them. Given its complex mountainous geography and tribal cleavages, even without this active involvement of a hostile power, holding the west in check was difficult enough.[13]

The Reforms of al-Muʿizz

With the coming-to-power of the fourth Fatimid caliph al-Muʿizz in 341/953, the fortune of the dynasty commenced its most impressive phase. The new imam, although relatively young when he began to rule, represented in many ways the culmination of his three predecessors and of their combined experience of governing a diverse and naturally fractious territory often under adverse circumstances partly caused and abetted by religious opposition among the native population. He also inherited their aspirations, in particular the goal of moving eastward to oust the Abbasid usurpers in Baghdad. His father's military successes had rid North Africa of the Kharijite threat. The long interlude of weakness caused by it was then at an end.

Under al-Muʿizz, who was to adopt a number of crucial reforms, the basic form of Fatimid rule continued. His main contribution added and built on the previous pattern. In contrast to the later Fatimids, none of those in North Africa delegated major responsibilities to a subordinate without close and careful supervision.

Al-Mahdī, perhaps because of his personal experience with those that had abandoned him or proven disloyal, had been noted for his evident distrust of his own agents. Both al-Qāʾim, mainly as the heir apparent, and al-Manṣūr spent a considerable period of their lives in the field at the head of an army. Thus, with these imam-caliphs, the sense of their direct involvement is noteworthy, even to the point that the absence from public duties of any one of them, as occurred during various periods, affected their rule directly. That would not be the case, or as much the case, if they had elected to depend on, for example, a wazir who could replace them or even assume full responsibility in their stead. But there were to be no wazirs in the Maghrib Fatimid state.

Al-Muʿizz continued this tradition of strong personal leadership. The historical record reflects this fact. In part because he actively sponsored the production of the documentation for his own rule, the picture of him as a hands-on leader both accords with reality and with the image he wished to leave behind. One prime source for the history of his period, and that just prior to him, comes from the memoirs of his majordomo, the eunuch Jawdhar, who held key assignments in the central administration. Jawdhar's 'autobiography' provides the story of his involvement in the government and preserves copies of many valuable decrees, letters and official and semi-official documents.[14] More importantly, however, and ultimately of greater significance, was the work of the famous Qāḍī al-Nuʿmān, who although he had been in Fatimid service to the first three caliphs, under al-Muʿizz occupied a new role as the author of a series of books and treatises that, in its totality, constituted a major effort at reform of the existing Ismaili attitude toward the public within the state the imam ruled.[15]

Qāḍī al-Nuʿmān had been appointed to a kind of supreme judiciary by al-Manṣūr, who summoned him from a provincial office to the new capital of al-Manṣūriyya. Already he had begun to compose a number of important works on law and on the imams. It was al-Muʿizz, however, who further encouraged al-Nuʿmān to expand these interests and to compose several works designed not only for an Ismaili audience but also for public consumption. In fulfilment of this commission, al-Nuʿmān created a new type of

Ismaili literature in which he offered both a system of Shiʿi (and Ismaili) legal doctrine and an exemplary record of the many achievements of the imams (and their supporters) up to his time. In a sense, because they were expressly approved by the Imam al-Muʿizz, after coming into existence, they thereafter constituted a kind of constitution for the Ismaili state. Law, rather than being the private tradition of Shiʿi scholars, would henceforth be accessible in the works of al-Nuʿmān; the legal school of the Ismailis would thereafter match, in its systematic delineation of jurisprudence, the rival schools of the Mālikīs, Ḥanafīs and Twelver Shiʿa. The history of past imams and their acts and deeds likewise became a matter of public record. Here then was, as if to reassure a sceptical audience, an account of what policies they had pursued and why, policies quite Islamic and certainly not inimical to the religious beliefs of their subjects.

In part al-Muʿizz hoped to dispel the mystery of the Ismaili past. Secrecy had once been essential to protect the programme of the movement from its many opponents and antagonists, especially hostile governments. However, with the unknown had come falsification and distortion, a tactic of the enemy to paint the Ismailis in the worst light possible. Also there had been alterations in the professed teaching of the movement over time in accord with changing circumstances. Yet, even in the era of al-Muʿizz elements of the older doctrines persisted; the Qarmatians in the east clung to what, from his vantage-point, were notions rejected by the Fatimids. Chief among these, aside from the Qarmatian refusal to recognise the Fatimids as imams, was an antinomian conception of the law of Islam in which its proponents claimed that the inner meaning behind the literal form of the law and of scripture had replaced the latter. For those privy to the hidden significance of the law, the law, as observed by ordinary Muslims, no longer applied. The obligation to perform Islamic rites and rituals had ceased accordingly.

As the ruler of an Islamic state with a diverse population, only a small portion of whom were Ismailis, al-Muʿizz could neither afford to proffer such a doctrine himself, nor could he allow it within his domain. No Ismaili writer of the Fatimid period supported such antinomianism; all insisted vehemently that both the outer and the inner aspects of the law and ritual must be scrupulously observed. However, al-Muʿizz's dilemma was how to bring the eastern Ismailis back given that many of them professed various forms of this same doctrine. That was a goal he never achieved in any major way. But, by promoting the work of al-Nuʿmān, al-Muʿizz, although wanting to attract the Qarmatians, could at the least convince his own subjects that, despite rumours and innuendo to the contrary, Ismaili law both existed and was to be followed. Abbasid propaganda about the lawless Ismailis was thereby proven to be nothing but false rhetoric, a deliberate misperception based solely on the Qarmatians.

Another aspect of this same initiative saw an adjustment in Fatimid doctrine about the nature of the imamate. Prior to the time of al-Muʿizz the movement witnessed several alternations in regard to the position of Muḥammad b. Ismāʿīl. The eastern Qarmatians said that he was (or had been) the expected messiah, a claim that, since it stopped the succession with this Muḥammad, effectively precluded the imamate of the Fatimids. Under al-Muʿizz, however, Muḥammad b. Ismāʿīl could continue to be regarded as a messianic figure whose functions as the *mahdī* were to be performed by his descendants, the Fatimids. Meanwhile, the imamate, the Fatimids now added, had continued among his descendants, one among whom was al-Muʿizz himself.

It is hard to say now whether this view represented a temporary compromise or how seriously it was taken in the inner circles of the movement. It did succeed, however, in attracting some of the dissidents, notably the philosopher al-Sijistānī, who now accepted al-Muʿizz. Al-Muʿizz, moreover, was the first of the Fatimids to tolerate openly the abstract Neoplatonising thought of those Ismailis, who like al-Sijistānī, had adopted it in their writings. His predecessors had remained unimpressed and preferred not to allow it. The teachings of the philosophically minded eastern thinkers added a sophisticated intellectual dimension to Ismaili doctrine that served it well. In al-Muʿizz's broad perspective this was important if he were to win over the east.

Preparations for Egypt

Although al-Muʿizz's immediate goal was the conquest of Egypt, he could not afford to ignore the western Maghrib any more than the Mediterranean sea, which constituted, in effect, his northern boundary. Just as essential as a strong naval presence in the face of both the Byzantines and the Umayyads, was firm control over the more remote towns to the west such as Tahart, Sijilmāsa and Fez, each of which initially opposed him. No move east would be possible without dealing firmly with the north and the west. After all al-Muʿizz was to rule from his North African capital al-Manṣūriyya for twenty years (341–361/953–972) prior to leaving for Egypt.

A major part of his preparation for the eastern venture thus involved the thorough subjugation of the west, a project he set upon with great care. In this he could count on another of the loyal Berber groups, the Ṣanhāja confederation and their prince Zīrī b. Manād of the central Maghrib (as well as fresh volunteers from the Kutāma). As commander of the whole expedition he was planning, he drew on the services of a remarkable Slav, a former slave and clerk, named Jawhar. The army included also a number of Slavic commanders and troops. Jawhar's subsequent two-year campaign in the west (347–49/958–60) achieved its purpose with remarkable efficiency; the entire area to the Atlantic ocean was brought under Fatimid rule. All of the rebels, false caliphs and religious dissenters were eliminated and loyal forces from the Ṣanhāja henceforth claimed the central Maghrib including most importantly the city of Tahart.

Relations with the Byzantines depended on how aggressive they were in asserting their claim to southern Italy and Sicily versus their own expansion in the east. Despite occasional signs of a Byzantine threat, however, Fatimid land and naval forces in Sicily and on the sea held the upper hand. On the whole the Byzantines were stronger on their eastern frontier where they actively moved into northern Syria.[16]

During the period of al-Muʿizz, Egypt itself, then under the generally able Ikhshīdid caretaker, Kāfūr, witnessed unprecedented natural catastrophes that weakened its resistance to the

Fatimid appeal. Ismaili agents operated there as they had all along, but now increasingly all but in the open. With Kāfūr's death in 357/968, which left a leadership vacuum, local sentiment turned in favour of al-Muʿizz and he was ready to accept. Already in 355/966 he sent his commander Jawhar to commence the recruiting of Kutāma troops for just such a purpose and to begin the gathering of new funds. By the winter of 358/968, his elaborate and intense preparations were complete. Ismaili agents were on full alert in Egypt itself; large sums of money were loaded for transport with the invading army; provisions and wells were in place all along the route from Tunisia to the Nile.

As Jawhar approached the Egyptian capital, Egyptian notables came to him; there was little active resistance. In a grand gesture, before an assembled delegation of the Egyptian elite, he signed a proclamation of security in which he outlined the reasons for the Fatimid conquest and what the aims of the new government would be: to insure the safety of the pilgrimage routes, to resume the holy war against the Byzantines, to reform the coinage, to abolish uncanonical taxes, to repair and maintain the mosques, to protect the non-Muslims, and to uphold the Sunna of the Prophet. This document, which was preserved verbatim and later copied into histories of the times, well illustrates Fatimid policy. It represented a claim to rule on principles that ought to be applicable in the case of any Islamic government, but by implication had not been true for the prior regime. Jawhar's forces then crossed the pontoon bridge from Gīza into Fusṭāṭ and set up camp to the north of the mosque of Ibn Ṭūlūn on the site of what was later to become the city of Cairo. Jawhar himself led prayers in the Old Mosque of ʿAmr in Fusṭāṭ and the preacher, dressed now in Fatimid white in place of Abbasid black, recited the Friday sermon in the name of al-Muʿizz for the first time in Egypt.[17]

Even though Jawhar's conquest had been peaceful for the most part, the task of governing Egypt would not be quite as simple. The Fatimids planned in advance many of the initiatives undertaken by Jawhar, such as building a separate capital as a residential enclave for the troops and the government. As they had done sixty years earlier in the Maghrib, they also re-employed the administration of the previous regime in the bureaucracy and the judiciary. Jawhar's efforts to stabilise the Egyptian economy and to restore prosperity were thus aided by maintaining administrative continuity with the former regime. He also conducted an aggressive military campaign against the brigands who had previously contributed to the general suffering and chaos.

Once assured of his control over the situation, however, the sizeable army of imported Berber troops that had come with him quickly became a burden both in terms of provisioning and interactions with the local populations. Jawhar dispatched them in the direction of Syria where they marched quickly through Palestine to Damascus, which they seized before raiding northward. Whether they were ultimately headed toward Baghdad or merely conducting the promised *jihād* against the Byzantine Christians, or both, is not clear. In any case northern Syria had to be taken first. Even so this initial raid collapsed almost at once. A Fatimid army in the far north constituted, moreover, a major penetration into the Byzantine sphere of influence. The Berbers soon not only suffered a defeat at the hands of the Byzantines, but next had to face an angry Qarmatian force shortly thereafter in front of Damascus where they were soundly beaten. The Qarmatians, who displayed no allegiance or special regard for their fellow Ismailis, had gathered a group of tribal forces out of the east and added to them renegade former soldiers from Ikhshīdid territories. This army now invaded Egypt, rampaged through the eastern Delta, and ultimately confronted Jawhar at his new encampment. The good fortune of the Fatimid commander did not desert him, however, and in Rabīʿ I 361/December 971, he finally expelled the Qarmatians from Egypt.

The fortified enclave he was then building along the Nile north of the Mosque of Ibn Ṭūlūn was of substantial benefit to Jawhar. It rapidly became a city and was then called al-Manṣūriyya in imitation of the city in Tunisia where the imam continued to reside. Jawhar brought the plan for this new capital with him. Like its namesake he gave it a northern gate called al-Futūḥ, a southern gate called al-Zawayla, and a central congregational mosque named al-Azhar.

Keeping the Shiʿi army separate from the crowded city of Fusṭāṭ also proved beneficial. Egypt was at the time almost totally Sunni as far as its Muslim population was concerned. Although the heads of both the local Ḥasanid and Ḥusaynid families eventually acquiesced in the rule of Fatimid imams, whom they appeared to accept as blood relatives, they showed little or no sign of adopting Ismaili Shiʿism. Jawhar therefore introduced Shiʿi ritual with care and caution. The Shiʿi formula in the call to prayer was used first in the mosque of Ibn Ṭūlūn (Jumādā 1/March 970) and only later in the Old Mosque of ʿAmr in Fusṭāṭ. The Ismaili method for determining the end of Ramaḍān caused difficulties in the earliest instance because it allowed the Shiʿa to break the fast one day ahead of the Sunnis. Later, additional Shiʿi practices entered Egypt including the celebration of the event of Ghadīr Khumm and the elaborate emotional mourning of ʿAshūrāʾ. When the Sunnis had little or no physical contact with the Shiʿa, the friction between them was relatively small. If the regime tried to force the issue publicly, troubles and violence always followed. Nevertheless, the chroniclers report waves of enthusiasm for the Ismaili religious appeal during the first decades of Fatimid rule. It would be impossible, however, to determine accurately what percentage of the population ever actually became Ismaili. In Egypt as a whole, the numbers certainly remained relatively small.

Jawhar's defeat of the Qarmatians and his growing ability in general to regulate the affairs of Egypt, added to his construction of a palace in the new city, convinced the caliph al-Muʿizz to transfer the court. As with the conquest before, he prepared this move meticulously. Revolts by the Zanāta Berbers in the central Maghrib caused serious difficulties at first and the Ḥamdūnids of Masīla, once quite loyal to the Fatimids, went over to the Umayyads. Zīrī b. Manād and other commanders sent after the rebels failed to subdue them; Zīrī himself was killed. Only after Buluggīn the son of Zīrī had won full revenge did quiet return to the western territories. Buluggīn was given the responsibility for the western domains of the Fatimids when al-Muʿizz departed. Sicily remained under its long-time governor, an amir from the family of al-Ḥasan al-Kalbī. As with the prior departure of Jawhar, al-Muʿizz collected great sums of money and made them ready for transport along with large quantities of valuables and, symbolically of the finality of this move, the coffins of the three deceased Fatimid caliphs. In Ṣafar 362/November 972, the party set off. They travelled slowly and along the way several important figures died, among them the majordomo Jawdhar and the famous Andalusian court poet Ibn Hāni'. In Ramaḍān 362/June of 973, the imam entered his new capital, which only then became the 'City of al-Mu'izz's Victory', al-Qāhira al-Mu'izziyya, or more simply, Cairo.

2 *A Century of Empire*

Cairo as the New Centre

For Ismailis the residence of the imam is literally the centre of the physical world. With his move to Egypt and to his newly created capital city, al-Muʿizz had shifted the focus of that devotion from the Maghrib to Cairo. Henceforth his followers would come here to learn what was and was not proper in Islam; their supreme guide in whom and from whom all spiritual and temporal authority radiated was present only in that city. It became therefore critical that the abode of the imam be suitably embellished both physically and administratively. Even for the supporters of the new regime who acknowledged its claim to rule but without accepting the Ismaili understanding of the imamate, Cairo became the seat of a powerful empire now encompassing within it much of North Africa, Sicily, large sections of Syria, the Red Sea and the Hijaz. For the first time under Islam Egypt was not simply a province but an independent state, one centred in fact on Cairo itself.

Perhaps as a consequence, economic patterns in the Mediterranean world shifted with the imam. More likely the prevailing directions of commercial trade were already changing. Over at least the century before, in part because of the spread of Islam westward across North Africa and into Spain, Qayrawān and its surroundings came to be a major entrepôt of this trade. Even in the late Aghlabid and early decades of Fatimid rule, that area held its own due, quite possibly, to the yield of warfare in Sicily and then Italy. However, the Christian north began, not merely to revive, but to pursue aggressively trans-Mediterranean trade with Egypt in particular, which, in turn, started to exploit more actively its access to the Red Sea, Yemen and from there to India. The Ismaili movement had long since followed this route as well. It was only natural for the Fatimids both to encourage the possibility of trading along it and to institute a means for controlling it. Significantly, the role once played by Qayrawān, now became that of Fusṭāṭ, the old commercial capital of Egypt, which lay directly on the Nile just south of Cairo. Goods coming from the east stopped there and were then transferred for export northward. It cannot have hurt that Egypt now became the centre of an empire just as this trade entered a more intense phase.

A fair question, but one ultimately difficult to answer, is whether or not the Fatimid imams intended Cairo to remain their capital had they managed to achieve the final step eastward and the conquest of Baghdad. Certainly Baghdad itself, the Abbasid city, would never have served in this capacity, but yet another, new urban creation could easily follow. Nevertheless, for all the evidence that the Fatimids pursued such a policy at least until the defeat in 451/1060 of al-Basāsīrī, the last champion of theirs who had a serious chance of permanently ousting the Abbasids, it remains unclear if they had thoughts of moving again rather than simply governing the east from Cairo.

As with their earlier imperial cities in the Maghrib, the new rulers spared little to adorn this later capital. The massive palace complex built by them in Cairo became almost legendary for its scope and opulence. There were in fact two palaces separated by a massive parade ground. Unfortunately, little or no trace of it survives and any attempt at reconstruction, even on paper or in theory, depends on approximations determined by the presence of later buildings that reportedly occupied some portion of the original palace area.[1]

The building of congregational mosques was an equally important element of this same policy. Fusṭāṭ, as the pre-existing capital, was crowded with inhabitants few of whom were Ismailis.

It was mainly a commercial centre and had a long-established tradition of Sunni Islam that considered its main mosque to be the one bearing the name of ʿAmr b. al-ʿĀṣ, the Muslim conqueror of Egypt, a person regarded by the Shiʿa as an arch-villain for his support of Muʿāwiya against ʿAlī. Therefore, almost immediately upon his arrival, Jawhar commenced construction of al-Azhar, which later became the most famous mosque in Egypt. For the first decades, however, it served as the principal mosque of the army, the government and the Ismaili community in Egypt. Already near the end of his reign, al-ʿAzīz started building yet another just north of the city wall which his son, al-Ḥākim, completed. Although only one mosque among several that al-Ḥākim sponsored, it eventually bore his name.

Various indications connected to early Fatimid projects of this kind suggest that they consciously hoped to create symbolically in Cairo a centre for pilgrimage much like Mecca and Medina, the holy cities of their ancestors, the founders of Islam itself. Still their intent was not to replace the older shrines but rather to add to them.[2]

New Institutions

As with the building programme, new institutions developed in Egypt as aspects of Fatimid rule that in part grew out of an earlier practice and yet became typical of it in its later phases. One example is the post of chief justice, the judge of judges (*qāḍī al-quḍāt*). In the Maghrib each city had its own judge with that of Qayrawān normally regarded as the most important. Sicily, for example, had its own judge who was not under the others. In Egypt the first Fatimid judge was a holdover from the prior government; he was not, needless to say, an Ismaili. Likewise, in fact, many of the judges appointed during the Maghribi period were not Ismailis, which suggests that the administration of the law, despite its close connection to religious policy, accommodated the other *madhhab*s and was generally tolerant.

The famous Qāḍī al-Nuʿmān, at least under both al-Manṣūr and al-Muʿizz, certainly held the highest rank possible in his time. Later in Cairo, however, two of his sons, one after the other, were accorded an even higher status and finally his grandson became the first appointed formally to the office that controlled all the judges of the empire, who were thus subordinate to him. As one aspect of this new role, the supreme judge was responsible for a number of administrative operations such as supervision of the coinage and of weights and measures. Another, however, involved religious policy more directly. These same descendants of al-Nuʿmān held, in addition to the judiciary, the office of chief *dāʿī* (*dāʿī al-duʿāt*) of the Ismaili religious organisation, the *daʿwa*, and therefore one of their regular duties included providing religious instruction both locally and abroad.

As head of the religious mission, the chief *dāʿī* was required by the nature of his office to compose and deliver, at least once a week, a lesson on Ismaili doctrine to the members of the Ismaili community. Away from Cairo, these lessons were provided by subordinate *dāʿīs* appointed by him. Strictly within previous Ismaili circles such an office was called the 'Gate' (the Gate of Gates, *bāb al-abwāb*), denoting a slightly different role, that of controlling access to the imam. Elements of the later practice had existed for a long time and Qāḍī al-Nuʿmān himself frequently taught in these formerly semi-public sessions. Under al-Ḥākim, however, they achieved a formal regularity that had then become characteristic of the Fatimids and was to last until the very end of their rule.

For the Ismaili adherents of the caliphs these weekly sessions, called the *majlis al-ḥikma*, were the principal focus of their communal devotions. At each session they paid a fee for the privilege (in accord with a Qur'anic injunction) and these funds, collected both locally and throughout the network of Ismaili communities world-wide, accrued to the treasury of the imams.

Another institution of special note was the imam's library and also his treasury, or rather treasuries, of which there were many, each holding different kinds of valuables. The library must have been astonishingly rich in terms of the number and variety of the volumes in it. Although each of the previous imams had added to it, in Cairo there were few limits to what it might contain. Certainly the occasional reports about what it held, even setting aside some exaggeration, suggest that there can hardly have been a more complete collection of books anywhere else in the world.[3]

The imam's library holdings, however, were not for public use and thus, although a magnificent treasury of books, documents and other writings, their presence did not necessarily add to the intellectual life of the capital. But, in the year 395/1005, al-Ḥākim created what appears to be an entirely new and all but unprecedented institution, the House of Learning (Dār al-Ḥikma or Dār al-ʿIlm), a public library-academy, to serve the general populace. He donated to it, for example, many volumes from his own collections and provided the means whereby ordinary folk might not simply read but also make copies of these same books. In addition he appointed for it a teaching staff of experts in various academic subjects. Curiously, when it was first founded, this institution was not specifically Ismaili in any way; most, if not all of the professors, were Sunni, a fact that has puzzled historians ever since.[4]

The institutions just discussed belong to the realm of culture and religion; but the main challenge for Fatimid rule – as with almost any other – remained what might be called the secular state. Even before the acquisition of Egypt and the eastern Mediterranean, the caliphs had added substantial numbers of non-Ismailis to the bureaucracy and the army. Among the Berbers only the Kutāma were clearly Ismaili and, in the various bureaux of government, Ismailis held office mainly in those dealing with religious affairs. In Egypt these trends accelerated. While the Kutāma came with the invading army, their preponderance increasingly diminished as other Maghribi groups arrived to form separate contingents. Moreover, in less than a decade, the participation of units of eastern origin, principally formed of Turks, had reached such a level that they threatened the North Africans – that is, the Westerners – who began to express their resentment of the newly arrived Easterners. Within the civilian departments, such as the chancery, finance and even the judiciary, most of the lesser offices – the clerks and accountants, for example – were in the hands of Christians, as had been true for Egypt in the pre-Fatimid period. When the Fatimids took Egypt, the Christian population was still fairly substantial.

Directing and regulating both the military and the civilian departments of government obviously was more complex in the Egyptian situation than previously in the Maghrib, if only because of the size and scope of what was involved. A prior policy of avoiding the delegation of power to a wazir could not continue, although al-Muʿizz, al-ʿAzīz, and especially al-Ḥākim, made a vain attempt to do so at least in part. Al-ʿAzīz, himself a fairly dynamic and active ruler, was eventually forced, however, to recognise reality. In 367/977, he raised to the post of wazir Yaʿqūb Ibn Killis, who was already heavily involved in the administration of the state, having worked in Egypt both before the Fatimids and having come back to it from the Maghrib along with al-Muʿizz. It was the first such appointment under this dynasty. Thereafter, with only two short temporary lapses, Ibn Killis managed the administration of the empire until his death in 380/991.

The case of Ibn Killis is instructive as a model of much later types and yet is also of special interest because of his unique situation in having converted from Judaism not merely to Islam but to Ismailism. He certainly knew Egypt and Syria in ways few authorities did; his understanding of revenues, expenditures and other financial matters aided the new government immensely as a result. Yet he also, once converted, played a part in the promotion of Ismaili legal and religious affairs. It was he who must be credited with the implementation of a formal system of the teaching of Ismaili law; he also composed a important textbook on the subject that after him was known as the '*Wazīr's Book*'.

Given Ibn Killis's unique talents, his great personal wealth and influence, and his 'Ismaili' interests, the chance of finding another like him was remote and, after his death, al-ʿAzīz made no attempt to replace him. This caliph, like his father al-Muʿizz and his son al-Ḥākim, obviously preferred if at all to rule without sharing power.

Following Ibn Killis, and until the reign of al-Ẓāhir, the demands of the day to day tasks of administrating the growing bureaucracy and the various, often mutually jealous, units of the army fell to the *wāsiṭa*, a kind of lesser wazir with poorly defined authority whose duties included immediate supervision of either the military or the civilian departments or both together. In any case no one who held that office lasted long in it. The next case more like that of Ibn Killis is the later career of al-Jarjarāʾī, who had served under al-Ḥākim, and then his son al-Ẓāhir, for whom he was first the *wāsiṭa* and then the wazir, and finally continued as wazir to al-Mustanṣir. During the later reigns and prior to his death in 436/1045, al-Jarjarāʾī eventually accumulated considerable power.

Later still is al-Yāzūrī, whose slow rise through various subordinate posts ultimately brought him to the wazirate and there to great influence until his eventual disgrace and execution in 450/1058. Most significantly, al-Yāzūrī took control also of the judiciary and the *daʿwa,* thus combining all three offices – the first to do so. Even under Ibn Killis the judiciary – including supervision of coinage and other matters – and the teaching mission remained independent. But, from about 441/1049 under al-Yāzūrī the centralisation of power in the wazirate became ever more complete.

With the dismissal of al-Yāzūrī, however, although subsequent holders of the wazirate often controlled these other offices as well, few of the individuals involved ever lasted more than a few months, some only a few days, prior to their own demotion. The institutions of government in this period of Fatimid rule were thus more often than not in a state of flux and change.

When the Fatimids first arrived in Egypt they accepted rule over a large number of Christians, predominantly Copts but also a not inconsiderable group of Melkites, and a thriving Jewish community. In general the new government's relations with these protected minorities was reasonably amicable. Both Christians and Jews served in the government, with substantial numbers in the lower bureaucracies. Under al-Ḥākim several holders of the office of *wāsiṭa* were unconverted Christians. Two Jews (converted) were wazirs in this same century. The sole period of hostility falls during one phase of al-Ḥākim's reign when the government went out of its way to enforce sumptuary laws that disadvantageously affected Jews and Christians. Then also many churches and synagogues were ordered destroyed by the state. Although most of these same regulations were later cancelled by al-Ḥākim himself, Christians and Jews naturally regarded these acts as deliberate persecution.

Still both communities preserve extremely valuable records and accounts that cover the early Fatimids in Egypt. This is particularly the case with the Jewish geniza, an incredibly important collection of discarded papers of all sorts, originally in a room of a synagogue in Fusṭāṭ that was rebuilt beginning under al-Ḥākim as a replacement for one destroyed some years prior. For a historical era that is so poorly represented by surviving documents – there is no archive of any kind from this period – the disorderly and chaotic debris preserved by chance in this one geniza represents a historical treasure-trove.[5]

The Ismaili Movement at Maturity

Within a new imperial centre now much closer to the heartland of Islam, the Ismaili movement reached its greatest successes in terms of spread and popularity. Over the initial decades of their rule in Egypt, the Fatimids attracted support both locally and abroad. In this period several important developments outside of the confines of the empire involved a declaration by a local ruler in favour of the Shiʿi Ismaili caliph. A notable case was that of the ʿUqaylid amir in Mosul, who on more than one occasion professed to accept Fatimid suzerainty. Another is the much more prominent, though temporary, conquest of Baghdad itself by al-Basāsīrī at mid-century. Even later, when the lines hardened internally, recruits continued to join the movement outside. In contrast to the situation in the Maghrib, where after the first wave of influx there are fewer signs of visitations by Ismailis from outside, many of the later converts actually came to Cairo to pay homage to the imam.

But not all of the new enthusiasm was completely welcome. Ismaili doctrine with respect to the imam could easily be distorted elevating his office above that of both the Prophet and ʿAlī, his successor. A living imam holds absolute authority in his time; why not insist therefore that he is thus of greater importance than his deceased ancestors? Beyond this almost natural enhancement of traditional Shiʿi teachings, messianic expectations with regard to this or that imam appeared regularly, especially in the midst of troubled or otherwise unusual circumstances.

The reign of al-Ḥākim was one of those special moments.[6] In part because of his unpredictable and unfathomable style, this caliph attracted more than his share of self-appointed agents all claiming to represent him although, in fact, many of them advocated a view of him quite at odds with that offered by others. Toward the end of his rule this tendency got out of hand and resulted in a major conflict within the Ismaili movement. On the one side a group or groups of supporters, led by several figures that had come to Cairo from the east, emphasised al-Ḥākim's divine nature with increasing boldness. On the other, apparently with official sanction and the power of the government behind it, the establishment denied this claim of al-Ḥākim's divinity. What survived of the former group later became the Druze, a name not of their own choosing but one associated with them because of al-Darazī, who was the first of this tendency to promote it publicly in Cairo. The other side, however, comprised individuals holding high posts in the regime, chief among them the head of the Ismaili mission itself, Khatkīn al-Ḍayf.

The issues at stake posed a serious threat both for the continuation and long term success of the Ismaili movement and for the immediate health and well-being of the caliphate. To counter it most effectively, Khatkīn and the central administration imported from the east the leading specialist in Ismaili doctrines, the formidable Ḥamīd al-Dīn al-Kirmānī, who happened to reside at that time in Iraq, most likely in Baghdad. He came to Cairo and began a programme of instruction that was, in part, designed to ensure the stability and continuity of the imamate against the dissidents' antinomian and messianic cult, which they were then developing around the personality of al-Ḥākim.[7] With the imam's mysterious disappearance in 411/1021, the Ismaili establishment finally achieved its aim in this conflict. After some slight hesitation, the succession to al-Ẓāhir passed relatively smoothly. The Druze were ousted from Egypt completely, to survive only in remote areas of Syria, hardly representing any longer a danger to the Fatimids.[8]

Cairo, however, continued to attract a stream of outsiders drawn there on behalf of the Ismaili cause. Two curiously parallel cases from the reign of al-Mustanṣir well illustrate what must be regarded as a general tendency. They are Nāṣir-i Khusraw and al-Mu'ayyad fi'l-Dīn al-Shīrāzī.[9] Both arrived in Cairo within a year of each other and both later rose to positions of extreme importance, for the first as a writer and missionary, and the second as a writer, government agent and ultimately as the *dā'ī*-in-chief. Significantly, both came from Iran. Nāṣir later returned there and, writing exclusively in Persian, became a major literary figure. Al-Mu'ayyad wrote principally in Arabic but his written works, too, attained among those later Ismailis who continued to study in Arabic the highest possible status.

Although unusually successful, the careers of these two *dā'īs* may be regarded as indicative of what happened with many others and of how Cairo, as the headquarters of the Ismaili movement, played a role well beyond the confines of the Egyptian state. But not all Fatimid supporters left home and travelled to Egypt. There were important pockets of Ismailis throughout the territories not under the direct control of the caliph, including Yemen, India, Khurāsān and, most particularly, sections of the areas immediately surrounding Baghdad, at the very heart of Abbasid rule.

The case of the Turkish *amīr* al-Basāsīrī is the most famous but lesser examples existed, among them some of those who aided al-Basāsīrī at various points in his revolt. The exact situation in his case was, however, extremely complex with numerous Arab tribal factions and Turkish mercenaries all acting in their own interests and that of the Fatimids only when advantageous to them. Against these groups were the Abbasid caliph, many of his retinue, and most significantly the Saljuk Turks under Tughril Beg, who first intervened in Iraqi affairs on the pretext of a campaign directed ultimately against Egypt and the Ismaili rulers there. But aside from Tughril and the Abbasid caliph, the other parties, including members of Tughril's own Saljuk family, frequently switched sides in the midst of the conflict.

Al-Yāzūrī, the wazir in Cairo at the time, preferred to wage the ensuing battle in the east. To that end he dispatched al-Mu'ayyad, himself originally once influential with Abū Kālījar, one of the last of the Buwayhid rulers in Iraq, as the Fatimid agent commissioned to foment a revolt to counter the moves of Tughril.

Al-Muʾayyad brought with him from Egypt a vast sum of money and weapons, and he attempted to use them and his own influence to create an anti-Saljuk, pro-Fatimid alliance. Al-Basāsīrī, who may have had Shiʿi leanings prior to this venture, was, in any case, already in rebellion against the Abbasids and Tughril. The combination of al-Muʾayyad's intrigue with al-Basāsīrī's troops, aided by tribes that joined him, allowed the rebels to take advantage when, to deal with a family revolt elsewhere, Tughril was forced to abandon Baghdad temporarily. Late in 450/1059, al-Basāsīrī captured the Abbasid capital and proclaimed that city's adherence to the Fatimids.

His success and that of al-Mustanṣir, whose name now appeared in the Friday sermon in Baghdad, was short lived. Forty weeks later, the affair was all but over. Cairo, once so eager to provide support, had long since come to regret what looked more and more like an ill-planned and ill-conceived adventure. Indeed later non-Ismaili historians writing in Egypt, such as al-Maqrīzī, noted that this incident marked both the greatest achievement of the Fatimids and yet also the beginning of their decline.[10]

Nevertheless, although the details of this venture differ from others, the hand of the Ismaili movement in them is clear; the Fatimids during this period did not regard themselves as rulers of a political state based solely in Egypt but as imams of a much broader claim to govern the whole of the Islamic domain. And, at least until schism again split one faction of the Ismaili community away from the others, the hope of an eventual triumph over the Abbasids persisted and was acted upon whenever a feasible opportunity presented itself. To that end, despite the disappointment of al-Basāsīrī's ultimate failure, recruits continued to sign up in the territories of the enemy and many of them, such as the famous Iranian Ḥasan b. Ṣabbāḥ and the Yemeni Lamak b. Malik, also made their way to Cairo in a later period.

Rivalries and Foreign Relations

With the initial thrust of their armies into Syria and with recognition of the dynasty in the holy cities of the Hijaz shortly after the conquest of Egypt, the Fatimids obtained the greatest extent of their political dominion. They had achieved an empire reaching, at least in theory, from the farthest Maghrib across North Africa to the Red Sea with appendages in Sicily, Palestine, Syria and the Hijaz. But, by the end of the following century, little of all that remained in their hands. Given the inherent difficulty of governing such a vast and disparate territory, it would have been quite remarkable had they managed otherwise.

An interesting case in point is Syria, which was certainly an object almost of obsession for the caliph al-ʿAzīz, who may have inherited his concern from his father. Syria lay along the only feasible route from Egypt to Abbasid Iraq and the east. If Baghdad was the urgent goal of the Fatimids, as much evidence indicates, then they had to master Syria. However, not unlike the Maghrib, Syria presented a complicated pattern of tribal control over rural areas and of major cities and towns each with their own internal and purely local factions. In the north, moreover, the Byzantines were constantly on the alert to protect their interests and take advantage of any opportunity allowed them for expansion. A Byzantine army under John Tzimisces was, for example, able to penetrate with relative ease into the south, almost within sight of Jerusalem in 975.[11] Despite the advice of the wazir Ibn Killis, who knew well the near impossibility of capturing and holding Syria, al-ʿAzīz persisted until, as he prepared for yet one more attempt, death overtook him.

Thereafter, under the later imams, the Fatimids pursued the road through Syria with less urgency. The dream of eastern conquests did not die but gradually the reality of Syrian politics forced them to accept a system of local allegiances among the nominal rulers of the cities and the princely families that dominated the local Arab tribes. Already, in the first years of their rule from Egypt, they realised that if Syria was the way to the east, it was also likely an avenue for the reverse, for an invading force coming against them, as had happened more than once with the Qarmatians. Gradually, in fact, Fatimid hegemony in Syria in its various forms, rather than part of an offensive strategy, became a line of defence protecting the caliphal state in Egypt. Even so, the increasing intrusion there of Turkish troops, first as mercenaries, some in the pay of the Fatimids themselves, and then of the Saljuks, steadily reduced their own presence. By 468/1076, for example, the Saljuks gained permanent control over Damascus.[12]

In contrast to Syria the far West posed little direct danger to Egypt. Its loyalty and continued attachment to the Fatimids, especially to the protection of Ismailis who still resided in the cities of the Maghrib, was, however, often in doubt. The caliph al-Muʿizz left behind him the emirate of the Zīrids, whose nominal rule was to last until 543/1148.[13] But this period was certainly not one of prosperity and the general decline of North Africa is noteworthy in many respects. By 407/1016 when the long reign of al-Muʿizz b. Bādīs began, the state he inherited was already divided between himself, holding the Tunisian heartland, and his uncle of the Ḥammādid branch, ruling over the territories to the west. A severely debilitating outbreak of plague and famine in 395/1004–05 had hurt everyone. Then shortly after this Zīrid al-Muʿizz assumed power, anti-Shiʿa riots in Qayrawān and some other cities decimated the remaining Ismaili communities there. The government was either too weak to prevent these horrors or possibly secretly connived in them hoping to gain by the distraction they offered. These two tendencies, economic failure that promoted a precipitous decline in the prosperity of the population, and the religiously based, xenophobic attacks on the adherents of the distant Ismaili imam, appear to have gone hand in hand. Over the long term, as the prevailing trade patterns shifted away from Ifrīqiya toward Egypt and from east-west to north-south, Zīrid North Africa suffered. As one consequence, the Ismailis also disappeared from the region altogether. Moreover, Muslim warfare against the Christians, once a rich source of money and slaves to fuel the local economy of, first the Aghlabids and then the early Fatimids, now turned in favour of the other side. As the various Christian powers to the north grew stronger and more able to raid both Sicily and the North African coast, what forces the Zīrids could maintain were increasingly required for basic defence, or even to prop up the Muslims of Sicily lest it should fall and thus move the enemy even closer.

The anti-Ismaili pogroms in the Maghrib did not end until all of the Ismailis were wiped out, leaving eventually nothing but the adherents of the Mālikī legal school. The same Mālikīs had for over a century cultivated a vision of themselves as the ascetically pious orthodox martyrs to cruel and irreligiously heretical Fatimids. Mālikī scholars lost no opportunity to record and to embellish with outright hagiography every example in which one of their own suffered. Given this situation, therefore, with less and less interest in preserving his ties to Cairo, that the Zīrid al-Muʿizz chose to break with the Fatimids and to recognise the Abbasids in their place is perhaps understandable. That he wavered back and forth following one policy and then cancelling it is, however, less so. A most curious example was one of his renunciations of the Fatimids that led to the wazir al-Yāzūrī's scheme to send in his direction the Arab tribe of Hilāl, which previously resided on Egyptian territory. Presumably, the motive of the wazir was revenge (either for a personal slight or for the Zīrid's disloyalty, or both). Whatever the exact cause, the net effect of the mass migration of these Arab tribes into the central Maghrib, already suffering severe economic ill-health and fragmentation, wrought unprecedented devastation.[14] The Zīrids survived, but just barely, confined to a few protected cities. Ironically, the Zīrid al-Muʿizz in 449/1057 finally reaffirmed his allegiance to the Fatimid caliph and remained loyal thereafter until he died in 454/1062.

Fatimid Sicily fared better but was, even so, not immune to long-term decline. The Fatimids had appeared on the scene not long after the final conquest of the island by the Muslims in 289/902. They, like their predecessors, continued to press forward against the Christians by raiding and, on occasion, occupying portions of the Italian mainland. In 322–324/934–935, a Fatimid fleet raided the Italian coast between Genoa and Pisa with great profit; even as late as the years 395–406/1004–1015, they did so again several times. As his vassal in control of Sicily, the caliph had appointed al-Ḥasan b. ʿAlī al-Kalbī, the son of the son-in-law of one of the first Fatimid governors there. This al-Ḥasan had most recently served with particular distinction in the fight against the Kharijite rebel Abū Yazīd. He was to commence a period of memorable success. His descendants, ruling from their capital in Palermo, witnessed an era of cultural brilliance. Relations between the Kalbīds of Sicily and the court in Cairo also included the active participation of senior members of this same family in Egypt. Upon the accession of the young al-Ḥākim, the North African contingents of the army insisted on having a local Kalbīd amir, al-Ḥasan b. ʿAmmār, as regent.

Eventually, however, the situation in Sicily, as in the Maghrib, deteriorated into fractious chaos. The island was ever more distant from Fatimid concerns, and its consequent autonomy, rather than allowing for the rise of a strong central leadership, yielded instead fragmentation. As the local powers split apart and commenced internal warfare against each other, the Zīrids at first attempted to intervene to preserve Muslim rule and thereby counter the Christians. The latter, however, were also not represented by a single force but by many: the city-states of Pisa, Genoa and Venice; the Byzantines, German emperors and the Normans, all in a shifting array of alliances and counter-alliances. Certain of the Christian powers were often associated with one Muslim faction or the other, and that form of access finally allowed the entry into the island of the Normans, who began in 464/1071 their own conquest of Sicily. Long before then, however, the Kalbīd reign had ended with the death in 445/1053 of the last *amīr* of this family.

Poorly settled and all but destitute, the holy cities of Mecca and Medina held little strategic value, except symbolically. With the establishment and embellishment of Cairo, moreover, the Fatimids created a new cult centre, one that might substitute for those in the older and less accessible Hijaz. For the Ismailis the living imam after all occupies a superior place; his abode stands, therefore, higher than the others. Yet, as the focus of the broadest measure of Muslim piety and as the common goal of pilgrimage rites, though seldom worth even a minimal military venture, the holy cities occupied a significant niche in Fatimid foreign policy.

Except for a brief direct intervention by the Ṣulayḥids of Yemen in the mid-fifth/eleventh century, and in the absence of genuine Ismaili sentiment in the Hijaz, the Fatimids relied on the favour of the local *sharīfs* for a symbolic acknowledgement of their hegemony in the Friday sermon. Most often the loyalty of the Ḥaramayn depended on the timely disbursement of cash and the transfer of goods without which the good will of the Meccans and Madinese was sorely tested both physically, due to the lack of foodstuffs in the vicinity, and morally, despite previous sympathy for Shiʿism (but of a non-Ismaili kind) in general.

Prior to the advent of the Fatimids, the Abbasids delegated control of the Ḥaramayn to their governor of Egypt. When the Fatimids subsequently assumed a similar role, the Abbasids were slow to react. With the coming of the Saljuks, however, and with the decline of Fatimid power in the second half of the reign of al-Mustanṣir, the situation reversed. Now the prestige of the Saljuk sultans, notably Alp Arslan, was reason for an active Abbasid campaign to supplant the Fatimids in the affections of the Hijazi *ashrāf.* The necessary monetary gifts now flowed from Baghdad and, except for a short intercession during the reign of al-Ḥāfiẓ, the Hijaz became once more unequivocally Abbasid.

Yemen was a different matter. Fatimid influence there came and went but never disappeared. Prior to the caliphate the whole country had once been all but entirely in the hands of the Ismaili movement. A clear revival of Ismaili activity began yet again with the rise about 439/1047, or possibly earlier, in Ḥarāz of ʿAlī b. Muḥammad al-Ṣulayḥī, who had been converted to Ismailism by the local agent of the movement.[15] From that beginning he went on to capture all of Yemen south of and including Ṣanʿāʾ by 455/1066. His sway, however, extended finally from Mecca in the north to Aden in the south as well as other parts of Arabia. ʿAlī's murder in 459/1006, en route to Mecca, did not end Ṣulayḥīd rule but set it back considerably. Whatever authority he might have exerted over the Hijaz ceased; likewise the north of Yemen subsequently fell out of the Fatimid sphere. Still, one century after the imam's entry into Egypt, of all the outlying territories once within the greater Fatimid empire, besides a few coastal towns of Syria and Palestine and Egypt itself, only parts of Yemen remained.

Signs of Weakness

Once in control of Egypt and the other regions connected with it, in addition to North Africa and Sicily, the Fatimids now possessed an impressive political domain. However, all along, aspects of the way the imams governed had indicated elementary weaknesses, in part traceable, ironically, to religious policy. As Shiʿa attempting to rule over territories in which the Muslim population was predominately Sunni, their prospects for longevity were never good unless they could manage to convert a substantial portion of their citizenry to Ismailism. The model for such a development must surely have been the Kutāma Berbers, whose continued religious devotion provided a strong foundation – especially in the military – for the Fatimids. Individual converts, while of immense benefit in propagating and spreading the Ismaili message and its doctrines intellectually, or by providing dependable administrative staff, could not substitute for troops either in the field or in policing areas only nominally under the direct control of the state. However, the situation with respect to the Kutāma was apparently unique; no other group or tribal body, particularly none that contributed major contingents to the army, ever converted in the same manner. The Ṣanhāja, for a long time a mainstay of the Fatimid military, were never truly Ismaili, for example.

Large parts of Egypt and Syria, mainly in the countryside, like the Maghrib, moreover, were dominated by Bedouin tribes, in this case Arabs not Berbers. The Fatimids gained no religious influence over them, nor curiously is there evidence that they attempted to foster Ismaili Shiʿism among them. One result was a failure to control them effectively. And frequently these same tribal groups either sided with an enemy when the opportunity arose, or rose in rebellion on their own. Two interesting cases of this kind in the reign of al-Ḥākim, moreover, had a religious dimension. Each was led in part by a sort of counter-imam, not dissimilar to the Fatimids. In this aspect they resembled several such events in the Maghrib, including that of Abū Yazīd, where one tribe and its imam revolted against the state in a movement that recalled the case of Abū ʿAbdallāh and the Kutāma.

The first of these later incidents is the rebellion of the Umayyad pretender Abū Rakwa Walīd b. Hishām. About 395/1005, with the support of Zanāta Berbers, he rose in the area of Barqa on the Libyan-Egyptian border. Soon he added the Arab tribe of Qurra in the Nile delta just east of Alexandria. One army sent against this combined force was defeated and Abū Rakwa began to move toward Cairo and Fusṭāṭ. The threat he posed was real and the Fatimids all but succumbed to panic. Although dramatic action by the army eventually put down this rebellion, that it could occur so close to Cairo revealed how unreliable al-Ḥākim's support was both among the rural tribes and in the general urban population of Egypt.

The other case involved the tribe of Ṭayy, which held sway over southern Palestine. During this period its leader was a member of the Jarrāḥid family – for much of it Mufarrij b. Daghfal b. al-Jarrāḥ – who played a wily game of picking his causes and forming allegiances to suit his own independent purposes. Previously an ally of the Qarmatians in their fight with the Fatimids, in 363/974, the Ṭayy switched sides quite opportunely during an invasion of Egypt that year, having accepted a bribe to do so from the caliph al-Muʿizz. But, although often useful to the Fatimids – they helped against Abū Rakwa, for example – they were never entirely trustworthy. During one of their several revolts, they sided, for example, with a Meccan *sharīf* whom they tried to set up in 403/1012 as the imam, in opposition to al-Ḥākim but based on a model of the imamate similar to his.

These cases are by no means the only ones; the loyalty of the Bedouin clans was a constant problem, and since they often served as an auxiliary military for the Fatimids, their support was frequently essential. Why none of these groups ever became Ismaili is, however, a puzzle. The same applies also to the contingents of the regular standing army, among whom likewise there is little sign, outside of the Kutāma, of the spread of Ismailism or of an obvious attachment to it. Where the Aghlabids had relied on Arab troops, the whole effort of Abū ʿAbdallāh and his appeal concentrated on this one Berber tribe, which, once fully converted to Shiʿism, henceforth not only defeated the Arab armies sent against them, but loyally supplied the Fatimids with a dependable army throughout their formative years in the Maghrib and even beyond. It can easily be shown, moreover, that the Fatimid military of this initial period could hardly have survived without the Kutāma. Although the new rulers quickly implemented a policy of creating a multi-ethnic army, the mounted component never expanded much beyond the addition of Berber units from closely neighbouring groups such as the Zawāwa and the Ṣanhāja, both related to the Kutāma. The two other major new elements were, first, various Slavs and other Rum, some eunuchs and some not, but all originally purchased slaves, whose functions included technical support and most especially command, and second, a large formation of foot soldiers known by the term 'Zawīla' or 'Zuwayla', apparently from the market region of the Fazzan south of Tripoli, where Sudanese slaves were bought for service in the Maghrib.

Despite a few problems of religion and loyalty even in this period, the adhesion of the Kutāma to the Fatimid religious cause was nearly total. The long preparation by Abū 'Abdallāh paid off. When the new state created a bureau of the government responsible for the pay of the troops, an individual Kutāmī, who had not previously been salaried, retained the designation of *mutaṭawwiʿ*, 'volunteer'. When the Fatimids instituted conscription to raise additional troops, the Kutāma still enlisted for service.

Of course, many peripheral questions about the fortunes of Fatimid military policy may influence the answer to this question. The Berbers, for example, proved weak outside of their original domain, as when they were sent into Syria. Not only did their foreignness cause friction with the local population but, most importantly, they failed in the face of superior Turkish arms, particular archery. Accordingly, the Fatimids, from the first encounters in Syria, began to add Turkish (and Daylamī) units to their army. Ultimately, although Nāṣir-i Khusraw could still count 20,000 Kutāma horsemen in the army of Cairo in about 439/1047, this group was decidedly, possibly even deliberately, reduced in importance. The trend toward professional, thoroughly trained and heavily armed, mounted troops with the obvious increase in cost associated with this development marginalised the tribal 'volunteers', no matter how committed they were on the basis of piety.

An incident from 376–377/986–87 may help offer another explanation. In that year al-ʿAzīz dispatched an emissary named Abu'l-Fahm Ḥasan, a Khurāsānī *dāʿī*, to the Maghrib. He was well received by the Zīrid ruler and allowed to travel on to Kutāma territory. Once there, however, instead of raising new enthusiasm for service in Egypt, which must have been his original purpose, he generated an appeal that apparently centred on himself. Ultimately he minted his own coins and rode about with numerous troops.[16] The old zeal of the Kutāma was apparently not diminished but had become slightly uncontrollable. How many of the Kutāma that Nāṣir-i Khusraw observed in Cairo in 439/1047 were recently arrived from Ifrīqiya and how many were merely descendants of an earlier first generation in Egypt? Nevertheless, even at the end of the Fatimid dynasty two centuries later, there were Kutāma in Egypt.

The Zuwayla contingents were likewise once numerous in Egypt but later disappeared. Instead Nāṣir mentions the *ʿAbīd al-shirāʾ* (purchased slaves), who by his time may have been predominately black like the Zanjīs, another group he lists. Similarly the later Fatimid army had units of Bāṭilīs and Masāmida, both North African tribal groups, but not Kutāma. It seems therefore that the Zuwayla, who were not specific in ethnic origin, in any case, were simply replaced in Egypt by blacks imported through the Aswan market (and thus not from Zuwayla). Also, in addition to the now problematic Kutāma, new Berber troops were being recruited in the farther Maghrib but by what process we do not know. Their religious affiliation is likewise undetermined. It would be interesting to know if any of the Zuwayla, or the Sudanese and Zanjīs, of the later period became active in the Ismaili cause in the religious sense. Several prominent officers of the state are said to have been blacks, but in every case there is virtually no information about religion. The same claim appears justified for nearly all of the Turkish army officers.

There are other unanswered questions about the Fatimid military and its religious loyalty. Much of the problem has to do with the nature of the sources that document so well the religious policy of the Fatimids in the Maghrib, and thus highlight the adherence of the Kutāma and many of the Slavs, but which, given also that the documentation itself is different for the later period, being largely non-Ismaili, fails to account for or to even notice what may have occurred later in regard to the interaction of religious and military institutions. Information in the earlier sources easily confirms that the Fatimids fully recognised what they owed to the Kutāma and, most importantly, they show the religious nature of this alliance between the state and its chief military support. What is lacking is a similar set of sources from later periods. It would be especially useful to have from Egypt Ismaili writings like those that cover the Maghrib. Unfortunately, nothing from later quite matches the material from North Africa. Therefore, the evidence for the later interaction of ideology and the military must be derived from a different kind of source, one that may have been blind to precisely that sort of religious policy.

A second kind of weakness that began to appear in the new situation concerns the formation of a social and bureaucratic elite in the capital that was both closely beholden to the state and could pursue its own interests even to the detriment of the caliphate. It is, of course, much harder to see how this class operated and to analyse its connection to government policy. In contrast to the military whose victories and defeats were public knowledge and of special interest to the chroniclers, the workings of the bureaucracy or the self-interested acts of members of the social elite entered history only in rare instances – the occurrence of a notable scandal, for example. They are almost always recounted in isolation from one another. Thus, in an era for which there are no personal memoirs, diaries, letters, or documents, patterns in the behaviour of the elite tend to be obscure, often completely so.

Still there are trends that can be observed for Fatimid Egypt in this period. A particularly important one is the rise and continued prominence of several families, members of which kept reoccupying certain key positions in the government. Another is the growing power of the caliph's extended family and other private retainers. Two cases illustrate the latter situation well. They are, first, the role of al-Ḥākim's much older sister, Sitt al-Mulk, in preserving the caliphate during the uncertainty surrounding his last years and eventual disappearance. It was she who orchestrated the transfer of rule to her nephew al-Ẓāhir. A closer look, moreover, reveals clear signs that she was the leading voice of a larger elite. It consisted of numerous members of the establishment and the caliph's family, who feared that the caliph, if he continued to follow the course he was then pursuing – such as appointing as his successor one or another of his cousins in place of his own son and lavishly giving away huge portions of his wealth and holdings – would bring down the empire and them with it. It is naturally impossible to say how else matters might have turned out but the power of the forces behind her shows what could happen. The interests of this new elite were not quite identical with those of the imam.

Another similar case involved the mother of al-Mustanṣir whose connection with her former master, a member of the powerful Tustarī family, long played an important role in the rule of her son, either directly or indirectly through agents who handled her affairs. And she and Sitt al-Mulk are by no means the only examples of powerful women who influenced the course of government in this period.

Slightly less powerful but in many ways more prominent because they held appointments to key public posts were several members of the families of Qāḍī al-Nuʿmān[17] and then of Saʿīd b. Malik al-Fāriqī.[18] Again these two cases are not unique except in the amount of information available about them. Starting in Egypt two of Qāḍī al-Nuʿmān's sons, two grandsons, and one great-grandson rose to the position of chief qadi and all five were also chiefs of the Ismaili mission, as the *dāʿī al-duʿāt*. Whether each was completely qualified for these appointments became less and less important against their illustrious pedigree and family name. The last of them, al-Qāsim b. ʿAbd al-ʿAzīz, in fact, was considered by many to be incompetent, most particularly as a judge, but also as head of the *daʿwa* which he, nevertheless, directed for over two decades. The al-Fāriqī family commenced its prominence with

Malik's promotion to supreme justice under al-Ḥākim. He was also in charge of the *daʿwa*. Although, like several members of al-Nuʿmān's family, he ran afoul of the caliph and was eventually executed – in Malik's case quite possibly for collusion with Sitt al-Mulk – his service thus ending in disgrace, again like them other members of his family took over. Malik's sons occupied lesser judgeships but his brother became chief justice in 419/1028 and lasted in that position until 427/1036, whereupon he fell from grace having been caught up in a scandal of his own. Still three of his sons rose to become chief qadi (one of them four separate times), two of them were also wazirs, and one the chief *dāʿī*. In the next generation one al-Fāriqī was appointed chief justice seven times in the space of six years and was also wazir during that same period on at least five occasions. It is essential to note these aspects of Fatimid rule and to see how they contributed to a steady decline in the viability of the state, a decline that became especially precipitous over the final decade of the first century in Egypt, a period known in the historical sources as the 'Days of Trouble' (*ayyām al-fitna*) or the 'Calamity' (*al-shidda, al-shidda al-ʿuẓmā*).

Commencing about 454/1062, Fatimid Egypt experienced a long period of such extensive chaos and disorder, of famine and plague, and of general economic decline and weakness that it was remembered for a long time as a great catastrophe. So pervasive was the resulting destruction that parts of the older city of Fusṭāṭ simply ceased to exist, having been depopulated. At one point the caliph al-Mustanṣir was reduced to accepting a handout of food from a better-off supporter. To maintain even the semblance of order in his administration and army, he was forced to hand over the greater share of his treasury, including objects of unique beauty and rarity and whole rooms full of valuable books. All in all there can be no doubt about the seriousness of these events and how close the Fatimids came then to being overthrown as a direct result of them. Units of the army in Egypt, though not in Cairo itself, at least once proclaimed their allegiance to the Abbasids. The caliph ultimately decided he had no other option but to call on his strongest military commander, Badr al-Jamālī, to intervene and to bring with him from outside sufficient force to restore order. His action seems fully justified under these circumstances.

That such a move would change the character of Fatimid rule forever may have then appeared less inevitable. But the problems that brought about the collapse were already there. It is usual to attribute these troubles to seven successive years of low Niles which caused in turn, according to this view, a corresponding period of famine leading eventually to the breakdown of general order. Certainly the annual rise of the river's level is crucial to the prosperity of Egyptian agriculture. Each year its crest was duly noted and proclaimed but the data for the period in question does not confirm any unusual occurrence of low readings. The years 453/1061 through 455/1063, for example, were not problems; 455 was especially high; 460 was quite low, but 461/1068–9 was high again. This explanation simply does not account for what happened.

The breakdown must be attributed to the failure of the government itself to deal with an increasingly fragmented military and to control a self-aggrandising, incompetent bureaucracy that often responded less to the needs of the state than to its own interests and the elite from which it came and to which it therefore owed its primary allegiance.[19] Much of the disorder also resulted directly from the rivalry of ethnically segregated troops, principally the black Sudanese against the Turks, occasionally in association with the Berbers and others, and vice versa. Commanders of these units saw an opportunity for gain and they took it without regard for the chaos that ensued. The civilian elite managed to put one of their own in high office and then almost at once regretted having done so and put up another. Wazirs were appointed and replaced so often it is almost impossible now to keep track of them. As the general population starved, the upper classes speculated in the grain trade by buying large parts of the annual crop and then hoarding it until the price rose during the inevitable scarcity that followed. There were signs of all this much earlier and these kinds of corruption and mismanagement were, moreover, not unique to the Fatimids. What is troublesome is why it took so long to act appropriately. By not dealing with it at all, the caliph merely postponed what had become inevitable long before he did. That aggravated the crisis and prolonged it until it became a major disaster.

3 *A Century of Military Wazirs*

The Innovations of Badr al-Jamālī

In the midst of all but complete chaos, with his standing army divided into warring factions, the economy in shambles, and most sections of Egypt in the hands of brigands or semi-independent Arabs tribes and local warlords, the caliph al-Mustanṣir finally chose to summon a saviour. Once he had two possibilities but, with the murder in 459/1067 of ʿAlī al-Ṣulayḥī, who had been eager to perform just such a mission in Egypt, the Yemeni option had now faded from view. By 466/1073 the caliph was left with no one other than Badr al-Jamālī, then in ʿAkka. It is doubtful that he could trust any other source that might have supplied a force of sufficient size to accomplish the immense task of ridding Egypt of what was by then, due to the failure to act sooner, a well entrenched system of corruption and lawlessness.

Badr already had a distinguished prior career in service to the Fatimids. Over the previous decade in Syria and Palestine, he had been governor of Damascus twice and, in the face of persistent encroachment by the Saljuks, had managed to hold several coastal cities. Nevertheless al-Mustanṣir did not call on him earlier. Yet the crisis was by then considerably worse than, for example, in 461/1069 when the caliph sent many members of his own family, including some of his sons, away from Cairo. In fact, one son was sent to the care of Badr himself in ʿAkka. Several female members went on to Baghdad, the seat of the enemy.

Now, however, al-Mustanṣir fully grasped what must happen, and Badr rightly insisted that he bring with him his own private army. Without it he could do nothing. The time was winter. Badr nevertheless risked a desperate gamble, a crossing from Palestine to Egypt by sea. Embarking over a hundred ships with a strong force of Armenian soldiers and others all beholden to him personally, he arrived unannounced and began a march on Cairo. Since the imam had summoned him, the local players dared not oppose him; few knew why he had come in any case. Once in the capital, the answer was soon apparent as Badr ordered his forces to eliminate the old regime ruthlessly. The commanders of various pre-existing contingents of troops were executed all in one evening. Leading members of the previous administration were arrested and killed. Badr then attacked the Arab tribes of the Delta, subdued rebels in Alexandria, and turned on the Sudanese and Arabs of upper Egypt, thereby asserting his firm determination to bring all of the country back under the control of the central government.

In his attempt to re-establish Fatimid rule he was, in this way, almost entirely successful within Egypt. But former territories in distant areas were by then lost forever. The one remaining contested domain was Syria and Palestine; and there Badr obviously intended to reclaim what he could. Still, although he expended great effort, in the end he hardly won more than he lost. The advance of the Saljuks proved relentless. They took Damascus away for good about 468/1076 and even invaded Egypt where Badr, with difficulty, eventually stopped them.

Once in control, Badr adopted, and the caliph accepted, the concept that he was the wazir. But, given that what he had accomplished could not have happened without the dependable support of his own private militia, his situation hardly resembles that of any of the previous wazirs. Instead, from the beginning he was known as the 'Commander of Armed Forces' (*amīr al-juyūsh*), a title more appropriate to a new style that his arrival, in fact, introduced for the first time. Where even the most powerful of the earlier wazirs – Ibn Killis or al-Yāzūrī, for example – came to office from within the clerical bureaucracy, Badr was a soldier and his authority depended on the strength of his own corps of troops, who in fact carried his name, the *Juyūshiyya*, in recognition that it responded to him and not, it would seem, to the government at large or even the caliph.

Most significantly, Badr pursued a deliberate policy of adding soldiers to his own regiments and they were often Armenian like himself. Though many of these soldiers were Muslim, either recently converted or born of converted parents, some others were certainly Christian. For Badr, however, they provided an element of secure loyalty to him personally. Once the opening for the Armenians existed, however, like other ethnic groups before, they flocked to Egypt in great numbers bringing with them not only professional military but tradesmen, clergy, and others as well. Many subsequently rose to high positions. There were to be six or possibly seven wazirs of Armenian extraction over the next century and one among them, Bahrām, remained a Christian even while holding that august office.

Thus not long after taking over, Badr acquired full control over all aspects of the government, save only the throne and person of the caliph. Eventually, he assumed the powers of a military dictator, holding even the offices of chief judge and chief *dāʿī*, which meant that the judiciary and the *daʿwa* were under his direct supervision. The latter position is noteworthy because, in Badr's assumption of this prerogative, he became the director of the Ismaili mission both in Egypt and abroad, although his own interest in Ismaili Islam is hardly apparent. Significantly, he did not assume that office as long as the great al-Mu'ayyad fi'l-Dīn al-Shīrāzī lived, but when the latter died in 470/1077, Badr immediately added that title as well. Henceforth he was 'The Illustrious Lord, Commander of the Armed Forces, Sword of Islam, Defender of the Imam, the Guarantor of the Judges of the Muslims, Director of the Missionaries to the Believers'. Naturally, he delegated certain of these functions to underlings. None the less his power was all but total.

Badr changed the way the Fatimids ruled and, except for a brief interlude or two much later, the new configuration remained in place to the very end of the dynasty. An Ismaili imam continued to be recognised as the caliph, and therefore his role as imam persisted. The religious character of that aspect of the government did not change, but the real power now resided in the hands of the wazirs whose claim to authority derived from personal military might, not necessarily from the approval of the caliphs, many of whom in later times were mere children in any case.

But the Fatimids in Egypt were, in this phase, not like their Abbasid counterparts in the east. The Buyids, for example, assumed control over the Abbasid caliphs in a similar way but they ruled rather more directly and in their own name. In fact the Buyid amirs appointed their own wazirs, who invariably came from the ranks of the scholars and the bureaucracy. The Saljuk sultans likewise had their own wazirs who, as in the case of the famous Niẓām al-Mulk, were men of the pen. Therefore, in the east, the caliph simply ceased to rule in almost every way, except in name, and the real power lay with the military. The wazirate was thus an office subordinate to the sultan, not to the caliph (until the caliphs began to appoint their own wazirs again). Under the later Fatimids, the caliph retained his theoretical superiority as head of the realm but lost it in practice to the Commander of Armed Forces who thus, while even so subservient to the caliph, assumed direct control over the whole of the government, often as a result of a forced *coup d'état*. Even when, nearer the end of the dynasty, these wazirs of the sword eventually added to their titles the term '*malik*', meaning something like 'king', they remained wazirs and thus deputies of the caliph-imam. But at the same time it is significant that several of the wazirs were decidedly not Ismaili and that the final 'wazir' was the famous Ṣalāḥ al-Dīn, the great champion of Sunni Islam and the person who ultimately rid Egypt of the Fatimids.

The reign of Badr al-Jamālī is thus obviously crucial to the understanding of the revival and further progress of Fatimid rule. His innovations, or those instituted to accommodate him, are clearly important and in many ways define not only the century following his arrival but carry over into subsequent periods. It is essential as well to find out to what extent the pattern of the earlier

Fatimids continued, what institutions remained and what changed. Here there is a major problem in the sources. Despite needing to know for all these reasons about Badr's actions and policies in as much detail as possible, there simply are no sources available to explain them. The two decades of his government, from 466/1073 to his death in 487/1094, are the worst documented of the whole Fatimid age. For four of those years the most astute of the later medieval chroniclers, al-Maqrīzī, could find no information at all; there were apparently no sources that he could draw upon.[1] This deplorable situation leaves the modern historian without any way of judging accurately the transition from the earlier phase to that of Badr and later. This defect is, moreover, compounded by a tendency to project backward what information does exist, often in quite specific detail, about later practices. The sources fall therefore unhappily into two groups or phases, one covering reasonably well the century of empire up to the 'Calamity' and the other from the reign of the caliph al-Āmir to the end. Some twenty-five years in between are by and large simply missing from the record.

Fortunately certain of Badr's accomplishments have left traces that did not depend on being preserved by contemporary historians. A prime example is a host of inscriptions on buildings erected by him that bear his name.[2] It is clear furthermore that, in restoring order throughout the realm, he reaped an immediate financial benefit given him by the security of both long- and short-range commerce, the regular collection of taxes that now once again flowed to the central government rather than to the pockets of local warlords and tribal chieftains, and as well by control over the expenditure of these same revenues. That Badr increased the income of the regime from two million to at least three million dinars – a figure often cited – appears quite likely.

An added benefit for the caliph was restoration of his non-governmental income, especially that contributed privately by his Ismaili followers either within Egypt or abroad. The security afforded by Badr's strong rule now permitted the imam's adherents once again to transmit their donations directly to him. This was not the case in the years just prior to Badr as is evident from the profuse praise and expression of thankfulness by the imam for Badr's having done exactly that in several of the caliph's letters from this period that were sent by him to his community in Yemen and which are luckily preserved as a part of a larger collection of them, the *Sijillāt al-mustanṣiriyya*.[3] In short both Egypt as a whole and the imam personally faced a new era of prosperity as a result of the measures undertaken by Badr.

The letters of al-Mustanṣir to the Ismailis of Yemen are one example of a source for this period that was not mined by the medieval historians, who may never have had a chance to see them. They are, however, of special value now, in part due to the lack of other sources. That they were addressed to the Yemeni community also highlights the importance to the Fatimids, even under Badr, of the Red Sea and the route there and on to India. Most distant territories, such as Iran, apparently were of little concern to the Egyptian government under Badr. He did preserve an abiding interest in taking Syria but he failed to realise it; he and the Fatimids had better fortunes in Yemen. Still the reality of Fatimid rule after Badr was that it was no longer an empire but rather an Egyptian state and little more.

This altered perspective may explain why one of Badr's main achievements was the embellishment of Cairo, around which he constructed a new, enlarged wall to fortify it and added at least three monumental gates, the Bāb al-Futūḥ, Bāb al-Naṣr and Bāb Zuwayla, all three of which survive until now.[4] He also put up a number of major buildings including the famous *mashhad*, an oratory bearing his name that sits atop the Muqaṭṭam plateau overlooking Cairo. In part these projects and his policies served to change the relationship between the newer city of Cairo and its much older neighbour Fusṭāṭ. Fusṭāṭ had remained the commercial capital and was even then an entrepôt for all trade coming from the Red Sea and going on to the Mediterranean and vice versa – a critical source of wealth for Egypt – but it had suffered severely in the years of the 'Calamity' when it shrank in size and lost much of its outlying suburban habitation. The area between Fusṭāṭ and Cairo, previously an appendage of the former, was decimated. With new-found prosperity following his restoration of order, the inhabitants began, in line with the policy of Badr, to build in and around Cairo. Before him the Fatimids apparently discouraged the general populace from moving in this direction, preferring to keep them in Fusṭāṭ and away from the palace and army in Cairo. The net effect of the changes was a general aggrandisement of Cairo and the further decline of Fusṭāṭ.

Problems of Succession

Remarkably, despite a strict doctrine that the previous imam must name his successor and that succession should pass from father to son, the Fatimids faced no major crisis in this regard until the death of al-Mustanṣir in 487/1094, a full two centuries after the elevation of al-Mahdī to the imamate. In contrast to the Abbasid caliph, who needed only to be a legitimate member of the Abbasid family, for the Ismailis there was no flexibility; each imam must of theological necessity have been the subject of the designation by his predecessor.[5]

This requirement does not, however, entail the choice or even preference for the oldest son over the younger. A paradigmatic case was that of the succession to the Imam Jaʿfar al-Ṣādiq, which also happens to be the point of origin for the Ismailis as a separate Shiʿi community. Jaʿfar, according to the most reliable information, chose his second son Ismāʿīl as the next imam. Although it is often claimed that Ismāʿīl was the eldest, that is disproved by Jaʿfar's *kunya* Abū ʿAbdallāh; ʿAbdallāh was, in fact, his eldest son. However, Ismāʿīl predeceased his father, leaving the succession an open question. The later Fatimid Ismailis asserted that the imamate then passed to Ismāʿīl's son Muḥammad and from him eventually to al-Mahdī.[6] In terms solely of the Fatimid caliphs, al-Qāʾim, al-Manṣūr, al-Muʿizz, al-Ḥākim, al-Ẓāhir and al-Mustanṣir were the oldest of their male siblings (where there were others). Al-ʿAzīz, however, was a noteworthy exception. His eldest brother was excluded fairly early although he was certainly still present and active. The reasons for ignoring him are not clear. A second son ʿAbdallāh appears to have been favoured by al-Muʿizz until this son's untimely death, after the move to Egypt. Only under these unusual circumstances was a third son, al-ʿAzīz, declared his father's ultimate choice.

The succession to al-Mustanṣir would not prove even that easy. In part this may have been due to his own longevity and a reign lasting almost sixty years (427–487/1036–1094). He was also fairly prolific, leaving behind a number of sons, several of whom apparently anticipated becoming imam in his place. Among the latter, two were old enough when the succession took place to have long been established in their own right, each with supporters in the Ismaili community and among the powerful elite. That the succession would result in a disagreement was certainly likely, particularly with respect to these two princes, Nizār and ʿAbdallāh, both of whom thought they had been chosen.

What actually happened, however, denied both; and it depended not, it would seem, on the explicit wish of their father, but on the actions of the son of Badr al-Jamālī, who had only recently won himself the right to inherit his father's power, titles and prerogatives. A key to this event therefore is this prior succession to the office of wazir. Badr died earlier in the same year as al-Mustanṣir and therefore his control over the government might have ended with him had not his son al-Afḍal successfully claimed his place. By the moment of the caliph's death, al-Afḍal held most certainly complete authority in respect to all that had once been in his father's hands, including most significantly the latter's private militia, previous known as the *Juyūshiyya* after the father and now to become the *Afḍaliyya* after the son.

It is impossible to know to what extent Badr himself determined the next imam; if he did his actions were quite circumspect. Those of al-Afḍal, however, once announced, were not. On the morning immediately following al-Mustanṣir's death, he proclaimed as imam and caliph the latter's youngest son Abu'l Qāsim Aḥmad with the regnal name al-Mustaʿlī. He was then slightly less than twenty and also al-Afḍal's own brother-in-law. Various parties protested, seeing in the selection a *coup d'état* in favour of the Jamālīs rather than a proper succession. Of those who dissented and rebelled, the most prominent was Nizār, who fled to Alexandria and openly defied al-Afḍal with noteworthy support both there and elsewhere, in Egypt and abroad. Even after al-Afḍal managed to suppress the dissenters and have Nizār murdered, the schism failed to heal. In Egypt the party of Nizār continued to threaten the government of al-Mustaʿlī and his successors. Outside, most particularly in Iran but also in Syria, under the quite capable direction of the famous Ḥasan-i Ṣabbāḥ, this group formed their own branch of the Ismailis, which long outlasted the Fatimids in Cairo.

Al-Mustaʿlī himself survived barely six years to be succeeded by a five-year-old son al-Āmir, who was likewise carefully supervised by the real holder of power al-Afḍal. The wazīr had a special riding saddle built to which he added a tiny seat in front of his own, so that the infant imam could appear with him in public. Only much later did the caliph finally escape from al-Afḍal by arranging the assassination of his wazir in 515/1121. Although under these circumstances a new wazir quickly assumed this same office, the stranglehold of the Jamālīs had thus come to an end.

Al-Afḍal's successor, al-Ma'mūn, had been the chief of staff for the former wazir but his elevation proved not nearly as effective in terms of power and authority. Moreover, once he was himself arrested in 519/1125 (and later executed), even the amount of power left him was reduced for those who acted in a similar capacity right after him. Possibly then the caliph al-Āmir was moving, albeit slowly, to reclaim from the wazirate the role of a true ruler.

When only four years later in 524/1130, al-Āmir was himself assassinated, however, another crisis of succession ensued, this time of even greater consequence. Al-Āmir had produced a son, known by the name al-Ṭayyib, only some months prior to his unexpected death, and the existence of such an heir was widely recognised at the time.[7] Nevertheless, at the moment of the caliph's murder, none of those concerned with the succession, the palace and court, the army and the Ismaili *daʿwa*, seemed by then able to admit to the son's existence, with one important exception. The Yemeni branch of the movement under the firm control and direction of the aged queen Arwa, widow of ʿAlī al-Ṣulayḥī's son, al-Mukarram, declared in favour of the infant, despite not knowing where he might be. Thereafter the main Yemeni Ismaili group refused to recognise the government in Egypt, even in the theological sense. For them al-Ṭayyib was or had been the imam after al-Āmir and as a consequence the imamate continued and will continue solely among the descendants of al-Ṭayyib.

That option was apparently not available to the Ismailis of Cairo or to the other supporters and beneficiaries of the Fatimid dynasty. If al-Ṭayyib was then alive, there is no evidence of his presence, even as an infant. Admittedly the historical record is scanty in the extreme and the situation that followed was chaotic and fraught with uncertainty. Still the palace clique, who had the most to gain or lose by the failure to find a legitimate heir and thus to perpetuate the dynasty, apparently decided to announce that the caliph had left behind a pregnant wife or concubine. Accordingly, they insisted on the elevation of a regent who would rule as a temporary expediency. The person chosen was ʿAbd al-Majīd, a grandson of al-Mustanṣir and thus a cousin of al-Āmir, who was also the oldest living male descendant of the Fatimid line. It needs to be stressed that the situation was without precedent; Ismaili doctrine demanded that the previous imam actually designate his successor, who by all customary expectation must be a son of the former. Here, as yet, they had no claim of such a designation.

Whether they actually had reason to expect the birth of a son posthumously, it did not happen. Moreover, the army declined to wait even that long; within weeks it staged a coup, soon after deposing ʿAbd al-Majīd. The leader of the coup was Kutayfāt, a son of al-Afḍal and the heir of the Jamālī legacy. Because the wholesale confiscation of his family's property and the execution of his uncles had accompanied the murder of his father, the new ruler had valid reasons to despise those around al-Āmir. He likewise realised that there was little hope, following a strict interpretation of Ismaili doctrine, of a valid succession to the imamate. Instead he pragmatically adopted another tactic, one quite common in Shiʿism, of announcing for the 'Expected (or Awaited) Imam' – a position that afforded him maximum flexibility while retaining the basic Shiʿism of both Ismaili and also Imami varieties that had by then spread in the army and among the general populace.

Kutayfāt's policies and actions, however, quickly alienated the palace including what was likely to have been a sizeable contingent of princes of the Fatimid line and, in general, the whole Ismaili establishment. Barely a year later this coalition, and others who saw Kutayfāt as a rival for power, brought him down. They reinstalled ʿAbd al-Majīd, who now dropped the fiction of being merely a regent and announced instead that he was the legitimate imam, having actually been designated by his predecessor, in a manner similar to the Prophet Muḥammad's declaration in favour of his cousin ʿAlī at Ghadīr Khumm, an event celebrated annually by the Shiʿa in Fatimid Egypt and elsewhere. Whether the new imam, who now adopted the name al-Ḥāfiẓ and subsequently held power for the next two decades and beyond, actually convinced a substantial body of Ismailis to accept his interpretation of the succession, the dynasty persisted and survived another thirty-five years.

Much of its earlier prestige, however, was lost; that it might be overthrown was henceforth a constant reality. Only a large, well-entrenched establishment in Cairo and the inertia of tradition continued to prop it up. Nevertheless, both in its outward forms and institutions, and for Ismailis loyal to it and to its local beneficiaries, it remained a government that no one dared eliminate. Al-Ḥāfiẓ was himself moderately active as a ruler, though not necessarily either effective or competent. Yet after him there were three more caliphs all of whom were mere children and were hardly noticed by an increasingly independent military. Even if the period from the death of al-Āmir to the end was no more than a third of a century, that is a not inconsiderable length. The subsequent longevity of a Shiʿi Ismaili dynasty in Egypt surrounded by a sea of Sunnis and other non-Ismailis surely requires an explanation.

A report from the reign of al-Ḥāfiẓ tells of a quite interesting attempt to depose the Fatimids and it may help provide a partial answer. This caliph appointed a series of powerful military commanders as his wazirs, one of whom, Riḍwān, was Sunni and thus eager to depose his patron. But he was unwilling to accomplish this aim by brute force. Instead he attempted to convene the leading authorities in Islamic law hoping they would provide him the validation for such a deposition of the caliph. Riḍwān himself considered al-Ḥāfiẓ nothing more than a regent acting for another (al-Ṭayyib?), who was himself, even so, not acceptable (or possibly even non-existent). The three legal authorities represented respectively the Sunnis, the Twelver Imāmīs and the Ismailis. The first of them, however, asserted that deposing a caliph in this case could only be done in accord with the stipulations of the law – that is, Sunni law – which, while it theoretically allows for such a disposition, once the caliph has taken office hardly offers any real means to accomplish it in actuality. The Twelver Imāmī argued that, since, in his view, al-Ḥāfiẓ was not a legitimate imam, it was not necessary to depose him – that is, he was not subject to being deposed by a legal decision because his rule had never been legally valid. The Ismaili said that al-Ḥāfiẓ could not be deposed because that would imply that they lied when they accepted him in the first place.[8]

An Egyptian State

With the downfall of al-Afḍal and the elevation of al-Maʾmūn al-Baṭāʾiḥī to the wazirate, the flow of information about the Fatimids begins to increase dramatically both in the surviving chronicles and in other kinds of sources. As one result the final years of their rule, despite the government's apparent weakness and decline relative to the earlier periods, are more accessible to historical inspection and analysis. They are therefore intrinsically of greater interest if only because for them the detail about what happened and why, exist, whereas for the prior eras it does not. But the profusion of sources that cover the end of the Fatimids also requires caution. Using them to judge the overall character of the dynasty is difficult. Thus it is helpful here to look closely at the kinds of questions that can be asked and what problems they might engender, even while admitting that they provide essential material both for the history of the Fatimids and, of equal concern, the transition to Ayyubid and Mamluk rule.

It is clear that the Fatimids once harboured aspirations as large as the Islamic world itself; their empire thus comprised both the territories they had conquered and over which they ruled politically and, as well, those areas where their movement existed as a clandestine appeal. Following the death of al-Āmir, however, the hope of expansion came to an end; only a tiny portion of Yemen and perhaps a few outposts in Syria responded thereafter to the imam in Cairo. Although the Ḥāfiẓī *daʿwa* certainly persisted, this branch of the Ismailis was limited in almost every way to Egypt alone. The Fatimids had become, despite their origin, a purely Egyptian phenomenon, confined to the Nile valley.

The state that the Fatimids created, with Cairo as its capital, had not existed before them and yet it was to continue from then into modern times. In a real sense the Mamluks, if not the Ayyubids, inherited that same state. Thus, for historians of either the Ayyubid or the Mamluk eras, the institutions and aspects of later rule that can be traced back to an earlier Fatimid period – or conversely clearly do not go back to it – help explain the character of subsequent developments. For these reasons – the relative abundance of information about it and its critical position for judgements about both the overall character of Fatimid rule and the continuity and change in subsequent periods – the final years of the dynasty are especially interesting.

One caution, however, involves determining whether, for example, an institution or a practice observable in these last decades actually continued from much earlier, or it represents an important change in Fatimid practice over time. The woeful lack of information about the era of the Jamālīs, even while noting its vital importance, makes assessments of this kind extremely difficult and uncertain. There are, none the less, several areas worth studying in the late Fatimid period. One is the continuation of the imamate as a religious institution even after the Nizārī, Ṭayyibī and Ḥafīẓī schisms. Moreover, despite the dominant role of the military wazirs from Badr to the end of the dynasty, occasionally the caliphs could and did reassert their authority. Al-Āmir's deposition of al-Afḍal, his wholesale confiscation of the Jamālī family holdings, and his subsequent execution of al-Ma'mūn suggest that an adult imam still held a substantial degree of power. In another way al-Ḥāfiẓ, the only other adult imam from the period, certainly played an active part in governing Egypt. He was noted, for example, for an interest in astronomy and in magic and chemical properties, the kind of personal traits that suggest evidence of a ruler who was more than an empty figurehead or a mere child.

As earlier, moreover, the two offices of chief qadi and chief *dāʿī* retained a high status in the apparatus of the state, and as before, the same person often held both, indicating the continuing importance of the Ismaili appeal. One characteristic aspect of the qadi's responsibilities had not changed: he continued to supervise the minting of coins as was Fatimid practice from the beginning. The mints under his control, it is true, by then reflected the narrow limits of the state; for al-Āmir they were Cairo, Fusṭāṭ, Alexandria, Qūs, ʿAskalan and Tyre.

One example of the altering of a long-established institution involves the Dār al-ʿIlm, first created by al-Ḥākim. When it began it was a secular, that is, non-religious, public academy; the professors who taught there were in fact Sunnis. After al-Ḥākim there is little or no detailed information about its fate for more than a century. As an endowment, however, it certainly persisted. Because the chief *dāʿī* al-Muʾayyad was buried in the building that housed it, scholars have assumed that it must have become the centre of the *daʿwa.* That fact is, however, not proven and appears unlikely, because, near the end of al-Afḍal's reign, he ordered it closed to prevent a group of populist, non-Ismaili heretics from teaching and meeting there. Under al-Maʾmūn it was reopened briefly only to attract the same anti-establishment element. Finally, the wazir decided to move it from its previous location in a section of the palace to a building outside the complex. He also then appointed a proper Ismaili *dāʿī* to supervise closely what went on in it. Thereafter it served as the headquarters of the *daʿwa* and its core staff, who were responsible for Ismaili legal and doctrinal matters, including supervising the preparation of the weekly Ismaili lessons for the *majālis al-ḥikma.*[9]

As with the assembly for these *majālis,* many of the ceremonies and practices of the Ismailis remained a feature of Fatimid rule to the end. These include a number, such as the feast of Ghadīr Khumm and the mourning of ʿAshūrāʾ, that were exclusively Shiʿi.[10] By contrast to these universal features of Shiʿi practice, the late period witnessed the growth in Cairo and Fusṭāṭ of the cult of several saints who were all descended in some fashion from ʿAlī b. Abī Ṭālib. Several important mausolea were constructed either to house the physical remains of these saints or to commemorate them. It is difficult, however, to see how this activity reflects Fatimid or Ismaili doctrine. The imams and their immediate family were buried elsewhere and those grave sites did not become centres of pilgrimage, at least not in any subsequent era. Moreover, while there are signs in this final period that Egypt was then attracting Shiʿa of a great variety – including Twelvers and Nuṣayrīs – not merely Ismailis, the cult of the ʿAlid saints that developed in and around Cairo appears to have appealed to the general public and perhaps to certain of the wazirs. Few of those involved directly in this activity were actually Ismaili.[11]

Another new institution that began in this period is the madrasa. A madrasa is often said to be a residential college designed solely for the teaching of Sunni law. Presumably there cannot be such a school for Shiʿi law and thus the Fatimids would not have sponsored a similar institution. That is not correct in two regards. First, the wazir Ibn Killis clearly once tried to create a madrasa adjoining the mosque of al-Azhar.[12] However it did not last and the only other obvious sign of a similar Shiʿi establishment is the much later version of the Dār al-ʿIlm as reformulated by the wazir al-Ma'mūn. Also regardless of these developments, several madrasas were set up during the period of al-Ḥāfiẓ and later, and in these cases, the law taught in them was Sunni. One was founded by the wazir Riḍwān b. Walakhshī, who was in fact himself Sunni.[13] Following the overthrow of the Fatimids, the building of such madrasas was to proliferate in accord with a policy of the Ayyubids to promote Sunni Islam and especially Shāfiʿī law.

Yet another feature of late Fatimid rule that needs to be examined as a possible root of later developments is the wazirate. While this office did not continue in the Ayyubid and Mamluk period as it was under the Fatimids, control of the government by the commanders of various private militias – especially those composed predominantly of *mamlūks*, that is, purchased slave soldiers and other indentured retainers – finds a definite echo in later practice. It is therefore not out of the question here to look carefully at the sequence of wazirs and the exact circumstances of their coming to power.

The case of Badr al-Jamālī contrasts sharply with that of Jawhar from the time of al-Muʿizz. Jawhar was in fact a purchased slave who, as a freedman, rose to the position of commander-in-chief. He never, however, replaced the caliph except under specific and quite temporary conditions. By contrast, Badr acquired full control over all offices of the government and he was backed by his own armed forces, principally troops that he either brought with him or imported subsequently, a majority of whom seem to have been Armenian. Curiously, Jawhar's son Ḥusayn, who was granted his father's title 'Commander-in-chief', thought at one point to form for himself a regiment of Slavs but nothing came of it. The pattern of creating personal armies, so apparent later, was in his time either not customary or not permitted. It is, however, a prominent feature of Fatimid rule in the final century of its existence. Creation of a private militia or control over one that already existed became an essential step leading to the office of wazir.

After the downfall of al-Afḍal, what remained of his militia passed first to al-Ma'mūn and then later to others. Kutayfāt could still reclaim it or more likely reconstitute it once he took over. The restoration of al-Ḥāfiẓ, now as caliph and no longer merely regent, was engineered by an Armenian amir named Yānis, who had been a *ghulām*, a retainer, of al-Afḍal, and presumably therefore a member of the private militia of the former wazir. Yānis's power, like that of his predecessors, derived from his militia, known appropriately as the *Yānisiyya*. For his role in rescuing the dynasty and in restoring to the Fatimids all the vast property confiscated from them by Kutayfāt, Yānis was thereafter made wazir. He lasted, however, only nine months, an indication that the instability of this office had now become characteristic of it.

Following Yānis, al-Ḥāfiẓ elevated to it a bureaucrat, Abu'l-Thurayyā Najm, who had risen from Ismaili *dāʿī* to qadi and finally to the equivalent of wazir, although without the exact title. Evidently the caliph hoped to avoid dependence on a wazir of the military type. For him, however, the trouble that threatened lay with his own sons, three of whom now contested with each other for precedence and authority. His first choice, Sulaymān, died in 528/1134 two months after having been given, along with the designation as the heir apparent, a position all but that of wazir. Next the caliph promoted his second choice, Ḥaydara, to the control of the courts of grievances (the *maẓālim*), which at that time included the bureau for confiscations (the *dīwān al-mufrad*), a major source of income for the government. At that moment yet another son, Ḥasan, who wanted it all for himself, took action. He prompted a fierce battle between two existing regiments of the army and then collected those who survived into his own organisation, the *Ṣubyān al-zarad*, so named because of the chainmail he supplied those who joined it. Because of the strength of this militia, al-Ḥāfiẓ could ill afford to oppose Ḥasan, until this son began to have his troops kill many of the elite commanders and other government officials, among them Abu'l-Thurayyā Najm, the *wāṣita*. Finally the caliph was forced by public pressure in 529/1135 to have Ḥasan poisoned and thus to be rid of him.

The next case is one of the most curious of all. Al-Ḥāfiẓ selected as wazir a prominent commander, Bahrām, another Armenian, but here a Christian, who, unlike Ibn Killis, for example, never converted. The situation was certainly strange. As wazir Bahrām was recognised as 'the Sword of Islam', a standard title of the office. But, by common consent, he could never be the 'Guardian of the Judges of the Muslims' or 'the Guide of the Missionaries to Believers', both also standard from Badr onward, and both apparently religious offices. As a Christian he could hardly be expected to mount the *minbar* in the congregational mosque on Fridays and thus take part in the collective worship by the community.

While it is evident that Bahrām was personally quite competent and had the confidence of the caliph, he was open to attack precisely because, although he now ruled an Islamic domain, he was not himself Muslim. To ensure his own survival, he attempted to promote the local Armenians both in the armies and in civilian life – his own brother was the patriarch of the Egyptian Armenian church – and to import many more of his countrymen. But the influx of Armenian Christians was apparently too obvious and the building of new churches for the immigrants quite noticeable. Many of the Armenian officers constructed for themselves houses that included, or had added to the side, a church.

Muslim alarm grew and when in 530/1136 the military commander Riḍwān b. Walakhshī tried to prevent the flow of Armenians, he became a local hero. As the situation worsened, Riḍwān then called for a holy war (*jihād*) against the Armenian Christians and, when Bahrām fled before him, he assumed the latter's place in Cairo (Jumādā II 531/March 1137), with the title of wazir to which was added that of 'Illustrious King' (al-Malik al-Afḍal). He was the first to be accorded that honour.

With the Sunni Riḍwān the situation swung decidedly in the opposite direction. He adopted a policy that reflected his own Sunni views, such as promoting the creation of a madrasa, enforcing repressive laws against Christians and Jews, and advocating a strong commitment to the war against the Crusaders. He, moreover, contemplated deposing the Fatimids altogether, or, once that seemed unlikely, replacing al-Ḥāfiẓ by another member of the family, one more pliant and thus more easily ignored. But, when he consulted the Ismaili chief *dāʿī* of the time about this latter project, he was told that the formal designation of another imam did not exist and he could therefore not replace the old one. Curiously, the same *dāʿī* also insisted that al-Āmir had in fact designated al-Ḥāfiẓ.

After the death of Riḍwān, al-Ḥāfiẓ managed for the short time left him to do without a wazir, although, when he saw his own end approaching, he made sure that his youngest son al-Ẓāfir would succeed and would have Ibn Maṣāl as wazir. This Ibn Maṣāl, like his father, was an important amir; they came from Lukk in the region of Barqa. Significantly, the father had supported Nizār in his ill-fated rebellion against al-Afḍal and had thus opposed the Mustaʿlī succession. Both he and his son escaped from Alexandria at that time. How exactly, many years later, the son rose to the position of wazir is not clear. He did not survive in that office long, however; again it was a prominent Sunni commander, al-ʿĀdil ibn Salār, who ousted him and took over (544/1149).

Prior to becoming wazir Ibn Salār was governor of Alexandria, where he, like Riḍwān, founded a madrasa for the study of Sunni law. His career with the Fatimids, however, began in his youth. Salār, the father, was originally acquired by al-Afḍal in Jerusalem and thereafter served him. The son was raised in the special military barracks schools (*ḥujar*) set up by al-Afḍal to train the sons of his commanders. Thus al-ʿĀdil grew up in the 'Barracks' Youth Corps' (the *ṣibyān al-ḥujar*), an elite unit of the army.

His murder in 548/1153 while still wazir is one of the stranger stories in Fatimid history, especially as he was killed by the same person who eventually murdered the caliph. Al-ʿĀdil's wife was the mother, from a previous marriage (to a descendant of the Zīrids of North Africa), of ʿAbbās, another important *amīr*, whose son, Naṣr (her grandson) was thereafter raised in the wazir's palace in Cairo. Seeking the wazirate for himself, this ʿAbbās prompted his son to murder his step-grandfather, which he did and the father then marched on the capital to claim the latter's office.

Not more than eight months later, embroiled in a sea of mutual suspicions and doubt, ʿAbbās with his son murdered the caliph, who was on intimate terms with the latter, in their home (Muḥarram 549/April 1154). Ostensibly to avenge this death, they compounded it by killing several members of the caliph's family before they allowed his infant son to succeed. The court was both alarmed and outraged. The governor of Upper Egypt, Ṭalāʾiʿ b. Ruzzīk, yet another of the many Armenians, was urged to intervene, which he did. The father and son hurriedly departed for Syria where they were apprehended, the father killed and the son delivered back to Cairo for execution there.

With the advent of Ṭalāʾiʿ came one more variation in the religious affiliation of this string of wazirs. He was widely known as a Twelver Shiʿi, but was quite likely actually a Nuṣayrī, an obscure sect that accepts the same twelve imams as the Imāmīs but with a different set of doctrines in many other regards.[14] The Nuṣayrīs were then confined mainly to Syria – an area where they still exist. As wazir, with the title al-Malik al-Ṣāliḥ, Ṭalāʾiʿ, who was the last true advocate of the dynasty to hold this office, survived more than seven years before falling prey to an assassin himself.

The End of the Fatimids

The premature death of the caliph al-Fā'iz in the summer of 555/1160 at the age of only eleven and a half brought the dynasty to yet one more test of its durability. There could be no question of a proper heir and, accordingly, the wazir Ṭalā'i' made little fuss about the formalities. He simply asked for and obtained a prince of the house, a grandson of al-Ḥāfiẓ, then nine years old, whose own father had been murdered by the earlier wazir 'Abbās in the aftermath of his killing of al-Ẓāfir. Ṭalā'i', and after him his son, Ruzzīk b. Ṭalā'i', who inherited the wazirate from his father, cared almost not at all about the person and attitudes of this imam-caliph. Still they preserved a sense of what the Fatimids meant as Shi'i rulers since they themselves were also Shi'a.

Moreover, while the caliphs were of small consequence, they were surrounded in the palace by a sizeable establishment consisting of numerous princes and other members of the royal family plus thousands of servants and retainers. This considerable body clearly sided with the dynasty and depended for their very existence on its perpetuation. Nevertheless, the weaknesses in the system of Fatimid rule had become obvious and the forces for its abolishment had grown considerably. Only inertia and the preponderance of ongoing tradition seem to keep it in place. But aside from the factors already explained here, the ultimate demise of the dynasty required the action of an outside force. That had been set in motion much earlier, in part by the arrival in Palestine and Syria of the European Crusaders.

When the Crusade movement first entered the equation, the Fatimids paid them only slight heed. Even when the Crusaders conquered Jerusalem in 492/1099, the reaction of the government in Cairo – although al-Afḍal certainly made an attempt to resist – was not by any means equal to the danger posed. Thereafter, despite an intermittent commitment of troops to the struggle for Palestine, over the next decades the Fatimids steadily lost their remaining footholds there. But, worst yet for the Fatimids, the presence of the Crusaders as a force occupying a key portion of the Islamic heartland stimulated among Muslims an increasingly militant counter movement making the holy war for the liberation of Syria and Palestine a consuming necessity and a potent political goal.

Naturally the holy war against the Christians could serve many secondary causes as well. One of considerable importance in this regard was the creation of a powerful state centred first on Aleppo under the amir Zangī and then later his son Nūr al-Dīn at Damascus. Both were ardently Sunni and both focused their attention on the interlocking goals of defeating the Crusaders and reuniting Syria and Egypt. In the long run these Zangids managed to deprive the Fatimids of their old claim – a part of their original propaganda from the time of Jawhar's conquest of Egypt and before – to leadership in the holy war. With the steady growth of Zangid power, Egypt began to appear ripe for annexation, not merely to the Syrian Muslims but also to the Christian Crusaders, who were, from their Kingdom of Jerusalem, in fact closer to Cairo than the Syrians. Thus there were two outside forces quite ready to intervene and, if possible, seize Egypt, a rich source of both revenue and produce.

The final dramatic struggle commenced with yet one more overthrow of a wazir. The palace clique in Cairo, one faction of which had arranged the assassination of Ṭalāʾiʿ, wanted to be rid of his son as well. They appealed to the governor of Upper Egypt, Shāwar, who then marched on Cairo, where he ousted Ruzzīk barely a year and a half later in 558/1163. But now six or seven months afterward, unhappy with Shāwar, the caliph urged yet another amir, Ḍirghām, to do the same. Rather than giving up easily Shāwar fled to Nūr al-Dīn Zangī and asked for his help to regain his previous office in Egypt. It was an excuse Nūr al-Dīn could not help liking. He dispatched with Shāwar a force of his own soldiers led by a Kurdish amir named Asad al-Dīn Shīrkūh, who in turn took with him his own nephew, Ṣalāḥ al-Dīn, the famous Saladin of subsequent crusading history. This was the first of three separate expeditions by the Syrians into Egypt.

In all three cases, their main enemy was not the Egyptian Fatimids, who were hardly a match for them, but the armies of Amalric I, King of Jerusalem. The first campaign of Shīrkūh, except in restoring Shāwar to the wazirate in the late summer of

559/1169, proved indecisive. The wazir had promised to pay the Syrians a substantial portion of Egypt's revenue but, once back in power, reneged and immediately sought the assistance of Amalric, who then sent an army of his own. After facing each other at Bilbays for a couple of months, all parties agreed to a settlement and the foreigners withdrew. The second expedition originated with the Syrians, who invaded Egypt in the winter of 562/1167. The perfidious Shāwar responded by calling in the Franks again. Both sides fought a number of battles, one involving the siege of Alexandria, which was then under the control of Ṣalāḥ al-Dīn, acting for his uncle, who was engaged elsewhere. In the end this campaign also culminated with a settlement; Shāwar promised to pay even larger tribute than before and to both the Franks and the Syrians. Unhappy with Shāwar's failures, Amalric's interference did not cease, however, and at one point he invested Cairo and threatened Fusṭāṭ. Shāwar then ordered Fusṭāṭ to be burned (Ṣafar 564/November 1168) to prevent its occupation by the Crusaders. The final campaign commenced with an invasion by Amalric. Enemies of Shāwar, who by then had lost all support in Egypt, urged him to attack. Yet again Shāwar followed his old pattern by seeking the aid of the Syrians, who responded this time with an especially large force, again under Shīrkūh and his nephew. When the new Syrian army reached Cairo mid-winter 564/1169, the Franks had already departed. Within days the Syrians lured Shāwar into a trap and assassinated him. In his place the caliph accepted the appointment of Shīrkūh as wazir, an odd choice but fully in accord with the reality of the situation. There had been Sunni wazirs before, why not now? The problem lay in Shīrkūh's primary allegiance to Nūr al-Dīn and, although the conditions of his coming were not materially different than had been those of Badr al-Jamālī, like his predecessor a century earlier, the absence of any need on his part for Egyptian support left him a free hand.

Shīrkūh, however, died suddenly two months later and his nephew took over both command of the Asadiyya regiment of his uncle and the wazirate by the appointment of al-ʿĀḍid himself. That occurred in Jumādā II 564/23 March 1169. Ṣalāḥ al-Dīn was thus, from that point onward, an office holder in the government of the Ismaili caliph and, in that one regard, not subservient to the ruler of Damascus, who had sent him to Egypt. But his position between the two involved a delicate balance; each contributed to his own independence from the other. There are signs, moreover, that, although he would eventually bring the Fatimid dynasty to a close, his relationship with al-ʿĀḍid was reasonably accommodating. On one occasion, when Nūr al-Dīn finally permitted Ṣalāḥ al-Dīn's son to join him in Egypt, the caliph actually rode out in formal procession to greet the son, a sure mark of respect for his new wazir.

The Abbasids in Baghdad understandably waited impatiently to be recognised in Egypt and they put pressure on Nūr al-Dīn. Yet, when the Zangid ordered his commander to do exactly that, the latter refused, claiming that the Egyptians themselves would not accept such a move. Nevertheless, in the year following his elevation to the wazirate, Ṣalāḥ al-Dīn commenced a series of measures to reduce sharply the Shiʿism of the state. He cancelled the Shiʿi call to prayer that proclaimed the phrase 'Come to the best of works, and Muḥammad and ʿAlī are the best of mankind'. Shortly thereafter he altered the Friday benediction (the *khuṭba*) so that it now mentioned the four 'rightly guided' successors of the Prophet in the order accepted by the Sunnis. Al-ʿĀḍid's status was reduced also. Ṣalāḥ al-Dīn also began to build Sunni (Shāfiʿī) madrasas, to remove Shiʿi judges from office, and to appoint in their place Shāfiʿīs. Soon he ordered the Ismaili *majlis al-ḥikma* stopped wherever it was still held. Finally he had the name of the Abbasid caliph proclaimed in the Friday sermon. By the time of that event, even the palace was under the watchful control of his own men. Al-ʿĀḍid was already known to be quite ill; he died a few days later on 10 Muḥarram 567/13 September 1171.

As with questions about later versus earlier Fatimid practice, which is a matter of considerable uncertainty owing to the lack of source material, there is a parallel problem in assessing the change and continuity between what Ṣalāḥ al-Dīn preserved of the state he once served as wazir and the new regime he created on his own. Some elements of Ayyubid rule were clearly new or predominantly so. These would include the adoption of a stridently Sunni (and Shāfiʿī) religious policy that both promoted Abbasid 'orthodoxy' and harshly suppressed all other tendencies. He did not hesitate to arrest and execute those he suspected of wanting to restore the dynasty that he had just abolished. But, in many other respects, he retained the old order in its essentials, often continuing to employ the bureaucrats who had run the Fatimid *dīwāns* in the same or a similar position and, if they proved loyal and effective, to promote them to even higher responsibilities.

With the advent of the Ayyubids, moreover, the sources multiply in sharp profusion compared with what is available to cover the Fatimids. Perhaps this relative abundance reflects a natural interest in the beginnings of a new venture and a new dynasty. For the commencement of the Fatimids in the Maghrib, there exists a similar, albeit poorer in its total extent, body of material. Still the wealth of sources for Ayyubid history is altogether enviable. And in part this is due to the status of Ṣalāḥ al-Dīn himself. For his apparent restoration of Sunnism, he was a hero to many Muslims of the time; for waging constant war against the Crusaders and eventually recovering Jerusalem from them, he was both then and later one of the great figures of Islamic history. The radiant glow that thus accrued to his name infused those close to him as well and they contributed this same attitude to his legend in the histories they and others wrote about him.

For the study of Fatimid history this tendency can prove quite useful, especially insofar as Ṣalāḥ al-Dīn and the Zangid amirate from which he came overlap the period of the last Fatimid caliphs. His career comprises in part an important segment of Fatimid history. In addition several officials of the previous regime continued in his service. One notable example is Qāḍī al-Fāḍil, who had entered the Fatimid chancery as far back as 543/1148. Under the wazir Ruzzīk b. Ṭalāʾiʿ, he ran the Bureau of the Army (*Dīwān al-jaysh*). But he is most famous for his role as advisor to Ṣalāḥ al-Dīn for whom he was almost the equivalent of a wazir (Ṣalāḥ al-Dīn, although once a wazir himself, appointed none as sultan).

There exist several other examples involving sources composed for one reason or another under the Ayyubids by officials and historians whose knowledge derived from their own experience in the administration of Egypt under the Fatimids. Two prime cases are the works of Ibn Mammātī and al-Makhzūmī, both connected with the administration of various governmental bureaux and the collection of taxes, and both therefore intrinsically interesting and instructive for what they reveal about Fatimid practice. Ibn Mammātī was himself the third in a line of government bureaucrats going back to the time of Badr al-Jamālī.[15]

Moreover, the establishment of Ayyubid rule did not occur all at once but rather evolved over the rest of its founder's lifetime. Initially he could not even publicly assert his own independence from Nūr al-Dīn. In addition there was no exact model for his actions. Luckily for him he had already assumed complete control over what remained of the Fatimid state and its assets, which were substantial, among these the great palace complex in Cairo and all that it contained. Within this sprawling palace area there were literally thousands of resident servants, both eunuchs and females, and a sizeable contingent of Fatimid princes, and other family members. It also contained an enormous library-archive and dozens of treasuries holding in them ceremonial gear and extremely valuable objects of art. All of this now belonged to the new regime and was thus its to dispose of.

To deal with what must have been an embarrassing mass of riches in the old palaces, Ṣalāḥ al-Dīn, having himself apparently no personal interest in it, simply proceeded to sell what he, or his agents, could. One figure given for the number of books is a staggering 1.6 million. While this is surely a wildly exaggerated number, the holdings of the Fatimid imams, who collected books and calligraphy avidly, was truly exceptional.[16] It is reported that it took Ṣalāḥ al-Dīn's agents ten years to dispose of everything.

As with the books and other treasures, the palace complex was of no special interest to the new ruler. As he did with grants of land revenues that he likewise took away from those who held them previously, he offered the palaces in separate portions to his high ranking commanders. Over the following decades these pieces of the palace complex suffered steadily from deterioration as they were broken up into smaller and smaller units. Some portions were simply pulled down and rebuilt. In the end no visible trace of either one of the Fatimid palaces survived at all.[17]

From the point of view of Fatimid history the end of the dynasty, even though reported by the sources in rich and enviable detail, appears sordid and dreary in comparison to prior periods. But the decline and fall of the Fatimids is the beginning of the Ayyubids and for the historiography of the successor regime, these were auspicious times and accordingly extremely important. Moreover, the Ismailis who remained loyal to the Fatimid imamate in Egypt over these last decades, the so-called Ḥāfiẓī branch, died out totally early in the medieval period. It left behind almost no trace of itself, no literature and hardly any historical sources at all. Thus, while it is relatively easy to reconstruct with precision the story of what happened, its meaning and significance, reveal as much about Ayyubid history as they do about the Fatimids as a whole.

Of major concern was the suppression of the Fatimid dynastic line. Ṣalāḥ al-Dīn rounded up all the princes of this house and sequestered them where they would have no access to females. Many years later, in fact, quite a number of them were still living and still under detention. This measure helped but did not quite eliminate either the rising of a pretender or other kinds of attempts at a restoration. But such events were both rare and feeble. The earlier Nizārī-Mustaʿlī and Ṭayyibī-Ḥāfiẓī schisms had already dispersed the bulk of the Ismailis that once inhabited Egypt. Nevertheless, Ismailis of the Ḥāfiẓī line, the only ones allowed in Egypt, were certainly present up to the end and pockets of them, particularly in Upper Egypt, continued to adhere to their religion well into the Ayyubid era.

II

Sources and Studies

4 *Coins, Building Inscriptions, Ṭirāz, Art and Archaeology*

Historians frequently divide their sources into those that are primary and those that are secondary, implying by the first category that the material in question is somehow closer to the original events and thus more trustworthy for accuracy. Too often in the study of the medieval Middle East this separation depends solely on the language of the source – a medieval work in Arabic, for example, having automatic precedence over a modern reconstruction of events. It is, however, simply not the case that the great composite histories assembled by the medieval chroniclers are necessarily better and more reliable than a modern work of history. Arabic sources for the history of the Fatimids, even in the medieval period, comprise a range of secondary – that is, second-hand, third-hand and more remote – witnesses. The information in them, unless quoted directly from a source contemporary to the events in question, does not constitute a primary account in any sense. Medieval chronicles are secondary histories in regard to the distant past quite as much as those of the present century. Their advantage, however, and what can make their testimony essential is their access to yet other sources now lost. Still it is important to remember that the Ayyubid and Mamluk era historians who supply most of the data from which Fatimid history is made are themselves basically no more omniscient than we are, and they, like us, have their own agendas, biases and prejudices.

The first category of sources to consider in the reconstruction of Fatimid history belongs to the objects, particularly those that actually date directly to the period and which carry information in the form of inscriptions. There are, of course, a wide variety of such items. Those most likely to convey useful factual data include coins, glass weights, textiles with embroidered writing (*ṭirāz*), building dedications, works of art and the artefacts having value to historians of art, and those unearthed by archaeologists. The range of items in the latter two categories is almost unlimited.

The subject of this chapter, therefore, concerns a category of source material that in its immediacy is truly primary. For a period from which so few documents survive and about which the written sources that were originally composed by eyewitnesses now exist either in late copies or in scattered and fragmented quotations embedded in a secondary context, the objects here, all of which date to the Fatimids, have a special value. They are, moreover, what are sometimes called 'unintentional' sources – a term that applies also to documents if, and when, they survive. In origin none of these items were, by and large, intended to serve a historical purpose. For the most part this means that the information they give can be taken at face value. The difficulty here therefore does not involve a test of accuracy. None the less, this material does raise complicated questions of meaning and relevance.

Coinage

Coins, even a complete corpus of all Fatimid issues, do not by themselves constitute a history of the dynasty. A similar judgement applies to the other kinds of objects under consideration. Nevertheless, Fatimid coinage is an important source in a number of ways, not least as an indication of economic and monetary history. Fatimid coins continue to exist in large numbers, most especially gold dinars, which are favoured by modern collectors.[1] Fortunately, as a result, significant numbers of them have entered the holdings of major museums and have been catalogued accordingly. Thus it is not impossible to draw up an extensive description – a true corpus – of what survives and the resulting body of data appears to match more or less what might be expected – in terms of dates, types of issue, and mints – from the known chronology and the references to coinage in the other historical sources.

Coins, by the nature of how and why they are collected, assume a life of their own, however, which involves a rationale not necessarily related to the requirements of historical research. The rarity of a certain coin issue now may or may not indicate a useful historical fact, for example. In general, collectors tend to ignore silver coins of any grade[2] and that is a matter of particular concern for monetary history for which the exchange rate from silver to gold and back is a key gauge.[3] The Fatimids did not issue copper coins and thus they are not a part of the picture. But for the general scope of Fatimid history coins can, and frequently do, offer significant information. One striking example is the coins issued in the years 334/946–947 and 335/947–948 that bear the name of the recently deceased caliph al-Qā'im and not that of his son al-Manṣūr, who for this period deliberately concealed his father's death until he had finally defeated the Kharijite rebel Abū Yazīd. Only then did he publicly claim the imamate and issue coins in his own name. His first issue was in fact inscribed with the month of his victory, even for those minted in Sicily at the time, as well as the year: Dhu'l-Qa'da 336/May-June 948, a practice then quite new to Fatimid coinage.

Another interesting case involves the coinage of al-Ḥākim for the years 404/1014 to 411/1020–1021 when this caliph had publicly recognised as his heir apparent (*walī ʿahd al-muslimīn*) his cousin ʿAbd al-Raḥīm whose name and this title appear thus on the coinage. The whole inscription ran as follows: 'The servant of God and His guardian [on earth] the Imam al-Ḥākim bi-amr Allāh, Commander of the faithful and ʿAbd al-Raḥīm, the Walī ʿahd al-muslimīn'. For the years 408/1017–1018 to 412/1021–1022, this was true as well for Fatimid coins issued in the Maghrib.

Yet another unusual situation occurred immediately after Abū ʿAbdallāh al-Shīʿī's victory over the Aghlabids. Lacking the authorisation to use the imam's name while he remained under house arrest in Sijilmāsa, Abū ʿAbdallāh issued coins in 296/909 bearing the legend *al-ḥamdu li-llāh rabbu'l-ʿālamīn* (Praise be to God, Lord of the Universe), which was then, or later became, the motto and signature for all of the Fatimid caliphs. Another legend in 297/909 reads 'The proof of God arrives and disperses His enemies'. There are still other instances where critical historical events were reflected in the coinage; one more example is the coins (and glass weights) of Kutayfāt, issued during his brief reign, on which he cited the 'Expected Imam', in the absence of a designated heir from the Fatimid line.[4]

When the caliph al-Mustanṣir's son Nizār retreated to Alexandria following the declaration in favour of al-Mustaʿlī by al-Afḍal, he ruled there briefly as the imam in his own right, minting coins thus in his own name. Although exceptionally rare, such coins do exist, thereby confirming this event. The Institute of Ismaili Studies is in possession of one such coin minted in 488/1095.

Of all the special problems, surely the most interesting revolve around the presence or not of some symbol of religious policy on Fatimid coinage. From 386/996 to the end of the dynasty all coins, in fact, carried the quintessential Shiʿi legend attesting to the *wilāya* of ʿAlī b. Abī Ṭālib by use of the phrase *ʿAlī walī Allāh.* Normally this is translated as "ʿAlī is the friend of God' and it appears after the standard testimony of faith (the *shahāda*). For the Shiʿa it means rather that ʿAlī was God's guardian (*walī*) of His earthly community in a way similar to Muḥammad's position as God's apostle (*rasūl*). That it might be taken in either sense, however, made it less offensive to Sunnis than more blatantly Shiʿi phrases that had appeared earlier on some Fatimid coinage.

But the first three caliphs hardly press the matter, preferring instead to employ Qur'anic phrases without adding an explicitly Shiʿi message. Al-Qā'im alone cited on his coins Qur'an 6:115: 'The words of your Lord are perfectly true and just; none can alter His words, for He is all-hearing and all-knowing'. Whether or not there is a special meaning to that is not clear; this is a case where the coins supply all the information and the other sources say nothing, although the same motto had once before been used by Abū ʿAbdallāh al-Shīʿī in the stamp seal on his official decrees (*sijillāt*) according to information recorded in Ibn ʿIdhārī's history of that period.

With the advent of al-Muʿizz the situation changed fairly dramatically. Al-Manṣūr had already altered the design of his coins to begin a distinctive style of Fatimid coinage that featured concentric circles of writing around a central field with a horizontal inscription. Al-Muʿizz now made an even more radical change both in design and in the Shiʿi content of the inscription. He dropped the horizontal field altogether in favour of a central dot surrounded by three concentric circular bands of writing that read from inner to outer: 'There is no god but God, alone without associate; Muḥammad is the apostle of God; and ʿAlī b. Abī Ṭālib is the heir (*waṣī*) of the Apostle and the most excellent deputy and husband of the Radiant Pure One'. The outermost margin had Qurʾan 9:33. The reverse side of the coin read in part: 'The servant of God Maʿadd Abū Tamīm, the Imam al-Muʿizz li-dīn Allāh, Commander of the Faithful; Revifier of the Sunna of Muḥammad, the lord of those sent [by God], and the inheritor of the glory of the Rightly Guiding Imams'. The mention on these coins of ʿAlī as the heir of the Prophet and his most excellent deputy and a connection so explicitly made to Fāṭima as the Radiant Pure One (*al-zahrāʾ al-baṭūl*) is highly unusual. These aggressively Shiʿi issues in fact continued for only two years, 341/952–953 to 343/954–955, to be replaced by a more moderate type that from 343 to the end of his reign, read in the corresponding space simply: 'And ʿAlī is the most excellent of the heirs and is the deputy (*wazīr*) of the best of those sent [by God]'. But al-ʿAzīz preferred to alter even this to ''Alī is the best of God's elite (*khayr ṣafwat Allāh*)'.

Without an explanation of them in the other sources, whether these overt proclamations of Shiʿi belief had special significance remains unclear. What is most obvious in them is none the less completely in line with Fatimid doctrine both before and after their use on the coinage. Therefore, the main unanswered questions are why al-Muʿizz decided to add them and also why he dropped them after such a brief run of only two years.

There are yet other curiosities about Fatimid coinage. One is al-Mustanṣir's issuing from 440/1048–1049 to 473/1080–1081 coins that seem purposely to imitate those of al-Muʿizz from the years 343/954–955 to 365/975. The later issues are in fact all but identical except for the regnal title al-Mustanṣir in place of al-Muʿizz. Al-Mustanṣir had the same name (*ism*) and patronymic (*kunya*) as the former caliph; both were Abū Tamīm Maʿadd. In this case it seems reasonable to speculate that, since the coinage of al-Muʿizz retained high repute for its purity and fineness, his successor hoped to ride that reputation in his imitation of it.

In fact, Fatimid coinage preserved its standard remarkably well over the length of their rule. That cannot have been easy especially in the later years when the resources of the state diminished substantially in comparison to the earlier period. But possibly the temptation toward debasing the coinage – lowering, for example, the gold content of the dinar – was held in check, in part, by religious policy and tradition. For the Fatimids control of the mint, as well as the bureau of weights and measures, fell under the domain of the qadi. Thus the chief justice of the empire controlled the minting of coins, evidently following an old concept that the purity of the coinage is essential for the fulfilment of obligations mandated in religious law. None the less, the great Mamluk historian, al-Maqrīzī, writing in an era when matters were quite different, expressed considerable admiration for Fatimid policy in this respect. One more impressive indication of the high reputation of Fatimid coinage was the deliberate imitation of it by the Latin Crusaders.[5]

Mints existed in a variety of cities yet presumably all were subject to the qadi's supervision. A list of these places serves to show the extent of Fatimid rule. Coins were minted in the name of the Fatimid caliphs in the following locations: Alexandria, Ayla, Aleppo, Damascus, Zabīd, Zawīla, Ṣabra (al-Manṣūriyya), Sicily (Palermo), Sanʿāʾ, Tyre, Tiberias, Tripoli in Syria, Tripoli in Libya, Barqa, Acre, ʿAscalon, Fez, Palestine (Ramla), Cairo, al-Qayrawān, Masīla (al-Muḥammadiyya), Medina, Baghdad, Qūṣ, Fusṭāṭ, Mecca and al-Mahdiyya.[6] Of course for certain of these places, such as Baghdad, the occasion for an issue with this particular place name was rather brief. It is also possible that there were additional sites of a mint that are not on this list because no coins of that type have come to light.

Alongside the coins there exist a fairly substantial number of glass weights that, like the coinage, bear inscriptions, usually the name of the reigning caliph and his titles.[7] Made of either clear glass or a combination of glass and paste, they range in size from nine to thirty-six millimetres in diameter. Only a very few have a place of manufacture (al-Manṣūriyya in the Maghrib and Fusṭāṭ and Alexandria in Egypt). In relative numbers they are quite abundant for the reign of al-Ḥākim, less for his predecessor and successor, and far less for the earliest and latest of the Fatimids. Previously the subject of disagreement about their original use, they have now been proven to be have been coin weights (rather than as some thought a substitute for metal money).[8]

Again as with the coins, these glass weights have a few curiosities. For example, those of the appropriate period have the name of al-Ḥākim's cousin ʿAbd al-Raḥīm as heir apparent. Under the rule of al-Afḍal b. Badr al-Jamālī, his name – that is, of the wazir – appears with the caliph. For the interregnum of Kutayfāt b. al-Afḍal, his name likewise appears in the company of the 'Expected Imam'. One quite unusual exception during the reign of al-ʿAzīz features the inclusion of the name of a qadi, Aḥmad b. al-Qāsim b. al-Minhāl, who had come to Egypt from the Maghrib and is thus known but who was ostensibly of a lesser rank than either of the sons of Qāḍī al-Nuʿmān from the same period.

Inscriptions on Buildings[9]

One of the earliest accounts of the beginning of Fatimid rule contains an unusually complete record of the mottoes and legends employed by Abū ʿAbdallāh al-Shīʿī on various objects; these were clearly intended to convey a public message.[10] One category was his coinage with the simple legend noted above. Among the others his personal seal used Qur'an 27:79: 'So put your trust in God; truly you are thereby upon the manifest truth'. As mentioned previously the stamp he used on his official decrees contained Qur'an 6:115 (a verse that later appeared on the coins of al-Qā'im). The thigh of his horse(s) had a brand with the words: 'To God belongs the kingdom' (*al-mulk li-llāh*); his standards and flags carried Qur'an 54:45, 17:83, and other verses. Unfortunately, there is no information of this kind for later periods that compares in the amount of detail given in this one instance.[11] Nevertheless, it should be clear that the Fatimids were keenly aware of the value of such pious slogans and of the importance of having them appear wherever possible, particularly on the facades and walls of public buildings throughout their realm. One of the first acts of al-Mahdī upon formally assuming the caliphate was to issue an order to remove from all of the mosques, cisterns, palaces, bridges and aqueducts the names of those who had built them and to inscribe his own name in their place.[12] Much later during the period of al-Ḥākim's rule when he had decreed the public cursing of those of the *ṣaḥāba* (Companions of the Prophet) who denied 'Alī his right to lead the Muslim community, this caliph made a point of insisting that these curses be written on the walls of mosques and other buildings and be boldly outlined with contrasting colours.

Naturally these examples of inscriptions and the use of public writing have all disappeared. Al-Ḥākim himself soon commanded that the curses he had ordered be effaced. The standards and flags of the Fatimid army long ago disintegrated. What does remain and therefore continues to function as an important source for Fatimid history are a number of building inscriptions, usually of its foundation, and a few carved wooden *minbar*s or portions of a *miḥrāb* that have survived by being moved to a secure setting in a museum. But even here the problem of survival presents a major difficulty. In several cases the text of the inscription for a given building, because it has disappeared since his time, now must be recovered from the record of it given by al-Maqrīzī. In yet other situations, as, for example, is true for a Fatimid mosque once adjacent to the famous Nilometer on the island of Rawḍa built in 485/1092 by Badr al-Jamālī, the inscription(s) were not, for some reason, recorded by al-Maqrīzī. They could still be seen, however, and copied, by a member of Napoleon's French scientific mission, J. J. Marcel, at the end of the eighteenth century.[13]

One Fatimid inscription that was lost long ago and for which al-Maqrīzī is the best witness concerns what was likely to have been the very first in Egypt.[14] It recorded the foundation of the mosque of al-Azhar in the name of al-Muʿizz 'at the hand of his servant Jawhar, the Clerk (*al-kātib*), the Sicilian (*al-ṣiqillī*), in the year 360'. That it has now disappeared makes the testimony of the later medieval witness critically important and yet emphasises at the same time how little of the Azhar mosque actually dates to the era of its founding.[15] With the exception of two surviving examples of carved wooden elements that once belonged to the mosque, almost nothing remains that actually dates to the Fatimid period. One is a pair of doors engraved with the name of al-Ḥākim and the other a wooden *miḥrāb* donated to al-Azhar by al-Āmir in 519/1125. The inscribed panel above the *miḥrāb* records al-Āmir's order to make it for al-Azhar and it gives the caliph's names and titles, noting that he is the son of the caliph al-Mustaʿlī who was the son of al-Mustanṣir.

Another case of a missing set of inscriptions comes from the next great Fatimid building to survive in part, the mosque of al-Ḥākim, the second major congregational *masjid* built for Cairo. In the year 393/1003, al-Ḥākim added over the principal entrance to the mosque a foundation inscription giving his name and the date.[16] Later in 403/1012, he dedicated a *minbar* pulpit to it as well. Both facts were noted by Ibn ʿAbd al-Ẓāhir and from him picked up by al-Maqrīzī. The *minbar* has long since disappeared. The entrance inscription, also now lost, the text of which was recorded by al-Maqrīzī, was still there in the early nineteenth century when it was seen by Gardiner Wilkinson and published by Hammer-Purgstall in 1838.

From the period beginning at the end of the reign of al-Ḥākim and continuing to the advent of Badr al-Jamālī, which includes the years of the so-called 'Calamity,' there are neither major new buildings nor evidence of important historical inscriptions on those that already existed. The era of Badr, by contrast, saw great activity in terms of construction. He built, renovated or embellished on a grand scale throughout his reign and he left an unusually large number of inscriptions which, for an era generally devoid of the other types of historical information, such as chronicles, assume incommensurable value as a result.

One of the earliest examples is Badr's renovation of the mosque of Ibn Ṭūlūn in Ṣafar 470/September 1077 noted in a commemorative inscription over the north-east doorway.[17] In this instance, in contrast to later usage, Badr lists his titles without mentioning his authority over either the judiciary or the *daʿwa.* In fact he was not granted that authority until six months later in the month of Shaʿban, a fact confirmed by the historian Ibn Muyassar, by one additional inscription, and by the text of a letter of the caliph to Yemen, all of that year. The additional responsibility of directing both the judiciary and most especially the *daʿwa* were not his until after the death of al-Mu'ayyad, which occurred only then.[18]

Several years later in 478/1085 Badr erected the imposing oratory, a '*mashhad*', that can still be seen atop the Muqaṭṭam overlooking modern Cairo. It, too, has an inscription recording Badr's role, although curiously not by mentioning his name, as was true in the former case, but by his titles, which now include 'Guarantor of the Judges of the Muslims' and 'Guide of the Missionaries to the Believers' – titles that from then on were standard for the wazir in such inscriptions.

The year 480/1087 witnessed the completion of Badr's vast project of providing a new defensive wall for Cairo, substantially enlarging its enclosed area and adding several monumental gates, on four of which, the Bāb al-Naṣr, Bāb al-Futūḥ, Bāb al-Barqiyya and Bāb Zuwayla, he placed foundation inscriptions.[19] The first three of these survive with the text more or less intact and, while not precisely identical, they are substantially alike. The last of the three – that for the Barqiyya entrance, one of two in the eastern wall – oddly was not described by al-Maqrīzī, who evidently never completed the entry destined for it in his *Khiṭaṭ*. Luckily the gate itself with its inscription was uncovered in modern times.[20] The fourth gate, called Zuwayla, which like the others still exists, once had an inscription. Al-Maqrīzī mentions this fact saying it contained the date, a reference to Badr and the name of the caliph. The actual plaque that gave the text is now gone although the place for it remains visible.

At least one more inscription of Badr contains important historical information. In the year 477/1084, he was forced to put down a revolt staged by his own son al-Awḥad. In the wake of this unpleasant event, he moved to raise his son al-Afḍal to the position of heir apparent (to the wazirate). Ibn Muyassar admits this fact and assigns it to Jumādā I of that same year. It is also confirmed in a letter of the caliph to Yemen for 479/1086.[21] Architectural evidence for it existed as well in an inscription, now lost, added by Badr to the mausoleum of Sayyida Nafīsa in 482/1089 the text of which was copied by al-Maqrīzī. In it he credits his son and heir, 'the Illustrious' al-Afḍal whom he cites in this manner along with his titles.[22]

For al-Afḍal in his own right there is an important inscription on the *miḥrāb* of the mosque of Ibn Ṭūlūn that, although it does not give a date itself, mentions both al-Mustanṣir and al-Afḍal. It must date therefore to 487/1094, the only year in which al-Afḍal served as wazir to this caliph who died in that same year.[23]

Al-Afḍal's successor as wazir, al-Ma'mūn, is represented by the inscription of the al-Aqmar mosque on which in two places a text gives the date 519/1125, the name and titles of the caliph al-Āmir, and the name of al-Ma'mūn, also with his titles, which are the same as those of Badr and al-Afḍal, including Commander of the Armies (*amīr al-juyūsh*).[24]

Recent excavations at the site of Ascalon have brought to light an inscription from the reign of al-Ẓāfir bearing the name of his wazir al-ʿĀdil b. Salār, the local governor Abu'l-Manṣūr Yāqūt and the qadi al-Ashraf, who supervised in 544/1150 the building of the tower at Ascalon on which it appeared. This qadi was in fact the father of the famous Qāḍī al-Fāḍil. As it happened the plaque that has this particular inscription was later reused by the Latin Crusaders who turned it on its side and carved over the Fatimid lettering the heraldic shields of the knight who had reused this particular piece of marble.[25]

Still later there is an inscription for al-Ṣāliḥ Ṭalā'iʿ.[26] During the reign of al-Fā'iz in the year 555/1160, Ṭalā'iʿ built the mosque that bears his name. Its inscription gives his name and titles as usual but with additions. He is not only the Illustrious Lord (*al-*

sayyid al-ajall) but the Noble Ruler (*al-malik al-ṣāliḥ*) and Defender of the Imams, Dispeller of Sadness, Commander of the Armies and so on. As was true of all the monumental inscriptions put up by the Fatimids, these were likewise written with a Kufic script, a fact all the more notable because their successors, the Ayyubids, who had come to Egypt from a different tradition, insisted on changing to a Naskhī script. Fatimid preference for Kufic, however, appears to represent nothing more than the persistence of a tradition.

Beyond the examples just cited there are a number of others, more than a few in Jerusalem, Hebron and several in the mosques of provincial cities of Egypt, such as Sohag, Damietta, Sinai and Mahallat al-Kubra. Also there exist a considerable number of tombstones that date to the Fatimid period. This latter kind of artefact which gives the name and death date of usually otherwise unknown individuals provides raw data for social history although, given the lack of a context for it, it is difficult to use. Still a comprehensive corpus of all Fatimid era inscriptions from buildings in the first instance and perhaps also from tombstones and epitaphs could be quite useful.[27] In part such a corpus already exists in previous publications such as the extremely important *Répertoire chronologique d'épigraphie arabe*,[28] which lists in chronological order all known Arabic inscriptions from any country that has them by year (or reign of the named ruler when the date of issue is missing).

Ṭirāz

Another category of inscribed artefacts is textiles. The flags and standards of the army, mentioned above, would be included here except that none survive. The same appears to be true of the *khilʿa*, a ceremonial robe of honour given by the ruler, for example, to foreign dignitaries, to military chiefs and to the holders of major offices in his realm. The Fatimids made good use of this practice from the very first moment of al-Mahdī's reign to the end of the dynasty. The chronicles and other written sources report any number of occasions during which the caliph bestowed his favour on a person so honoured by giving that person a *khilʿa*. Presumably such a robe carried on its fringes or borders an inscription containing the caliph's name and titles.

As a sub-category of such presents, the ruler also gave to an even larger number of his subjects and other honoured persons gifts of fine linen cloth also bearing an embroidered inscription with his name and titles. The general term for such inscribed cloth is *ṭirāz*.[29] Because this type of cloth was often employed as a burial shroud, far more examples of it survive than for any other, such as the *khilʿa* or carpets to name only two.[30]

Ṭirāz production, although a controlled state monopoly, was also fairly big business for the Fatimids. Obviously gifts of such cloth with the name of the imam woven or embroidered on them conferred a favour eagerly sought, especially by the faithful as well as, possibly, many of the non-Ismaili elite. Curiously, whereas coins never carry the name of the wazirs, *ṭirāz* was by tradition considered theirs. An early report contained in the announcement of al-Manṣūr's formal accession following his victory over Abū Yazīd specifically allows the majordomo Ustādh Jawdhar the right to put his name on the *ṭirāz* along with the caliph's which was only at that moment made public. Jawdhar already supervised the *ṭirāz* workshops, among the rest of his considerable responsibilities. Thus, although he was never actually a wazir in the full sense of the term, he was afterward, at least under al-Manṣūr, close to it.[31]

The first wazir for whom pieces of *ṭirāz* survive is Ibn Killis. He was also known to have tightly controlled the imperial workshops,[32] which were in his time mainly located in the eastern Egyptian delta towns of Tūna, Shaṭā, Tinnīs, Būra, Dabqu (Dabīq), Dumayra, Dīfū and Damietta.[33] Typically the inscription on such pieces includes general pious benedictions, the full name of the imam with an extensive list of titles and salutations on him and his family, plus, if there was a wazir and if he had ordered the work, a statement of that fact ending with the kind of workshop – public or private – the place of manufacture and the date. All in all the large number of examples that now exists provides an important source of historical information in part precisely because of this connection to the wazirs.

A curious case comes from the year 386 immediately after the succession of the young al-Ḥākim when the amir Ibn ʿAmmār served as a sort of wazir-regent. A piece of *ṭirāz* with that date names the Imam al-Ḥākim but indicates that the Amīn al-Dawla Abū Muḥammad al-Ḥasan b. ʿAmmār had ordered it made in the public workshop of Tūna.[34]

As with coins and glass weights, during the final years of al-Ḥākim, the *ṭirāz*, which no longer cites a wazir (quite likely because al-Ḥākim had none), explicitly names the heir apparent (w*alī ʿahd al-muslimīn wa khalīfat amīr al-muʾminīn*) ʿAbd al-Raḥīm b. Ilyās b. Aḥmad b. al-Mahdī bi-llāh.[35]

For the wazir al-Jarjarāʾī there are many examples from the years 425/1034 to 436/1045. Interestingly this man's full titles now read *al-wazīr al-ajall al-akmal al-awḥad ṣafīy amīr al-muʾminīn wa khāliṣatihi* Abu'l-Qāsim ʿAlī b. Aḥmad, showing a tendency toward title inflation that seems characteristic of the Fatimids in the same period.[36]

For al-Yāzūrī the only examples come from the year 450/1058 which was also the year he was deposed. From the following period of rapid change and the constant turnover of wazirs, there are few examples of *ṭirāz*. A couple cite the wazir by title but not name; one contains the titles and name of the wazir Ibn al-Maghribī.[37] For Badr al-Jamālī there are even fewer and none with a date or complete name or title.[38]

Ironically, while from Badr onward there exist relatively few examples of *ṭirāz*, building inscriptions increase substantially and most of them carry the name of the wazir in addition to the caliph. Nevertheless, among the *ṭirāz* that survive from this late period there are examples with the names of al-Mustaʿlī and al-Afḍal, with al-Afḍal alone (fragments only that presumably, judging from the date, also originally named al-Āmir), al-Āmir and al-Maʾmūn, and a couple with the name of al-Ḥāfiẓ. The most famous of these is the so-called Veil of St. Anne in the Vaucluse (France) which, although it survives in a European reliquary, is actually a piece of Fatimid *ṭirāz* woven in Damietta and bearing the names of the caliph al-Mustaʿlī and the wazir al-Afḍal.[39]

Works of Art

Except for the architectural inscriptions just discussed and those on textiles, generally classed under the term *ṭirāz*, few art objects convey historical information directly and immediately enough to serve the needs of conventional history.[40] But, for various as yet imprecisely articulated reasons, the historians of art, particularly Islamic art, have shown great interest in the Fatimid period, a concern that stands out in comparison with all other categories and subjects of history. The literature on aspects of Fatimid art far surpasses that on any other. And the art historians seem to agree the material they study in this regard holds a special place and that it can more or less be separated from the art of the period before the Fatimids and of other non-Fatimid geographical regions.[41]

Naturally their attention to the Fatimids depends on and derives principally from the scrutiny of objects that by date and provenance belong to this period and to the produce of the territories under Fatimid rule. Except for what might be written on an object, such as the name of the maker, the place of manufacture, or the person to whom the object is dedicated or who was its original owner, art history can and does exist in the absence of textual evidence. But there happen to be two rather important exceptions to this general observation in the case of the Fatimids. These are first the massive topographical compilation of textual descriptions for Egyptian monuments in al-Maqrīzī's *Khiṭaṭ*, which quite rightly has attracted considerable interest from architectural historians. The existence of this *Khiṭaṭ*, the scope of which is most impressively comprehensive, has itself worked especially well to bring a major textual source together with the study of this one aspect of art and material culture. The other written source is what survives of an eyewitness account that described in detail a whole list of precious objects taken from the caliph's palace treasuries to pay off government officials and the military at one point in the midst of the 'Calamity' under al-Mustanṣir. Al-Maqrīzī is again one source for this account; another was his neighbour and fellow historian al-Awḥadī, who compiled one version of it. Whatever its exact source, the list and its descriptions of the objects that came from the royal collections constitute an invaluable tool for the art historian.[42]

Judging solely on the quality, quantity, and diversity of the art that remains from the Fatimid era, it appears now to have been the beginning of a remarkable change. Art historians see in it the first flowering within the Islamic realm of, for example, the *muqarnas* pendentive, the mausoleum, and representational art in general. But there are serious questions about whether or not these developments owe their existence to the Fatimids, or to a time and place, or to the accident of survival. Possibly this art remains merely because it was produced or assembled in Egypt during a period of relative security and prosperity. Egypt did not suffer the extreme devastation, for example, that befell many areas both in the east and in the west, both then and later.

The range of art attributable to the Fatimid centuries is quite noteworthy and much of it has been preserved either *in situ*, as is the case with several important buildings (some discussed above), or in museums throughout the world. A good deal of Fatimid art found its way into the treasuries of European churches long ago, having come there perhaps as a result of the Crusades. Altogether the material for analysis and study includes manuscript drawings, calligraphy, and inscribed textiles; rock crystals, glass, carved ivories, wood work, metal work, and pottery, and each of these has its own specialists and an extensive literature. Much, if not most of it, however, concerns the narrower field of art history for which this kind of research is quite legitimate. In part because social history and art history are disciplines that rarely overlap, it offers the general historian far less than might be expected.

A central question about the art concerns its original audience. It is, for example, amply clear from the histories that the exchange of lavish gifts was common between, say, the Byzantine ruler and the Fatimid caliph. The Zīrids in the Maghrib, who were subordinate to the Fatimids, regularly sent to Cairo presents of a kind deemed worthy of this relationship. At the appointment of a new governmental office holder such as the chief qadi, or the chief *dāʿī*, the appointee visited the royal treasury where he was given ceremonial robes plus other objects of great value.

Merchants of the time obviously understood the market for luxury goods and many of them specialised, for example, in trafficking between Cairo and Baghdad. If an item of exceptional value came their way, they could and did choose either of these cities as the market of best price depending on current conditions, tastes, and availability. Cairo for much of the Fatimid period was the home of a wealthy elite that included not only the caliph but a substantial contingent of his extended family – several wives and mothers of caliphs possessed enormous fortunes, as so noted in the obituaries for them in the chronicles of the era. Wazirs, qadis, even physicians, were quite often holders both of vast estates and city dwellings full of rich furnishings. A great source for this information is the obituary notice, but even more telling are the records of confiscation. Al-Ḥākim, for example, had a special bureau, the *dīwān al-mufrad*, to perform the auditing and appropriation of the estates of those he did away with. The property of al-Afḍal was obviously extensive – his library alone is said to have contained half a million books. All that was confiscated by the caliph upon his death.

And naturally, perhaps accordingly, above all else, the treasury – or rather treasuries, since there were many – belonging to the imam-caliph held a fantastic collection of art, books and furnishings. In part these items came to him as gifts, many from his Ismaili followers, both within Fatimid domains and abroad. It appears certain as well that the imams assembled the royal treasuries based on personal interests. It is notable, for example, that several reports about what the treasuries contained specifically cite a large collection of the calligraphy of Ibn al-Bawwāb and Ibn Muqla. In the decades following Badr al-Jamālī, an all but unforgivable sign of corruption on the part of any official was to be caught with an object that had been taken, however many years before, from the royal treasury during the 'Calamity'.

This review of only a small part of the evidence for Fatimid connoisseurship of the arts does not, despite proving that there existed both an interest and a market for it in Cairo, establish an intrinsic connection between the art in question and the Fatimids themselves. Is Fatimid art 'Fatimid', or merely a set of objects that derive from the period? How much of it was, in fact, produced on Fatimid territory? And even when that was the case, was the maker of it perhaps imported as, for example, seems to have been the case with the architects (or builders) of the great gates for Badr's new city wall who came to Cairo from northern Syria?

One answer is negative: the available evidence does not support the concept of a Fatimid art. There is little or no reason to credit the Fatimids, either as imams, caliphs, or as a government, with sponsoring or propagating, or even favouring, a specific style. The fact that all public building inscriptions were written in Kufic script points only to a conservative tradition for such writing. But, at the same time, it is important to see that there is no sign of a puritanical opposition to art among the Fatimid imams. Strong objections to figural depictions, to lavish ornamentation, the wearing of silk fabrics, public pomp and display, which are relatively common in the most conservative circles of Islam – as for example among the Mālikīs and Ḥanbalīs – found no support in Fatimid domains. For al-Mahdī, the very first of the imam-caliphs, there exists ample evidence of his choice of an imperial style over the simple ascetic comportment of many of his own followers, who were observably puzzled and perplexed by his behaviour in this regard. It is thus quite possible that Fatimid art differs from what preceded it simply because the new dynasty allowed it to exist, or to come into being, or, better still, to revive traditions in art that, under previous Islamic rule, had by that time been long dormant or suppressed.

One final question about this art is whether or not it served a special religious purpose. Is there an Ismaili connection, an Ismaili art? Several art historians have tried to establish just such a relationship by attempting to show how various elements of Fatimid art convey a doctrinal message. Unfortunately, the links that have been proposed between Ismaili teachings and the art that supposedly depends on it are purely speculative and thus lack a solid foundation either in the art or in the textual evidence about the Ismaili mission.

Archaeology

There have been quite a number of archaeological excavations carried out on important Fatimid era sites, including most significantly al-Mahdiyya and al-Manṣūriyya in the Maghrib, and Fusṭāṭ in Egypt. Although the full publication of the results of this work tends to appear slowly and is often incomplete when it does, archaeology clearly produces information about the Fatimid period that cannot be obtained otherwise.[43] Where the art historians must rely for the most part on evidence provided by an object that was long ago removed from its cultural context and now sits in isolation either in a museum or a private collection, the archaeologist has a chance to discover such items surrounded by what remains of the physical evidence of the culture from which they derive. Unfortunately, however, except in rare instances, archaeology by its very nature deals solely with the abandoned debris of a given site and a situation where the context can be defined only in relatively gross terms. In regard to the study of the history of a period narrowly restricted chronologically, as is, for example, the case in trying to answer meaningful questions about specific changes or events that occurred during the seven decades of direct Fatimid rule in North Africa or Sicily, or even the two hundred years of their control over Egypt, aside from architectural remains, little else surveyed by this discipline provides the precision required for integration with the information supplied by other sources. This judgement should certainly not be taken as excluding archaeology as a source; there are in any case many instances of finds that involved the recovery of inscribed objects, among them coins and glass weights, and even of letters and documents. But in general archaeology has to this point not supplied as much useful information as some of its advocates may have hoped. Not unlike art history, archaeology tends to serve itself, as if it is a separate discipline with its own agenda and results, and not as an adjunct to a broader historical investigation.

5 *Letters and Documents*

Almost any study of the Islamic medieval period suffers considerably from the near total absence of original documents and archives. The Islamic world was for most of its history, moreover, fully literate and written documents of all kinds played an essential role in it. Almost all Islamic governments had a chancery in charge of drafting and archiving a constant supply of governmental edicts, decrees, regulations, correspondence, and other written records. The judges of every rank and location likewise depended on written materials, some they produced themselves and others they consulted or were presented to them in the course of litigation. The Fatimids were no exception. For them there is ample evidence concerning their use of documents at all levels of their administration of public affairs.

Most certainly archives of these documents and records once existed; in fact quite probably such collections contained a vast accumulation of what was then the work of various bureaucracies and courts, each with its own substantial army of officials and clerks. A simple amassing of these records, which surely commenced immediately upon the advent of the Fatimid state in the Maghrib, up to and including its final years prior to the Ayyubids, would have constituted an immense treasure trove for the future historian. But such collections would also have been of considerable size, possibly involving hundreds of thousands of individual items or copies of them that occupied great storerooms. It is quite conceivable that the reports of huge library holdings in the Fatimid palace in Cairo reflect not merely a library comprised of volumes of literature but also of archived documents and records.

Unfortunately the truth is that such archives have now disappeared completely both with respect to the Fatimids and in the case of all other Islamic governments of their time and earlier. How serious this lack of archival sources can be is obvious in comparison with the study of medieval Europe where, in numerous situations, both private and public, the records of given institutions survived. Accordingly, they can and do offer extremely valuable information to the historian, particularly for social history, most especially in regard to social classes not a part of the highest elites. But why do these archival sources exist in Europe and not in the Middle East? There is no easy answer to this important question except to note the evident fact of dramatic transitions from one regime to another in which the succeeding government apparently saw no reason to preserve the records of the one it replaced. Such, in any case, is a possible explanation for the disappearance of the Fatimid archives. Ayyubid era sources report the wholesale emptying of Fatimid storerooms and presumably this action, which is said in one account to have consumed ten years running, must have, in respect to the non-literary holdings, consisted of selling off the contents for scrap. Given that the Ayyubids came to power utterly opposed to the Fatimids and their memory, that they had no interest in retaining their archives seems probable.

Still, relative to other Islamic governments contemporary to the Fatimids, the situation is for them not nearly as hopeless. To be sure no archive, private or public, remains and thus the kind of statistical sampling undertaken by European historians in such archives is impossible. Nevertheless, a considerable number of documents issued by Fatimid governmental sources do exist, not enough to allow a detailed survey of their contents over time, but enough to provide solid evidence of how they were produced and recorded. In several important instances, an original chancery document survives; in others a copy of it that dates to the same time; and in yet others a copy of its textual content exists as preserved in a secondary context such as a later historical compilation.

For the Fatimid period in addition there is the extraordinarily rich treasury of papers, letters, documents and books that constitute the Cairo geniza, a truly astonishingly fertile source for the history of the Jewish community in Egypt and elsewhere during the eleventh, twelfth and thirteenth centuries. The Cairo geniza, in part by accident, also preserves a surprising number of documents relating to matters that did not involve Jews even indirectly. Of course, there are many as well where both Jews and non-Jews were common parties to the event that led to the production of such materials. In any case, the geniza constitutes a major source for just about every matter its contents touched. It was never, however, by the very nature of how it came to be, an archive. All of the items in it were taken out of their original context and discarded haphazardly, almost at random, in the lumber storeroom of the Palestinian synagogue in Fusṭāṭ. It is likely that this material was simply thrown into the room completely without regard for what should happen to it next, except with the (possible) expectation that these papers would be buried eventually.

A geniza ordinarily represents an accumulation of papers with some sacred content, generally all written in Hebrew. To avoid possible desecration they are commonly collected and ritually buried. Several unusual factors set the Cairo geniza apart from the many other genizas elsewhere both then and now. In the first place the Jewish community in Egypt apparently included in theirs a wide array of secular items. Such materials might have comprised only those that, although composed in the Arabic language, had been written with the Hebrew script except for the presence of quite a few in Arabic script. The latter may have found their way into the geniza by accident. There are many examples at any rate of Arabic documents written on the back of another in Hebrew script.

The second factor is preservation. Why did this particular geniza remain unburied contrary to the common practice that was followed in all other instances? There seems to be no answer to this important question. All this needs to be examined in greater detail later. Here it is important to see that, rich and extensive as it is, the geniza was not an archive and the exploration of its contents bears greater resemblance to archaeology than it does to normal archival research.

Therefore, the most productive sources of documents and letters for the Fatimid period depends on the recovery of such materials from a second-hand context, either as they now exist in later compilations and histories or as brought to light by archaeological methods.

Still a handful of original chancery items exist even now in the hands of the very institutions – principally minor religious establishments – that received them at the time of issue. Accordingly, they, like coins, *tirāz* and building inscriptions, are truly primary, preserving all the data that originally accompanied them such as, in this case, the marks of registration and authentication. As well the material from the geniza, along with papers and other written items that have been uncovered in archaeological excavation, such of those at Fusṭāṭ, are certainly primary in the sense that they all date to the period under study. Less immediate are those copied long after the time when they were issued and where there is no way to confirm independently the accuracy, or often even the authenticity, of the copy now available. Nevertheless, where the latter exist, especially as they tend to have been highly important or they would not have been preserved at all in this fashion, they demand attention and consideration. To see how much is available and what might be done with them, it is useful to review here these categories one by one.

In addition for the subject of public, particularly chancery documents, there are several important medieval textbooks and manuals designed to teach the art of drafting and processing such documents, which was the work of the clerks in the various bureaux responsible for them. For the Fatimids two such manuals survive, one from the eleventh and the other from the twelfth century, both composed by officials highly placed in the chancery. Beyond these, later examples of this type of literature, such as the massive compilation by the Mamluk chancery expert, al-Qalqashandī, in his *Ṣubḥ al-ʿashāʾ*, contain a fair number of copies of Fatimid decrees of various kinds, including, for example, imperial edicts, diplomas of appointment to office, and deeds of endowment.[1]

Although nothing like a complete study of Fatimid documents has been attempted to this point, a great deal of preliminary work on what survives in one form or another already exists. Of those that remain in their original context – that is, those documents housed now in the same institution that received them directly from the Fatimid chancery – only the eight examples from the monastery of St. Catherine on Mount Sinai form a set. A few others found individually add to this basic group. Ten in all were studied and published by S. M. Stern in his *Fāṭimid Decrees: Original Documents from the Fāṭimid Chancery* (London, 1964). There are yet others, though few enough in total, that emanate from a different organ of the government, in this case the qadi's court. An important example of the latter is a report issued in 429/1038 of the court's proceedings in a case involving responsibility for a Rabbinite synagogue, an official copy of which is still held by the Cairo Rabbanite community.[2]

While a few more may exist, the aggregate of such documents is hardly sufficient to allow for a more complete analysis than to provide a tiny sample of documents of this kind. Fortunately there are additional items both in the geniza and other archaeological contexts, as well as a substantial number that were copied verbatim into later post-Fatimid works. It is important to remember also that the writers of manuals on chancery practice have left fairly detailed descriptions of its procedures. Therefore the manner in which the government drafted, issued and archived its documents is known; what is missing, except in the few cases just noted, are actual examples that confirm these literary accounts.

Archival Copies

It is obvious that the various bureaux of the Fatimid state that issued documents of almost any type had to retain in their own files a complete and accurate copy of the same. Often several different departments and perhaps a number of individuals involved also each required a copy. This was clearly necessary, for example, with public decrees that were sent to be read out in various regions of the empire. Archival copies had to be available for later reference as well. There now exists one quite interesting example, not of the original, but of the archived copy. Geoffrey Khan published this document along with a detailed study of it.[3] In his own commentary on it Khan cites an essential passage from Ibn al-Ṣayrafī's chancery manual, the *Qānūn dīwān al-rasā'il* – one of the two mentioned above. Al-Ṣayrafī, who was himself a career official in the Fatimid chancery, explains the procedure for making archival copies:

> When the clerk of state documents, or the official in charge of correspondence addressed to kings, finishes a letter, he hands it over to the clerk in charge of copying, who then copies it letter by letter. At the top he writes: Copy of such and such a letter, issued at such and such a time, giving the full date with day, month and year. This copy is then taken by the archivist who puts it together with other copies of the same kind into the file for that year. Similarly, when the clerk whose duty it is to deal with the correspondence of the dignitaries of the state, its great men and amirs, or the official in charge of public decrees and others writes a document of the kind for which he is responsible, the copyist copies it letter by letter and writes the aforementioned formula on top. The archivist puts together all the copies that are of the same kind, keeping each year apart, divided into twelve sections, each month having a separate file, so that if he must search for any of them he can find it with a minimum of trouble.[4]

As it turns out, the Cairo geniza contains an example of just such a copy. It consists of a single piece of paper folded over once to yield four writing surfaces. The copy runs consecutively *recto, verso, recto, verso* and thus neatly occupies the one sheet that could be sewn conveniently into the volume that formed the collected documents for that month or year. Khan's geniza example reveals small perforations along its fold indicating that it came from a bound volume. But how such an archival copy got into the geniza is a mystery. It represents nevertheless an important find because, although it is a copy and not the primary document, which in this case has not come to light, it provides some evidence of exactly how copies were made and kept. An active chancery (or another bureau of the government) over the course of two centuries and a half obviously amassed a gigantic archive of state documents and copies thereof. Yet curiously almost none survive and, of the thousands and thousands of archival copies, only this one instance remains and that in the geniza where it is totally out of place.

Petitions

Yet another type of state document concerns the petition. Petitions were a standard method of bringing a problem to the attention of the government. Presumably in most cases petitions were needed in those situation where the ordinary administration of affairs had failed to deal with the issue at hand. Normally, for example, the dispensation of justice and legal matters in general fell under the jurisdiction of the qadis and their courts. For the redress of a grievance, however, it was often necessary to appeal to a special Court of Grievances, the *maẓālim*, a common institution in Islamic lands. Most governments prided themselves on their willingness to listen to such complaints and to grant redress to any and all citizens with a valid case. The ruler himself appeared with some regularity in person to hear such appeals; his willingness to do so is frequently cited as a mark of good government. Clearly the number of appeals to the state for help and the righting of a real or perceived wrong must have been considerable. More often, however, the system for handling such complaints involved the use of written petitions that were brought to the *maẓālim* courts, supervised in most situations by a qadi, frequently acting on behalf of the chief qadi, although in other instances under the control of a special judge appointed to that jurisdiction alone. Not infrequently also this responsibility belonged to the wazir rather than the qadi and, from the reign of al-Ḥākim, there are several reports of periods when the caliph himself would receive such petitions personally despite the obvious burden it imposed on him.

Fortunately a fair number of examples of such petitions survive. Only a few were of the importance required to find a place in the standard chronicles. And in fact the vast majority of these cases concern a matter of interest for a limited number of individuals who might have been directly involved in the particular case.

In answer to the most important of these petitions, the state might issue a special decree ordering, for example, its own officers to rectify the situation. In such cases the original petition asking for this action would reappear merely as a recapitulation of the grievance repeated within the body of the final edict. The original petition and the resulting decree or orders were separate documents. For lesser cases, however, the standard practice was for the person hearing the complaint to hand the original petition to the first of two clerks who sat with him when he heard the case. That official was called the Clerk of the Thin Pen; it was his responsibility to note with his 'thin pen' on the same document that had been presented the basic facts and disposition of the case. Subsequently, the second clerk drew up a formal statement of what was to happen as a result of the decision, that is, to 'translate the Clerk of the Thin Pen's notes into an administrative order'. He used a thick pen to distinguish his orders from the rest of the writing on the petition and he was thus called, accordingly, the Clerk of the Thick Pen. In such cases the original piece of paper served for three separate stages of the process, the intermediate and final disposition of which were often written out on the back of it on the left and right hand, in parallel columns. Luckily several of these petitions and their 'small decrees', namely the order for the disposition of the case (composed by the Clerk of the Thick Pen), exist and have been published along with a detail analysis of the process by Stern, Khan, and D. S. Richards.[5]

Non-Archival Copies

In regard to this subject, the modern scholars just cited, as well as S. D. Goitein, Richard J. H. Gottheil and others, have in the main concerned themselves principally with the surviving documents as opposed to those now found only as copied in later histories and in the chancery manuals. This does not imply that they have ignored the latter sources but that none attempted a systematic review of all the copied material, a task that remains, in fact, to be done. It would be highly useful for someone to collect in one place all of the Fatimid documents of the various categories that are preserved in contemporary and later histories. Such a project was announced and begun by the Egyptian historian Jamāl al-Dīn al-Shayyāl and he subsequently published an initial volume containing twenty-three examples out of the one hundred and ten that he had located.[6] Evidently he did not pursue the matter beyond this quite preliminary step and did not in any case publish the volume(s) that might have included the rest of the documents he found. Still his attempt is interesting on several counts.

In the first place al-Shayyāl proved he could readily assemble a fairly large corpus of official Fatimid documents using almost exclusively major Egyptian and Syrian works. Those he listed are by al-Suyūṭī, al-Qalqashandī, Ibn al-Ṣayrafī, al-Maqrīzī,[7] Ibn al-Qalānisī, al-Ḥanbalī, Ibn Wāṣil, Abū Shāma, Ibn al-ʿAdīm, Ibn Taghrī Birdī, and finally the Ismaili text *al-Hidāya al-āmiriyya*, which is in itself an example of an imperial Fatimid decree.[8] Al-Shayyāl himself admitted that his collection did not draw on the examples contained in a number of additional Ismaili works, such as the *Sīra* of al-Mu'ayyad, the *Sīra* of Ustādh Jawdhar, and most importantly the *rasā'il* (letters) of al-Mustanṣir (*al-Rasā'il* [*al-Sijillāt*] *al-mustanṣiriyya*). Jawdhar's 'autobiography' consists, in fact, largely of copies of letters and documents that had come to him from the imams or which mentioned him. Thus al-Shayyāl did not examine a considerable number of sources particularly for the earliest phase of Fatimid history in the Maghrib, such as Qāḍī al-Nuʿmān's *Iftitāḥ al-daʿwa* and *Majālis wa'l-musāyarāt,* or Idrīs ʿImād al-Dīn's *ʿUyūn al-akhbār.* These Ismaili works may not have been available to him but are published and thus accessible now. This is not to fault the effort of al-Shayyāl but to illustrate how extensive the corpus of extant Fatimid decrees and other documents is likely to be when fully assembled. Al-Shayyāl could locate a hundred and ten; the total is quite likely well more than triple that figure.

Another aspect of al-Shayyāl's inventory are the types and categories of those he found. Again, merely as an illustration, here is his list for the full one hundred and ten: ten concerning the caliphate and the designation of a successor to it; thirteen referring to the wazirate and the wazirs; nine about the judiciary and the judges; two on market inspection (*ḥisba* and the *muḥtasib*s); one on the *daʿwa* and the *dāʿīs*; twenty regarding financial and economic matters; nine dealing with social affairs; three concerning internal affairs and security; fourteen on administrative matters, bureaux of government, and the governorate of the capital and other districts; two on intellectual life, teaching and the schools; seven relating to the army; six that constitute assurances of personal security (*amānāt*); and fourteen concerning external relations. There is no reason to believe that the relative distribution of these categories will remain true of a much larger sampling but Shayyāl's results are nevertheless interesting as a specimen of what might exist.

Not all of these documents (either those noted by Shayyāl or the many others) have the same value for the reconstruction of Fatimid history but among them several are of considerable interest for one reason or another. What follows are a few examples.

Several edicts and letters of instruction and proclamation had been sent by the Imam al-Mahdī even before his arrival in Raqqāda[9] at the commencement of his reign as caliph. However, the formal pronouncement of it came in a signed order to the preachers of the various mosques of the land to be included in the Friday service on 5 January 910. The text of this short benediction to the new caliph, complete in its appropriate rhetoric, is preserved in Qāḍī al-Nuʿmān's *Iftitāḥ*.[10] In the next passage al-Nuʿmān records a second decree, a letter to be read from the minbar in Qayrawān 'copies of which were dispatched to various territories', to be read in the mosques. This second document issued from the servant of God, Abū Muḥammad, the Imam al-Mahdī bi-llāh, Commander of the Faithful, and was addressed to his followers (his *shīʿa*) among the believers and to all Muslims. Longer than the first, it set out the very conditions and reasons for Fatimid rule and in particular a direct assertion of the right to the imamate by virtue of inheritance through the family of the Prophet himself.[11] Given its basic claims, it is unlikely that a non-Ismaili source would have transmitted it and yet there is no reason to doubt its authenticity or that al-Nuʿmān's copy is inaccurate.

A later Maghribi example, also of extraordinary importance, comes from Idrīs's history of the Imams, his *ʿUyūn al-akhbār*. In it he records nearly verbatim the text of al-Manṣūr's proclamation of his accession, which he issued only after he had defeated and killed the Kharijite rebel Abū Yazīd on 29 Muḥarram 336/19 August 947. Until then, to avoid giving comfort to the enemy, he had carefully concealed the death of his father, who had died on 13 Shawwāl 334/17 May 946 well over a year earlier. This document also commands for the first time use of the throne name of the new caliph, which he adopted only then, al-Manṣūr bi-Naṣr Allāh (Victor by the Aid of God). Like other proclamations it was sent to all regions and governorates, and this document itself specifically mentions that from then on the titles of the new caliph are to appear on the coinage and on the *ṭirāz*.[12]

For the reign of al-Ḥākim an unusual amount of material survives in part due to the work of the amir al-Musabbiḥī, who was intimately associated with the government of this caliph and who also left an extensive record of what he observed personally and heard from others he knew. For that reason al-Maqrīzī, who consulted it, records a great deal of information about the occasions for the issuing of decrees, letters of appointment, guarantees of personal security (*amānāt*), and other documents in that period. In a number of cases these sources state specifically that al-Ḥākim wrote out the original copy of some of these decrees in his own hand, a practice that by its obvious rarity, indicates how seriously he perceived the matter before him. Normally the most important documents that emanated from the caliph, or were issued following upon his explicit order, were drafted by the clerk in charge of the *Dīwān al-inshā'* (the chancery) who for most of that reign was Ibn Sūrīn, a Christian.

There is an interesting example of Ibn Sūrīn's work in the text of the *sijill* (decree) that al-Ḥākim commanded be issued to explain why it had been necessary to execute his former tutor Barjawān. The latter was put to death pursuant to the youthful imam's order in Rabīʿ II 390/April 1000. Because Barjawān had accumulated considerable power and employed many who were beholden to him personally, and because the caliph was relatively young, al-Ḥākim felt that the situation required an official public explanation, which Ibn Sūrīn then composed and dispatched according to the imam's instructions to all of the congregational mosques of Fusṭāṭ, Cairo, Gīza, and Rawḍa. A copy is preserved in al-Maqrīzī's history of the Fatimids[13] and he states explicitly that a number of copies of this *sijill* were made from the original and sent as well to the other districts and governorates.

In view of the gradually increasing importance of the wazirate and its eventual centrality, evidence for the major steps in the development of this institution assumes a critical place in the history of the Fatimids. Thus, although there are copies of the edict of appointment for several of the later wazirs, the one raising al-Jarjarā'ī to this office under al-Ẓāhir represents a document of special significance. The text, however, comes now from the history of the Syrian (Damascene) Ibn al-Qalānisī (*ca.*465–455/1073–1160), which is not where it might be most expected.[14] As mentioned earlier in part one, with the exception of Ibn Killis, there were no wazirs in the real sense of the term under al-Ḥākim or any of the caliphs before him. In fact the first true appointment to this office (after Ibn Killis) is that of al-Jarjarā'ī in Dhu'l-Ḥijja of 418/January 1028. Therefore the *sijill* composed and read on that occasion holds particular value. The text drafted by the supervisor of the chancery Walī al-Dawla Abū 'Alī b. Khayrān,[15] for example, refers specifically to 'Alī b. Abī Ṭālib as both the brother and the deputy (*wazīr*) of the Prophet. It quotes, moreover, the Qur'anic passage about Joseph who said, 'Set me over the storehouses of the land; truly I am a knowing guardian' (Qur'an 12:55), and the words of Moses when he asked God to grant him a wazir, 'Give me of my family a deputy (*wazīr*), Aaron, my brother; add to my strength through him and make him share my task' (Qur'an 20:29–32). The text, which also reviewed the many qualifications of al-Jarjarā'ī for the wazirate and listed his newly acquired titles, was read out in the presence of the caliph to the leading commanders and others of the elite before it was copied and sent elsewhere (one copy obviously went to Syria).

The case of al-Jarjarā'ī is interesting for yet another reason. He had lost both his hands and forearms as a result of penalties for crimes – malfeasance in office – committed during the reign of al-Ḥākim. Although he could not have personally held the *sijill* granting him the highest office in the government – someone always accompanied him to write for him[16] – he had none the less risen steadily through the ranks and ultimately to the wazirate itself. And, moreover, he continued to hold it until his own death in 436/1045 – a tenure of more than seventeen years.

The latter half of the eleventh century is not as well represented by documents of most types. One category of *sijill*s, however, exists in relative profusion thanks in part to the actions of the recipients who collected and thus preserved them, in this case in Yemen. These are the so-called 'letters' of al-Mustanṣir (*al-Sijillāt al-mustanṣiriyya*). In reality they are various letters, instructions, and decrees issued by the imam in Cairo to his *daʿwa* in Yemen, plus one by al-Mustaʿlī, and four by al-Mustanṣir's mother, sister, and al-Mustaʿlī's mother. The whole collection contains sixty-six items ranging in date from 445/1053 to 489/1095; and it is particularly rich for the period of Badr al-Jamālī (466–487), who is always mentioned in these documents with special praise.

It is curious that such a collection even exists because there is nothing like it before or after. Moreover, it does not contain all of the *sijill*s that are known to have been sent from Cairo to Yemen in this same period. The standard Ismaili history of this period, volume seven of Idrīs's *ʿUyūn al-akhbār*, contains five that are the same but also at least four that are not,[17] including an extremely important letter that announces the birth of the future al-Mustaʿlī in 467/1074.

Another document of major importance that was preserved solely within the Ismaili community is the *Hidāya al-āmiriyya* issued following a special session of the royal court to hear the evidence against the claims and propaganda of the Nizārī Ismailis. It was composed for public distribution by the head of the chancery Ibn al-Ṣayrafī about 516/1118. Somewhat later the government added to it a *Risālat īqāʿ ṣawāʿiq al-irghām* as a refutation of the Nizārī refutation of the former proclamation. While both documents come now from Ṭayyibī Ismaili sources, the original event that generated it is well-attested in non-Ismaili histories.[18]

Commencing with the reign of al-Āmir documents from the imperial chancery, whether originals or copies, seem to become more common. Based simply on the materials studied by Stern and al-Shayyāl, there are six for al-Āmir, seven for al-Ḥāfiẓ, six for al-Ẓāfir and al-Fā'iz, and seven for al-ʿĀḍid. These numbers, however, indicate merely that the later documents were more likely to survive. It is also noteworthy that several of these were issued by al-ʿĀḍid in favour of Ṣalāḥ al-Dīn or his uncle Shīrkūh; all of them were in fact composed by al-Qāḍī al-Fāḍil who was to continue on in the service of the Ayyubids. The very situation that saw a Fatimid Ismaili imam appoint an ardently Sunni wazir – one who was to annul the Shiʿi caliphate itself – must seem strange. These decrees appointing either Ṣalāḥ al-Dīn or Shīrkūh, as with the earlier one in favour of Ridwān b. Walakhshī, as wazir, are Shiʿi in content, although written by Sunni clerks, and the appointee in each case was Sunni. But they prove that the tradition of the Fatimids and the rhetoric used to support them was alive and active right to the end of the dynasty.

Documents from the Qadi's Court

The chancery was, of course, not the only organ of the state to issue documents. Many came from the qadi's courts including some of great importance. The following items represent but two examples. The first is one of the precious few original documents that was preserved by the same institution to whom it was given when issued, in Shaʿban of 429/May of 1038, quite early in the reign of al-Mustanṣir. The matter before the court concerned a dispute about a Rabbinite synagogue in the Zuwayla quarter of Cairo. The main question was whether it was newly built or was old; if new it might accordingly be destroyed according to Islamic law which tends to forbid the construction of new houses of worship for either Christians or Jews. The judge in the case was al-Qāsim, who was not only the chief judge of the empire at the time and also its chief *dāʿī* but was, moreover, the great grandson of Qāḍī al-Nuʿmān. When the head of the Jewish community in Cairo, with others, testified that the building in question was old and their opponents could not prove the opposite, the judge had a written decision allowing the synagogue to continue drawn up in the name of the caliph (and of himself), witnessed by notaries and given to the Rabbinite community which is still in possession of it.[19]

The second example comes from the notes of the Mamluk statesman and writer Ibn ʿAbd al-Ẓāhir as appended to one version of his *al-Rawḍa al-bahiyya al-zāhira*, the earliest of several topographical works (a *khiṭaṭ*) on Cairo and an important source for al-Maqrīzī and others.[20] As a final chapter to that work Ibn ʿAbd al-Ẓāhir provided a copy of a deed of endowment (*waqf*) – one of several he found in a volume of such deeds (*waqfiyya*s) – that were all created by al-Ḥākim. The one he selected to copy was drafted and attested to by the chief judge Mālik b. Saʿīd al-Fāriqī in Ramaḍān of the year 400/April-May 1010. In it the imam deeded a number of his own properties in perpetuity to the support of three mosques, namely al-Azhar, al-Anwār al-Ḥākimī (later known simply as the mosque of al-Ḥākim) and al-Maqs, plus, most significantly, the recently established Dār al-ʿIlm (also known as the Dār al-Ḥikma). The division of the annual proceeds of the endowment and how it was to be spent and on which of these institutions is spelled out carefully. Although the use of such *awqāf* and *aḥbās*, another term for such endowments, is well attested for the Fatimids, almost no specific details about how it was done and what actually happened exist. For the later periods of Egyptian history this kind of document provides a rich source for social history, especially in regard to educational institutions such as the madrasa. For the Fatimids little or nothing survives and accordingly this one example assumes unusual importance.

Archaeological Materials

Turning now to written materials that have surfaced in an archaeological context, more needs be said about this category of documents, especially about what was found in the geniza. Excavations undertaken on sites from the Islamic period often come upon bits and piece of papyrus, parchment, or paper on which there is writing of some kind. And in some cases such excavations by chance encounter large quantities of it. The process is, however, quite random. None the less, it is always possible that an important new find will shed valuable light on an historical problem. Even a seemingly minor scrap of paper might yield tantalisingly intriguing evidence once expertly read and analysed.

Egypt, moreover, has an ideal climate for the preservation of such documents. As a result the Fatimid period has produced an unusually large amount of excavated material – especially from the area of Fusṭāṭ where over the past century there have been several sustained attempts to recover what remains of the Fatimid city. Fusṭāṭ, it should be remembered, fell into serious decline in the middle of the eleventh century and was later burned by order of the wazir in 564/1168. Although it did not disappear completely, much of the sizeable ruin surrounding the tiny enclave now called 'Old Cairo' therefore dates to the Fatimid period and earlier.

Although the excavation of this site has recovered a body of documents, one example – a small one at that – may suffice to illustrate what can be done with this material. In 1991 D. S. Richards, whose name has already appeared here as an expert on Arabic documents, published a paper fragment uncovered during the Fusṭāṭ excavations directed over several seasons by George Scanlon. Richards had already provided a preliminary assessment of the written materials from Scanlon's excavations in reports printed in the *Journal of the American Research Center in Egypt*, along with the other results of the project. In this later article he provided the text of what appears to be one or two bits from the daybook of a slave trader. It consists of two pieces of paper once folded at several intervals over each other. The larger is no more than fourteen by twelve centimetres and yet Richards found on it and its companion fascinating details of the dealer's accounts: dates, sex, race and condition of the slaves, the seller, the purchaser and the price paid. As expected from so tiny a fragment, not all of this information remains for each sale. But, as an example, one line reveals that on Sunday, the eighteenth day of a month the name of which is missing, the qadi of Tripoli, Ibn Ḥaydara, bought a particularly valuable girl who was not a virgin for 110 (presumably dinars). A certain Manṣūr, the agent of Abū Isḥāq, was the seller who brought her to the market.[21] It is not entirely clear that any of this information fits other known historical facts or even what are the precise dates involved. Nevertheless, it provides a good example of what can and often does turn up under these circumstances.

The Geniza

The geniza by its sheer size and volume, although generally just as haphazardly arranged and preserved, represents, of course, a different situation. While it contains countless fragments much like the one just mentioned, written both in Hebrew and in Arabic letters, it also provides larger, longer, and substantially more complete items, including in some cases major portions of whole books or enough materials from single family's records over time to suggest that the aggregate originally came from a private archive. S. D. Goitein, who has done the most work on this material (and also the most to promote the study of it), estimated that the whole geniza preserves some 10,000 documents that are larger than mere scraps and of these 7,000 are self-contained and of such a size to constitute items of distinct historical value. There are, he also notes, as many as 250,000 leaves of literary works.[22]

Given its size, the geniza must loom quite large in the reconstruction of the Fatimid period. It is therefore especially important to see what kinds of information it is likely to offer and about what aspects of that history. As Goitein was careful to point out, there are a number of limitations to this material. One already noted is its archaeological character; by its very nature it comprises only the refuse, the discarded records of the community that created it. The chaos that resulted from random and disinterested disposal of the items in the first instance was, moreover, compounded by the process of its recovery. Starting about 1890 the earliest collectors of geniza materials to gain access to it were treasure hunters seeking the most valuable literary manuscripts, mainly sacred texts. The storeroom was thus often ransacked prior to the later more conscientious efforts of serious scholars like Solomon Schechter and Charles Taylor, who, in 1897, together managed to transfer what remained in Egypt to the University Library of Cambridge University. Of the many depositories that exist elsewhere including several in the UK, in Russia and the US, the Taylor-Schechter Collection at Cambridge is by far the largest.[23]

Another important limitation of the material is its source as a geniza for only one of the three Jewish groups in Fusṭāṭ, 'the Palestinians'. It thus excludes the Iraqis (Babylonians) and the Karaites, not to mention all the Jews of Cairo and other cities. Each of these had their own synagogues with, presumably, their own genizas none of which have survived. In chronology also there are serious limitations. The three synagogues of Fusṭāṭ, as was the case with a number of churches there and elsewhere, were destroyed about 403/1012 by order of the government. Near the end of his reign the same caliph, al-Ḥākim, gave permission to the communities so affected to rebuild which most did thereafter. The new Palestinian synagogue carried an inscription that mentions the date 416/1025, which seems to be approximately when the restoration was complete. It follows therefore that material discarded in its geniza could not have arrived there prior to this date. However, since placing what was discarded in the geniza occurred only after the material in question had ceased to be useful, documents older than 416/1025 could have and clearly did enter the collection. Nevertheless, Goitein regarded the period from about 393/1002 up to 665/1266, when there seems to be a break, as what he called the 'classical' geniza, an era best represented by the documents in it.

Another serious restriction is its limitation solely to the Jewish communities from which the overwhelming majority of the items in it stem. Those written in Hebrew script, moreover, although composed in the Arabic language commonly used even by Jews at that time, can have only been circulated by and for Jews. There are others in Arabic script but substantially fewer. It is obvious therefore that the geniza will have the most to say about life in the Jewish community, for which, however, it represents an incredibly valuable source. Nor is the information limited to the Jews of Egypt. It comprises in addition a fair amount about Jewish communities in the Maghrib as well as trading outposts all along the route to India.[24] A major question is how much it indicates about either the Muslims (or Christians) in general or the Fatimid state in particular. Using the geniza Goitein produced a massive study of the Jewish communities it represented and to be sure much of the information in his work helps explain the others. None the less, the direct cross-confessional benefits of having the geniza as a source are not yet clear.

The work more recently of Geoffrey Khan, however, also already mentioned, on the Arabic documents in the geniza – that is, those written in Arabic script – has revealed a good deal more of what it offers in this latter category.[25] His volume on *Arabic Legal and Administrative Documents in the Cambridge Genizah Collections* (Cambridge, 1993) includes important examples of the following types: documents of sale, lease, endowment, marriage contracts, acknowledgements, testimonies and depositions, declarations, court records, powers of attorney, contracts of tax farmers, questions posed to jurisconsults, petitions to government officials (caliphs, wazirs, judges, *amīrs*), reports, reports of death, accounts and orders for payment and receipts. Thus, however slowly, it seems that, despite the lack of archival resources in the manner found in Europe, the number of Fatimid-era documents available to the modern researcher has expanded steadily and, as with materials from the geniza, occasionally in dramatic fashion.[26]

6 *Memoirs, Eyewitnesses and Contemporaries*

There is little doubt that an eyewitness account commands greater credence than a report related second- or third-hand, or even more distant, from the events in question. This is as basic a principle in the reconstruction of history as it is in legal proceedings, except that in the latter situation the value placed on such testimony may possibly determine a matter of life and death. The work of the historian normally does not carry so serious a consequence. Nevertheless, as in the examination of a witness in a court case, it is essential both to admit the likelihood of greater credence and accuracy and at the same time the possibility of error, deliberate or otherwise. Eyewitnesses are not automatically immune to failed memory, self-serving fancies and purposeful lies. Yet, when compared to the evidence from sources far less immediately connected to the subject of the reporting – an unfortunately common element in the determination of what happened as much as a millennium ago – eyewitness accounts must assume tremendous importance. They can be overturned or disregarded only rarely and solely on the basis of compelling documentation suggesting the contrary.

For Fatimid history in general, the eyewitnesses whose accounts survive and are now available are the exception. This scarcity is partly a result of the historiographical process itself rather than mere survival. Few observers bothered to write an account of what they saw and heard, and of those that did only a tiny handful ever entered the public domain. The kind of autobiographical memoir that becomes more common in later periods was not unknown, but even in the highly literate Islamic society of the fourth/tenth through the sixth/twelfth centuries, it was unusual. Even so, biographical – as opposed to autobiographical – literature for the period abounds. In part, it came into being as a way of recording the passing of learning and knowledge by one generation of scholars to those that came next. Moreover, there are numerous instances of historians who gathered information and composed an ongoing written record of contemporary events. In a sense, in those situations where it has been taken from a report related directly to the author from an eyewitness, much of the material in such accounts has itself the value of an eyewitness, especially where the details of its transmission – who it came from and under what circumstances – are known.

Many additional bits and pieces of first-hand information come from the writings of persons who happened to live within Fatimid territories or, in some other case, who worked for the Ismaili missions elsewhere. To a degree, any example of information related personally and directly by an author from the Fatimid period may possibly provide historical evidence, sometimes of exceptional value, but also of trivia and of a less consequential character.

The evaluation of evidence is, of course, a major aspect of the historian's task. Even recognising the importance of the eyewitness's testimony does not guarantee its total reliability and the problem, moreover, of sifting what is in fact a first-hand account from the material in which it is imbedded or which surrounds it is often difficult. And, even with some assurance of its authenticity as an eyewitness, the question of what motivated the respondent to report and why further complicates how it was, and now may be, used. In what follows in this chapter, it is essential to remember these problems even while conceding the exceptional value of this type of material.

It is useful to survey all instances where there exists anything like an eyewitness account from the Fatimid period. Given the nature of such information, however, which comprises often not more than a footnote to the larger sweep of major events and trends, it is impossible to cover here the entirety of what exists or might exist. It makes good sense therefore to begin with those of greatest value and work toward those with less to offer – that is, to commence with those few sources that are actually a form of personal memoir and which provide highly significant data about crucial events and turning points in Fatimid history. But it is also necessary in the process to glance at the material from the same time frame that appears in perhaps less secure sources.

The Maghrib

For reasons not obvious the distribution of such memoirs is vastly uneven over the course of the dynasty's two centuries and a half. Some periods have none. It is therefore notable that for the founding of the state, there are several. Two of these – by Ibn al-Haytham and Jaʿfar al-Ḥājib, respectively – come from the literature of the Ismaili movement where they were preserved exclusively. It is likely that others once existed and that traces of them may have entered the work, for example, of Qāḍī al-Nuʿmān, who wrote the main Ismaili history of that earliest period. Moreover, in contrast to the situation in Egypt later, the Sunni opposition in the Maghrib, namely the Mālikīs, composed their own accounts of what happened to them. While nothing in this material constitutes by itself a personal memoir, it is full of individual accounts and intimate recollections of what transpired. Although often embellished and given a deliberately polemical slant, behind much of it lies the genuine testimony of persons who were present and who experienced first-hand what happened.

For the advent of Fatimid rule in the Maghrib, two Mālikī authors – al-Khushanī and ʿArīb b. Saʿd – provide the most essential information. The first, al-Khushanī, was in fact living in Qayrawān quite near his native city when the Fatimids took over. In the aftermath, like many other Mālikī scholars, he left North Africa in 311/923 for the Umayyad court in Spain where he served until his death in 371/981. ʿArīb (d. *ca.*370/980), his younger contemporary, wrote his own history of the Maghrib also at the same court. In contrast to al-Khushanī, ʿArīb was a chronicler with no first-hand experience of the Fatimids. Nevertheless, both men quite likely relied heavily on the reports of Mālikī refugees coming at the time from North Africa to Spain. Later Mālikī compilers of biographical dictionaries – works of the classes or generations of scholars (*ṭabaqāt*) – also had access to the direct testimony of those of their own *madhhab* who had previously or continued to live under the Fatimids. But, in part to justify later Mālikī persecution of the Ismaili communities that remained in the Maghrib, much of this later material is blatantly hostile and distorted, not infrequently even highly hagiographic rather than historical. Nevertheless, where the polemical rhetoric and exaggeration can be excluded, the information in this literature is as a whole extremely valuable. This judgement applies most particularly to the work of al-Khushanī whose *ṭabaqāt* of the scholars of Qayrawān features, quite exceptionally for the Mālikīs, biographies of many Ḥanafīs and even a list of those scholars who converted to the Ismaili cause. In many cases al-Khushanī could claim that he knew the men he wrote about personally.[1]

Abū ʿAbdallāh Jaʿfar b. al-Aswad b. al-Haytham (Ibn al-Haytham) came from the same elite community of scholars in Qayrawān as al-Khushanī and most of those he wrote about. Ibn al-Haytham's family took up residence in the city over a century before. They were wealthy landowners of obvious prominence. Nevertheless, although living among Sunnis, Ibn al-Haytham reports that his father was a Zaydī and that a number of his friends and acquaintances were Shiʿa, a faith they observed with due circumspection and caution. Although still in his early twenties when Abū ʿAbdallāh entered Raqqāda in victory, Ibn al-Haytham eagerly sought to join the new movement. The great *dāʿī* obviously sensed a special opportunity and without hesitation commenced to induct the young man into the *daʿwa* and put him to service. Over the next approximately ten months during precisely that period when the two brothers in succession governed the Maghrib pending the arrival of al-Mahdī from Sijilmāsa, Ibn al-Haytham was frequently in attendance on first one and then the other brother, either in the company of others or often alone. Long afterward in the midst of the revolt of Abū Yazīd and the transition from al-Qā'im to al-Manṣūr, for reasons not perfectly clear but likely connected to an attempt to promote himself, Ibn al-Haytham wrote a detailed memoir of his conversations with the two brothers, adding many personal observations and recollections of people and events. The resulting work is astonishingly rich in information about a crucial period in the first phase of the Fatimid revolution, most particularly as a record of the thoughts and deeds of the new government and its leaders prior to the advent of the imam himself. Although it was composed almost four decades after the time it describes when nearly everyone mentioned in it was long dead, what it reports is confirmed in the other sources. There appears to be no reason to doubt its essential accuracy.[2]

Slightly less certain is the other memoir, that of Ja'far,[3] the manservant of the imam who accompanied him during his flight from Salamiyya to Egypt and on to Sijilmāsa and finally to his installation as caliph in Raqqāda in 297/910. Once rescued by the army of Abū 'Abdallāh, Ja'far began to serve his master as chamberlain and was thereafter known as al-Ḥājib (chamberlain) accordingly. In origin, however, he was a eunuch slave in the imam's household born approximately at the same time as al-Mahdī, that is in about 260/874. Even on the eventful journey across North Africa, although entrusted on occasion with high responsibilities, he was merely one of several servants of the imam; he played no role, for example, in the *da'wa*. Nevertheless, he was present at important moments and when not actually on the scene reported what happened from another person who was. Still his autobiographical recollections, which commence with a few details of life in Salamiyya, covers only their travels after leaving it and ends with their arrival in Raqqāda. And, this account comes now from a record made of it by Muḥammad b. Muḥammad al-Yamānī, a writer from the era of al-'Azīz. It is clear, moreover, that Ja'far had trouble recalling exactly what had happened and sometimes in precisely what order. If he was still alive in the reign of al-'Azīz, he was then over a hundred years old. More likely the old chamberlain dictated his recollections much earlier. Nevertheless what he reported is in the main highly important regardless of when it was initially transmitted and exactly how.

Following these two Ismaili texts, there is nothing like them covering the next thirty-five years or more. That does not mean that none were written but only that the next signs of such direct material appear much later. Coincidentally, the next flurry of such activity comes on the heels of the extremely dangerous revolt of Abū Yazīd. On this incident itself Qāḍī' al-Nuʿmān composed a substantial work, now lost; this is according to his own testimony.[4] Idrīs's *ʿUyūn al-akhbār* certainly seems to preserve a considerable record of a first-hand observation of al-Manṣūr's long and relentless pursuit of the rebels. One possible source for all this could be an account of it by the qadi in the army, Aḥmad b. Muḥammad al-Marwadhī (al-Marwarrudhī).[5]

It is somewhat ironic that this period is also the time when Ibn al-Haytham decided finally to write his own memoirs, not to describe these events, but to recall the earliest heady days of the new regime. It is noteworthy as well that the advent of al-Manṣūr and the changes that followed upon the victory over Abū Yazīd brought to the fore both Qāḍī' al-Nuʿmān, who only then attained special prominence and high rank, and Ustādh Jawdhar, a eunuch slave whose previous position within the caliph's family and inner circle was now augmented considerably. In the wake of the young caliph's victory, Jawdhar was granted his freedom and at last recognised as a sort of majordomo – a quasi-wazir, in fact – whose name was accordingly thereafter to be seen on the imperial *ṭirāz*.

Jawdhar is particularly important here for the *sīra* (biography, autobiography) written about him by his personal clerk, Abū ʿAlī al-Manṣūr al-Jawdharī.[6] Neither technically a memoir nor an eyewitness account, the *Sīrat Ustādh Jawdhar* is a difficult work to categorise. Its author, Abū ʿAlī Manṣūr, however, entered the service of his master in 350/961 and remained with him until the latter's death en route to Egypt with al-Muʿizz in 362/973. Thereafter he inherited several of the positions formerly held by Jawdhar, also adding the name al-ʿAzīzī, which indicates his service to this caliph. What the clerk Manṣūr had to work with was not a narrative of his master's life but a personal archive of letters and documents, a significant number of which had been sent to Jawdhar by the caliphs. It is clear, moreover, that Jawdhar's archive was far more extensive than the material from it selected by Manṣūr to prove his master's importance and high honour under the imams he had served. In that sense much in this *Sīra* belongs to the material of the previous chapter on government documents. It constitutes, however, equally a record of Jawdhar's personal activities and what he saw and did, albeit not related as a narrative but through copies of the documents that were an essential part of them.

In origin Jawdhar came to the Fatimids already a young slave of the Aghlabids. He therefore began his service under al-Mahdī. Each succeeding caliph gave him a greater degree of authority. Eventually he controlled the private monetary resources of the caliphs and supervised their personal treasuries. He was deeply involved in maritime affairs as well and that activity among others made him rich. Commencing with the succession of al-Manṣūr, he seems to have been asked to monitor and, if necessary, hold in check the other members of the royal family. It was he who was privy to the secret designation of the succeeding imam. All of his responsibilities were not quite so important, but it is true that, even in its trivia, his 'biography' preserves almost uniquely an insider's view of the government at its highest level.

Qāḍī al-Nuʿmān, although a contemporary who worked for the same four caliphs, represents a considerable contrast to Jawdhar. From the scholarly elite and thus both freeborn and privileged, he entered government service under al-Mahdī in 313/925. Until promoted by al-Manṣūr, his role was that of a district judge and jurisprudent. Eventually, however, he rose to a position of the highest judicial authority under al-Manṣūr and then al-Muʿizz, both of whom, but especially the latter, urged him to compose works on law and history. In the end his output was vast, covering law and legal theory, the history of the imams and the Ismaili *daʿwa*, the Qurʾan and interpretation, various polemics against and refutations of opponents, and others. One interesting treatise of his covers the proper comportment of the followers of the imam. Because he composed these works for the imam and often at his specific request, they all represent evidence of the direct interaction of the Fatimid caliph with an author who put the imam's teachings and instructions down on paper. Nevertheless the kinds of material al-Nuʿmān produced are considerably diverse, ranging from a history of the mission of Abū ʿAbdallāh and the founding of the Fatimid state – his *Iftitāḥ al-daʿwa wa ibtidāʾ al-dawla*[7] – to a comprehensive collection of the materials of Shiʿi (and Ismaili) legal doctrine (*fiqh*) in some 3,000 folios – his *al-Īḍāḥ* – and the critically important handbook of the same – his *Daʿāʾim al-Islām.*[8] Given his central position within the hierarchy of the state and the Ismaili *daʿwa* – although he was never regarded as the head of the latter – his writings must be taken as the equivalent of an eyewitness in one sense or another. It is significant, moreover, that, unlike many works produced by members of the *daʿwa* that were not intended for public use but were carefully guarded from unwanted exposure, those of Qāḍī al-Nuʿmān – at least most of them – were widely circulated, perhaps as a part of a deliberate policy designed to spread the state's appeal more broadly.

While there is information in many of his works about matters that he observed, or that arose out of concerns of the time he was writing, one in particular comes closer than the rest to what is normally considered an eyewitness report. That is his *Kitāb al-Majālis wa'l-musāyarāt* (Book of Sessions and Excursions) in which he provides a lengthy record (292 separate episodes) of the audiences of the imam in which he was present, mainly those of al-Muʿizz.[9] Altogether this book constitutes a remarkable account of the imam in action, facing the constant duty of receiving his followers, counselling them and ruling on all manner of issues brought before him. Naturally as a loyal adherent of the imam, al-Nuʿmān relates nothing to discredit him but instead only what will show him as the very model of the supreme spiritual and political leader. The book certainly had as its purpose the portrayal of Fatimid rule in its best light. Yet there is enough incidental information in it about historical events and what was said about them or in explanation of them to make of it also a highly useful source for much more than how the Fatimids hoped to appeal for the sympathy and political loyalty of their subjects.

One other Ismaili authority from this same period should be mentioned. He is Jaʿfar b. Manṣūr al-Yamān, the son of Ibn Ḥawshab the head of the *daʿwa* in the Yemen over the last decades of the third/ninth century. It was Ibn Ḥawshab who dispatched Abū ʿAbdallāh on the mission that eventually resulted in the North African state. After him the *daʿwa* in the Yemen fell into disarray, partly as a result of family feuding. Jaʿfar eventually left the country and moved to al-Mahdiyya, arriving there just as al-Qāʾim ascended to the caliphate. Although usually regarded as a specialist in esoteric forms of knowledge and the allegorical interpretation of Qurʾanic matters, his many works, all of which were composed under the Fatimids, do contain information of historical value. Unfortunately, most of them have never been published.[10]

In yet another category, though perhaps not entirely outside of Ismaili influence, there is the geographical work of Abu'l-Qāsim Ibn Ḥawqal. Although Ibn Ḥawqal came from Naṣībīn in Mesopotamia, in the course of his personal journeys to verify the information he assembled in his *al-Masālik wa'l-mamālik*[11] (or with the alternative title *Kitāb Ṣūrat al-arḍ*), he visited much of the Islamic world of his time. He was in North Africa and Spain about 336–40/947–51, Egypt slightly later, and Sicily in 362/973, to name only areas of prime Fatimid interest. While it is not clear exactly what relationship he had with the Ismaili movement – some suspicion exists that he was in fact a *dāʿī* – he was certainly in sympathy with the Fatimids religiously and he does appear to have obtained information in person from highly placed Ismaili authorities.[12]

The Earliest Phase in Egypt

As with the foundation of the Fatimid state, the conquest of Egypt by Jawhar and the transfer of the imam's residence from the Maghrib to Cairo constituted an event of such magnitude that it should have produced an impression on contemporaries so momentous as to generate a clear reflection in the literature of the time. There is, in fact, considerable evidence of just such a reaction. For example, there once existed three biographical works on Jawhar alone. Yet, despite reports of a number of works that covered either the career of Jawhar or of the first caliphs in Egypt, strangely not one of these survive. Therefore, in dealing with the period from Jawhar's victory in 358/969 through the reign of al-Ẓāhir, nearly all eyewitness material now comes second-hand in the form of quotations that appear in works of later authors. None the less it is possible to describe the source of many, though certainly not all, of these reports and to recognise, at the least, the origin of it and to assign it an appropriate value accordingly.

When the Fatimid army reached Egypt, the leading historian there was Ibn Zūlāq the author of a continuation of al-Kindī's work on the governors and judges of Egypt and others including a history of the Māzarā'ī family, a *khiṭaṭ,* his *Akhbār Sībawayh al-miṣrī,*[13] a book on the excellences of Egypt, and others.[14] To these he added, according to reports, biographies of al-Muʿizz, al-ʿAzīz, and one on Jawhar, prior to his own death in 386/996. The latter three, all of which cover a period that he witnessed personally, would have been particularly interesting. However, they are not extant now, and it is not completely clear in what manner they were available to any of the later writers.

One of the other two contemporary biographies of Jawhar was composed by a certain Abū ʿAbdallāh al-Yamanī, a historian who also wrote on the history of grammarians and died in the year 400/1009,[15] but about whom nothing else is known. The other was Abū Manṣūr al-Farghānī. He was the son of another historian originally from Baghdad who settled in Egypt. The father wrote a continuation of al-Ṭabarī's great history and the son a continuation of his father's continuation. He also composed biographies of al-ʿAzīz and of Jawhar.

Another important witness to the initial phase of Fatimid rule in Egypt was Ibn al-Muhadhdhab whose family came from Qayrawān with al-Muʿizz. His *Siyar al-a'imma* (Biographies of the Imams) covered apparently all of them through to al-ʿAzīz, but it served the later author Ibn Saʿīd especially well as a source for al-Muʿizz. One more was al-Uswānī whom Jawhar dispatched at some point between 359/969 and 363/973 on a mission to Nubia about which he wrote an *Akhbār al-Nūba.*[16] Yet another was al-ʿUtaqī who covered the earlier phase up to the time of al-ʿAzīz under whom he fell into disfavour. He died in 384/994. For the final period of al-ʿAzīz, perhaps the most important was al-Rūdhbārī, whose *Balashkar al-ʿudabāʾ* contained essential information about that caliph as well as al-Ḥākim and at least the first years of al-Ẓāhir.

Unfortunately all of the sources just mentioned are lost; they serve here only as evidence of what once existed and to indicate that the advent of Fatimid rule clearly elicited its share of historical reports. Yet one more survives as yet unpublished; it is the collection of biographies assembled by Abu'l-Qāsim Yaḥyā Ibn al-Ṭaḥḥān (d. 416/1025). The author attempted to extend an even earlier work of the same kind by Ibn Yūnus (d. 347/958) and he thus added material for the years 340 to 410, roughly his own lifetime.[17]

By the reign of al-Ḥākim, which in any case left a vivid, if often painful, impression on those who wrote about it, several contemporary accounts survive at least in part. One of considerable importance is Abu'l-Faraj Yaḥyā b. Saʿīd al-Anṭākī's *Taʾrīkh* (History) which he thought of as a continuation of that by Ibn al-Baṭrīq.[18] His own, however, runs to the year 425/1034, almost a century beyond the former. He had already composed one version of it as early as 397/1006. Yaḥyā was a member of the Melkite Christian community in Egypt, which he left in the year 405/1014, moving thereafter to the north Syrian city of Antioch. Therefore, for his account of Egypt prior to the year of his departure, he constitutes an eyewitness. With regard to the information in his history for Egypt after that, although much of it is invaluable, he does not have the same degree of authority. Moreover, the reason for his leaving was connected in some way to the persecution of the Christians prior to 404/1013. In that year al-Ḥākim offered to let depart any of them who wished to and most importantly to take with them those possessions they could transport. Still, despite his evident hostility to this ruler, Yaḥyā had himself known highly placed members of the government, among them one of the caliph's personal physicians.[19]

In contrast to Yaḥyā's history, which survives, that of the amir al-Mukhtār ʿIzz al-Mulk Muḥammad al-Musabbiḥī has for the most part all but disappeared. His life spanned the period 366/976 – 420/1029 and his history the years 368/978 – 415/1024 (at least), for which except the earliest of them he was obviously an eyewitness.[20] The main work in question, his *Akhbār Miṣr,* was in fact more of a day by day diary of events and other matters of interest to him than a history in the normal sense of the word. Although medieval historians typically lay out their material annalistically in chronological order year by year (and not infrequently month by month, if possible), al-Musabbiḥī's was evidently even more finely detailed. It also obviously constituted a massive accumulation of entries by the time, perhaps not long after 415/1024, the year of the last known portion, when he ceased to record them. It is reported that the total work rose to an astonishing 13,000 folios, a figure so large that it is little wonder that volumes of it were seldom copied and eventually became separated, scattered and ultimately lost. Now, of the whole, only the portion covering the year 414 and part of 415 exists.[21] Still, later medieval historians – among them Ibn Muyassar, Ibn Ẓāfir, Ibn Khallikān and al-Maqrīzī – could find some volumes of it and they put them to good use.[22]

Two additional examples of lost histories for this period are, first, a work on the Kutāma by a certain Ḥaydara b. Muḥammad b. Ibrāhīm, who lived during the reign of al-Ḥākim, and second, a history written by the Maghribi Zīrid official Abū Isḥāq Ibrāhīm Ibn al-Raqīq. The latter's multi-volume *Ta'rīkh Ifrīqiya wa'l-Maghrib* would not itself constitute an eyewitness account as a whole. However, the author did work for the Zīrids and in 388/998 was sent by them to Cairo and to their nominal overlord at the time, al-Ḥākim. Ibn al-Raqīq, who was Shi'i, apparently prolonged his stay in Egypt in part accordingly.

Another source that needs to be cited here is the *History of the Patriarchs of Alexandria* (*Siyar al-bī'a al-muqaddasa,* also known as *Ta'rīkh baṭāriqa al-kanīsa al-miṣriyya*), a semi-official history of the Coptic church, composed over several centuries by a number of authors. For the Fatimid period it contains important information often from a first-hand witness. The appropriate section dealing with the years from the conquest to 438/1046 were written by Michael, the Bishop of Tinnis. He wrote that part in Coptic about 443/1051 (or 450/1058) and it was later translated into Arabic under the direction of one of the continuators, Mawhūb b. Manṣūr b. Mufarrij.[23]

Finally, the Ismaili *daʿwa*, in sharp contrast to the situation obtaining earlier in the Maghrib, apparently produced little or nothing that can be used as a historical source during the reigns of the first four imams in Egypt. Several works by the great *dāʿī* Ḥamīd al-Dīn al-Kirmānī, who came to Egypt from Iraq about 406/1015 in the latter years of al-Ḥākim, are an important exception. While all of his writings constitute a major source for Ismaili thought and doctrine during that period, those few that mention his activities in Egypt in one way or another also have the value of an eyewitness.[24] In fact his testimony is vitally important in regard to the state of the *daʿwa* and its opposition to the insurgent heresy of factions within it that wanted to proclaim al-Ḥākim's divinity. What survived of the latter group eventually became the Druze. Al-Kirmānī and his associates, as his own words seem to suggest, were instrumental, though not without some serious difficulty, in keeping this heresy from permanently tainting the Ismaili *daʿwa*.

The Reign of al-Mustanṣir

For the following period roughly commensurate with the long reign of al-Mustanṣir, the situation becomes more and more desperate as those few sources that exist for the earlier portion of it come to an end without any to succeed them. Even so from 427/1035 (or 1036) when the youthful al-Mustanṣir came to power until the advent of Badr al-Jamālī, the lack of historical information is serious enough, but in contrast to the next two decades, it appears relatively rich. This judgement applies both to the availability of eyewitness accounts and to all other types of historical materials. The era of Badr, by contrast, is a historical wasteland and the early years under al-Afḍal are hardly better.

One of the best and most important eyewitnesses to the reign of al-Mustanṣir was Nāṣir-i Khusraw, the famous Persian traveller and Ismaili *dāʿī*, who arrived in Egypt in 439/1047 and stayed there for several years in between pilgrimages to Mecca and

Medina. By 444/1052 he had returned to his native Iran. Although he was a member of the Ismaili *daʿwa* for which he wrote numerous doctrinal treatises, he also composed a travelogue of his journey to Egypt and what he saw there and along the way both coming and going. That book, his *Safarnāma*, reveals almost no trace of his Ismaili loyalties, except perhaps in its rather extravagant and entirely laudatory depiction of Egypt and its capital city, which he offers, even so, without any comments that indicate a religious bias.[25] In that work he says nothing, for example, to indicate his special relationship to the imam and his Ismaili followers. Nevertheless, there is little reason to doubt or reject his descriptions. Cairo and Fusṭāṭ were then at the height of a prosperous era, and the latter city would never again be so well off. Twenty years later Fusṭāṭ, and most of Egypt were in the midst of chaos and decline. Fusṭāṭ simply never recovered.

A second major eyewitness was also a Persian who came to Egypt. A poet, *dāʿī* and prolific author like Nāṣir-i Khusraw, al-Muʾayyad fi'l-Dīn al-Shīrāzī had departed his native land after being forced to flee. He reached Cairo in 438/1046 quite nearly the same time as Nāṣir. In contrast to his fellow Persian *dāʿī*, al-Muʾayyad soon began to play a role in local Egyptian affairs. Later he became the leading intermediary between Cairo and the anti-Saljuk forces centred around al-Basāsīrī. At about the time of al-Basāsīrī's brief success in Baghdad, in 450/1059, al-Muʾayyad, then back again in Cairo, rose to the position of chief *dāʿī*, the *dāʿī al-duʿāt*. He was to hold that rank, with some slight interruptions, until his own death in 470/1078 two decades later. Throughout all of these momentous changes, he was also active as a writer composing, for example, at least 800 lessons for the weekly *majlis al-ḥikma*, and a *dīwān* of poetry, plus many other works. One among them is an autobiographical account of his coming to Egypt, what he saw there, and a record of his later efforts to enlist the *amīr*s of the east in the coalition he tried to put together against the Saljuks. Unfortunately, it comes to an end in year 450/1058, which is likely when he wrote it hoping through it to justify his previous activities on behalf of the Ismaili mission and the imam.[26]

1. Dated 296/909 and struck in Qayrawān by the *dāʿī* Abū ʿAbdallāh al-Shīʿī without naming the Imam, this is an example of the very earliest Fatimid coinage. The obverse, shown here, has a three-line inscription in the centre field:

lā ilāha illā
Allāh waḥdahu
lā sharīka lahu

(There is no god but God, alone without associate)

encircled by a marginal inscription that reads:

Muḥammad rasūl-Allāh
arsalahu bi'l-hudā wa dīn al-ḥaqq li-yuẓhirahu ʿalā al-dīn kullihi

(Muḥammad is the messenger of God; God sent him with the guidance and religion of truth to proclaim it above every religion)

2. The reverse of the coin has a five-line inscription in the centre field:

al-ḥamdu lillāh
Muḥammad
rasūl
Allāh
wa rabb al-ʿālamīn

(Praise be to God, the Lord of the worlds; Muhammad is the messenger of God)

encircled by a marginal inscription that reads:

In the name of God, this dinar was struck in Qayrawān in the year 296.

3. An example of the first Fatimid coinage struck in Egypt. It bears the name of Imam al-Muʿizz and is dated 358/969. On both sides the legends are inscribed in three concentric circles. On the obverse, from the inner to the outer, the circles read:

There is no god but God; Muḥammad is the messenger of God.
ʿAlī is the most excellent of executors and deputy to the best of those sent by God.
Muḥammad is the apostle of God; God sent him with the guidance and religion of truth to proclaim it above every religion despite the opposition of the idolators (Qurʾan 9:33 and 61:9)

4. On the reverse, from the outer to the inner, the circles read:

In the name of God, this dinar was struck at Miṣr in the year 358
The Imam Maʿadd summons to the absolute oneness of God the Eternal.
al-Muʿizz li-Dīn Allāh, amīr al-muʾminīn

5. Cairo, Bāb al-Futūḥ, Gate of Victories, one of four surviving Fatimid gates to the medieval city.

6. (*Above*) Cairo, part of the foundation inscription from 480/1087 on the Bāb al-Naṣr, naming both al-Mustanṣir and Badr al-Jamālī, the latter with full titles.

7. (*Left*) Cairo, the *miḥrāb* of the *mashhad* of al-Juyūshī erected by Badr al-Jamālī in 478/1085 above Cairo on the Muqaṭṭam.

8. Cairo, the *miḥrāb* from 487/1094 in the Mosque of Ibn Ṭūlūn with the names of both the caliph al-Mustanṣir and the wazir al-Afḍal.

9. Fatimid inscription found at the site of Ascalon from the reign of al-Ẓāfir and bearing the name of his wazir al-ʿĀdil b. Salār, the local governor, and the qadi. The same piece of marble was later reused by the Latin Crusaders who turned it on its side and carved over the Arabic letters their own heraldic shields.

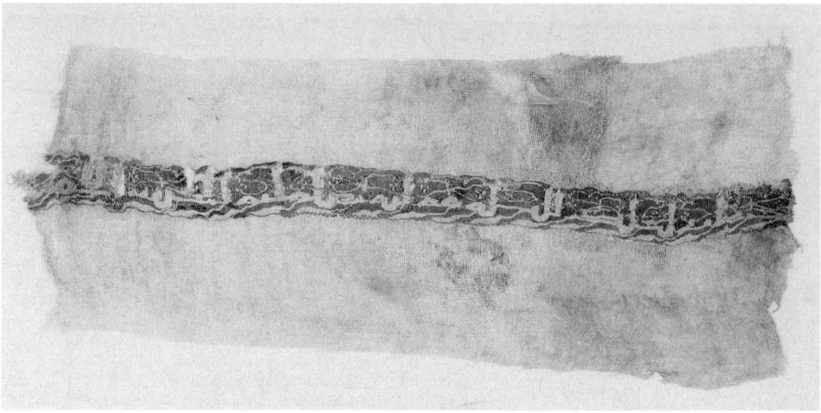

10. Rectangular *ṭirāz* textile fragment, linen with tapestry, woven with a single line of Kufic inscription. 24 x 10 cm. Fatimid Egypt, 4th/10th-5th/11th century.

11. *Ṭirāz* textile fragment, a tripartite frieze comprising a central band with lozenge interlace and a repeating pattern of hares within medallions, flanked by two lines of inscription: Kufic text, red on gold, with the repeat phrase *Naṣr min Allāh.* 17.5 x 12 cm. Fatimid Egypt, 5th/11th century.

12. A page from a manuscript of the *Khiṭaṭ* of al-Maqrīzī, dated 966/1558, from Egypt or Syria.

Beyond these two essential witnesses, neither of which was readily accessible to most later medieval writers in any case, there are several works that are now lost. Two of them were, however, used and are cited by later Egyptian sources. One was the *khiṭaṭ* (of Fusṭāṭ) by al-Quḍāʿī, *al-Mukhtār fī dhikr al-khiṭaṭ wa'l-āthār.* Al-Quḍāʿī was a Shāfiʿī but he had been a deputy qadi under the Fatimids; he died in 454/1062.[27] His topography of Fusṭāṭ was thus completed prior to the decline of that city during the years of 'Calamity' which began not long after his death. His work was therefore of major importance for al-Maqrīzī and others in their attempt to understand the layout of that city before it fell into ruin. Another source from the same period was a biography of the wazir al-Yāzūrī consulted by later medieval writers but for which not even the name of the author is known now. Yet one more that ought to be mentioned is 'Alī b. Khalaf's *Mawādd al-bayān,*[28] which, although a work on the technical aspects of writing for the chancery, is none the less, based on the author's personal experience of Fatimid practice. His dates centre around or before 437/1045 the last date known for him.[29] Another is the relatively brief necrology of Sunni hadith transmitters, mainly of Egypt, by al-Ḥabbāl (or Ibn al-Ḥabbāl), who was born in 391/1001 and died in 482/1089 (or 483/1090) all the while, except for trips abroad to hear hadith, living under the Shiʿi regime of the Fatimids. His *Wafayāt al-Miṣriyyīn* includes the names and occasionally a detail or two about the life and death of those who died in the years between 375/985 and 456/1063, many of whom the author must have known personally.[30]

An incidental source that would normally be of only minor interest resulted from a cantankerous exchange that took place in Egypt between two quite prominent physicians, Ibn Riḍwān and Ibn Buṭlān. A Muslim, Ibn Riḍwān was born in Egypt (Gīza), grew up there, and though almost entirely self-taught succeeded in becoming a prolific author and the leading doctor in the capital. He died in 468/1068. Prior to his visit, Ibn Buṭlān, a Christian, taught medicine and philosophy in Baghdad, from which he departed in 440/1049 for Cairo. In Egypt, and before he moved on to Constantinople in 446/1054, he and Ibn Riḍwān, proceeded to attack each other over matters of scientific principle in a series of pamphlets. All of this material survives and is a testimony to what appears to have been, at the time, a lively intellectual climate, if slightly uncivil in this one case.[31] Ibn Riḍwān also wrote a curious treatise 'On the Prevention of Bodily Ills in Egypt' which also survives.[32]

In the same year that saw Ibn Buṭlān arrive, yet another prominent scholar living in Egypt, al-Mubashshir b. Fātik, composed his *Mukhtār al-ḥikam wa maḥāsin al-kalim* (Choice Wise Sayings and Fine Statements), the only work of his to survive but one that earned him lasting fame. Like Ibn Buṭlān and Ibn Riḍwān, he was a physician and a philosopher; supposedly he had once been a student of both Ibn Riḍwān and of the mathematician and physicist Ibn al-Haytham. Unlike them he was a historian as well who wrote what he called a 'great history'. Another historical work consisted of a biography in three volumes of al-Mustanṣir, *Sīrat al-khalīfa al-Mustanṣir.* The latter, were it not lost, would now be of incomparable value. Unfortunately, however, there seems to exist no trace of it, not even quotations from it. It is reported, perhaps apocryphally, that when the author died, his wife, whom he had always neglected in favour of his books, took her revenge by throwing them all into the pool in the courtyard of their house.[33]

One other source from the middle of al-Mustanṣir's reign – the year 461/1067 – is the highly unusual *al-Dhakhā'ir wa'l-tuḥaf* (Book of Treasuries and Rarities) by an unknown author. The original form of this work is likewise not clear.[34] It was, however, an eyewitness account of the items taken from the caliph's various storehouses and treasuries to pay, in the absence of normal revenues during the period of the 'Calamity,' the salaries owed army officers and other government officials. Later historians found this information fascinating and they picked it up; it also served as fodder for a genre of writing about elaborate luxuries and especially extravagant gifts. A later example was the *Hadāyā wa'l-tuḥaf* of the Qāḍī al-Rashīd b. al-Zubayr (d.562/1167). Much later still al-Maqrīzī's neighbour and fellow historian al-Awḥadī compiled a volume of selections from such sources, including that describing the emptying of al-Mustanṣir's treasuries in 461/1068. In that form and in numerous quotations used by al-Maqrīzī in both his *Khiṭaṭ* and his *Ittiʿāẓ*, at least some, if not all, of that earlier work survived.

Following those sources just mentioned, the situation becomes so desolate and barren that even minor and at first sight unpromising sources command attention. The *History of the Patriarchs of Alexandria*, particularly for its biographies of Christodoulus (1047–1077) and Cyril II (1078–1092), both written by the contemporary Mawhūb b. Manṣūr, and that of Michael IV (1092–1102), composed by Mawhūb's successor Yūḥannā b. Sāʿid Ibn al-Qulzumī, assume unusual importance.

The Wazirates of al-Afḍal and al-Maʾmūn

For the era of the wazir al-Afḍal much more information exists than for his father, although the situation is, even so, not comparable to the period that follows his own. One important eyewitness for the years 489/1096 to 506/1112 is the *Risāla al-miṣriyya* of Umayya b. ʿAbd al-ʿAzīz b. Abi'l-Ṣalt.[35] This Andalusian author came to Egypt and stayed for these years under al-Afḍal, who, in fact, forcefully detained him in Alexandria for three of those same years. Ibn Abi'l-Ṣalt was interested in music, medicine and astrology and he was a poet of some note, friend to other poets and a collector of verse. In this treatise he left a description of what he saw in Egypt, the scholars and poets he met, and his assessment of the state of letters there in his time.[36]

Although material about the earliest period under al-Āmir is rare, with the assassination of al-Afḍal and the elevation of al-Maʾmūn al-Baṭāʾiḥī in his place, historical details become exceedingly rich and voluminous. That situation is due mainly to the work of al-Maʾmūn's son who was himself a historian.[37] He died in 588/1192 well into the rule of the Ayyubids, but his four volume history was used heavily by most of the later writers precisely for what it reported about the years 515/1121 to 519/1125, the very period of his own father's wazirate which he presumably witnessed first-hand and close up.

From the final years of al-Afḍal and the transition to al-Maʾmūn comes what remains of a curious work, the *Kitāb ʿAmal al-raṣad*

(On the Making of the Observatory). It is an account, apparently by someone closely connected to the project, of how these wazirs tried to have an astronomical observatory built by a committee of local scholars and engineers. Al-Maqrīzī much later picked up this material for his *Khiṭaṭ* (and also his *Ittiʿāẓ*).[38]

Other cases of works from the period now lost but used by later writers included a biography of al-Afḍal, a *Sīrat al-wazīr al-Afḍal*, by an unknown author copied in part by Ibn Ẓāfir al-Azdī. From slightly later there was a *Taʾrīkh Miṣr* (History of Egypt) by al-Qurṭī. The author in this work made an attempt to cover all periods of the history of Egypt down to his time; he presented it finally to Shāwar the wazir of al-ʿĀḍid. But perhaps the most important was another history, the *Taʾrīkh khulafāʾ Miṣr* by the qadi al-Murtaḍā Abū ʿAlī Muḥammad al-Aṭrābulsī, known as al-Muḥannak. He had been a ranking administrator in the various departments of the government prior to his death in 549/1154. His work became a major source for Ibn Muyassar and several others.

From another angle, Christian historians continued their *History of the Patriarchs* throughout the final phase of Fatimid rule and beyond. Ibn al-Qulzumī was the author of the biographical entry for Macarius II (495/1102 – 522/1128), Patriarch Mark III b. Zurʿa wrote the entries covering the period 527/1131 – 563/1167, and finally Maʿānī Abū al-Makārim for the years 562/1166 – 585/1189.

Like ʿAlī b. Khalaf over a century earlier, Abu'l-Qāsim ʿAlī Ibn al-Ṣayrafī worked in and later directed the chancery until his death in 542/1147. Two treatises of his survive, one on chancery practice, the *Qānūn dīwān al-rasāʾil*,[39] and the other a small history of the wazirs from Ibn Killis to al-Maʾmūn, *al-Ishāra ilā man nāla al-wizāra*.[40]

The Final Phase of the Fatimids

The historiography of the last period of the Fatimids, especially that concerning the final decades of their rule and the assumption of power by Ṣalāḥ al-Dīn and the Ayyubids, is considerably more complicated than any previous to it. In part this development stems from the simple fact of better and more complete preservation of the sources. But it involves as well a larger field of players and parties, each with their own interests and reasons for recording what happened to them. First, the Latin Crusaders entered Palestine and then confronted Fatimid armies there and later even in Egypt itself and, next, following them, the Zangids rose to power in Syria aspiring to check the Crusaders which almost inevitably brought them to engage the Fatimids. The historical writings of both the Crusaders and the Zangids and the sources for them soon become intertwined with those produced in Egypt. The history of the very last Fatimids must thus include both the Crusaders and the Zangids.

The enormous field of crusade history and the scholarly analysis of its sources is beyond the scope of this study. Suffice it here to note that, insofar as the Crusaders either directed their attention to their Fatimid enemy and were conscious of that fact, their witnesses have a place in the history of the latter. The main crusader history of the period 538/1143 onward is William of Tyre's *Historia rerum in partibus transmarinis gestarum.*[41] This very work began as a commission in 562/1167 from King Amalric I to record his various campaigns in Egypt. Only later did it grow into a much larger project.

Another important witness to the earlier period of the Crusades was the Syrian historian Ibn al-Qalānisī whose *Dhayl ta'rīkh Dimashq* (Continuation of the History of Damascus)[42] depended heavily on what its author saw, heard of, or experienced for its coverage of the years he lived through, namely 465/1073 to 555/1160.[43] Material in it for the period prior to his own lifetime is also quite valuable but not as an eyewitness.[44]

A good example of Syrian involvement, though not always necessarily tied directly to the Zangids, except peripherally, is the memoir of Usāma b. Murshid b. ʿAlī Ibn Munqidh, a member of the Banū Munqidh of Shayzar. Once a part of the entourage of Zangī, at one point he was banished from Syria from where he travelled to Egypt and attached himself to the wazir al-ʿĀdil b. al-Salār. His ten-year stay in Cairo ended in 549/1154, when he fled back to Syria in the aftermath of a plot to murder his patron and then the caliph al-Ẓāfir, in which he was deeply involved personally. All this and much more he recounted in detail in his *Kitāb al-Iʿtibār* (Book of Examples) composed long afterward in 579/1183.[45] He died in 584/1188.

Yet another author who came to Fatimid Egypt from outside was ʿUmāra b. Abi'l-Ḥasan al-Ḥakamī al-Yamanī. He was a well-known poet and littérateur, who after having been sent for a second time on a diplomatic mission from the Sharīf of Mecca to Cairo, eventually settled there in 552/1157. As a court poet he eulogised several of the Fatimid wazirs including Ṭalāʾiʿ, Ruzzīk, Ḍirghām, Shīrkūh and Ṣalāḥ al-Dīn. He wrote also an autobiographical work *al-Nukat al-ʿaṣiyya fī akhbār al-wuzarāʾ al-miṣriyya* covering the years 558/1162 to 564/1169.[46] All this as well as his *History of the Yemen* and more survives. Curiously, although ʿUmāra was not himself Shiʿi, his sympathies for the Fatimids caused his execution by Ṣalāḥ al-Dīn when he became involved in a conspiracy to revive the dynasty.

Not all those who saw the end of the Fatimids expressed their regrets at their demise. Many made the transition to the new dynasty with relative ease and a few of them, as was the case with Qāḍī al-Fāḍil, attained an enviable status in the inner circle of the Ayyubid ruler. Those most adversely affected were the Ismailis and other Shiʿa, all of whose institutions and means of communal support were eliminated or closed down. In addition, because of the crusader threat, the ardently determined Muslim opposition under the Ayyubids tended to deal roughly with the local Christians. By contrast the Jews did well. One among them who witnessed the change of regime was the great Maimonides, by then living in Egypt and about to become head of the Jewish community there.

Another relatively high ranking figure under the later Fatimids and then the Ayyubids was Ibn al-Ṭuwayr (525/1130 – 617/1220),[47] whose long life reached well into the Ayyubid period. He composed a history, the *Nuzhat al-muqlatayn fī akhbār al-dawlatayn* (History of the Two Dynasties) to chronicle both the last Fatimids and the Ayyubids he had seen. Quite possibly he intended it as a comparative study of the two. Though lost for the most part, it was consulted and copied extensively by later writers in regard to its information about the Fatimids.[48]

These final examples do not exhaust all of the eyewitness material from the very end of the Fatimids,[49] but to continue involves more and more historiographical questions related to Ayyubid history rather than the dynasty they replaced.[50] And in any case works composed after the Fatimids will be considered in the following chapter on later chronicles, histories and biographical dictionaries.

7 *Histories, Topographies and Biographical Dictionaries*

As noted before, the writings of the ninth/fifteenth century Egyptian Mamluk historian Taqī al-Dīn Aḥmad b. ʿAlī al-Maqrīzī play an excessively large part in the historiography of the Fatimids.[1] To them al-Maqrīzī dedicated an individual work, his *Ittiʿāẓ al-ḥunafāʾ bi-akhbār al-aʾimma al-Fāṭimiyyīn al-khulafāʾ* (Lessons for the True Believers in the History of the Fatimid Imams and Caliphs), the more famous *Khiṭaṭ*, also in so many ways a work on the achievement of the Fatimids who had founded Cairo, and finally, a biographical dictionary, the *Kitāb al-Muqaffā al-kabīr*. Thus al-Maqrīzī is both one of the last chronologically, of the medieval historians to compile important studies of the Fatimids that contain information not otherwise available and, also, the only one to write major works in three main categories of Islamic historiography: chronicles, topographies and biographical dictionaries. His effort to comprehend Fatimid history, therefore, certainly requires special attention.

But writing well over two centuries after their demise, al-Maqrīzī had little direct connection with the period. Even much of the physical evidence of the Fatimids had by his time been replaced by later buildings or had fallen into ruin. Like the modern historian he was forced to search for information in whatever documents and chronicles he could find that were either witnesses contemporary to the events of Fatimid history or preserved some portions of that kind of record. His advantage was, in the first instance, access to works now lost, some – for example, the chronicles of al-Musabbiḥī, Ibn al-Ṭuwayr, Ibn al-Ma'mūn and Ibn Muyassar – of inestimable value. Another was his relative proximity to the culture of the Fatimid era; the language of his sources and the facts they spoke about were more often something he understood better than any modern scholar. Of course that is not always and invariably true. Al-Maqrīzī's view of history had serious limitations. To cite but one example, he knew little about genuine Ismaili literature, either doctrinal or historical. His writing on the Fatimids, whatever his strengths and flaws as a historian, nevertheless serves here as quite possibly the most important representative of the medieval sources that, rather than providing crucial eyewitness testimony, are compilations assembled by authors writing long after the events they chose to chronicle.

Although he was among the last, many others came before him including a number who wrote such accounts during the Fatimid period itself. In regard to the historians who came after the Fatimids yet prior to al-Maqrīzī, it is customary to group them either by dynasty – Ayyubid or Mamluk, for example – or roughly by century. Judging in part from the titles of works mentioned by later writers, originally there were a number of histories that had the Fatimids as their central focus. In almost all instances of works that survive more or less intact, however, the Fatimids are not the main subject. Of those available now, most cover the Fatimid period as only one portion of a much longer time frame, frequently a self-styled universal history of the world down to the author's own immediate era, or in many other cases a continuation of someone else's universal history. As another example the important history of the Coptic patriarchs commences long before the Fatimid period and thus its coverage of the later era is incidental to its main purpose. Even so, several examples of these larger works contain a major section, often a separate volume, on the Fatimids. Many of the chronicles, at any rate, tried to provide a year by year account of all significant events for whatever period they cover. The universal history of Ibn al-Athīr, for example, records what took place in each year, in general combining in one yearly entry all important events in the several countries and geographical regions of the Islamic world. The Fatimids were therefore not accorded a separate treatment in his history. Similarly, the biographical dictionaries, even those like the *Wafayāt* of Ibn Khallikān that offered biographies for each of the individual Fatimid imams, did not deal with the Fatimids as such but rather with important single figures who happen to have lived in territories controlled by them and in their period. There also exist a number of local histories for towns or regions that were at one point within or adjacent to the Fatimid empire. Information in them concerns, but the work itself is not about, the Fatimids. The *khiṭaṭ* genre, a study of the topography of a city or region, belongs in this category. But for Egypt the earliest examples covered Fusṭāṭ and not Cairo; only with the work of Ibn ʿAbd al-Ẓāhir and al-Maqrīzī did the primary focus shift to Cairo.

North Africa

Again, as with eyewitness accounts and other contemporary sources, *post-facto* histories tend to concentrate either on the Maghrib (and Spain) or on Egypt and the east but, with notable exceptions, not both. Al-Maqrīzī tried to cover the Maghribi period of Fatimid rule in his *Ittiʿāẓ* and Ibn al-Athīr attempted to be truly universal in scope, but others were interested solely in one region and not the other. In several cases, however, what survives or what has been published of a given work represents solely the limited portion of it that covered one particular geographical area.

For the Fatimids in the Maghrib, the historical works of the Ismaili authorities Qāḍī al-Nuʿmān and Idrīs ʿImād al-Dīn are as important as any of the later non-Ismaili histories of that region. But, among the latter, the chronicle of Ibn ʿIdhārī is none the less indispensable. Abu'l-ʿAbbās Aḥmad b. Muḥammad b. ʿIdhārī al-Marrākushī lived long after the Fatimids; he was active in the second half of the seventh/thirteenth and early eighth/fourteenth century.[2] His *al-Bayān al-mughrib*,[3] however, is based on and thus contains a good deal of invaluable information from older chronicles, most notably, for the coming of the Fatimids, the chronicle of ʿArīb b. Saʿd. An Andalusian native, ʿArīb, who died about 370/980, wrote his own history of the Maghrib for the Umayyad court in Cordova and his basic outlook was thus pro-Umayyad. Because Ibn ʿIdhārī inserted whole passages from ʿArīb in his own work,[4] it is now the major source for the history of the later Aghlabids and the North African Fatimids. No other source provides as much information over the whole of the relevant time frame or as wide a geographical range.[5]

Quite separate from Ibn ʿIdhārī, the Mālikī *Ṭabaqāt* of Abū ʿAbdallāh Muḥammad b. al-Ḥārith al-Khushanī, who was born near Qayrawān where he was educated prior to departing in 311/923, offers, as noted previously, a near contemporary eyewitness account of the lives and activities of many of the figures he thought fit to include in it. Most importantly, in contrast to the *ṭabaqāt* works of the other Mālikī authorities, which naturally focus almost exclusively on the scholars and notables of this *madhhab*, al-Khushanī added to his own various sections on the Ḥanafīs, as well as accounts of those *fuqahā*ʾ of Qayrawān who converted to the Ismaili cause and also a special list of the scholars who were persecuted by the government. Later Maghrib *ṭabaqāt* compilations, which were all Mālikī, never failed to point out the repression of their own by the Fatimids. The most important of these works, al-Mālikī's *Riyāḍ al-nufūs* and Qāḍī ʿIyāḍ's *Madārik*,[6] although rich in information about what happened to the members of this particular school under the Fatimids, both tend toward exaggeration and hagiography.[7] They also depend on al-Khushanī for the details of the earliest encounters with the Ismailis as well as for the biographies of any of the scholars from Qayrawān under the last Aghlabids. Al-Khushanī's work therefore has a historical value that is not always characteristic of items in the *ṭabaqāt* genre. He was certainly not unbiased and most of the information he gives needs to be treated with caution. Nevertheless, he provides a viewpoint not given by ʿArīb or by the Ismaili sources. But the same is even more true of al-Mālikī and Qāḍī ʿIyāḍ and those who came still later in the same tradition such as al-Dabbāgh and Ibn Nājī.[8]

Another non-Ismaili historian of some importance is Abū

ʿAbdallāh Muḥammad b. ʿAlī b. Ḥammād al-Ṣanhājī (Ibn Ḥammād or also Ibn Ḥamādu). A Berber and a qadi, who died in 628/1231, this man wrote a now lost history of the Ṣanhāja Zīrids that was used by Ibn Khaldūn. In addition, he composed a surviving short account of the Fatimid imams entitled *Akhbār mulūk banī ʿUbayd wa-sīratihim.*[9]

Finally, the famous Ibn Khaldūn, who died in 808/1406, by then a resident of Mamluk Cairo, himself falls into this category. His own universal history, the *ʿIbar*, of which the introduction (the *Muqaddima*) is properly applauded for what it says about the historian's craft and science, deals extensively with the long history of the Maghrib up to his own time, including the Fatimids and Zīrids, though with less of value to offer for them than for later periods.

For North Africa, of the works now apparently lost, the history of Ibn al-Raqīq, *Ta'rīkh Ifrīqiya wa'l-Maghrib,* cited in the chapter on eyewitnesses, even though much consulted by later writers, was likely pro-Shiʿi, even Ismaili. Ibn al-Raqīq, who died after 418/1027–8, worked for the Zīrids at a time when they were still ostensibly loyal and subservient to the Fatimids. He is also thought to have visited Cairo during the reign of al-Ḥākim. Accordingly, he likely had access to some Fatimid works, quite possibly those of Qāḍī al-Nuʿmān, but perhaps others.[10]

Another writer, the Qayrawānī physician Ibn al-Jazzār (d.*ca.*395/1004) is known to have composed a history of the Fatimids called *Kitāb Akhbār al-dawla.*

The Ismaili *daʿwa* itself, due largely to the efforts of Ṭayyibī scholars in the Yemen, made a special attempt to recover and thus preserve both doctrinal and historical works from all periods prior to their own. Qāḍī al-Nuʿmān's invaluable account of Abū ʿAbdallāh al-Shīʿī's mission to the Maghrib and the founding of the caliphate, the *Iftitāḥ*, may owe its survival to this very effort. The same is true of the *Munāẓarāt* of Ibn al-Haytham, the *Sīra* of Jaʿfar al-Ḥājib and the *Sīra* of Ustādh Jawdhar, which have already been discussed. Unlike these latter works, al-Nuʿmān's *Iftitāḥ al-daʿwa wa'l-ibtidā' al-dawla* is not an eyewitness account or a memoir but rather, despite its great authority, a history composed substantially after the events it covers. It was certainly, however, based on older contemporary sources and accounts.

It is quite likely that this list does not exhaust either what the archives of the *daʿwa* once contained for this period or even what these Ṭayyibī scholars possessed. The principal history of their own imams and the Ismaili movement is Idrīs's *ʿUyūn al-akhbār*, itself a massive compilation of historical information for all periods prior to the eighth/fifteenth century when it was written. Idrīs, who lived from 794/1392 until 872/1468, was the nineteenth chief *dāʿī* of the Ṭayyibī Ismailis in the Yemen.[11] While his history deals with the whole Fatimid period, the volumes on the Maghribi phase – now properly edited and published by Muḥammad al-Yaʿlāwī – contain, in addition to long sections taken from Qāḍī al-Nuʿmān and others that are known, passages from original works not yet recovered. Unfortunately what it reports about later periods appears in portions either poorly published or still unpublished.

Egypt and the East

In regard to Egypt and the East the situation should have been to a degree different due to the length of direct Fatimid rule there. The two hundred years of their reign ought to have attracted the interest of any number of chroniclers. To be sure some are known by name if not by their work, such as Ibn Zūlāq, al-Musabbiḥī, Ibn al-Ma'mūn, Yaḥyā of Antioch, the contributors to the *History of the Patriarchs*, Ibn al-Qalānisī and others. Most of these writers were also either eyewitnesses or contemporary with the events they report. As such they appeared in the previous chapter. However, it should be noted here that they were also historians of the period before their own. But in several cases even the evidence for the original scope of these histories is uncertain. One partial exception is the *History of Damascus* by Ibn al-Qalānisī, which purports to be a 'continuation' of an older chronicle once thought to be that of Hilāl al-Ṣābi'.[12] For the period prior to his own lifetime, all but the opening pages of which exist, Ibn al-Qalānisī's work rather depends on Egyptian-Syrian archival materials and minor chronicles available to him the information from which is of exceptional value. The second portion of this same history covers his own lifetime and is thus an eyewitness and/or a contemporary account.

From a quite different perspective and on a limited topic, there is the *History of the Churches and Monasteries of Egypt* from about 555/1160–565/1170 whose main author was Abu'l-Makārim Saʿdallāh b. Jirjis.

Histories from the Ayyubid Period

The last period of Fatimid rule and the commencement of the Ayyubids contains almost a plethora of sources and works of a special kind, in addition to a number of histories. Observers at the time and those who were to chronicle the period later – particularly as it concerned the career of Ṣalāḥ al-Dīn – did not necessarily separate what happened under the Fatimids from what came later. Thus works like those of Ibn Mammātī and al-Makhzūmī deal with administrative matters both before and after. Similarly there is an important treatise on market supervision (*ḥisba*) by al-Shayzarī (d.589/1193)[13] and the famous collection of sixth/twelfth century Arabic poetry *Kharīdat al-qaṣr* by Ṣalāḥ al-Dīn's secretary, al-ʿImād al-Isfahānī (d.597/1201), as well as the correspondence of al-Qāḍī al-Fāḍil. Most of these are in essence Ayyubid but they cover aspects of the Fatimid period as well.

Yet another example is the *Nuzhat al-muqlatayn fī akhbār al-dawlatayn* by Abū Muḥammad ʿAbd al-Salām Ibn al-Ṭuwayr (d.617/1220). Although now lost it was, as its title indicates, an account of the two dynasties, the Fatimids and the Ayyubids, both of which Ibn al-Ṭuwayr knew well. He had been, in fact, a high official under the Fatimids. His history was used by many later historians among them Ibn al-Furāt, al-Maqrīzī, al-Qalqashandī, Ibn Taghrī Birdī, and even Ibn Khaldūn.

Two more Egyptians from the Ayyubid period wrote important historical studies that had, in these cases, a universal rather than particular scope. One is the famous biographical dictionary of learned men, the *Taʾrīkh al-ḥukamāʾ* by Jamāl al-Dīn Abu'l-Ḥasan ʿAlī Ibn al-Qifṭī (d.646/1248).[14] The other is the *Kitāb al-Duwal al-munqaṭiʿa* by Jamāl al-Dīn Abu'l-Ḥasan ʿAlī Ibn Ẓāfir, who was born in Cairo in 567/1171. One section of this work, which survives, covered the Fatimids.[15]

Several universal histories from the same period were composed outside of Egypt by non-Egyptians. The viewpoint of these authors in part reflects where they lived and what sources were available to them locally. One among them, however, was himself a Shiʿa – a fairly rare condition in that place and era – and that allowed him to express much greater sympathy for the Fatimids than those, like the ardently Ḥanbalī Ibn al-Jawzī, who were notably anti-Shiʿa. This Shiʿi historian, Yaḥyā Ibn Abī Ṭayyi', lived in Aleppo (575/1180 to *ca.*625–30/1228–33) under Ayyubid rule. His now lost *Maʿādin al-dhahab fī ta'rīkh al-mulūk wa'l-khulafā' wa dhawi'l-ratab* is of special value for the final years of the Fatimids and the transition to the Ayyubids. Despite its Shiʿi leanings, it was none the less consulted by Ibn al-Furāt and Abū Shāma, both themselves Sunni, for what it reported, especially about the sixth/twelfth century.

The most famous of the universal histories from this period, one generally highly regarded, is the *Kāmil* of ʿIzz al-Dīn Abu'l-Ḥasan ʿAlī Ibn al-Athīr (d.630/1233). He was from Mosul and tended to dislike Ṣalāḥ al-Dīn. Despite its outside perspective Ibn al-Athīr's work contains valuable information for nearly all periods of the Fatimids including the Maghribi phase.

Two other prominent historians both with a viewpoint even farther east, in this case, Baghdad itself, are first ʿAbd al-Raḥmān b. ʿAlī Ibn al-Jawzī (d.597/1200), the famous Ḥanbalī preacher and prolific author, who was so stridently anti-Shiʿa. When he received news of the overthrow of the Fatimids, for example, he composed a work of celebration. His universal history, *al-Muntaẓam fī ta'rīkh al-mulūk wa'l-umam*, however, is useful precisely for its perspective. It survives for the years 257/871 to 574/1179. Sibṭ ibn al-Jawzī, the author of the equally famous *Mir'āt al-zamān*, was the former's grandson, the son of his daughter. Following the death of his grandfather, Sibṭ left Baghdad and settled in Damascus where he died in 654/1256. His history preserves older material that he had apparently copied in large quantities. The parts of it that cover the crusade period have been published and studied, but it contains important information also about the second half of the fifth/eleventh century which has not all been published.[16]

Yet another important writer, like Ibn al-Athīr originally from Mosul, was Bahā᾽ al-Dīn Abu'l-Maḥāsin Yūsuf Ibn al-Shaddād, who composed an important biography of Ṣalāḥ al-Dīn whom he served in close attendance over the final years of this ruler's life. Thereafter Ibn al-Shaddād moved to Aleppo still in service to various Ayyubids. There he died in 632/1235. His biography of Ṣalāḥ al-Dīn relied on second-hand information for the earlier period and it is of less value with regard to the Fatimids for that reason. Like the work of Ibn al-Shaddād, the later history of the Damascene Shihāb al-Dīn Abu'l-Qāsim ʿAbd al-Raḥmān, known as Abū Shāma (d.665/1268), focused closely on the careers respectively of Nūr al-Dīn Zangī and Ṣalāḥ al-Dīn. His *Kitāb al-Rawḍatayn fī akhbār al-dawlatayn*, although not specifically on the Fatimids, nevertheless preserves important information from Ibn Abī Ṭayyi᾽ and Qāḍī al-Fāḍil among others.

From roughly the same late Ayyubid era, there is a work that has in general greater value for the whole of Fatimid history. That is the *Kitāb al-Mughrib fī ḥulā'l-Maghrib* by the Andalusian Abu'l-Ḥasan ʿAlī b. Mūsā Ibn Saʿīd al-Maghribī (d.685/1286). Completed while the author was in Egypt in 641/1243,[17] it is a massive accumulation of data on the western regions of the Islamic world, including most importantly Egypt. That latter portion of it, for which Ibn Saʿīd used sources now otherwise lost, has been published separately.[18]

Histories from the Mamluk Period

With the end of the Ayyubids and the beginning of the Mamluk period starting in 648/1250, direct contact with the Fatimids had long ceased except for the accounts of earlier writers and the physical remnants of their capital city Cairo. For Fatimid history, therefore, what is significant in the later histories is the information they preserve from older works. But it must be noted that, given how many of those older sources no longer exist and also how little in general remains of what once might have existed, the work of the Mamluk era historians, although they are not by any means of equal value, is quite often simply indispensable.

Two highly important biographical dictionaries were both compiled in the first decades of the Mamluks. The *ʿUyūn al-anbāʾ fī ṭabaqāt al-aṭibbāʾ* by Ibn Abī Uṣaybiʿa (d.668/1270) is devoted to the lives of prominent physicians, including a number who were active under the Fatimids. The final recension of this work was completed in 667/1268. The other is, however, of even greater value for Fatimid history. It is the famous dictionary of notable men, *Wafayāt al-aʿyān wa anbāʾ abnāʾ al-zamān,* by Aḥmad b. Muḥammad Ibn Khallikān (d.681/1282).[19] Originally from Irbil, the author moved to Cairo in about 646/1249 where, interrupted by several appointments as chief qadi in Syria, he eventually finished the work in 672/1274. Justly acclaimed for the range and detail of its coverage, Ibn Khallikān's *Wafayāt* is exceptionally rich in Fatimid material. It contains, for example, a separate biographical entry for each of the fourteen imam-caliphs and likewise for many of the wazirs, among them, Ibn Killis, al-Jarjarāʾī, al-Afḍal, Ḍirghām, Shāwar, Ṭalāʾiʿ b. Ruzzīk, Shīrkūh, Ibn al-Salār and Ibn Maṣāl. Many of the men outside of Egypt who were important to the Fatimids also appear such as al-Basāsīrī, ʿAlī al-Ṣulayḥī, Abū ʿAbdallāh al-Shiʿi, most of the Zīrids and many more. From within the state there are biographies for Jawhar, Barjawān, Jaʿfar b. Falāḥ al-Kutāmī, Abu'l-Qāsim al-Maghribī, al-Qāḍī al-Fāḍil, Qāḍī al-Nuʿmān and his sons and grandsons, as well as the poets Tamīm b. al-Muʿizz, Usāma b. Munqidh, Ibn Abi'l-Shakhbāʾ, ʿUmāra, Ibn al-Hāniʾ, Ibn Qalāqis, the astronomer Ibn Yūnus and several historians such as, for example, al-Musabbiḥī, whose own history was an important source of information for the author. And the foregoing list does not exhaust those Fatimids who receive treatment; all in all the *Wafayāt* contains substantial amounts of material not available elsewhere.

From almost precisely the same generation, the Egyptian historian Tāj al-Dīn Muḥammad b. Yūsuf Ibn Muyassar's *Taʾrīkh Miṣr,* to judge from the evidence of it that survives, may well have been one of the most important works to cover the Fatimid period. As a whole it is now lost but al-Maqrīzī found a copy and took notes for his own purpose including, apparently, whole sections either verbatim or in précis. A direct copy of al-Maqrīzī's own notes exists and has been published twice, once edited by H. Massé and later by Ayman Fu'ād Sayyid.[20] It consists of the portion for the years 439/1047 to 553/1158, minus the period from 502/1108 to 514/1120. In addition there are small bits of it for the periods 362/973 to 365/976 and 381/991 to 387/997, these ultimately having come from Ibn Zūlāq and al-Musabbiḥī respectively. For the later period Ibn Muyassar's main source may well have been al-Muḥannak. Despite its importance for the Fatimids, it is hard to know now what was the overall scope of the original. Certainly it continued into the Ayyubid period and may have commenced earlier than any of the surviving parts – that is, prior to the Fatimids. It was heavily used by al-Maqrīzī and also by al-Nuwayrī.

Three more historians whose death dates put them in the latter half of the thirteenth century deserve to be noted. They are Ibn al-ʿAdīm from Aleppo whose work centred on the history of his native city, for which it is extremely important, although he himself died in Cairo in 660/1260, a refugee from the Mongol onslaught in Syria. He composed a massive biographical dictionary the *Bughyat al-ṭalab fī ta'rīkh al-Ḥalab* and a chronicle the *Zubdat al-ḥalab fī ta'rīkh Ḥalab,*[21] the latter covering the history of Aleppo down to 641/1243. The ultimate value of either work for the Fatimids is substantially less than for Syria in general. The second is Ibn Wāṣil (d.697/1297), the author of a history of the Ayyubids, the *Mufarrij al-kurūb fī akhbār banī Ayyūb,*[22] which is again of marginal interest for Fatimid history. The third is Ibn ʿAbd al-Ẓāhir [23] (d.692/1292), a high-ranking official in the Mamluk administration of the time whose biographies of the sultans he served personally are especially important. In regard to the Fatimids he was the first to compose a work in the *khiṭaṭ* genre specifically on Cairo, as opposed to Fusṭāṭ, which had been the focus of those written earlier. One version of this, *al-Rawḍa al-bahiyya al-zāhira fī khiṭaṭ al-muʿizzīya al-Qāhira,* has now been edited and published by Ayman Fu'ād Sayyid.[24] Although it is in its total extent a mere fraction of his, al-Maqrīzī credits it with, in part, inspiring his own efforts in the same direction.

From at least one whole generation later still come two major universal histories, both by Egyptians, those of Shihāb al-Dīn Aḥmad al-Nuwayrī (d.733/1333) and Abū Bakr b. ʿAbdallāh Ibn al-Dawādārī (d.after 736/1335). Al-Nuwayrī's work, the *Nihāyat al-arab fī funūn al-adab*, is actually an encyclopaedia of some 9,000 pages on all of the arts and sciences of which only one is history. However, the latter subject occupies a major part of it and volume 28 of the published edition contains a lengthy section devoted to the Fatimids.[25] Ibn al-Dawādārī's universal chronicle, finished in 736/1335, likewise has a substantial segment on the Fatimids. It is part six of the *Kanz al-durar wa jāmiʿ al-ghurar*, which is entitled *al-Durra al-muḍiyya fī akhbār al-dawla al-fāṭimiyya*, now available separately in an edition by Ṣalāḥ al-Dīn al-Munajjid.[26] Much later is the universal history by Nāṣir al-Dīn Muḥammad Ibn al-Furāt (d.807/1405), his *Taʾrīkh al-duwal wa'l-mulūk*, of which he completed only the volumes covering the years from 500/1106 onward. Unfortunately the earliest part of it, that dealing with the Fatimids, remains unpublished. However, it is known that Ibn al-Furāt used Ibn Abī Ṭayyiʾ and Ibn al-Ṭuwayr extensively and thus, since both are now lost, it could be of great value.[27] From almost exactly the same time there is the great history of Ibn Khaldūn (d.808/1406), which, though often cited, is of less value for the Fatimids since its perspective is North Africa and the Fatimid presence there was relatively brief. Although Ibn Khaldūn died in Egypt and was influential in the formation of historical scholarship there, he composed his history prior to coming to Cairo.

Ibn Ḥajar al-ʿAsqalānī, who died in 852/1449, was a major scholar from the next generation – the generation of al-Maqrīzī – and is justly famous for his voluminous writings on hadith and hadith sciences. Concerning the Fatimids he would be of only minor interest except for a curious work of his on the judges of Egypt, his *Rafʿ al-iṣr ʿan quḍāt Miṣr*, which contains important information about this subject for the Fatimid period; parts, but not all, of it have been published.[28]

Before turning again to take a closer look at al-Maqrīzī, who follows next in the natural chronological order, it is useful here to complete this survey of fifteenth-century historians. Though of far less importance than his predecessor, the Mamluk historian Abu'l-Maḥāsin Ibn Taghrī Birdī (d.874/1470), whose *al-Nujūm al-zāhira fī mulūk Miṣr wa'l-Qāhira* is a complete history of Egypt from the year 20/641 down to his own time, preserved valuable information not included in earlier works.[29] In his coverage of the Fatimids, in contrast to al-Maqrīzī, however, he shows a distinct tendency to draw heavily on the non-Egyptian historians Ibn al-Qalānisī, Ibn al-Athīr and especially Sibṭ b. al-Jawzī, and therefore to echo the anti-Fatimid bias of these outsiders.

The last historian of special note for Fatimid history chronologically is also one of the first to be discussed here. Idrīs ʿImād al-Dīn, the Ṭayyibī Yemeni authority whose *ʿUyūn al-akhbār* is critically important as the main Ismaili account of the imams throughout the Fatimid period, was himself contemporary with these last Mamluk historians. He died in 872/1468. Given his access to Ismaili sources, as well as many available to the Sunnis, his history ought to be especially valuable. And as mentioned earlier it is certainly essential for the North African phase, but it remains to be seen exactly what it contains for the Egyptian period. The earlier editions by Mustafa Ghalib of some portions are generally unreliable and incomplete. In any case volume seven on the reign of al-Mustanṣir has not yet appeared in print in any form.[30]

Al-Maqrīzī

Of all the writers discussed above, al-Maqrīzī (d.845/1442) stands alone in many respects. A Mamluk historian and himself a Sunni, he is remarkable in this context for his unusually keen interest in the Ismaili Fatimid dynasty and its role in Egyptian history.[31] On it he composed a separate and quite substantial chronicle, the *Ittiʿāẓ*. He was practically the only later scholar to do so. Why should he celebrate the Fatimids in an era of staunch Sunni rejection of all Shiʿism, most particularly of the Ismaili brand of it? The fairly extravagant attention of al-Maqrīzī to the details of Fatimid history certainly appears out of place. His interest seems to demand an explanation; even his contemporaries wondered why he had devoted so much of his concern to them.

In addition to the *Ittiʿāẓ*, which has been available in a complete, though faulty, edition since 1973, his more famous *al-Mawāʿiẓ wa'l-iʿtibār bi-dhikr al-khiṭaṭ wa'l-āthār* – the *Khiṭaṭ* – is likewise a work on the achievement of the Fatimids. First printed by the Bulaq press in 1853, it remains al-Maqrīzī's great monument of scholarship, although, as with the *Ittiʿāẓ*, the edition is notoriously unreliable. Because of the great number of manuscripts that remain, so huge is the undertaking necessary to redo it correctly that the old Bulaq text has not been supplanted. Recently Ayman Fu'ād Sayyid produced a good edition of al-Maqrīzī's own first draft of this work, his *musawwada*,[32] to which the author eventually added considerably, before releasing the ultimate version of it. Finally, in addition to a number of lesser treatises that might bear occasionally and in part on events in the era of the Fatimids,[33] al-Maqrīzī compiled a massive biographical dictionary, the *Kitāb al-Muqaffā al-kabīr*. His intention in this case was to provide a notice in it on everyone who had a connection of some sort with Egypt in the period from the Islamic conquest until just before his own time.[34] He managed to finish only sixteen volumes out of what a contemporary historian, al-Sakhāwī, estimated would have comprised eighty and of those only a few survive, even though in the printed edition by al-Yaʿlāwī they take up eight volumes.[35] Nevertheless its importance for Fatimid history is considerable when and where the biographies in it cover appropriate figures.

Al-Maqrīzī knew of the *Wafayāt al-aʿyān* of Ibn Khallikān, also his contemporary's biographical dictionary of Egyptian judges, the *Rafʿ al-iṣr*. Thus the motivation for the *Muqaffā* need not be sought nearly as much as the *Khiṭaṭ*, first, and most of all the *Ittiʿāẓ*, second. While it is true that al-Maqrīzī himself recognised the *Khiṭaṭ* of Ibn ʿAbd al-Ẓāhir as the pioneering effort it had been, the existing text of the latter work is puny by comparison to that of al-Maqrīzī. It contains less than 140 pages to the 435 pages of the *musawwada* of al-Maqrīzī's *Khiṭaṭ*, which is still a fraction of the full (Bulaq) version. Ibn ʿAbd al-Ẓāhir has but one line on al-Azhar, for example.[36]

Writing the *Khiṭaṭ*, as al-Maqrīzī himself seems to say in its introduction, may have begun as an expression of nostalgia. He was born in the Barjawān quarter of Cairo and he obviously felt a strong, almost youthful loyalty to his home and to its urban setting. Also the plan for the *Khiṭaṭ* grew enormously over time. The earliest version may have been inspired by finding the notes on the same subject compiled by his neighbour al-Awḥadī following the latter's death. Al-Maqrīzī credited al-Awḥadī but not in his introduction where he probably should have. Al-Sakhāwī accordingly accused him of plagiarism or its equivalent. However, it does not appear that al-Awḥadī's work was ever completed or published. Since it was therefore unknown, it could not very well be cited. And since, moreover, it, like al-Maqrīzī's own early draft, was likely full mainly of quotations from older works, citing the originals of these, as al-Maqrīzī certainly did in his own *Khiṭaṭ*, was more appropriate under the circumstances. Even so this hardly explains how the author moved from his original, limited plan to the full-blown compendium it became and which, significantly, contained a substantial history of the Fatimids in addition to its voluminous entries on individual institutions and monuments.

The great value of the *Khiṭaṭ*, in the first instance, is its quotations of older sources with accompanying citations and references. That allows a modern researcher to trace the information to its primary context in the work of an original author. Care needs to be taken always in observing the chronological facts, however. Al-Maqrīzī mixed sources in the *Khiṭaṭ* in such a manner that he jumped back and forth between al-Musabbiḥī (early fifth/eleventh century) and Ibn al-Ṭuwayr (mid sixth/twelfth century), thereby perhaps inadvertently confusing material about a single institution from vastly differing periods. Nevertheless, in the *Khiṭaṭ* usually the origin of a piece of information is clearly marked and that is of major importance. In addition, narrative portions of the *Khiṭaṭ* also have value for the history of the Fatimids. One section of it covers the doctrines supposedly advocated by the Ismaili *daʿwa.* He reports that, because the people of his time are ignorant of their beliefs, he wants to explain them in accord with what he found in their books on that subject, although he himself will have none of it personally.[37] Al-Maqrīzī's attitude to the Fatimids is thus surely ambivalent. He is concerned to include all the information about them that he can find and yet he expresses his own distance from them.

It is known, however, that he apparently confessed to some associates that he thought himself related to the Fatimid imams through the son of al-Muʿizz, Tamīm b. al-Muʿizz.[38] Ibn Ḥajar reported that someone had seen in a work of al-Maqrīzī a note about being related to this Tamīm but that the author had later scratched it out. Al-Sakhāwī, however, repeated a genealogy for him that goes back to Tamīm. Ibn Ḥajar likewise related a story in which al-Maqrīzī was told by his father once on entering the mosque of al-Ḥākim, 'My son, this is the mosque of your ancestor'. Furthermore, Ibn Ḥajar claimed that the father said that they were descendants of Tamīm but that they should not reveal this fact to any person they could not trust. Whether any of this is true is impossible to determine and it may mean little. Ultimately it would be hard to conclude that al-Maqrīzī conceived any more than an antiquarian interest in the Fatimids. His main concern seems more likely to be the meaning they and their city might have for the present, that is, for Mamluk Egypt and its role in Islam.

Still he did write a single work on the Fatimids as no other non-Ismaili historian had done or would do. It should be noted that it is, however, one of a series of three works on the history of Egypt from the Arab conquest until the year of his own death. The first, his *ʿIqd jawāhir al-asqāṭ min akhbār madīnat al-Fusṭāṭ*, ran up to the year 358/969.[39] Next is the *Ittiʿāẓ*, his history of the Fatimids, and finally his *al-Sulūk li-maʿrifat duwal al-mulūk*, for the Ayyubids and Mamluks. The pattern of these histories thus suggests that the Fatimids were not accorded as much special attention as might be supposed from the one work in isolation.[40]

What survives of the *Ittiʿāẓ* is, like the older version of the *Khiṭaṭ*, a *musawwada*, a first draft, although the only complete text of it is a copy of al-Maqrīzī's original and not the actual autograph. Apparently, the author would have added to it and filled in a number of blanks. Since there are only two manuscripts of it and the other is woefully incomplete, it seems that the work, in stark contrast to the *Khiṭaṭ*,[41] did not find much favour and was not read or consulted by many others. It must also be admitted that the modern edition, especially of volumes two and three, lacks a good deal.[42] An editor of the *Ittiʿāẓ*, and therefore anyone using it, must know of each and every parallel passage in al-Maqrīzī's other writings and it is the duty of that editor to either include them in the apparatus or cite them. For the *Khiṭaṭ*, which is uncontrollably immense and still lacks a perfect index, that task is regrettably formidable. The *Khiṭaṭ*, by its very nature, contains material tucked away in odd corners under headings and subtopics that are not obvious.

Nevertheless, it is essential to have control over both, even if neither presents a sound text. The *Ittiʿāẓ* is often critically important for the chronological context of a given report. Because al-Maqrīzī follows there a careful time line, he not infrequently puts the information from quotations of the older sources in the temporal order they should have had but which, in the topographical arrangement of the *Khiṭaṭ*, they lack. Conversely, in the *Ittiʿāẓ*, as also in the *Muqaffā*, the author rarely credits his sources. With both at hand, however, one complements the other; and where there are difficulties in reading the manuscript(s), they provide often valuable, even essential, checks on the wording of the text itself.[43]

Thus it is extremely useful to confront all instances of the material when al-Maqrīzī included more than one version somewhere in his writings. The chronological context of the *Ittiʿāẓ* naturally provides a check on the source citation of the *Khiṭaṭ*, but there are other benefits as well. And when the same material appears three times in three different works, the opportunities for cross-checking and expanded understanding become even more advantageous. No one work of al-Maqrīzī, even if edited properly, will or should suffice. At the moment, therefore, with both the *Ittiʿāẓ* and the *Khiṭaṭ* in serious textual disarray, this is all the more necessary. In addition, because the history of the Fatimids in Egypt depends so heavily on the contribution of later Ayyubid and Mamluk writers, al-Maqrīzī's unusual attention to them – and the sheer volume of his works in which they play a major role – make of him the pre-eminent source for it. All that he had to say, therefore, in whichever context – and in all of them together – must be carefully compared prior to a final judgement about almost any detail that he relates.

Given the basic fact that the history of the Fatimids depends heavily on the recovery of lost materials that, by purpose or chance, may have been collected and preserved in almost any of the works composed long after them, this limited review of the principal medieval sources does not exhaust by any means what likely exists. For example, as definitive as the various writings of al-Maqrīzī are in regard to the Fatimids, even later Egyptian historians who had access to the some of the same materials, such as al-Suyūṭī (d.911/1505) and Ibn Iyās (d.930/1505), may have, even so, occasionally recorded a detail or two that he missed. Likewise Ṭayyibī Ismaili scholars in the Yemen and later in India, other than Idrīs, certainly came upon and likely copied sources that are not as of now published and perhaps not even as yet recognised for their historical value. One more category is important: that comprises the many histories written outside the main sphere of Fatimid influence but which, as with those just mentioned, could well contain bits and pieces of vital information. One significant example is the great history by the Damascene al-Dhahabī (d.748/1348), the *Ta'rīkh al-Islām*, and the various abridgements of it.

8 *Literature and the Sciences*

The writings of poets, scholars and other practitioners of various literary arts constitute yet another category of historical material. The work of the historian is often counted as a part of it, but this kind of literature in general is not primarily and formally historical. Thus, except in special cases where the relevance of the information in it has a direct bearing on events, it tends to be ignored in the construction of narrative history. Generally speaking, poetry or philosophical doctrine or entertaining stories, or even the treatises of hard science, do not provide evidence for social, economic or political history. They do, however, offer crucial testimony about culture and about intellectual trends.

For the Fatimids, whose very claim to rule depended not merely on genealogy but on knowledge of ultimate (religious) truths, the latter, more ideological aspect of both public and private policy carries with it a special importance. Intellectual history is thus a subject particularly germane to the Fatimids. In respect to the propagation of religious ideology this point should be obvious. Because of the broad, almost universal, scholarly interest that lies behind Ismaili doctrine at large, they might have, as a part of their general intellectual attitude, been expected to encourage a true renaissance of learning within their domains. It is often said to have been the case. Whether or not the Fatimids actually encouraged or promoted the world of letters, either by direct patronage on the part of the imams themselves, or by another agent acting on behalf of the government, or even simply by providing an atmosphere conducive to it, requires, however, additional investigation. Ultimately, it is not immediately clear that, leaving aside the work of a few key members of the *daʿwa*, the Fatimid era was one of special intellectual brilliance. But this is in part an open question that needs to be revisited. As one example of the problem, certain evidence about the holdings of the caliph's royal libraries indicates an eclectic taste for learning that must have been behind the creation of these vast repertoires of culture. Nevertheless, of all their rich contents that which was actually produced under the Fatimids was likely quite limited.

In general the subject matter of this chapter is properly subsumed under the Arabic term *adab*, taken here in its broadest sense to include all the written arts and sciences, what is sometimes called *humanitas*, that is, all that makes humans cultivated and knowledgeable. The English word 'letters', again broadly construed, likewise fits. Although *adab* might comprise writings in many areas, under the Fatimids some flourished and others did not. But there certainly exist important examples of poetry and epistolary compositions, studies of grammar, music, medicine, astronomy and mathematics and optics, all in addition to the legal and doctrinal works of the *dāʿīs*. The writing of history also belongs in this category.

Fatimid Patronage of the Arts and Sciences

In part, the encouragement of the literary arts and letters depended then on the patronage of a powerful ruler or interested members of a wealthy elite. For the Fatimids there were notably moments when such conditions applied, the two most prominent cases being Ibn Killis as wazir and al-Ḥākim as imam, both of whom actively supported a whole body of scholars and writers. To a lesser extent the same is true of al-Muʿizz and al-Afḍal, to cite two more not quite so obvious examples, again one an imam and the other a wazir. But the question of patronage in the arts and sciences raises in this instance the problem of religious loyalty. As Ismaili imams, or as wazirs of an Ismaili Shiʿi government, could such patronage extend to non-Ismailis? What effect did religious policy have on the promotion of *adab* under the Fatimids? Surely at a minimum a considerable number of the scholars who might have sought support from the Fatimids had these caliphs been Sunni, for religious reasons did not. Also a good proportion, perhaps the major portion, of Fatimid resources in this area went to the *daʿwa* and to the promotion of its work. Still, one of the key institutions created by the state for the academic community was al-Ḥākim's Dār al-ʿIlm and it, when first established, was entirely non-sectarian. The imam gave employment in it to many scholars; those whose names are now known happen, in fact, to have all been Sunni.

Another question about patronage involves the purpose of the patron. The actions of any government in supporting the arts are obviously related to its interest in the product. The wazir al-Afḍal provided funds to create an astronomical observatory, the data from which could then carry his own name and thus add to his personal fame. Naming a work after its patron, who thereby earns part of the acclaim it generated, was then common. More straightforward motives involve a desire for favourable publicity. Such was often the case with poets whose laudatory proclamations of a ruler's glory or, conversely, of the vile and base nature of his opposition, were likewise standard. Such motives are quite noticeable, for example, in the poetry of the famous Andalusian, Ibn Hāniʾ, who became the court poet and eulogist of al-Muʿizz.

Poetry and the Poets

Poetry in fact serves well as a beginning point for this examination of the literary arts and sciences under the Fatimids.[1] And the case of Ibn Hāniʾ is an especially interesting place to start. Prior to Ibn Hāniʾ there were other poets at the Fatimid court who composed pieces of praise on important occasions. One example is instructive. Al-Fazārī was a minor poet from Qayrawān who dedicated a poem of celebration to al-Manṣūr for his victory over Abū Yazīd, but, as a Mālikī himself, this poet also wrote bitter and quite hostile verses against the Fatimids.[2] Ibn Hāniʾ by contrast was evidently ardently pro-Shiʿi, even prior to his close association with the court. His father Hāniʾ is thought to have been a Fatimid agent working in Spain. Still the poet himself appeared in the direct service of the Fatimids only after Jawhar's great campaign to subjugate the furthermost Maghrib. Ibn Hāniʾ then went to the court of the Hamdūnids in Masīla and from there was summoned to the capital al-Manṣūriyya by al-Muʿizz.[3] Thereafter, as the most widely recognised and acclaimed of the Fatimid poets, Ibn Hāniʾ wrote for al-Muʿizz verses of such extravagantly bold hyperbole, they earned both him and his patron fame accordingly. What these pieces said about the Fatimids and their aspirations served as a clear message that proved singularly effective precisely because they commanded the attention of an audience quite outside of the Ismaili community. But the poet himself was to die murdered en route to Egypt with al-Muʿizz in 362/973, and there are suspicions that the cause might have been a growing disenchantment with the imam. Unfortunately so little is actually known about Ibn Hāniʾ and his life, it is difficult to judge accurately about his supposed 'Ismaili' affiliation beyond the words in his poems and they may reflect only his desire to please his patron.

No such questions concern the next major Fatimid poet, Tamīm b. al-Muʿizz. As the reigning imam's eldest son, Tamīm was a prince of the royal family. He might have succeeded his father as imam, except for a clear indication fairly early that he would be passed over. The cause of his exclusion is not certain: one report suggests that he was involved in a plot set in motion by his cousins; another states that since it was known that he would not produce an heir, he could not become imam, whatever that may imply. Prior to his own death in Cairo in 375/985 during the reign of his brother al-ʿAzīz, Tamīm, however, flourished as a poet, leaving in the end a full *dīwān* of poems that were collected later and preserved among the Ṭayyibī Ismailis.[4]

From al-Musabbiḥī's history of Egypt, which originally included an annual accounting of the best poetry produced each year,[5] it is clear that any number of poets were active during the years he covered. However, the next major figures are the two Persian *dāʿīs*, Nāṣir-i Khusraw and al-Mu'ayyad fi'l-Dīn al-Shīrāzī, both of whom have already been mentioned for writings other than their poetry. It may be difficult to count Nāṣir as a Fatimid poet since he wrote in his native Persian and did so predominately, if not exclusively, well away from the areas of direct Fatimid control. Still, as remote as he was from Fatimid domains, he was acting on their behalf. His poetry, however, shows that allegiance less clearly than his doctrinal treatises. Perhaps for that very reason coupled with his special gift for poetry, his verse achieved an unusual renown, which ranks him among the greatest of the Persian poets.[6] Al-Mu'ayyad's poetry, which was composed in Arabic, did not fare as well in relation to the larger body of poetry in that language. However, for later Ismailis, who continued to use Arabic, the writings of al-Mu'ayyad – his poetry included – represented the high point of Fatimid letters. Among Ṭayyibī Ismailis the *dīwān* of al-Mu'ayyad holds a place comparable to that of Nāṣir for the Nizārīs.[7]

Following the four poets just mentioned, Fatimid poetry ceases to come from authors intrinsically linked to the Ismaili movement.[8] There was, however, no lack of poetry in the final century of the Fatimids, although, even when intended to serve a panegyric role in support of the imams, it was written in that period almost exclusively by non-Ismailis. Several of the more famous of these poets, such as 'Umāra al-Yamanī and Ibn al-Munqidh, were in fact Sunni by religious inclination. None the less 'Umāra composed odes in praise of his Fatimid patrons and finally died in a failed attempt to reinstate them. The case of Ibn al-Munqidh, by contrast, reveals little more than a limited connection between him and any of the Fatimids whom he served relatively briefly in comparison to the other patrons in his life. There is no reason to expect this temporary allegiance to show up in his poetry.

From the years of Badr al-Jamālī, the poet Ibn Abi'l-Shakhbā' (alternately al-Shakhnā', al-Shaḥnā' or al-Shajnā') was originally from Askalon but died (or was put to death) in Cairo in either 482/1089 or 486/1093. Ibn Khallikān provided an entry for him (under the name al-Mujīd al-Askalānī) and he notes that he was the author of quite famous epistles and poetry. Like many others he earned his living in the Fatimid chancery.[9]

One curious case demands special attention. That is Ṭalāʾiʿ b. Ruzzīk and his son Ruzzīk b. Ṭalāʾiʿ, most particularly the father who was not only an important poet himself but an avid patron of poets.[10] His retinue included ʿUmāra, who wrote several long *qaṣīdas* in praise of Ṭalāʾiʿ, and al-Qāḍī al-Jalīs (Ibn al-Ḥubāb), al-Muwaffaq b. al-Khallāl, Ibn Qādūs, al-Muhadhdhab b. al-Zubayr, al-Rashīd b. al-Zubayr, Ibn Nujayya, and others. Ibn Khallikān, who devoted a substantial entry to Ṭalāʾiʿ, noted that he had seen his *dīwān* in two volumes.[11] What makes him a curiosity is his attachment to Twelver Shiʿism – or more likely to Nuṣayrī Shiʿism. The latter sect claims the same twelve imams and thus might easily be confused with the Twelvers.[12]

Previous to the wazirate of Ṭalāʾiʿ but also like him a devoted fan of poets and poetry, al-Afḍal established his own reputation as a patron of the literati. At least ten poets whose names are known merited a place in his circle, some of them moderately famous in their time although little of their poetry survives. A key source for it and for information about al-Afḍal's patronage in this area is *al-Risāla al-miṣriyya* of Umayya b. Abi'l-Ṣalt who was himself one of the ten and thus knew the others well.[13] Naturally praise for the wazir was an important element in the work of these poets.[14]

One final poet from this period of Fatimid decline is Ibn Qalāqis (532/1137 - 567/1172), for whom in contrast to most of the others, a *dīwān* survives.[15] Although noted for his travels outside of Egypt – to the Yemen (in 565/1169 – 566/70) and to Sicily (in 564/1169) – and for verse in praise of various rulers elsewhere, his collected works include poems he wrote to extol important figures in his native land, among them the wazirs Ibn Maṣāl, Shāwar and his son, and al-Qāḍī al-Jalīs and al-Qāḍī al-Fāḍil.

Works of *adab*

The general field of *adab* even in the narrower sense of belles-lettres is represented by several examples each within a special genre. One is an odd item in Islamic literature since it comprises a book on the subject of monasteries. Al-ʿAzīz's personal librarian, Abu'l-Ḥasan ʿAlī al-Shābushtī, composed several books himself;

one is his *Kitāb al-Diyārāt* (Book of Monasteries) which survives and has been published.[16] Christian monasteries occupied a liminal space within the Islamic realm; they were places of escape and relative freedom from ordinary social conventions. Regardless of his connection to the Fatimid court or to Egypt, al-Shābushtī was interested in this subject as a literary matter. In this book he covered a large number of monasteries in Iraq, the Jazīra and Syria, but only a few in Egypt.[17] Also from the reign of al-ʿAzīz there is a work on falconry by the ruler's keeper of falcons; the author's name has been lost though not his treatise a *Kitāb al-Bayzara*.[18] Another important example and another field is represented by the famous *Mukhtār al-ḥikam wa-maḥāsin al-kalim* by al-Mubashshir b. Fātik. The author composed this collection of mainly Greek wisdom concerning ethics and moral behaviour in Egypt in 440/1048 during the reign of al-Mustanṣir about whom he also wrote a biography (now lost). Widely popular in the Muslim world, the *Mukhtar al-ḥikam* was the only work of this author to survive.[19]

In the area of manuals about epistolary arts and diplomatic, which was primarily the work of the chancery, there are two treatises from the Fatimid period. One is ʿAlī b. Khalaf's *Mawādd al-bayān* from the first half of the fifth/eleventh century and the other is Ibn al-Ṣayrafī's *Qānūn dīwān al-rasāʾil* from the first half of the next. Both were composed by heads of the chancery and both were major sources of material for the justly famous encyclopaedic multi-volume work on the same subject by al-Qalqashandī, his *Ṣubḥ al-aʿshā fī ṣināʿat al-inshāʾ*, completed in 814/1412,[20] which, as a result, constitutes in itself a great treasure-trove of Fatimid items in this genre.[21]

So many of those like the two just mentioned who wrote works of *adab* of one kind or another also spent most of their careers in the Fatimid chancery. One more is Abū Saʿīd Muḥammad al-ʿAmīdī (d.433/1042) who was a supervisor (*mutawallī*) in the *dīwān al-inshāʾ* (chancery) and later in 432/1040 appointed its head. A number of his writings survive but perhaps the best known is a curious work on the plagiarisms by the great poet al-Mutanabbī (*al-Ibāna ʿan sariqāt al-Mutanabbī*).[22]

The most important grammarian from the Fatimid period was Ibn Bābashādh. Like others he was an employee of the chancery until he withdrew from public life and thereafter spent most of his time atop the minaret of the mosque of ʿAmr in Fusṭāṭ from which he fell and died in 469/1077. Two of his grammatical studies survive, one a commentary on the *Jumal* of al-Zajjājī[23] and the other a better known *Muqaddima* to the subject of grammar.[24]

Music

There were two treatises on music. An earlier one was composed about 427/1036 by a certain Abu'l-Ḥusayn Muḥammad Ibn al-Ṭaḥḥān, who was a practising court musician in the reign of the caliph al-Ẓāhir and was himself from a family of musicians. At some point after al-Ẓāhir's death, he wrote *Ḥāwī al-funūn wa salwat al-maḥzūn* (Compendium of the Arts to Comfort Sad Hearts),[25] a work that combines both music theory and practice in contrast to the more famous, but purely theoretical treatments of the subject by, for example, al-Fārābī. Much later, in the period between 489/1096 and 506/1113, Ibn Abi'l-Ṣalt, whose poetry was already noted, composed a work on musical theory, perhaps as one part of a larger encyclopaedia of the sciences. Although the Arabic of it is now lost, a Hebrew translation at least of portions survives. Based on the evidence of this translation, the debt of Ibn Abi'l-Ṣalt to al-Fārābī in this area is clear.[26]

Medicine

From the beginning medicine and medical science were vitally important to the Fatimids and a long list of prominent physicians who served the caliphs and their court could be drawn up without much difficulty. Ibn al-Haytham's memoirs of his first encounters with the brothers Abū ʿAbdallāh and Abu'l-ʿAbbās indicate a special role for the physician Ziyād b. Khalfūn, who accompanied the army when it travelled west to rescue the imam from Sijilmāsa. Presumably Ziyād continued to serve as the chief court physician until his death in 308/920. But he, like many others, did not compose works on medicine itself, at least none that survive. By contrast early in North Africa the Jewish philosopher and physician Isaac Israeli, who was himself attached at some point to the imam's court, wrote, in addition to a number of interesting philosophical treatises, several works on medicine: books on fevers, urine, nutrition and others (many translated later into Latin).[27] The latter earned him a high reputation in this field.[28] The limited biographical data about Israeli, however, claims that he lived to be over a hundred and spent only the later portion of his life in the Maghrib. His writings may have come from the earlier years when he was not in the service of the Fatimids. Hence they may or may not be regarded as a product of their patronage.

Better examples might include the medical writings of Ibn Riḍwān (d.460/1067), who was appointed chief of Egyptian physicians by al-Mustanṣir. In addition to his well known pamphlets against Ibn Buṭlān and his *On the Prevention of Bodily Ills in Egypt*, there is his as yet unpublished *Kitāb al-Nāfiʿ*, plus a list of nearly one hundred works credited him by later authorities, most of which are now lost.[29] His *Prevention of Bodily Ills in Egypt* was an answer to a work by the North African Ibn al-Jazzār (d.369/979), who was another earlier Fatimid-era medical author of considerable importance. He had been a student of Israeli. In fact, along with numerous treatises on medical subjects, this Ibn al-Jazzār, as noted before, wrote a history of the Fatimid dynasty which is, however, now lost.[30]

The Sciences

In the pure sciences of mathematics and astronomy, the Fatimids happened to employ two of the most outstanding figures in all of the medieval period: ʿAlī b. ʿAbd al-Raḥmān b. Yūnus (d.399/1009) and Abū ʿAlī al-Ḥasan Ibn al-Haytham (d.430/1039). Both of them came to Cairo in the time of al-Ḥākim, quite likely in his service. Ibn Yūnus called his extremely important astronomical work the *Zīj al-ḥākimī al-kabīr* in honour of this patronage. A major portion of it survives.[31] Ibn al-Haytham was a highly regarded mathematician and physicist, who is often said to have been the best physicist in the Islamic world in that era. That he came to Egypt under al-Ḥākim and remained (or came back again) under his successors, suggests that the Fatimids, at least at that time, tried actively to foster the sciences.[32] Unfortunately, the towering achievements of these two scholars have no parallels either before or after their period. A later attempt by the wazirs al-Afḍal and al-Ma'mūn to construct an astronomical observatory and to patronise such scholarship – as described in a contemporary report called *The Making of the Observatory* (no longer extant but copied extensively by al-Maqrīzī) – appears lame by comparison.[33]

Politics

One category of letters not mentioned as yet is well represented by the *Sirāj al-mulūk* (The Lamp of Kings),[34] a work on politics and good government by the Spanish Mālikī Abū Bakr Muḥammad al-Ṭurtūshī, also known as Ibn Abī Randaqa. Having come to Egypt and settled permanently in Alexandria, the author completed it in Fusṭāṭ in 516/1122 and dedicated it to his patron the Fatimid wazir al-Ma'mūn; it is thus in that sense Fatimid. Al-Ṭurtūshī was, however, a Sunni, and like the important contemporary hadith specialist, Abū Ṭāhir Aḥmad al-Iṣfahānī al-Silafī, he belonged to a growing circle of scholars and teachers in Alexandria who, as Sunnis, did not subscribe to the Ismaili Shiʿism of the caliphs in Cairo. Nevertheless, they seemed to have flourished. The few Sunni wazirs under the Fatimids even endowed *madrasas* for them. Although al-Ṭurtūshī died as early as 520/1126,[35] al-Silafī (d.576/1180) witnessed the advent of the Ayyubids under Ṣalāḥ al-Dīn, who was Shāfiʿī like himself and who eventually imposed that *madhhab* everywhere he could.[36]

The Literature of the *daʿwa*

With the exception of the poetry of al-Mu'ayyad and Nāṣir, possibly that of Ibn Hāni' and Tamīm, most of the foregoing examples of Fatimid letters, even those directly under the patronage of the caliphs, had little connection to the Ismaili movement as such. Meanwhile, the *daʿwa* continued its own programme, both within the domain of the state and outside. Composing various kinds of written works was quite obviously an essential aspect of it. But, of the considerable number of books and treatises authored by the *dāʿīs* during the Fatimid period, many of which have been recovered fairly recently from modern Ṭayyibī collections in India, some have greater claim to represent the Fatimids than others. For yet others, particularly in regard to works written outside the areas of Fatimid control, evidence of Fatimid sponsorship and the imam's authority over the product, is uncertain. That problem, however, is not at issue in many other cases where the imam's influence is more or less clear. By and large, the literature of the *daʿwa*, which all served in one way or another to promote Ismaili Shiʿism at large, must nevertheless, be approached with caution in regard to the Fatimid regime and its policies.

An instructive example of how this literature was created and later used comes from the early writings of various *dāʿīs* in the East where the direct control of the Fatimid caliph was initially not generally acknowledged. That trend applies to the interval from the moment of al-Mahdī's announcement of his intention to claim publicly the imamate and establish the state until well into the reign of al-Muʿizz and even beyond. The dissident wing of the *daʿwa*, generally subsumed under the term Qarmatian, refused to admit to al-Mahdī's position. None the less, members of that faction composed important works of doctrine and thought, among them some of considerable influence for subsequent writers. The best known of these are the *Maḥṣūl* of Muḥammad al-Nasafī, who was martyred in an anti-Ismaili pogrom at Naysābūr in 332/943, and the writings of Abū Ḥātim al-Rāzī (d.322), especially his *Kitāb al-Zīna, Kitāb al-Iṣlāḥ* and *Aʿlām al-nubuwwa.* The *Maḥṣūl* is unfortunately no longer extant but the three books of al-Rāzī survive at least in major part.[37] Even so their connection to the Fatimids is suspect because of the Qarmatian leaning of their authors. Like other works with a similar pedigree, the *Maḥṣūl* was quite possibly later purposely disregarded by Fatimid authorities. Others, however, as was the case with the works of al-Rāzī, were subsequently incorporated in the literature of the Fatimid *daʿwa*, often apparently in an edited form that made them more acceptable in terms of doctrine and attitude toward the imamate.

Available evidence strongly suggests that the Imam al-Mahdī in particular made no effort to accommodate the dissidents and that only with al-Muʿizz and his policy of broader tolerance was the eastern Qarmatian wing brought back into the fold in this manner. Still not all the Ismaili writers of that period were supporters of the Fatimids even after al-Muʿizz's attempted reformation. One notable success was the Iranian Abū Yaʿqūb al-Sijistānī, who responded positively. All, or nearly all, of his works, at least in their extant form, bear testimony to his having recognised the Fatimid caliphs. At the same time they also suggest in subtle ways that he formerly had not. None the less, despite al-Sijistānī's later clear expression of loyalty to the Fatimids, what he wrote even after his acceptance of them was likely not influenced by them directly.[38] Thus his works are less Fatimid in that sense than Ismaili and Shiʿi in the broadest understanding of these terms.

There are several additional writers in this category, among them the largely unknown – except from a work of his called the *Kitāb al-Shajara* – eastern *dāʿī*, Abū Tammām, an important disciple of al-Nasafī. Given that another book by the same author was strongly criticised by al-Muʿizz, Abū Tammām's position is at best uncertain. He was most likely also one of the dissidents.[39]

In this early period with the situation so unclear in many cases, only those that involve writers who actually lived and worked in the Maghrib directly under the imams are safely known. Chief among these are the many compositions of Qāḍī al-Nuʿmān and Jaʿfar b. Manṣūr al-Yaman, both of whom attended the imam in person and thus could be expected to have responded directly to his wishes. Jaʿfar was the son of the famous Yemeni *dāʿī* Ibn Hawshab. Following his father's death, his own brother defected during the reign of al-Mahdī putting Jaʿfar in peril from which he escaped by leaving Yemen for North Africa. There he served al-Qāʾim, al-Manṣūr and al-Muʿizz by writing a number of treatises on the art of esoteric interpretation, an issue of some secrecy among Ismailis. Accordingly, the works of Jaʿfar never became public and even now have largely remained unpublished and unstudied.

By contrast, and perhaps intentionally, those that Qāḍī al-Nuʿmān was asked to write in the field of both law and in history were always considered at least semi-public. Neither subject involved esoteric doctrines in any case. In law, for example, al-Nuʿmān first assembled a massive corpus of Shiʿi hadith material from the Shiʿi imams up to and including Jaʿfar al-Ṣādiq but none from a later period. That compilation, his *Īḍāḥ*, drew on common Shiʿi sources among which were many of Zaydī provenance. Accordingly, the law that al-Nuʿmān sought to anchor in this material, rather than having a specifically Ismaili colouring, was generically Shiʿi and thus hardly offensive to the Shiʿa at large or completely unfamiliar to legal scholars in general.[40] Out of the *Īḍāḥ* al-Nuʿmān created a series of handbooks and summaries, the most famous of which is his *Daʿāʾim al-Islām* (The Pillars of Islam), which later became the standard textbook of Fatimid law. Al-Nuʿmān's historical writings similarly were for public consumption in part. They show the imams and the movement supporting them in an exemplary fashion.

In the era of al-ʿAzīz, the wazir Yaʿqūb b. Killis attempted to play a corresponding role by encouraging the work of the many scholars he hired or added to his personal retinue and those he employed at the legal college he set up at al-Azhar. One treatise on law that came from this effort was called after him the 'Wazir's Epistle' (*al-Risāla al-wazīriyya*) but several others were on medicine, on law, religion, Qurʾanic readings and other topics.[41] Also from about the same time there are a few minor treatises by members of the *daʿwa*, such as the *Ithbāt al-imāma* and *Istitār al-imām* both by al-Naysābūrī,[42] and the more important *sīra*s of both Jaʿfar al-Ḥājib and Ustādh Jawdhar.

From the years of al-Ḥākim comes yet another small epistle on the imamate[43] by Abu'l-Fawāris (d.413/1022) and the many major and minor works of al-Kirmānī. Although al-Kirmānī was active for the most part in Iraq and the east, his loyalty to al-Ḥākim was never in doubt; this imam was cited by him in virtually every treatise he composed. His output was, moreover, considerable. In addition, in contrast to his predecessors such as al-Sijistānī, he came to Cairo to teach there under the chief *dāʿī* Khatkīn al-Ḍayf from about 406/1015 to 410/1019 (the latter date is uncertain). As with the writings of al-Sijistānī before him and al-Muʾayyad later, the work of al-Kirmānī was so important that it defines a crucial stage in the evolution of Ismaili thought. In philosophy, unlike al-Sijistānī who was heavily influenced by Neoplatonism, al-Kirmānī favoured an Aristotelianism much like that of his even more famous contemporary Ibn Sīna (Avicenna). Many doctrines of al-Kirmānī therefore were at odds with his own Ismaili predecessors and in his writings he attempted to correct them, almost always, however, with due respect and appreciation for what they had achieved. Nevertheless, although the later Ṭayyibī *daʿwa* regarded him highly, al-Kirmānī's interpretations of Ismaili teachings were not accepted by the next generation which preferred those of al-Sijistānī instead. Still al-Kirmānī is now represented by an unusually complete corpus of surviving works, among them his *Kitāb al-Riyāḍ*, on a dispute within the *daʿwa*, his *al-Aqwāl al-dhahabiyya,* written in refutation of Abū Bakr al-Rāzī, *Maʿāṣim al-hudā*, on the virtues of ʿAlī over against those of Abū Bakr, his *Tanbīh al-hādī, al-Waḍīʾa fī maʿālim al-dīn,* several smaller treatises and finally his magnum opus, the *Rāḥat al-ʿaql.*[44]

The next period of great literary activity comes a full generation later with the careers of al-Muʾayyad and Nāṣir, both of whom have already been cited as eyewitnesses for their autobiographical accounts and as poets. Each one also wrote a number of doctrinal works. Those of al-Muʾayyad, particularly his massive collection of 800 homilies and sermons from the *majālis al-ḥikma* that he had taught personally during his years in Egypt from 450/1058 until his death in 470/1078, provide essential evidence of Ismaili doctrine and thought, as expressed at the capital itself, in the era of al-Mustanṣir. The doctrinal writings of Nāṣir-i Khusraw, by contrast, although certainly valid indications of Ismaili teachings, were composed away from the direct influence of the court since he spent the greater part of his career as a *dāʿī* in Central Asia.

The *majālis* of al-Muʾayyad also contain the textual evidence of his disputes and correspondence with others of his time, most notably with the great blind poet Abu'l-ʿAlāʾ al-Maʿarrī. This one exchange became well known long before any section of the whole collection became available in general scholarship because it had appeared also in Yāqūt's biography of al-Maʿarrī in the *Muʿjam al-udabāʾ* and from there was picked up by Margoliouth and published as early as 1902.[45]

Also from this period a small epistle by another *dāʿī* Shahriyār b. al-Ḥasan survives as one item in a collection of thirteen treatises, most of the rest by al-Kirmānī.[46] From an even later period as yet only names of writers and a few titles of their works exist, including examples that appear to have constituted lectures in the *majlis al-ḥikma* – given, for example, by Abu'l-Barakāt, the leading *dāʿī* under al-Āmir and a certain Mufliḥ b. ʿAbdallāh, a *dāʿī* in Damietta about 508/1114.[47]

From here on, partly as a consequence of the schisms first of the Nizārīs and second of the Ṭayyibīs, the literature of the Ismailis in Egypt, who had no successors, disappears from view. The Nizārīs, of course, continued and they subsequently produced their own literature, although almost entirely outside of Fatimid territory. The Ṭayyibīs in the Yemen also commenced their own *daʿwa* with a literature of its own. Unlike that of the Nizārīs of Iran and India, however, it largely continued the traditions, including most significantly the Arabic language, of its predecessor. The Ṭayyibīs, moreover, soon after their break with Cairo and the Ḥāfiẓīs, began a sustained attempt to recover all the writings of the Ismailis before them. The main records of the Ismaili *daʿwa*, meanwhile, and thus copies of what existed in its headquarters remained presumably in the hands of the last Fatimids in Cairo. Those records were eventually destroyed *in toto* along with the Fatimids upon the advent of the Ayyubids, who had neither interest in nor use for such literature.

This brief review of literature and the sciences under the Fatimids indicates most of what survives and some of what likely existed formerly. With some notable exceptions – the scientific work of Ibn Yūnus and Ibn al-Haytham, the poetry of Ibn Hāniʾ (and perhaps Nāṣir-i Khusraw and al-Muʾayyad), plus the doctrinal writings of several members of the *daʿwa* (including both Nāṣir and al-Muʾayyad) – the evidence does not allow for a conclusive or unambiguous judgement about the role of letters and the literati in the period as a whole, especially not in comparison with a number of other Muslim states and dynasties. The brilliance of Fatimid rule in terms solely of its sponsorship of arts and letters is thus not as clear as often claimed. But possibly additional research and study will put the matter in a different light.

9 *Modern Studies*

The modern historiography of the Fatimids has benefited from steady progress in the recovery of sources of all kinds and in the improvement of their accessibility. But the most dramatic advances have often depended on texts and the information in them found in the libraries of the Ṭayyibī Ismailis, mainly now located in India. Discovery of such materials, which were by and large unavailable prior to the middle of the twentieth century, has changed the perspective from which Fatimid history can be written. Previously, in many ways, all questions involving religion and religious policy – a subject of particular importance in dealing with the Fatimids – were answerable solely on the basis of non-Ismaili Sunni accounts that were quite hostile and biased against the Shiʿa. Recovery of substantial numbers of authentic Ismaili works from the Fatimid era has, therefore, changed the whole character and approach of the contemporary historian.

It has also complicated matters in special ways. Formerly the history of the Fatimids was more accessible to investigation than the Ismaili movement behind the same caliphate. With the opening of the Ṭayyibī libraries and the publication of their contents however, it is currently becoming relatively easy to study the Ismailis, their spread and the development of their doctrines. To an extent such progress helps explain the Fatimids, who certainly formed one aspect of the larger Ismaili picture and, insofar as the caliphs were also the imams in charge of the Ismaili community wherever it might exist, Fatimid history and Ismailism were and are inextricably intertwined. But as rulers of territories in which there existed considerable populations of non-Ismailis, the Fatimid caliphs were not only Ismaili imams. Much of Fatimid history had little to do directly with Ismailism. Moreover, the exact relationship of religion and public policy within the empire is as yet in need of its own careful investigation. Knowing the history of Ismaili thought and its various manifestations in different regions and in varying circumstances does not always aid in explaining how the Fatimid caliph dealt with, for example, his subjects, his army, his bureaucracy, or his foreign adversaries and allies.

A good example of a religious issue that confounds Fatimid historiography is the question of the dynastic origin of the Ismaili imams themselves. This is an area where the recovery of genuine Ismaili material has also proven to be of little help, and has possibly even added to the confusion that already existed. Traditionally no one took up the subject of the Fatimids without a lengthy examination of the question of whether or not the caliphs were, in fact, actually descended from ʿAlī and Fāṭima as they claimed. Because this matter ultimately goes back to the various polemical positions of the rivals for the caliphate and for religious superiority at the very time these claims first surfaced publicly centuries ago, medieval literature on the subject is full of rhetoric for and against the Fatimids. Medieval polemics were followed successively by others and ultimately they appear once again in modern historiography. Accordingly, all the reasons given for or against a false or spurious genealogy, even in blatantly biased sources, come up once more. Unfortunately, Ismaili sources contain an equally perplexing array of opinion and surmise, some instances of which ostensibly derive from the very pronouncements attributed to the imams themselves. But it has become far too easy to dwell on this matter as the possible interpretations of what might have been the case have multiplied, many with fairly solid evidence behind them. One document even purports, for example, to be a letter from al-Mahdī to his followers in the Yemen in which he seems to indicate that he thought himself descended from ʿAbdallāh, the oldest son of the Imam Jaʿfar al-Ṣādiq (rather than his second son

Ismāʿīl).[1] Certainly, if this information represents an accurate reflection of the true facts, it does not accord well with the more common Ismaili understanding of this matter. There are, as well, other troubling pieces of evidence, each supporting it seems a different conclusion. As a result it is simply impossible to sort out this problem to everyone's satisfaction; and with each new bit of information the issue becomes more and more intractable.[2]

But is it really necessary to confront the issue at all beyond simply noting that it exists? To the extent that uncertainty about their genealogy may have compromised the Fatimids and made their rule more difficult, it must, of course, be taken into account. However, that conclusion should be established first. A considerable amount of evidence that the Fatimids were treated by their subjects as caliphs and imams with a reasonable genealogical claim to be descendants of the Prophet argues against it. The caliphs, moreover, evidently preferred not to provoke such controversies. Thus, in regard to the religious issue as such, rather than attempting to find one solution amid a bewildering array of conflicting assertions of fact, a far more useful approach is that of Madelung in his masterful study 'Das Imamat in der frühen ismailitischen Lehre' published in *Der Islam* in 1961. Madelung simply provided a complete survey of all of the varying claims and pronouncements given in one place or another, one situation or another, one text or another, and he showed in the process how the public and private teaching about the nature of the imamate changed over time. For a problem that has no final solution, this is the only fruitful approach and it has the added benefit of clarifying as much as possible a critically important – perhaps the central core – doctrine of Ismailism in the process. This is not to denigrate the important studies of the genealogical problem by B. Lewis, W. Ivanow, H. Hamdani, A. Hamdani and de Blois and others but to suggest that a definitive answer is not essential to the further progress of Fatimid history.

None the less, parallel to this kind of investigation, there is a topic where Ismaili sources have proven to be of immense value. That is the pre-history of the movement and its leaders. Attempts by the scholars who have examined the genealogical problem often commence, perhaps out of necessity, with the era of Jaʿfar al-Ṣādiq and then trace the imamate, or claims to it, from this imam to al-Mahdī – a time span of almost a hundred and fifty years. Ismaili accounts, however, provide little dependable information on the earliest portion of this process; non-Ismaili sources similarly have not much to say that is helpful in this regard. But, among the records and accounts preserved by the Fatimids, there is a surprising abundance of material about the Ismaili *daʿwa* in the period immediately preceding the caliphate. Non-Ismaili sources, principally those collected by Abbasid authorities in the east, also contain reliable information. Many of the accounts that stem from Fatimid sources were brought together by Ivanow in his *Ismaili Tradition Concerning the Rise of the Fatimids* (1942), including key portions of unpublished Arabic texts. More were to follow, among them the critically important work of Qāḍī al-Nuʿmān on the 'Commencement of the *Daʿwa* and the Establishment of the *Dawla*' (*Iftitāḥ al-daʿwa wa-ibtidāʾ al-dawla*) and now, much later, Ibn al-Haytham's *Kitāb al-Munāẓarāt.* With the information in many of these and other sources in hand, S. M. Stern, M. Canard and W. Madelung were at last able to begin to sort out with precision the sequence of events leading up to the victory of Abū ʿAbdallāh in the Maghrib. What they learned, especially Madelung, shows up clearly in the treatment of this period in F. Daftary's *The Ismāʿīlīs* and in H. Halm's *Empire of the Mahdi.* Both of these later scholars have added the results of their own investigations to this discussion as well.

Fatimid history could once be written without Ismaili sources, as was done by F. Wüstenfeld, the first European author to compose anything like a history of the dynasty. Wüstenfeld in his 1881 *Geschichte der Faṭimiden-Chalifen, nach arabischen Quellen* provided data excerpted from the works of ʿArīb, Ibn al-Athīr, Ibn ʿIdhārī, Ibn Khallikān, Ibn Khaldūn, the *Khiṭaṭ* of al-Maqrīzī, Ibn Taghrī Birdī, al-Suyūtī and some others; plus Silvestre de Sacy's *Exposé de la religion des Druzes* (1838), which had been a seminal study of monumental importance in stimulating Western interest in the Ismailis and the Fatimids. Along with the work of Wüstenfeld, C. H. Becker's *Beiträge zur Geschichte Ägyptens unter dem Islam* (1902),

Stanley Lane-Poole's *A History of Egypt in the Middle Ages* (1901; rev. ed. 1914), Gaston Wiet's volume of the *Précis de l'histoire de l'Égypte* (1932–35) on the medieval period and De Lacy O'Leary's *A Short History of the Fatimid Khalifate* (1923) once together constituted the standard bibliography on the Fatimids. All of them depended exclusively on non-Ismaili, mainly Sunni, sources.

Even so what was then available is reasonably impressive. In addition to the works used by Wüstenfeld, named above, O'Leary could consult Nāṣir-i Khusraw's *Safarnāma*, al-Nuwayrī, 'Usāma b. Munqidh and al-Qalqashandī. He also used Wüstenfeld, although apparently not Becker. Becker, however, had access to the first part of al-Maqrīzī's *Ittiʿāẓ*, some of the same author's *al-Muqaffā*, Ibn Saʿīd and most importantly the surviving portion of al-Musabbiḥī. The first volume of Becker's *Beiträge*, which is the one on the Fatimids, is, in fact, a detailed study of the reign of al-Ẓāhir in the year 415/1024 based on al-Musabbiḥī.

It should be noted, however, that none of the modern works just cited really serves as a complete history of the Fatimids. Becker did not attempt such a project, nor did Wüstenfeld. Wiet and Lane-Poole wrote histories of Egypt in the medieval period, not of the Fatimids *per se*. O'Leary himself admitted that his book was merely a 'brief outline' of its subject. But curiously, even with the virtual flood of Ismaili materials and substantially improved access to both them and the many other sources, a complete modern history of the Fatimids does not yet exist. The only candidate is Ḥasan Ibrāhīm Ḥasan's *Ta'rīkh al-dawla al-fāṭimiyya fi'l-Maghrib wa Miṣr wa Sūriya wa bilād al-ʿarab*, originally published in 1932, though revised later. By the time of his third edition in 1964, Ḥasan could cite an impressive array of Ismaili texts that cannot have been available to him when he first composed it. A more recent book by Ayman Fu'ād Sayyid on the Fatimids in Egypt, *al-Dawla al-fāṭimiyya fī Miṣr: tafsīr jadīd* (1992; rev. ed. 2000) is much better in terms of its scholarship, but does not aim to be nearly as comprehensive. Halm's *Empire of the Mahdi*, which is limited to the background of the caliphate and the North African period, set the right standard in its masterful integration of Ismaili and non-Ismaili sources, with full documentation and a fine narrative. It is evidently the first of additional volumes yet to come. If so, it will suffice nicely, although English readers must hope somehow that Halm's German will again find an English translator, as was the case, courtesy of Michael Bonner and Brill Publications, with the first volume.

Meanwhile, not only have Ismaili sources become available in bulk, but also the tools for access to them have seen dramatic improvement. The great pioneer of modern Ismaili studies, Wladimir Ivanow, long ago extracted from the Ṭayyibī collections he was able to examine their inventories of their own literature. Based largely on them, particularly the *Fihrist al-kutub wa'l-rasā'il* compiled by the twelfth/eighteenth century Ṭayyibī authority known as al-Majdūʿ,[3] plus information he obtained from helpful Ismaili scholars, he published first in 1933, *A Guide to Ismaili Literature*, and much later in 1963, *Ismaili Literature: A Bibliographical Survey* (a second amplified edition of the *Guide*). As useful as either was when it appeared, neither offered information about editions and manuscripts (of which not many were even available to the academic public when he first began). Finally, however, a noted Ismaili scholar, Ismail Poonawala, professor of Arabic at the University of California, Los Angeles, issued in 1977, his monumental catalogue, the *Biobibliography of Ismāʿīlī Literature*, a truly impressive survey of some 300 authors and their works from the earliest period prior to the Fatimids until modern times. Chapter one (pp.31–132) of that work covers the Pre-Fatimids and Fatimids, listing all titles either presently existing in Ismaili collections or cited in one place or another in this same literature. Poonawala's *Biobibliography* instantly became indispensable for the study of the Fatimids, as well as of the Ismailis at large. Unfortunately, it has also done its job only too well. Over the more than two decades since its appearance, there has been considerable progress in the recovery of this same material and in the discovery of new items or the clarification of the data about those previous known, making it now in many ways almost out-of-date.[4]

A good portion of the credit for the recent, quite striking advance in Ismaili studies and in particular the recovery of the older texts or copies of them is due to the establishment of The Institute of Ismaili Studies in London. The head of the Institute's academic and research programmes is Farhad Daftary, whose own massive history of the Ismailis has already become the standard reference on all phases of the subject (including what the author calls 'Fāṭimid Ismāʿīlism'). His *The Ismāʿīlīs: Their History and Doctrines* (1990), as well as his more recent *A Short History of the Ismailis* (1998), are invaluable. Would only that Fatimid history as such could have received the same meticulous and knowledgeable treatment and in such exemplary detail as exhibited in these two books, especially the first. Daftary is also the general editor of the Institute's Ismaili Heritage Series, and Ismaili Texts and Translations Series. But even prior to Daftary's joining the Ismaili Institute, his predecessors there had made the collecting of Ismaili manuscripts a priority. The Institute's librarian then, Adam Gacek, produced in 1984–85 a scholarly *Catalogue of Arabic Manuscripts in the Library of The Institute of Ismaili Studies*, volume one of which deals with the Ismaili works of importance in this regard. Quite recently (2000) Delia Cortese published an additional volume covering new acquisitions to this same collection. Also, while the Institute's holdings are quite significant and continue to grow, it has undertaken to acquire also photocopies of any and all of those known to exist elsewhere, including the important collection in Tübingen University and the Fyzee Collection in the Bombay University Library.

Even with full access to these collections of Ismaili sources, however, it is ultimately odd how limited this material is in terms of what it contributes to the ordinary history of the Fatimids. While at this point no study of the Fatimid period can do without it, certain subjects require it more obviously than others. Even in the investigation of Fatimid religious policy and the role of ideology in the state, an area where such materials ought to have the most to contribute, there are many gaps in the record available purely from Ismaili sources that must be filled with information in the non-Ismaili chronicles. An issue such as succession to the imamate whether in theory or in actual individual cases is hardly intelligible without consulting both. Moreover, as the following list indicates, for reasons unknown, the Ismaili *daʿwa* wrote and preserved few histories at all, as if the writing of history, except in the notable case of Qāḍī al-Nuʿmān, was of low priority. If the Ismaili works that are personal memoirs rather than histories as such are removed from the list, precious little remains.

Leaving aside those predominantly or exclusively devoted to doctrinal topics, here then are the principal Ismaili sources for Fatimid history:

Ibn al-Haytham's *Kitāb al-Munāẓarāt*
Qāḍī al-Nuʿmān's *Iftitāḥ al-daʿwa* and *Kitāb al-Majālis wa'l-musāyarāt*
Sīrat Jaʿfar al-Ḥājib
Sīrat Ustādh Jawdhar
al-Naysābūrī's *Istitār al-imām*
Nāṣir-i Khusraw's *Safarnāma*
Sīrat al-Mu'ayyad fi'l-Dīn al-Shīrāzī
al-Sijillāt al-mustanṣiriyya
al-Hidāya al-āmiriyya

This list in all likelihood does not exhaust either what is yet to be uncovered or all the bits and pieces of valuable historical information in other works. Several items that are cited by Idrīs in his *ʿUyūn al-akhbār*, for example, but which have not yet come to light may be presumed to exist even now. One example would be Ḥaydara b. Muḥammad Ibrāhīm's *al-Sīra al-kutāmiyya*, which has thus far not surfaced. It is equally possible that any one of several as yet unstudied treatises that appear now from their titles alone to contain only doctrinal material will ultimately prove to have significant historical value. The *Munāẓarāt* of Ibn al-Haytham was long ignored for this very reason. And yet it was all along a major historical source in its own right. The works of Jaʿfar b. Manṣūr al-Yaman, Qāḍī al-Nuʿmān's *Sharḥ al-akhbār*, certain of al-Kirmānī's treatises, particularly his *Mabāsim al-bishārāt*, written in answer to the preaching of the proto-Druze dissident al-Akhram, plus several epistles said to have been written by various of the imams themselves are examples of works that also have historical merit in part.

But given the list as it stands, it is remarkable first that it consists almost entirely of personal memoirs and not histories. Allowing some flexibility in the definition of memoir, moreover, it might comprise not only the *Munāẓarāt* of Ibn al-Haytham, the *Sīra*s of Jaʿfar, Jawdhar and al-Muʾayyad, but also al-Nuʿmān's *Majālis* and Nāṣir's *Safarnāma*, both of which reflect the first person viewpoint of the author. The *Sijillāt* of al-Mustanṣir and the *Hidāya* of al-Āmir are official documents issued by the imam and are thus also not histories. The sole history among this group is the *Iftitāḥ* of al-Nuʿmān.

Another striking fact is how many of them belong to the North African phase of the Fatimids even if, as is apparently the case with the *Sīra*s of Jaʿfar and Jawdhar and the *Istitār*, they were finally recorded during the reign of al-ʿAzīz. None, moreover, were composed prior to the reign of al-Manṣūr and nothing, save the *Hidāya*, after al-Mustanṣir.

A judgement of this kind does not take into account the writings of the later Ṭayyibī authorities, who, after the Ḥāfiẓī-Ṭayyibī schism, were not technically Fatimid in the strict sense.[5] Nevertheless, Ṭayyibī scholars were quite active both in collecting and preserving older material and in writing new works. Idrīs, the author of the essential history of the imams, the *ʿUyūn al-akhbār*, was the nineteenth *dāʿī muṭlaq* of the Ṭayyibīs and in many ways represents the culmination of the same Ṭayyibī tradition that favoured the writing of history and the collecting of the past.

While not a history, the *Daʿāʾim al-Islām* is a special case. As the standard textbook of Fatimid (and Ismaili) law, it is both a historical document and a work of legal doctrine. Accordingly, because its role is so central to the Fatimids, it serves many different functions for the historian.

Fortunately, at present all of the Ismaili works cited above have been published and the editions of them are reasonably sound – a condition not common in many of the editions of Ismaili doctrinal materials. The one exception is Idrīs's *ʿUyūn al-akhbār* where the older publications of various volumes by Mustafa Ghalib are generally unreliable and where the important volume seven, which covers the reign of al-Mustanṣir, has yet to appear. In 1985 the Tunisian scholar, Muḥammad al-Yaʿlāwī, issued a new, complete, and much improved edition of those portions of the *ʿUyūn* that deal with the Maghrib – that is, from the coming there of the

Ismaili mission, through the rise of the state up to and including the reign of al-Muʿizz. He gave it a separate title: *Taʾrīkh al-khulafāʾ al-Fāṭimiyyīn biʾl-Maghrib* but indicated its contents in its subtitle, *al-Qism al-khāṣṣ min Kitāb ʿUyūn al-akhbār.* This edition now supersedes all others. An edition of the seventh volume is at the moment in preparation by Ayman Fuʾād Sayyid, to be published with its English summary by The Institute of Ismaili Studies.

As for translations, there are English versions only for Ibn al-Haytham, the *Sīrat Jaʿfar,* the *Istitār* and the *Safarnāma.* Prior to his death Asaf Fyzee had begun to translate the *Daʿāʾim* into English, a worthy project later taken up by Ismail Poonawala, who has now completed the first of the two volumes. Given its importance it is strange that the *Iftitāḥ* has never been translated, not even into French, although there are French translations of the *Sīra*s of Jaʿfar and Jawdhar (both by M. Canard) and of the *Safarnāma.*

Still, despite these major advances in the recovery of Ismaili sources, it remains quite obvious that solely from them no history of the Fatimids is possible. Having the full text of the *ʿUyūn al-akhbār* will not change this fact; there are simply too many gaps and missing pieces and its purpose in any case was to construct an exemplary account of the imams and their respective eras, not to chronicle the Fatimid state. Therefore, the investigation of Fatimid history continues to depend on non-Ismaili sources many of which have their own problems of access, reliable editing and translation. Certainly not all of the known texts are published even now and thus there is much basic work to be done on these non-Ismaili sources as well.

One highly significant example may suffice in this instance to illustrate a persistent problem of this kind. Early in the twentieth century, al-Maqrīzī's history of the Fatimids, his *Ittiʿāẓ,* was known solely from a fragmentary manuscript. Following the discovery of the complete text, the Egyptian scholar Jamāl al-Dīn al-Shayyāl, who had already published an edition of the fragment, was then able to revise that portion and to complete volume one of the whole which he published in 1967. Several years later in 1973 another Egyptian, Muḥammad Ḥilmī Muḥammad Aḥmad, finally finished the rest of the task by issuing the remaining two volumes of it. At last the whole of al-Maqrīzī's invaluable history of the Fatimids was available for general use. Unfortunately, however, while the effort of these editors was laudable, their edition, which remains the only one to this day, suffers from many problems and badly needs to be corrected and redone. They had tried to determine a sound reading of the *Ittiʿāẓ* without also carefully consulting any and all parallel material in either the same author's *Khiṭaṭ* or his *al-Muqaffā* (where it overlaps). But it is true at the same time that the nineteenth-century Bulaq edition of the *Khiṭaṭ* is likewise full of defective readings and it, moreover, as yet, partly for the same reason, has defied proper indexing. Although highly desirable as a preliminary step, a critical edition of the *Khiṭaṭ*, moreover, is at the moment all but impossible due to the existence of 170 manuscripts, far too many for easy comparison and collation. And, beyond these works of al-Maqrīzī, there are a number of others that are relevant.

One scholar now active who seems to have control over all this material is Ayman Fuʾād Sayyid. He has to this point published editions or re-editions of all that remains of al-Musabbiḥī, Ibn al-Maʾmūn, Ibn Muyassar, Ibn al-Ṭuwayr, and al-Ṣayrafī's *Qānūn* and his *al-Ishāra ilā man nāla al-wizāra*, more recently an edition of Ibn ʿAbd al-Ẓāhir's *al-Rawḍa al-bahiyya al-zāhira fī khiṭaṭ al-muʿizziyya al-qāhira*, and finally a critical edition of al-Maqrīzī's own first draft (his *musawwada*) of this same *Khiṭaṭ*. All these bear directly on the Fatimids. Sayyid's contribution to Fatimid history is, therefore, already enormous. Would only that he continue his work and that he re-edit also the *Ittiʿāẓ*, as well possibly as Ibn Ḥajar's *Rafʿ al-iṣr* (now incomplete), perhaps also the Fatimid years for Ṣibt b. al-Jawzī and Ibn al-Furāt, to name two more on this wish-list.

With respect to modern studies of the Fatimids, aside from editions and translations, a meaningful way to assess the state of the field is to look at individual scholars of the last few generations who have devoted a significant portion of their work to the subject. Several of those who have been the most productive over the middle decades of the twentieth century are now deceased. For them some final assessment is possible. Moreover, in a half dozen cases the writings of some of these figures remain almost as valuable as when written. It is also useful to divide them by language, thus separating those who write in French, for example, from those using Arabic or English. The French speaking world has traditionally maintained a strong historical interest in the areas of France's colonies and protectorates, which once included the Maghrib (Tunisia, Algeria and Morocco) and Syria. Certain aspects of scholarship in Egypt likewise fell within the domain of the French, in part as a long-term consequence of the French scientific expedition that accompanied Napoleon's army.[6]

Whether that fact explains the career of either man, two of the most important scholars of the Fatimids were Marius Canard (1888–1982) and Claude Cahen (1909–1991), both within the French tradition. Canard, who was a professor in the Faculté des Lettres of Algiers, was an authority on the history of both the Maghrib and Syria, as well as on Byzantine-Fatimid relations in Sicily, Italy and across the Mediterranean. Several of his studies also dealt with the Fatimids in Egypt. Although most famous for his massive work on Sayf al-Dawla and the Ḥamdānids of northern Syria, he also wrote at least a dozen individual articles on Fatimid topics, many but not all of which were later collected in 1973 in two volumes of the Variorum reprint series (*Byzance et les musulmans du Proche Orient* and *Miscellanea Orientalia*).[7]

Like Canard, Cahen produced a book-length study on an aspect of northern Syria, his *La Syrie du nord à l'époque des croisades* (1940). In addition, he devoted a considerable amount of his fine scholarship to economic history, including most importantly Egypt at the end of the Fatimid period and the beginning of the Ayyubids, on the sources for which he was more knowledgeable than anyone else. One of his special interests was al-Makhzūmī, for example.[8]

Yet another scholar who belongs here is Hady Roger Idris who specialised in the Zīrid period. Besides a half dozen articles, he wrote a two-volume study of this North African dynasty, *La Berbérie orientale sous les Zirides, Xe-XIIe Siècles* (1962). Though both are still living one might include as well Farhat Dachraoui whose *Le Califat fatimide au Maghreb, 296–362/909–973: histoire, politique et institutions* (1981) was the first comprehensive study of the Fatimids in the Maghrib, and Mohamed Talbi for his meticulously detailed book on the Aghlabids, including most particularly his section on their decline and collapse under the pressure of Abū ʿAbdallāh's onslaught. That work, *L'Emirat aghlabide* (Paris, 1966), has much to say therefore about the rise of the Fatimids.

Of those who represent the English writers, S. M. Stern (1920–1969) is the most important purely in terms of his contributions to the study of the Fatimids. In contrast to either Canard or Cahen, moreover, Stern was an authority on the Ismaili movement quite outside of issues that pertained directly to the Fatimid state in North Africa or in Egypt. In all, he wrote a dozen articles about aspects of either subject and contributed an important book-length work, *Fāṭimid Decrees: Original Documents from the Fāṭimid Chancery* (1964).

S. D. Goitein (1900–1985) the greatest of all the scholars of the geniza deserves to be cited here as well. However, in part, because of the ambiguous nature of the relationship between the geniza materials and what they reveal about the Fatimids at large, which is as yet an open question, Goitein's role in the study of Fatimid history as such is not clear. Nevertheless, in respect to his own incredible achievements, among them his monumental multi-volume *A Mediterranean Society*, he was certainly a towering figure.

W. Ivanow (1886–1970) has already been mentioned in connection with his *Ismaili Tradition Concerning the Rise of the Fatimids* and his *Ismaili Literature*, both of considerable importance for Fatimid studies. Beyond those two works and a couple of articles, however, most of Ivanow's many contributions to scholarship came in areas of Ismailism that are not truly germane to the Fatimids as such.

Of those who have written in Arabic, most are Egyptian. But currently Ayman Fu'ād Sayyid so dominates Fatimid studies in Egypt, no other figure has attained prominence. However, one or two generations ago that was not the case. There were then at least four major scholars working on the Fatimids: Jamāl al-Dīn al-Shayyāl (1911–1967), Ḥasan Ibrāhīm Ḥasan (1892–1968), ʿAbd al-Munʿim Mājid (1920–1999), and Muḥammad Kāmil Ḥusayn (1901–1961). Ḥasan's history of the Fatimids was mentioned previously, as was al-Shayyāl's work on the first volume of al-Maqrīzī's *Ittiʿāẓ*. Ḥasan also wrote book-length biographies of al-Mahdī and al-Muʿizz (both with Ṭaha Aḥmad Sharaf).[9] Al-Shayyāl compiled an important collection of Fatimid documents culled from later sources, the *Majmūʿat al-wathāʾiq al-fāṭimiyya* (1958). Mājid was an authority on Fatimid ceremonies about which he wrote *Nuẓum al-Fāṭimiyyīn wa rusūmuhum fī Miṣr* (*Institutions et Cérémonial des Fatimides en Égypte*).[10] He also published *Ẓuhūr khilāfat al-Fāṭimiyyīn wa suqūṭuhā fī Miṣr: al-taʾrīkh al-siyāsī* (1968), *al-Imām al-Mustanṣir bi-Allāh al-fāṭimī* (1961), and *al-Ḥākim bi Amr Allāh al-khalīfa al-muftarā ʿalayh* (1959), as well as an edition of the *Sijillāt al-mustanṣiriyya.* But perhaps the most important figure in this group was Ḥusayn. His *Fī adab Miṣr al-fāṭimiyya* (Cairo, 1963) remains the only work of its kind. He also produced editions of both al-Muʾayyad's *Dīwān* and his *Sīra*, as well as al-Kirmānī's *Rāḥat al-ʿaql* (the latter with Muḥammad Muṣṭafā Ḥilmī), *al-Majālis al-mustanṣiriyya, Sīrat Ustādh Jawdhar,* al-Nuʿmān's *Kitāb al-Himma* and others.

Beyond the four just mentioned several other Egyptian scholars have worked on the Fatimids, among them Rāshid al-Barrāwī and Muḥammad Jamāl al-Dīn Surūr; more are cited in the Bibliography of Modern Studies below.[11]

Two scholars from the Indian subcontinent, Husayn Hamdani and A. A. A. Fyzee, wrote both in English and Arabic and might have been considered in those categories above. They were also members of the extremely important modern Ṭayyibī Bohra communities, as are Abbas Hamdani and Ismail Poonawala, still to be discussed. One more is Zāhid ʿAlī, a scholar who wrote mainly in Urdu.[12] For all of them knowledge of and access to the sources preserved by these groups over the long interval between the collapse of the Fatimids and now has been, in a sense, continuous. For them, in that they are at the present end of a long line of scholarship within the same tradition, there has been no 'recovery' or 'discovery' of such materials. They deserve therefore to be regarded separately for this reason. Fyzee (1899–1981) specialised in law in accord with his own training and it was thus fitting that he produced an edition of the *Daʿāʾim al-Islām.* Husayn

Hamdani (1901–1962) contributed a number of important papers, but is perhaps best known for his *al-Ṣulayḥiyyūn wa'l-ḥaraka al-fāṭimiyya fi'l-Yaman* (1955).

Of those scholars who are still active at present, several have made important contributions to Fatimid studies but have not necessarily continued those efforts. Bernard Lewis is a good example here. Lewis properly deserves credit for his work on the Nizārī Ismailis of the Alamūt period, *The Assassins: A Radical Sect in Islam* (1967), for example, which will last better than his much earlier *The Origins of Ismā'īlism* (1940), which is now largely out of date. More recent examples include Thierry Bianquis and Paula Sanders. Bianquis has already published at least ten major papers plus his valuable two-volume study of *Damas et la Syrie sous la domination fatimide (359–468/969–1076)* (1986 and 1989). Sanders, who has a particular interest in court ceremonial, as witnessed in her book *Ritual, Politics and the City in Fatimid Cairo* (1994), has written less thus far. Two more in this category are Ismail Poonawala and Abbas Hamdani both of whom continue to work on Ismaili topics which is the area of their interest and speciality. To an extent such investigations overlap with Fatimid studies, but not always.

Wilferd Madelung occupies a special class by himself. His interests range so widely over almost the entirety of Islamic studies, the Fatimids are practically incidental to the many other areas that may from time to time attract his attention. However, no living scholar knows as much as he does, nor has his ability to extract information from the sources available. In part because Madelung began early in his career to investigate Ismaili doctrines and the relationship of the Fatimids to the Qarmatians, these topics remain areas he returns to frequently. One example of his recent contribution to Fatimid studies is the edition and translation of Ibn al-Haytham's memoir. Madelung currently serves as Senior Research Fellow at The Institute of Ismaili Studies as well as consulting editor for its Ismaili Texts and Translations Series.

With respect to the major players in Fatimid studies at the present time – those who have already published on more than one topic and in several areas either in time or geography, and who therefore may properly be regarded as Fatimid specialists, Heinz Halm and Ayman Fu'ād Sayyid have contributed by far the most. Four others, Michael Brett, Daniel De Smet, Muhammad al-Yaʿlāwī and Yaacov Lev, come next.[13] Halm has published at least fifteen papers and several books. His *Das Reich des Mahdi: Der Aufstieg der Fatimiden* (1991), translated into English as *The Empire of the Mahdi: The Rise of the Fatimids* (1996) set the standard for the writing of Fatimid history. In contrast to several in this group of historians, moreover, Halm has a solid background in early Shiʿism, supported by extensive experience with Shiʿi and Ismaili sources – a subject on which he has also published extensively. Sayyid does not work on the Ismailis as such but on Egypt (and to a lesser extend the Yemen). Nevertheless, on Egypt in the Fatimid period he has a commanding knowledge of the sources, for many of which, as noted earlier, he has produced new editions. He has also published two important books: *al-Dawla al-Fāṭimiyya fī Miṣr: tafsīr jadīd* (1992; second revised ed. 2000) and *Le Capitale de l'Égypte jusqu'à l'époque Fatimide* (1998).

Brett's publications on the Fatimids include at least eleven articles and a major book, *The Rise of the Fatimids: The World of the Mediterranean and the Middle East in the Fourth Century of the Hijra, Tenth Century CE* (2001). Lev has twelve articles and two books: *State and Society in Fatimid Egypt* (1991) and *Saladin in Egypt* (1999). De Smet published a fine book on the great *dāʿī* al-Kirmānī from the era of al-Ḥākim, which is, however, less of a contribution to Fatimid history, than a number of his many articles. Al-Yaʿlāwī's name has already been mentioned as the editor of the North African portion of Idrīs's *ʿUyūn al-akhbār*. He also edited and published al-Maqrīzī's *al-Muqaffā* (in eight volumes) and served as one of the editors of Qāḍī al-Nuʿmān's *Kitāb Majālis wa'l-musāyarāt*. Ibn Hāni' has also been the subject of his scholarly work, about whom he published a book-length study: *Un Poète chiite d'occident au IV/Xè siècle: Ibn Hani' al-Andalousi* (1976), Arabic translation, *Ibn Hāni' al-Maghribī al-Andalusī shāʿir al-dawla al-fāṭimiyya* (1985). Another relevant book from the same author is his *al-Adab bi-Ifrīqiya fi'l-ʿahd al-Fāṭimī* (1986).

The preceding account of modern Fatimid studies does not acknowledge by name literally dozens and dozens of quite valuable articles and some books on single topics, nor did it take notice of the work of many scholars just now entering this field. To do so would involve, in part, a comprehensive accounting of studies recently completed or in progress. A brief review of the field cannot accomplish that, most especially if it tries to cover successfully many areas that are connected with, but often peripheral to, the core themes of Fatimid history. One example of the latter kind is the Crusades. Another is art and archaeology. Instead, in keeping with the purpose of this book, which seeks to encourage further inquiry and exploration, the bibliography at the end lists an array of modern studies that serve as a guide to what has been achieved and what remains undone. Contributions of many scholars not previously named appear in that bibliography, including among them many authors of doctoral dissertations. Therefore, for additional reading and information on almost any facet of this field, readers should turn to the Bibliography of Modern Studies.

Notes

Chapter 1: The Maghrib

1. The dates that follow normally express both the Muslim *hijrī* era first, as is nearly always the case with the historical sources, and the Christian or Common Era equivalent second (unless the context is otherwise clear).

2. On the advent of Fatimid rule in the Maghrib and its background there, see M. Talbi, *L'Emirat aghlabide* (Paris, 1966); Heinz Halm, *Das Reich des Mahdi: Der Aufstieg der Fatimiden* (Munich, 1991), English tr. M. Bonner, *The Empire of the Mahdi: The Rise of the Fatimids* (Leiden, 1996); Ibn al-Haytham, *Kitāb al-Munāẓarāt,* ed. and tr. W. Madelung and Paul E. Walker in *The Advent of the Fatimids* (London, 2000).

3. The greatest advance in the understanding of this background came with the work of W. Madelung, particularly his articles 'Das Imamat in der frühen ismailitischen Lehre', *Der Islam,* 37 (1961), pp.43–135; 'Fatimiden und Baḥrainqarmaṭen', *Der Islam,* 34 (1959) pp.34–88; slightly revised English tr. 'The Fatimids and the Qarmaṭīs of Baḥrayn', in Farhad Daftary, ed., *Mediaeval Isma'ili History and Thought* (Cambridge, 1996), pp.21–73; and 'Ḥamdān Qarmaṭ and the Dā'ī Abū 'Alī', *Proceedings of the 17th Congress of the UEAI* [Union Européenne des arabisants et islamisants] (St. Petersburg, 1997), pp.115–24. Both Farhad Daftary and Heinz Halm have subsequently used most of this information profitably and added to it in the process of their own work.

4. On these sources, in addition to the studies cited previously, see

W. Ivanow, *Ismaili Tradition Concerning the Rise of the Fatimids* (London, 1942).

5. On the story of this man it is essential to consult Madelung's 'Ḥamdān Qarmaṭ and the Dāʿī Abū ʿAlī', cited previously.

6. The basic source is Qāḍī al-Nuʿmān's *Iftitāḥ al-daʿwa*.

7. *Sīrat Jaʿfar al-Ḥājib*, Arabic text ed. W. Ivanow, *Bulletin of the Faculty of Arts, University of Egypt*, 4 (1936), pp.107–33; English tr., Ivanow in *Ismaili Tradition Concerning the Rise of the Fatimids*, pp.184–223; French tr. M. Canard, 'L'Autobiographie d'un chambellan du Mahdī 'Obeidallâh le Fâṭimide', in *Hespéris*, 39 (1952), pp.279–330, repr. in his *Miscellanea Orientalia* (London, 1973), no.5.

8. See now especially Ibn al-Haytham's *Kitāb al-Munāẓarāt*, ed. and tr. Madelung and Walker in *The Advent of the Fatimids*, but also al-Nuʿmān's *Iftitāḥ al-daʿwa*.

9. Chiefly these are the product of Mālikī scholars beginning with the *ṭabaqāt* of al-Khushanī, *Kitāb Ṭabaqāt ʿulamāʾ Ifrīqiya* (*Classes des savants de l'Ifrīqiya*), ed. Mohammed Ben Cheneb (Paris, 1915), French tr. Ben Cheneb (Algiers, 1920).

10. For a recent reassessment of this event see Madelung and Walker, *Advent of the Fatimids*, introduction, pp.31–41.

11. The most recent study of Abū Yazīd's revolt is Halm's *Reich*, pp.265–89, tr. pp.298–325, but see also R. le Tourneau, 'La Révolte d'Abu-Yazid au Xme siècle', *CTI* (1953), pp.103–25.

12. On al-Sijistānī, see Paul Walker, *Early Philosophical Shiism: The Ismaili Neoplatonism of Abū Yaʿqūb al-Sijistānī* (Cambridge, 1993), *Abū Yaʿqūb al-Sijistānī: Intellectual Missionary* (London, 1996), and *The Wellsprings of Wisdom* (Salt Lake City, 1994).

13. On Fatimid policy toward the western Maghrib and the Umayyads, see in addition to the relevant sections of Halm's *Reich*, the articles by F. Dachraoui, 'Tentative d'infiltration shiʿite en Espagne musulmane sous le règne d'al-Hakim II', *al-Andalus*, 23 (1958), pp.97–106; M. al-Yaʿlāwī, 'Controverse entre le Fatimide Al-Muʿizz et l'Omeyyade Al-Nasir, d'après le *Kitab al-majālis wa-l-musāyarāt* du cadi Nuʿmān', *CT*, 26 (1978), pp.7–33; M. al-Yaʿlāwī, 'Les Relations entre Fatimides d'Ifriqiya et Omeyyades d'Espagne à travers le *Diwan* d'Ibn Hani', in *Acta 2 Coloquio Hispano-tunecino* (1972), pp.13–30; and most recently P. Guichard, 'Omeyyades et Fatimides au Maghreb: Problématique d'un conflit politico-idéologique (vers 929–vers 980)', in Marianne Barrucand, ed., *L'Égypte fatimide: son art et son histoire* (Paris, 1999), pp.55–67.

14. *Sīrat Ustādh Jawdhar*, Arabic text ed. M. K. Ḥusayn and M. ʿAbd al-

Hādī Shaʿīra (Cairo, 1954); French tr. M. Canard, *Vie de l'ustadh Jaudhar* (Algiers, 1958).

15. For a complete list see Ismail Poonawala, *Biobibliography of Ismāʿīlī Literature* (Malibu, CA, 1977), pp.48–68. On al-Nuʿmān, his biography and role, see also the several articles of Poonawala, 'al-Qāḍī al-Nuʿmān's Works and the Sources', *BSOAS*, 36 (1973), pp.109–15; 'A Reconsideration of al-Qāḍī al-Nuʿmān's Madhhab', *BSOAS*, 37 (1974), pp.572–9; 'Al-Qāḍī al-Nuʿmān and Ismaʿili Jurisprudence', in Daftary, ed., *Mediaeval Ismaʿili History and Thought*, pp.117–43.

16. See among other studies of Fatimid-Byzantine relations, A. Hamdani, 'Some Considerations on the Fatimid Caliphate as a Mediterranean Power', in *Atti Terzo Congresso de Studi Arabi e Islami* (Naples, 1967), pp.385–96; A. Hamdani, 'Byzantine-Fatimid Relations before the Battle of Manzikert', *Byzantine Studies*, 3 (1974), pp.169–179; M. Canard, 'Deux episodes des relations diplomatiques arabo-byzantines au Xe siècle', *BEO*, 13 (1949–1950), pp.51–69; M. Canard, 'L'Impérialisme des Fatimides et leur propagande', *Annales de l'Institut d'Études Orientales de la Faculté des Lettres d'Alger*, 6 (1942–1947), pp.156–93; S. M. Stern, 'An Embassy of the Byzantine Emperor to the Fatimid Caliph al-Muʿizz', *Byzantion*, 20 (1950), pp.239–58; Amin Tibi, 'Byzantine-Fatimid Relations in the Reign of Al-Muʿizz Li-Din Allah (r.953–975 AD) as Reflected in Primary Arabic Sources', *Graeco-Arabica*, 4 (1991), pp.91–107; Paul Walker, 'A Byzantine Victory Over the Fatimids at Alexandretta (971)', *Byzantion*, 42 (1972), pp.431–40; and Paul Walker, 'The "Crusade" of John Tzimisces in the Light of New Arabic Evidence', *Byzantion*, 47 (1977), pp.301–27.

17. On the Fatimid conquest of Egypt see, in addition to Halm's *Reich*, Th. Bianquis's 'La Prise du pouvoir par les Fatimides en Égypte (357–363/968–974)', *AI*, 11 (1972), pp.48–108.

Chapter 2: A Century of Empire

1. There are a number of studies devoted to reconstructing the Fatimid palaces on paper. For the most complete and most recent see Ayman Fu'ād Sayyid, *La Capitale de l'Égypte jusqu'à l'époque fatimide, al-Qāhira et al-Fusṭāṭ: essai de reconstitution topographique* (Beirut, 1998), pp.209–326. On the question of what of it might survive see, for example, the archeological evidence gathered by Nairy Hampikian and Monica Cyran, 'Recent Discoveries Concerning the Fatimid Palaces Uncovered During the Conservation Works on Parts of al-Ṣāliḥiyya Complex', in Barrucand, ed., *L'Égypte fatimide*, pp.649–63.

2. The main studies of this aspect of the Fatimid city are those of Jonathan Bloom. See his 'Meaning in Early Fatimid Architecture: Islamic Art in North Africa and Egypt in the Fourth Century AH (Tenth Century AD)' (Ph.D. dissertation, Harvard University, 1980), and 'The Mosque of al-Ḥākim in Cairo', *Muqarnas,* 1 (1983), pp.15–36.

3. On the libraries and treasuries, as well as the *majālis,* see Paul Walker, 'Fatimid Institutions of Learning', *JARCE,* 4 (1997), pp.179–200, pp.182–6 and pp.193–7.

4. Again see Walker, 'Fatimid Institutions of Learning', pp.189–93. Also Halm's *The Fatimids and their Traditions of Learning* (London, 1997), pp.71–8.

5. On the geniza and its role in Fatimid historiography, see chapter 5.

6. On the reign of al-Ḥākim, see the following studies: Sadik A. Assaad, *The Reign of al-Hakim bi Amr Allah (386/996–411/1021): A Political Study* (Beirut, 1974); Josef van Ess, *Chiliastische Erwartungen und die Versuchung der Göttlichkeit: Der Khalif al-Ḥākim (386–411),* (Heidelberg, 1977); Heinz Halm, 'Der Treuhänder Gottes: Die Edikte des Kalifen al-Ḥākim', *Der Islam,* 63 (1986), pp.11–72; Paul Walker, 'The Ismaili Daʿwa in the Reign of the Fatimid Caliph al-Ḥākim', *JARCE,* 30 (1993), pp.160–82; and Paul Walker, *Ḥamīd al-Dīn al-Kirmānī: Ismaili Thought in the Age of al-Ḥākim* (London, 1999).

7. Specifically on the role of al-Kirmānī, see the two studies by Walker cited in the previous note.

8. On the origin of the Druzes in Fatimid Egypt and the fate of their original leaders, see first David R. Bryer, 'The Origins of the Druze Religion', *Der Islam,* 52 (1975), pp.47–84 and 239–64; and 53 (1976), pp.5–27, and more recently Heinz Halm, 'Der Tod Ḥamzas, des Begründers der drusischen Religion', in Urbain Vermeulen and Daniel De Smet, ed., *Egypt and Syria in the Fatimid, Ayyubid and Mamluk Eras* II*: Proceedings of the 4th and 5th International Colloquium organized at the Katholieke Univeriteit Leuven in May 1995 and 1996* (Louvain, 1998), pp.105–113.

9. On both whose works are numerous and generally well known, see the basic biobibliographical information in Poonawala's *Biobibliography of Ismāʿīlī Literature,* pp.111–25 (Nāṣir) and pp.103–9 (Mu'ayyad).

10. Al-Maqrīzī, *Ittiʿāẓ,* vol.2, p.257.

11. See Walker, 'The "Crusade" of John Tzimisces in the Light of New Arabic Evidence', *Byzantion,* 47 (1977), pp.301–27.

12. The basic work on the Fatimids in Syria is Th. Bianquis, *Damas et la*

Syrie sous la domination Fatimide (359–468/969–1076) (Damascus, 1986–1989).

13. The standard work on the Zīrids is Hady Roger Idris, *La Berbérie orientale sous les Zīrīdes, Xe-XIIe siècles* (Paris, 1962).

14. Exactly how severe the devastation was, what caused it and what its consequences were for later Maghribi history is a matter of intense debate in contemporary scholarship. See, for example, J. Poncet, 'Le Mythe de la catastrophe hilālienne', *AnnalesESC,* 22 (1967), pp.1099–120; J. Poncet, 'Encore à propos des Hilāliens: La «Mise au point» de R. Idris', *AnnalesESC,* 23 (1968), pp.660–2; Hady Roger Idris, 'Hilāl', *EI2*; Idris, 'L'Invasion hilālienne et ses consequences', *Cahier de civilisation médiévale,* 11 (1968), pp.336–69; Idris, 'De la réalité de la catastrophe hilālienne', *AnnalesESC,* 23 (1968), pp.390–96; Radhi Daghfous, 'Aspects de la situation economique de l'Égypte au milieu du Vè s/ milieu du XIè s/: Contribution a l'étude des conditions de l'immigrations des tribus arabes (Hilal et Sulaym) en Ifriqiya', *CT,* 25 (1977), pp.23–50; Daghfous, 'De l'Origine des Banu Hilal et des Banu Sulaym', *CT,* 23 (1975), pp.41–68; Michael Brett, 'Ibn Khaldūn and the Arabisation of North Africa', *The Maghreb Review,* 4 (1979), pp.9–16; Michael Brett, 'Ibn Khaldun and the Invasion of Ifriqiya by the Banu Hilal, 5th century AH/11th century AD', in *Actes de colloque international sur Ibn Khaldoun, 1978* (Algiers, 1982); Michael Brett, 'Fatimid Historiography: A Case Study – The Quarrel with the Zīrids, 1048–58', in D. O. Morgan, ed., *Medieval Historical Writing in the Christian and Islamic Worlds* (London, 1982), pp.47–59; Michael Brett, 'The Execution of al-Yāzūrī', in Vermeulen and De Smet, ed., *Egypt and Syria in the Fatimid, Ayyubid and Mamluk Eras* II, pp.15–27; J. Thiry, 'L'Égypte et le déclin de l'Afrique du Nord (XIe–XIIe siècle)', in Vermeulen and De Smet, ed., *Egypt and Syria in the Fatimid, Ayyubid and Mamluk Eras* II, pp.237–48; and A. Hamdani, 'Did the Turkicization of Asia Minor lead to the Arabization of North Africa?', *The Maghreb Review,* 24 (1999), pp.34–41.

15. The classic study of the Ṣulayḥids is Husayn Hamdani, *al-Ṣulayḥiyyūn wa'l-ḥaraka al-fāṭimiyya fi'l-Yaman* (Cairo, 1955).

16. Al-Maqrīzī, *Ittiʿāẓ,* vol.1, p.263.

17. On the careers of al-Nuʿmān's descendants, see R. Gottheil, 'A Distinguished Family of Fatimide Cadis (al-Nuʿmān) in the Tenth Century', *JAOS,* 27 (1906), pp.217–96.

18. On the al-Fāriqīs, see P. Walker, 'Another Family of Fatimid Chief Qadis: The al-Fariqis', *Journal of Druze Studies,* 1 (2000), pp.49–69.

19. Two interesting attempts to explain this failure are Daghfous, 'As-

pects de la situation economique de l'Égypte au milieu du Vè s/ milieu du XIè s', pp.23–50, and Brett, 'The Execution of al-Yāzūrī'.

Chapter 3: A Century of Military Wazirs

1. To the extent that al-Maqrīzī depended at this point on the older chronicle of Ibn Muyassar, the same was obviously true of the latter historian as well.

2. Few of the earlier Fatimid building inscriptions have survived. By contrast for Badr some twenty are known. See Gaston Wiet, 'Nouvelles inscriptions fatimides', *BIE,* 24 (1941–42), pp.145–58.

3. Ed. 'Abd al-Mun'im Mājid (Cairo, 1954).

4. There is a fourth but it is largely inaccessible. See Gaston Wiet, 'Une Nouvelle Inscription fatimide au Caire', *JA* (1961), pp.13–20, and Ayman Fu'ād Sayyid, *Capitale de l'Égypte,* pp.418–24.

5. On the general subject of Ismaili successions to the imamate and the details of each specific case in the Fatimid period, see Paul Walker, 'Succession to Rule in the Shiite Caliphate', *JARCE,* 32 (1995), pp.239–64.

6. This is true primarily of later Fatimid Ismailis but not necessarily of the earliest. There is considerable confusion and disagreement among both Ismaili and non-Ismaili sources about the exact line of imams from Ja'far to al-Mahdī, or even to al-Qā'im, whose own line was said, by some, to differ from al-Mahdī's. About all this there exists an extensive literature, both scholarly and polemical, the most important of which are the following: Husayn F. Hamdani, *On the Genealogy of Fatimid Caliphs* (Cairo, 1958); Abbas Hamdani and F. de Blois, 'A Re-examination of al-Mahdī's Letter to the Yemenites on the Genealogy of the Fatimid Caliphs', *JRAS* (1983/2), pp.173–207; and the relevant sections of Madelung, 'Das Imamat in der frühen ismailitischen Lehre'; Farhad Daftary, *The Ismā'īlīs: Their History and Doctrines* (Cambridge, 1990), and Halm, *Reich.*

7. On this succession, see in addition to the study by Walker cited previously, S. M. Stern, 'The Succession to the Fatimid Imam al-Āmir, the Claims of the later Fatimids to the Imamate, and the Rise of Ṭayyibī Ismailism', *Oriens,* 4 (1951), pp.193–255.

8. al-Maqrīzī, *Itti'āẓ,* 3, pp.166–7.

9. On this development, see Walker, 'Fatimid Institutions of Learning', pp.191–3.

10. See Paula Sanders, 'Claiming the Past: Ghadîr Khumm and the

Rise of Ḥâfiẓî Historiography in Late Fâṭimid Egypt', *SI,* 75 (1992), pp.81–104.

11. There is a minor controversy about this issue. See the following articles by Caroline Williams, 'The Cult of Alid Saints in the Fatimid Monuments of Cairo, Part 1: The Mosque of al-Aqmar', *Muqarnas,* 1 (1983) pp.37–52; 'The Cult of Alid Saints in the Fatimid Monuments of Cairo, Part 2: The Mausolea', *Muqarnas,* 3 (1985) pp.39–60, 'The Qur'anic Inscriptions on the *Tabut* of al-Husayn', *Islamic Art,* 2 (1987), pp.3–14, and the critique of them by Christopher Taylor, 'Reevaluating the Shiʿi Role in the Development of Monumental Islamic Funerary Architecture: the Case of Egypt', *Muqarnas,* 9 (1992), pp.1–10.

12. See Walker, 'Fatimid Institutions of Learning', pp.186–9.

13. On the early development of Sunni madrasas in Egypt, see the several studies by Gary Leiser: 'The Madrasa and the Islamization of the Middle East: The Case of Egypt', *JARCE,* 22 (1985), pp.29–47; 'Muslims from al-Andalus in Late Fāṭimid and Early Aiyūbid Egypt', *al-Qantara,* 20 (1999), pp.137–59; and 'The Restoration of Sunnism in Egypt: Madrasas and Mudarrisūn 495–647/1101–1249' (Ph.D. dissertation, University of Pennsylvania, 1976).

14. On the Banū Ruzzīk and the Nuṣayrism of this family, see the evidence gathered by Seta B. Dadoyan, *The Fatimid Armenians: Cultural and Political Interaction in the Near East* (Leiden, 1997), pp.154–78.

15. On al-Makhzūmī, see the various studies by Claude Cahen, among them, 'L'Administration financière de la armée fatimide d'après al-Makhzūmī', *JESHO,* 15 (1972), pp.163–82; 'Al-Makhzūmī et Ibn Mammātī sur l'agriculture égyptienne médiévale', *AI,* 11 (1972), pp.141–51; and *Makhzūmiyyāt: Études sur l'histoire économique et financière de l'Égypte médiévale* (Leiden, 1977). Also Gladys Frantz-Murphy, *The Agrarian Administration of Egypt from the Arabs to the Ottomans* (Cairo, 1986). Ibn Mammātī's *Kitāb Qawānīn al-dawāwīn* was edited by A. S. Atiya (Cairo, 1943) and translated into English by R. Cooper in his Ph.D. dissertation.

16. See here Walker, 'Fatimid Institutions of Learning', pp.196–7, and Halm, *The Fatimids and their Traditions of Learning,* pp.90–3. In regard to the possibility that some copies of books that were once in these Fatimid libraries may still exist, see Ayman Fu'ād Sayyid, 'Khizānat kutub al-Fāṭimiyyīn, hal baqiya minhā shay'?' *Majallat Maʿhad al-Makhṭūṭāt al-ʿArabiyya,* 42 (1998), pp.7–32, and Sayyid, 'L'art du livre' in *Dossiers d'Archéologie,* 233 (May 1998): *Égypte, l'âge d'or des Fatimides,* pp.80–3.

17. On what if anything may survive, see D. Russel, 'Are there any Remains of the Fatimid Palaces of Cairo?', *JARCE,* 3 (1964), pp.115–21,

and more recently Nairy Hampikian and Monica Cyran, 'Recent Discoveries Concerning the Fatimid Palaces Uncovered During the Conservation Works on Parts of al-Ṣāliḥiyya Complex', in Barrucand, ed., *L'Égypte fatimide*, pp.649–63.

Chapter 4: Coins, Building Inscriptions, *Ṭirāz*, Art and Archaeology

1. The material that follows here on Fatimid coins derives for the most part from information passed to me from Michael Bates, the curator of Islamic coins at the American Numismatic Society, either in the form of a draft of an unpublished paper on the subject or his own personal notes. Unfortunately, as yet there is no published corpus of Fatimid coins although N. D. Nicol has been preparing one for several years. Meanwhile it is necessary to consult published catalogues of the major collections and the following articles or books: George C. Miles, *Fatimid Coins in the Collections of the University Museum, Philadelphia, and the American Numismatic Society* (New York, 1951); J. Farrugia de Candia, 'Les Monnaies fatimides de Musée du Bardo (Premier supplément)', *Revue tunisienne*, 15 (1948); 'Les Monnaies fatimides du Musée de Bardo', *Revue tunisienne* (1936), pp.333–72; (1937), pp.89–136; Aimee Launois, 'Catalogue des monnaies fatimites entrées au Cabinet des Medailles depuis 1896', *BEO*, 24 (1971), pp.19–53; W. A. Oddy, 'The Gold Content of Fatimid Coins Reconsidered', in *Metallurgy in Numismatics*, 1 (London, 1980), pp.99–118; Māysa Maḥmūd Dāwūd (Mayssa Mahmoud Daoud), *al-Maskūkāt al-Fāṭimiyya bi-majmūʿat Mathaf al-Fann al-Islāmī bi'l-Qāhira: dirāsa athariyya wa fanniyya* (Cairo, 1991); and the numerous articles by Paul Balog listed in the bibliography here.

2. The Fatimids used both *waraq dirhams* with less silver content which therefore tended to turn black and the full silver *nuqra dirham.*

3. See, for example, S. Goitein, 'The Exchange Rate of Gold and Silver Money in Fatimid and Ayyubid Times', *JESHO*, 7 (1965), pp.1–80; plus additions *JESHO*, 9 (1966), pp.67–8 and errata *JESHO*, 12 (1969), p.112.

4. See Ayman Fu'ād Sayyid, *al-Dawla al-fāṭimiyya fī Miṣr: tafsīr jadīd* (Cairo, 1992), pp.181–4 and the citations given there.

5. On these imitations see A. S. Ehrenkreutz, 'Arabic Dinars Struck by the Crusaders', *JESHO*, 7 (1964), pp.167–82.

6. This is the list given by George C. Miles, *Fatimid Coins in the Collections of the University Museum, Philadelphia, and the American Numismatic Society* (New York, 1951), pp.50–1. Add to it Barqa (noted by M. Bates).

7. The basic survey of Fatimid glass weights was done by Paul Balog, mainly on the basis of his own collection. See his *The Fatimid Glass Jeton* (Naples, 1974–75), originally published in *Annali dell'Istituto Italiano di Numismatica*, 18–20 (Rome, 1971–73).

8. On this issue see Michael Bates, 'The Function of Fatimid and Ayyubid Glass Weights', *JESHO*, 24 (1981), pp.63–92, and 'How Egyptian Glass Coin Weights Were Used', *Rivista Italiana di Numismatica e Scienze Affini*, 95 (1993), pp.539–45.

9. In general on Islamic inscriptions of this and other types, see Sheila S. Blair, *Islamic Inscriptions* (Edinburgh, 1998).

10. Ibn 'Idhārī, *Bayān*, vol.1, p.151.

11. Another less informative example of such inscriptions, however, comes from the *Safarnāma* of Nāṣir-i Khusraw who remarked on the saddle-blankets of the riders in a procession all of which carried the name, at least, of the ruler woven into the cloth (Thackston tr. p.48).

12. Ibn 'Idhārī, *Bayān*, vol.1, p.159.

13. Published by Marcel in the *Description d'Égypte – état moderne*, vol.15, p.506. See also Ayman Fu'ād Sayyid, *Capitale de l'Égypte*, pp.447–51; *MCIA*, 1, pp.64–6.

14. Al-Maqrīzī (*Khiṭaṭ*, vol.1, p.362) mentions another inscription that he had seen on what remained in his time of the first Bāb al-Futūḥ and that might have been earlier. Unfortunately, he does not give the text. See Sayyid, *Capitale de l'Égypte*, pp.152–3.

15. *MCIA*, 1, pp.43–4.

16. *MCIA*, 1, pp.50–1. See J. Bloom, 'The Mosque of al-Ḥākim in Cairo', *Muqarnas*, 1 (1983), pp.15–36.

17. *MCIA*, 1, pp.54–5.

18. On this inscription, see Sayyid, *Capitale de l'Égypte*, pp.432–3; on Badr's assumption of these prerogatives, see pp.379–80.

19. *MCIA*, 1, pp.56–62.

20. Sayyid, *Capitale de l'Égypte*, pp.418–24.

21. Ibn Muyassar, 47; *Itti'āẓ*, vol.2, p.321; *al-Sijillāt*, no.15.

22. Sayyid, *Capitale de l'Égypte*, pp.441–6; *MCIA*, 1, 63–4.

23. Sayyid, *Capitale de l'Égypte*, pp.460–2.

24. See Sayyid, *Capitale de l'Égypte*, pp.524–6; *MCIA*, 1, pp.67–9.

25. Moshe Sharon, 'A New Fâṭimid Inscription from Ascalon and Its Historical Setting', *'Atiqot*, 26 (1995), pp.61–86.

26. On which see Sayyid, *Capitale de l'Égypte*, pp.547–8; *MCIA*, 1, pp.73–5.

27. See, for example, how such material was used in the study of S.

Gellens, 'Scholars and Travellers: The Social History of Early Muslim Egypt, 218–487/833–1094'. (Ph.D. dissertation, Columbia University, 1986.)

28. Ed. Ét. Combe, J. Sauvaget, G. Wiet, et al. Cairo, 1933– .

29. In general see 'Ṭirāz' by A. Grohmann, *Encyclopaedia of Islam* (first ed.); 'Ṭirāz' by Yedida Stillman and Paula Sanders in the *EI2*; Ernst Kühnel and Louisa Bellinger, *Catalogue of Dated Tiraz Fabrics: Umayyad, Abbasid, Fatimid* (Washington, DC, 1952); and Blair, *Islamic Inscriptions*, pp.164–9, and the numerous references listed in them.

30. I am assuming here that the *khilʿa* is a highly restricted form of *ṭirāz* and therefore may be treated as a separate class of such objects. It should be noted, however, that some scholars consider the *khilʿa* as simply equivalent to the *ṭirāz*.

31. *Sīrat Ustādh Jawdhar*, text p.52, tr. p.75. See also text p.88, tr. pp.129–30 and Halm, *Reich*, p.287, tr. p.322 (and index).

32. See Ibn Ḥawqal, ed. Kramers, pp.152ff. *Khiṭaṭ*, vol.2, p.6.

33. Serjeant, 'Islamic Textiles', p.89, p.94.

34. *RCEA*, 6, no. 2048 (from the Tano collection).

35. Examples made at Tinnīs in the year 410 in *RCEA*, 6, no.2212.

36. For example *RCEA*, no.2417.

37. *RCEA*, no.2632.

38. For example *RCEA*, nos.2810 and 2828.

39. On it see Georges Marçais and Gaston Wiet, 'Le Voile de Sainte Anne d'Apt', *Monuments et Mémoires Fondation Piot*, 34 (1934), pp.177–94; H. A. Elsberg and R. Guest, 'The Veil of St. Anne', *The Burlington Magazine*, 68 (1936), pp.140–5; and Georgette Cornu, 'Les Tissus d'apparat fatimids, parmi les plus somptueux le «voile de Saint Anne» d'Apt', in Barrucand, ed., *L'Égypte fatimide*, pp.331–7.

40. It might be noted here that, among the many thousands of objects ascribed to the Fatimid period there is one inscribed ivory casket, three rock crystals inscribed with the names of caliphs or titles of major figures, and two ceramics with historical inscriptions that allow them to be dated with some precision. Information supplied by J. Bloom.

41. A complete bibliography of work on Fatimid art would run to a considerable length in part because it must include a great many small publications of individual pieces as well as catalogues of exhibitions that include such items. Moreover, the interest of art historians in the Fatimid period has in general exceeded that of the specialists in other fields. However, a good place to see what has been and what can be done is

Marianne Barrucand's edition of the papers from the 1998 Paris conference entitled *L'Égypte fatimide: son art et son histoire* (Paris, 1999).

42. Because the original author of this material is unknown, citations of it are difficult. One version, however, was compiled by al-Awḥadī, and it has been edited and most especially translated into English with commentary and a discussion of authorship. It is now the best place to begin. See, therefore, Ghāda al-Ḥijjāwī al-Qaddūmī, *Book of Gifts and Rarities* (Kitāb al-Hadāyā wa al-Tuḥaf): *Selections Compiled in the Fifteenth Century from an Eleventh-Century Manuscript on Gifts and Treasures,* tr., intro., annotations, Harvard Middle Eastern Monographs, 29 (Cambridge, MA, 1996).

43. As with the studies of Fatimid art, the archeology is difficult to represent in a simple bibliography. However, there is a quite useful list (mainly for Syria and Egypt) appended to Marie-Odile Rousset's 'La Céramique des XIe et XIIe siècle en Égypte et au Bilād al-Shām', in Barrucand, ed., *L'Égypte fatimide,* pp.258–64. For the Maghrib see, as examples, Lucien Golvin, *Le Magrib Central a l'époque des Zirides: recherches d'archeologie et d'histoire* (Paris, 1957); Lucien Golvin, *Recherches archéologiques à la Qalʿa des Banû Hammâd* (Paris, 1965); Alexandre Lezine, 'Notes d'archéologie ifriqiyenne, 4: Mahdiyah, quelques precisions sur la «ville» des premiers fatimides', *REI, 35* (1967), pp.82–101; and Alexandre Lezine, *Mahdiya: Recherches d'archeologie islamique* (Paris, 1965).

Chapter 5: Letters and Documents

1. It is, however, not always clear how such material reached al-Qalqashandī. Certainly, in part, he copied some of these documents from his Fatimid predecessors, the work of 'Alī b. Khalaf, for example. Still, others examples may have survived in one archive or another even in his time.

2. This document was published by Richard J. H. Gottheil, 'An Eleventh-century Document Concerning a Cairo Synagogue', *Jewish Quarterly Review* (1907), pp.467–539.

3. 'A Copy of a Decree from the Archives of the Fāṭimid Chancery in Egypt', *BSOAS,* 49 (1986), pp.439–53.

4. For stylistic purposes I have slightly altered here the translation of Khan.

5. S. M. Stern, 'Three Petitions of the Fāṭimid Period', *Oriens,* 15 (1962). pp.172–209; Geoffrey Khan, 'The Historical Development of

the Structure of Medieval Arabic Petitions', *BSOAS*, 53 (1990), pp.8–30; and D. S. Richards, 'A Fāṭimid Petition and "Small Decree" from Sinai', *Israel Oriental Studies*, 3 (1973), pp.140–58. See also G. Khan, 'A Petition to the Fāṭimid Caliph al-'Āmir', *JRAS* (1990), pp.44–54.

6. Al-Shayyāl, *Majmūʿat al-wathāʾiq al-fāṭimiyyin, I, wathāʾiq al-khilāfa wa wilāyat al-ʿahd wa'l-wizāra* (Cairo, 1958, reissued 1965).

7. Both the *Khiṭaṭ* and the *Ittiʿāẓ*, the latter partly available to him only in manuscript.

8. See al-Shayyāl's introduction, p.13, n.1.

9. See al-Nuʿmān, *Iftitāḥ*, pp.289–92 (para.262), for one example. Yet another pp.281–2 (para.253).

10. Ed. Dachraoui, pp.293–4 (para.265). See also Halm, *Reich*, p.138, tr. p.147.

11. Pp.294–9 (paras. 267–71).

12. *'Uyūn al-akhbār*, ed. al-Yaʿlāwī, pp. 459–61.

13. *Ittiʿāẓ*, vol.2, pp.27–9. It was duly noted and published earlier by al-Shayyāl. See his document no.12 (pp.131–5, 307–11).

14. Ibn al-Qalānisī, *Dhayl taʾrīkh Dimashq*, ed. H. F. Amedroz (Leiden and Beirut, 1908), pp.80–3. But also noted by al-Shayyāl (his document no.13), see pp.136–9, pp.313–21.

15. This Ibn Khayrān was already supervisor of the chancery in the year 414/1023 and he was still in charge of it in 443/1051 in which year he composed the *sijill* appointing al-Yāzūrī wazir.

16. Even in order to sign a document attesting to his approval of it. His signature (*'alāma*), *al-ḥamdu li-llāh shukran li-niʿmatihi*, was signed for him by the qadi al-Quḍāʿī. See Samuel M. Stern, *Fatimid Decrees: Original Documents from the Fatimid Chancery* (London, 1964), p.130.

17. Husayn Hamdani, 'The Letters of Al-Mustanṣir bi-llah', *BSOAS*, 7 (1933–35), pp.307–24, p.309; and *al-Ṣulayḥiyyūn wa'l-ḥaraka al-fāṭimiyya fi'l-Yaman* (Cairo, 1955). Copies of the additional items appear in the latter work on pp.303–20.

18. For the texts see the edition by A. A. A. Fyzee (also al-Shayyāl's *Majmūʿa*, pp.47–67). On the context see the study by S. M. Stern, 'The Epistle of the Fatimid Caliph al-Amir (al-Hidāya al-Amiriyya – Its Date and Its Purpose)', *JRAS* (1950), pp.20–31, and Walker, 'Succession to Rule in the Shiite Caliphate', pp.256–8.

19. Gottheil, 'An Eleventh-century Document Concerning a Cairo Synagogue'.

20. Ibn 'Abd al-Ẓāhir, *al-Rawḍa al-bahiyya al-zāhira fi khiṭaṭ al-muʿizziyya al-qāhira*, Arabic text edited by Sayyid (Cairo, 1996), pp.143–50. Most of

this document appears in al-Maqrīzī's *Khiṭaṭ*, bit by bit, in the entry for each of the four institutions granted an endowment in it.

21. D. S. Richards, 'Fragments of a Slave Dealer's Day-book from Fusṭāṭ', in Yūsuf Rāghib ed. *Documents de l'Islam Médiéval: Nouvelles perspectives de recherche* (Cairo, 1991), pp.89–96 + plates 3 and 4.

22. See S. D. Goitein's introduction to *A Mediterranean Society* (Berkeley, CA, 1967–1993), vol.1.

23. There is a growing body of scholarship on the geniza and it is by now not easy to keep track of all of it. For major examples, however, see the references in the bibliography here under the following names: E. Barekat, M. Cohen, M. Gil, Y. Stillman, N. Stillman, J. Mann, R. Gottheil, S. Shaked, and G. Khan.

24. There also exists, somewhat more incidentally, material concerning Jews in Spain, Europe and other areas of the Near East.

25. There are apparently some 7,000 fragments written in Arabic script or 5 per cent of an estimated total of 140,000. For a general assessment of the Arabic materials in the geniza, see G. Khan, 'The Arabic Fragments in the Cambridge Genizah Collections', *Manuscripts of the Middle East*, 1 (1986), pp.54–60.

Chapter 6: Memoirs, Eyewitnesses and Contemporaries

1. Muḥammad b. al-Ḥārith b. Asad al-Khushanī, *Kitāb Ṭabaqāt ʿulamāʾ Ifrīqiya* (*Classes des savants de l'Ifrīqiya*), ed. Mohammed Ben Cheneb (Paris, 1915); French tr. Ben Cheneb (Algiers, 1920).

2. Abū 'Abdallāh Jaʿfar Ibn al-Haytham, *Kitāb al-Munāẓarāt*, ed. and tr. Madelung and Walker in *The Advent of the Fatimids.*

3. *Sīrat Jaʿfar al-Ḥājib*, Arabic text ed. W. Ivanow, *Bulletin of the Faculty of Arts, University of Egypt*, 4 (1936), pp.107–33; English tr., Ivanow in *Ismaili Tradition Concerning the Rise of the Fatimids*, pp.184–223; French tr. M. Canard, 'L'Autobiographie d'un chambellan du Mahdī 'Obeidallâh le Fâṭimide'.

4. *Iftitāḥ*, p.334.

5. On this see Halm, *Reich*, pp.285–6, p.439, tr. pp.320–1, p.426.

6. Arabic text ed. M. K. Ḥusayn and M. 'Abd al-Hādī Shaʿīra (Cairo, 1954); French tr. M. Canard, *Vie de l'ustadh Jaudhar* (Algiers, 1958).

7. Qāḍī al-Nuʿmān, *Iftitāḥ al-daʿwa wa ibtidāʾ al-dawla*, ed. Wadad Kadi (Beirut, 1970), and Farhat Dachraoui (Tunis, 1975).

8. Qāḍī al-Nuʿmān, *Daʿāʾim al-islām*, ed. A. A. A. Fyzee (Cairo, 1951–61).

9. Qāḍī al-Nuʿmān, *Kitāb al-Majālis wa'l-musāyarāt*, ed. al-Ḥabīb al-Faqī, Ibrāhīm Shabbūḥ, and Muḥammad al-Yaʿlāwī (Tunis, 1978).

10. For a list see Poonawala, *Biobibliography*, pp.70–5.

11. Ed. de Goeje (Leiden, 1873) and J. H. Kramers (Leiden, 1938); French tr. Kramers and G. Wiet, *Configuration de la terre* (Paris and Beirut, 1964).

12. On him in general see 'Ibn Ḥawḳal' by A. Miquel, *EI2*.

13. Abū Muḥammad al-Ḥasan Ibn Zūlāq, *Akhbār Sībawayh al-miṣrī*, ed. Muḥammad Ibrāhīm Saʿd and Ḥusayn al-Dīb (Cairo, 1933).

14. See R. H. J. Gottheil, 'Al-Hasan ibn Ibrahim ibn Zulaq,' *JAOS*, 28 (1907), pp.217–97.

15. *Ittiʿāẓ*, vol.2, p.83.

16. See G. Troupeau, 'La Description de la Nubie d'al-Uswani,' *Arabica*, 1 (1954), pp.276–88.

17. Apparently there is a copy of it in the Zāhriyya in Damascus.

18. Yaḥyā of Antioch, Yaḥyā b. Saʿīd al-Anṭākī, *Ta'rīkh*, ed. I. Kratchkovsky with French tr. A. Vasiliev, *Patrologica Orientalia*, 18 (1924), pp.699–833 and 23 (1932), pp.347–520; part 3, ed. Kratchkowsky, French tr. F. Michaeu and G. Troupeau, *Patrologica Orientali*, 47 (1997), pp.373–559. There is another edition by ʿUmar ʿAbd al-Salām Tadmūrī (Tripoli, Lebanon, 1990).

19. There is a fairly complete study of Yaḥyā's history by John Harper Forsyth, 'The Byzantine-Arab Chronicle (938–1034) of Yaḥyā b. Saʿīd al-Anṭākī'. (Ph.D. dissertation, University of Michigan, 1977).

20. On him see 'al-Musabbiḥī' by Th. Bianquis in the *EI2*.

21. Al-Musabbiḥī, *al-Juz' al-arbaʿūn min Akhbār Miṣr*, part 1 (the historical section), ed. Ayman Fu'ād Sayyid and Th. Bianquis (Cairo, 1978); part 2 (literary section), ed. D. Ḥusayn Naṣṣār (Cairo, 1984).

22. Whatever survives of it as quotations in these later works has been collected by Ayman Fu'ād Sayyid and published separately. See Sayyid, 'Nuṣūṣ ḍā'iʿa min akhbār Miṣr li-l-Musabbiḥī,' *AI*, 17 (1981), pp.1–54.

23. On this work and its various authors, see Johannes den Heijer, 'Coptic Historiography in the Fāṭimid, Ayyūbid and Early Mamlūk Periods', *Medieval Encounters*, 2 (1996), pp.67–98, and den Heijer, *Mawhūb ibn Manṣūr ibn Mufarrig et l'historiographie copto-arabe: Étude sur la composition de l'Histoire des Patriarches d'Alexandrie* (Louvain, 1989), as well as the appropriate entries (also by den Heijer) in the *Coptic Encyclopedia*.

24. On this aspect of al-Kirmānī, see now Walker, *Ḥamīd al-Dīn al-Kirmānī*. Also van Ess, *Chiliastische Erwartungen und die Versuchung der Göttlichkeit*.

25. Nāṣir-i Khusraw, *Safarnāma*, ed. with French tr., Charles Schefer, *Sefer nameh: relation du voyage de Nassiri Khosrau* (Paris, 1881); English tr. W. M. Thackston Jr., *Nāṣer-e Khosraw's Book of Travels* (Albany, NY, 1986).

26. Al-Mu'ayyad fi'l-Dīn al-Shīrāzī, *Sīrat al-Mu'ayyad fi'l-dīn dāʿī al-duʿāt*, ed. Muḥammad Kāmil Ḥusayn (Cairo, 1949).

27. On him see Ibn Khallikān, *Wafayāt*, vol.4, pp.212–13, English tr. vol.2, pp.616–17; Ayman Fu'ād Sayyid, introduction to the *musawwada* of al-Maqrīzī's *Khiṭaṭ*, pp.11–13.

28. See S. A. Bonebakker, 'A Fatimid Manual for Secretaries', *Annali Istituto Orientale di Napoli*, 37, NS, 27 (1977), pp.295–337. The existing text of the *Mawādd al-bayān* has been published in fascimile (Frankfurt, 1986), ed. Ḥusayn 'Abd al-Laṭīf (Tripoli, Libya, 1982).

29. Note also the *Rasāʾil* of al-ʿAmīdī, for which see P. Sanders, 'A New Source for the History of Fāṭimid Ceremonial: The *Rasāʾil al-ʿAmīdī*', *AI*, 25 (1991), pp.127–31.

30. Al-Ḥabbāl's *Wafayāt* was edited and published by Ṣalāḥ al-Dīn al-Munajjid in *Revue de l'Institut des Manuscrits Arabes*, 2 (1956), pp.286–338. Although the editor, relying on other sources, gives al-Ḥabbāl's death as 482, al-Maqrīzī in the *Ittiʿāẓ* (vol.2, p.326) places it in the year 483 (the published text must be corrected to read the name properly). See also Sayyid, 'Lumières nouvelles sur quelques sources de l'histoire fatimide en Égypte,' *AI*, 13 (1977), pp.1–41, p.32.

31. For the treatises (both the Arabic original and English tr.), the men involved, and the background, see Joseph Schacht and Max Meyerhof, *The Medico-Philosophical Controversy Between Ibn Butlan of Baghdad and Ibn Ridwan of Cairo* (Cairo, 1937).

32. *Medieval Islamic Medicine: Ibn Riḍwān's Treatise 'On the Prevention of Bodily Ills in Egypt'*, tr. Michael W. Dols, Arabic text ed. Adil S. Gamal (Berkeley, CA, 1984).

33. See F. Rosenthal, 'al-Mubashshir b. Fātik,' *EI2*; and 'Al-Mubashshir ibn Fātik,' *Oriens*, 13–14 (1961), pp.133–58. The *Mukhtār al-ḥikam* was edited and published by 'Abd al-Raḥmān Badawī (Madrid, 1958), and a portion tr. by Rosenthal in his *Classical Heritage in Islam* (London *c.*1992), pp.124–44 (corresponding to pp.296–322 of the Arabic).

34. On the work and the problem of authorship, see Ghāda al-Ḥijjāwī al-Qaddūmī, *Book of Gifts and Rarities* (Kitāb al-Hadāyā wa'l-tuḥaf) (Cambridge, MA, 1996).

35. Published by 'Abd al-Salām Hārūn first in *al-Kātib* (1947–48) and then repr. in *Nawādir al-makhṭūṭāt* (Cairo, 1951), pp.3–56.

36. On Ibn Abi'l-Ṣalt see Muḥammad Kāmil Ḥusayn, *Fī ādāb Miṣr al-*

fāṭimiyya (2nd ed., Cairo, 1963), pp.212–21; Sayyid, 'Lumières nouvelles', pp.19–20; and the entry on him under 'Umayya' in the *EI2*.

37. His full name is Jamāl al-Dīn Abū 'Alī Mūsā b. al-Ma'mūn al-Baṭā'iḥī. The major surviving parts of his history were collected and edited by Ayman Fu'ād Sayyid, *Nuṣūṣ min Akhbār Miṣr li-ibn al-Ma'mūn* (Cairo, 1983).

38. *Khiṭaṭ* (Bulaq), vol.1, pp.135–8; see also Aydin Sayili's *The Observatory in Islam* (Ankara, 1960), pp.167–75. Also Walker, 'Fatimid Institutions of Learning', pp.197–9.

39. Ibn al-Ṣayrafī, *al-Qānūn dīwān al-rasā'il,* ed. 'Alī Bahjat (Cairo, 1905); and Ayman Fu'ād Sayyid (Cairo, 1990); French tr. Massé, 'Code de la chancellerie d'état,' *BIFAO,* 11 (1914), pp.65–120.

40. Ibn al-Ṣayrafī, *al-Ishāra ilā man nāla al-wizāra,* ed. 'A Mukhliṣ (Cairo, 1924); and Ayman Fu'ād Sayyid (Cairo, 1990).

41. English tr. E. A. Babcock and A. C. Krey as *A History of Deeds Done beyond the Sea* (New York, 1943).

42. Ibn al-Qalānisī, *Dhayl ta'rīkh Dimashq,* ed. H. F. Amedroz (Leiden and Beirut, 1908).

43. There is an English translation of this portion by H. A. R. Gibb, *The Damascus Chronicle of the Crusades* (London, 1932).

44. Even so some of it may well have been taken from eyewitnesses whose identities are not now known.

45. Ibn Munqidh, *Kitāb al-I'tibār,* ed. Ph. Hitti (Princeton, NJ, 1930); English tr. Hitti, *Memoirs of an Arab-Syrian Gentlemen* (New York, 1927; repr. Beirut, 1964).

46. *'Oumâra du Yémen: Sa vie et son oeuvre* (*al-Nukat al-'aṣriyya fī akhbār al-wuzarā' al-miṣriyya, qaṣā'id min shi'rihi, wa maqāṭī' min nathrihi*), ed. Hartwig Derenbourg (Paris, 1897).

47. Full name Abū Muḥammad 'Abd al-Salām b. al-Ḥasan al-Fihrī al-Miṣrī, Ibn al-Ṭuwayr al-Murtaḍā al-Qaysarānī.

48. Ayman Fu'ād Sayyid has collected and published the various pieces of this work that survive in later compilations. See Ibn al-Ṭuwayr, *Nuzhat al-muqlatayn fī akhbār al-dawlatayn,* ed. Ayman Fu'ād Sayyid (Beirut, 1992). See also Sayyid, 'Lumières nouvelles', p.28.

49. Yet one more minor example is the small book composed by Benjamin of Tudela to record his travels through the various Jewish communities of the eastern Mediterranean, including Egypt, and elsewhere. He visited Egypt at the end of the Fatimid period. See *The Itinerary of Benjamin of Tudela,* English tr. (n.p., 1983).

50. One more item worth citing is the *Akhbār al-dawla al-miṣriyya wa mā jarā bayn al-mulūk al-khulafā' wa'l-fitan wa'l ḥurūb min ayyām al-Āmir ilā*

ayyām Shīrkūh. Its author, who is not known, lived during the wazirate of Ḍirghām. The later historian Ibn al-Furāt copied most if not all of it into his history from which it was published by Cahen, 'Un Récit inédit du vizarat de Dirghām,' *AI,* 8 (1969), pp.27–61. Also Cahen, 'Quelques chroniques anciennes relatives aux derniers Fatimides', *BIFAO,* 37 (1937–38), pp.1–27, pp.15–16.

Chapter 7: Histories, Topographies and Biographical Dictionaries

1. On al-Maqrīzī, see in general the following: al-Sakhāwī, *al-Ḍawʾ al-lāmiʿ li-ahl al-qarn al-tāsiʿ* (Cairo, n.d.), vol.2, pp.21–6; *al-Tibr al-masbūk,* pp.21–4; Franz Rosenthal, 'Al-Maḳrīzī, Taḳī al-Dīn Abū'l-ʿAbbās Aḥmad b. ʿAlī b. ʿAbd al-Ḳādir (766–845/1364–1442)' in *EI2;* Jean-Claude Garcin, 'Al-Maqrīzī: un historien encyclopédique du monde afro-orientale' in Ch.-André Julien ed., *Les Africains* (Paris, 1990), vol.9, pp.195–223; and A. F. Sayyid's 'Introduction' to his edition of the *musawwada* of the *Khiṭaṭ.*

2. On him see 'Ibn ʿIdhārī' by J. Bosch-Vilá in the *EI2.*

3. Ibn ʿIdhārī, *al-Bayān al-mughrib fī akhbār al-Andalus wa'l-Maghrib.* Vol.1, ed. G. S. Colin and É. Lévi-Provençal (Leiden, 1948).

4. On this see Madelung and Walker, *The Advent of the Fatimids,* pp.41–2 and n.79.

5. One other important source for Ibn ʿIdhārī was the *History* (*Taʾrīkh Ifrīqiya wa'l-Maghrib*) of Ibn al-Raqīq, which is itself apparently lost.

6. Abū Bakr ʿAbdallāh b. Muḥammad al-Mālikī, a native of Qayrawān, died about 460/1068 (according to Bakkūsh, the editor of his *Riyāḍ al-nufūs*) and the Qāḍī ʿIyāḍ b. Mūsā al-Sabtī (from Ceuta) died in 544/1149. On the latter see the article by M. Talbi in the *EI2.*

7. These later Mālikī writers, beginning with al-Mālikī's *ṭabaqāt,* were evidently under moral pressure to justify the horrible massacres of Ismaili communities throughout the Maghrib instigated by the Mālikī *ʿulamāʾ.* This may explain why they quote at length lurid and obviously fictitious tales about Fatimid atrocities and about Ismaili heresy and atheism.

8. Abū Zayd al-Dabbāgh (605/1208–699/1300) from Qayrawān wrote a large compilation of biographies for the scholars associated with his native city which he called *Maʿālim al-īmān.* Abu'l-Qāsim Ibn Nājī (d. *ca.*839/1435), a later scholar from the same tradition in Qayrawān, copied it and added biographies and his own comments. That latter version, entitled *Maʿālim al-īmām fī maʿrifat ahl Qayrawān,* was edited by Ibrāhīm

Shabbūḥ and others (Cairo, 1968–78). See 'Al-Dabbāgh, Abū Zayd' by M. Talbi in the *EI2, Supplement.*

9. *Histoire des Rois 'Obaïdides* (*Akhbār mulūk banī 'Ubayd wa sīratihum*), ed. and tr. M. Vonderheyden (Algiers and Paris, 1927); ed. 'Abd al-Ḥalīm 'Uways (Cairo, 1980[?]).

10. See 'Ibn al-Raḳīḳ' by M. Talbi in the *EI2*.

11. On him see Poonawala's *Biobibliography*, pp.169–75 and 'Idrīs b. al-Ḥasan' also by Poonawala in the *EI2, Supplement.*

12. Hilāl b. al-Ṣābi' (359/969 – 448/1056), a native of Baghdad, wrote several works on chancery matters and a *History*. The latter is now lost except for a short fragment.

13. *Nihāyat al-rutba fī ṭalab al-ḥisba*, ed. al-Sayyid al-Bāz al-'Arīnī (Cairo, 1946).

14. Ibn al-Qifṭī, *Ta'rīkh al-ḥukamā'*, ed. J. Lippert (Leipzig, 1903).

15. Ibn Ẓāfir died in either 613/1216 or, according to another source, 623/1226. The portion of his history on the Fatimids was edited and published by André Ferré (Cairo, 1972).

16. Sibṭ b. al-Jawzī, *Mir'at al-zamān fī ta'rīkh al-a'yān*; years 345–447, ed. J. J. M. al-Hamawundī (Baghdad, 1990); *al-Ḥawādith al-khāṣṣa bi-ta'rīkh al-salājiqa bayna al-sanawāt 1056–1086*, ed. Ali Sevim (Ankara, 1968, also in *Belgeler: Türk Tarik Belgeri Dergisi*, 14 [1989–92]: pp.1–260); years 495–654, facsimile ed. J. R. Jewett (Chicago, 1907); printed ed. (Hyderabad, 1951–52).

17. On him see 'Ibn Sa'īd al-Maghribī' by Ch. Pellat in the *EI2*.

18. *Al-Nujūm al-zāhira fī ḥulā ḥaḍrat al-Qāhira, al-qism al-khāṣṣ bi'l-Qāhira min Kitāb al-Mughrib fī ḥulā al-Mahgrib*, ed. Ḥusayn Naṣṣār. Cairo, 1970.

19. Ed. Iḥsān 'Abbās (Beirut, 1968); English tr. M. de Slane (Paris, 1842–71).

20. *Al-Muntaqā min Akhbār Miṣr*, ed. Ayman Fu'ād Sayyid (Cairo, 1981).

21. Ibn al-'Adīm, *Zubdat al-ḥalab*, ed. Sāmī Dahān (Damascus, 1951–68), 3 vols. On him see 'Ibn al-'Adīm' by B. Lewis in the *EI2*.

22. *Mufarrij al-kurūb fī akhbār banī Ayyūb*, vols.1–3, ed. J. al-Shayyāl (Cairo, 1953–60).

23. Muḥyi'l-Dīn Abu'l-Fatḥ 'Abdallāh al-Rawḥī.

24. Cairo, 1996. It is likely that this version was not the final one. See Sayyid's introduction.

25. Ed. Muḥammad Muḥammad Amīn and Muḥammad Ḥilmī Muḥammad Aḥmad (Cairo, 1992).

26. Cairo, 1961.

27. See 'Ibn al-Furāt' by Cl. Cahen in the *EI2*.

28. *Raf' al-iṣr 'an quḍāt Miṣr. al-juz' al-awwal fī qismayn*, ed. by Ḥāmid 'Abd al-Majīd, et al. (Cairo, 1957–61).

29. Ibn Taghrī Birdī, *al-Nujūm al-zāhira fī mulūk Miṣr wa'l-Qāhira* (Cairo, 1929–49 and Cairo, 1963–71).

30. However Ayman Fu'ād Sayyid is currently preparing an edition of it.

31. Garcin, 'Al-Maqrîzî: un historien encyclopédique du monde afro-orientale'; Rosenthal, 'Al-Maḳrīzī, Taḳī al-Dīn Abū'l-'Abbās Aḥmad b. 'Alī b. 'Abd al-Ḳādir (766–845/1364–1442)'; Ayman Fu'ād Sayyid, 'Early Methods of Book Composition: al-Maqrīzī's Draft of the Kitāb al-Khiṭaṭ' in *The Codicology of Islamic Manuscripts, Proceedings of the Second Conference of Al-Furqān Islamic Heritage Foundation, 1993* (London, 1995), pp.93–101 and Sayyid, 'Remarques sur la composition des Ḫiṭaṭ de Maqrīzī d'après un manuscrit autographe', *Hommages à la mémoire de Serge Sauneron, II, Égypte post-pharaonique, IFAO* (1979), pp.231–58 + plates.

32. London, 1995.

33. Such as, for example, his *Ighāthat al-umma bi-kashf al-ghumma* ed. Muḥammad Muṣṭafā Ziyāda and J. al-Shayyāl (Cairo, 1957), French tr. G. Wiet 'Le Traité des famines de Maqrīzī', *JESHO*, 5 (1961), pp.1–90; English tr. A. Allouche, *Mamluk Economics: A Study and Translation of al-Maqrīzī's* Ighāthah (Salt Lake City, 1994).

34. Another work the *Durar al-'uqūd al-farīda fī tarājim al-a'yān al-mufīda* covered his contemporaries.

35. A. F. Sayyid reports that Leiden University has a *musawwada* version of the manuscript used by al-Ya'lāwī that he did not consult. In addition the same manuscript contains more biographies that appear to add to the entries previously available.

36. P.85.

37. *Musawwada*, p.94. See Sayyid's introduction, p.45.

38. On this see the material assembled by Sayyid, 'Introduction' pp.44–5.

39. This work is now lost.

40. The title of the *Itti'āẓ* apparently also changed. Originally, al-Maqrīzī thought to call it *Itti'āẓ al-ḥunafā' bi-akhbār al-khulafā'*. Later he added to it '*al-a'imma*' and then '*al-fāṭimiyyīn*' evidently to avoid ambiguity and, perhaps, to lessen the presumption implied in the term '*al-khulafā'*' or '*al-a'imma*' alone. On this and the appropriate citations, see al-Shayyāl's introduction to his edition of volume one (Cairo, 1967), pp.22–3.

41. There are 170 manuscript copies of the *Khiṭaṭ*.

42. Some students of Cl. Cahen tried to emend it and they published

a list of corrections separately (*Arabica*, 22, pp.302–20). Unfortunately, these corrections, which cover in any case only volume 2, are themselves not always 'correct.'

43. But it is equally important not to over-correct. It might be assumed, for example, that the wording of a passage in the *Khiṭaṭ* must be original and therefore more accurate, simply because it purports to be a quotation directly from the source. From other cases, however, we know better, or at least enough to tread cautiously. Of concern as well is the intention of al-Maqrīzī. Is he quoting or paraphrasing? If he paraphrases material, it might contain a hint as to how he understands what he reports. One may presume in many cases that he knew best what his source was trying to say. A quotation indicates only what the actual words convey but the paraphrase may reveal more, particularly about what al-Maqrīzī perceived as the implication of the material he reported.

Chaper 8: Literature and the Sciences

1. On Fatimid poetry in general see the following: Ḥusayn, *Fī adab Miṣr al-fāṭimiyya*, Muḥammad Yaʿlāwī, *al-Adab bi-Ifrīqiya fi'l-ʿahd al-fāṭimī* (Beirut, 1986), and the articles by Pieter Smoor listed in the bibliography below.

2. On this poet see al-Yaʿlāwī's *al-Adab bi-Ifrīqiya fi'l-ʿahd al-fāṭimī*, and his article 'al-Fazārī' in the *EI2, Supplement*.

3. On Ibn Hāni', see his *Dīwān* (Beirut, 1964), and the following by al-Yaʿlāwī, 'Ibn Hani, poète chiʿite et chantre des Fatimides au Maghreb', in Julien, ed., *Les Africains*, vol.6, pp.97–125, and *Un Poète chiite d'occident au IV/Xè siècle: Ibn Hani' al-Andalousi* (Tunis, 1976); Arabic translation of the same, *Ibn Hānī' al-Maghribī al-Andalusī shāʿir al-dawla al-fāṭimiyya* (Beirut, 1985). See also Canard, 'Ibn Hānī' al-Andalusī', *EI2*, and 'L'Impérialisme des Fatimides et leur propagande', in *Annales de l'Institut d'Études Orientales de la Faculté des Lettres d'Alger*, 6 (1942–47), pp.156–93; repr. in *Miscellanea Orientalia*, 2 (London, 1973).

4. *Dīwān Tamīm b. al-Muʿizz li-Dīn Allāh al-fāṭimī*, ed. M. H. Aʿẓamī, A. Y. Najātī, M. A. al-Najjār and M. Kāmil Ḥusayn (Cairo, 1957).

5. The only portion of it to survive in anything like its original state contains just such an account of poetry for the year 415. Al-Musabbiḥī, *al-Juz' al-arbaʿūn min Akhbār Miṣr*, part 2 (literary section); ed. Ḥusayn Naṣṣār (Cairo, 1984).

6. His *dīwān* was edited by Naṣr Allāh Taqavī et al. (Tehran, 1304–1307/1925–28), and ed. by M. Mīnuvī and M. Moḥaghegh (Tehran,

1974); partial English tr. P. L. Wilson and G. R. Aavani, *Forty Poems from the Divan* (Tehran, 1977), and Annemarie Schimmel, *Make a Shield from Wisdom* (London, 1993; repr. 2001).

7. *Dīwān al-Mu'ayyad fi'l-Dīn dā'ī al-du'āt*; ed. Muḥammad Kāmil Ḥusayn (Cairo, 1949).

8. For two additional examples of (minor) Ismaili poets not cited here, see Poonawala, *Biobibliography*, pp.92–3 (Ḥusayn b. 'Āmir from the reign of al-Ḥākim), p.109 (Ḥasan b. Maḥbūb from the reign of al-Mustanṣir).

9. Ibn Khallikān, vol.2, pp.89–91. See also Ibn Muyassar (ed. Sayyid, p.52) where the editor supplies several additional references.

10. See the comments of Ibn Khallikān, vol.2, pp.526–30 and 658–61; De Slane, vol.1, 658; Ḥusayn, *Fī adab Miṣr al-fāṭimiyya*, pp.228–38.

11. There are two editions of Ṭalā'i''s *dīwān*: *Dīwān al-wazīr Ṭalā'i' al-malik al-ṣāliḥ* by Aḥmad A. Badawaī (Cairo, 1958) and *Dīwān Ṭalā'i' ibn Ruzzīk*, by Muḥammad Hādī al-Amīnī (al-Najaf, 1964).

12. On his Nuṣayrī leanings see Dadoyan, *The Fatimid Armenians*, pp.154–78 and appendices.

13. On Umayya, who besides being a noted poet, wrote on astronomy, medicine, music and logic, see the article about him by Ibn Khallikān, vol.1, pp.243–7, de Slane, vol.1, pp.228–32. A small collection of his poetry – that now available – was published by Muḥammad al-Marzūqī, *Dīwān al-Ḥakīm Abi'l-Ṣalt Umayya b. 'Abd al-'Azīz al-Dānī* (Tunis, 1974).

14. The ten were Mas'ūd al-Dawla, Abū 'Alī Ḥasan b. Zubayr, al-Qāḍī Ibn al-Naḍar al-Adīb, al-Nājī al-Miṣrī, Sālim b. Mufarrij b. Abī Ḥusayma, Maḥmūd b. Nāṣir al-Iskandarānī, Marwān b. 'Uthmān al-Lukkī, Ibn al-Barqī, Ẓāfir al-Ḥaddād, and Umayya. See the list given by Ḥusayn, *Fī adab Miṣr al-fāṭimiyya*, p.212. On Ẓāfir al-Ḥaddād see Ḥusayn Naṣṣār, 'Ẓāfir al-Ḥaddād', *EI2* and *Ẓāfir al-Ḥaddād* (Cairo, 1975), and his *Dīwān*, ed. Ḥusayn Naṣṣār (Cairo, 1969).

15. Edited by Khalīl Maṭrān in *Jarīdat al-ahrām*. In general see Ḥusayn, *Fī adab Miṣr al-fāṭimiyya*, pp.258–62; and 'Ibn Ḳalāḳis' by U. Rizzitano in the *EI2*; Ibn Khallikān, vol.5, pp.385–.

16. Ed. by Gūrgīs 'Awwād(Baghdad), 1966.

17. He died in Fusṭāṭ about 388/988. On him, see 'al-Shābushtī' by C. E. Bosworth in the *EI2*; Ibn Khallikān, vol.3, pp.319–20, de Slane, vol.2, pp.262–3.

18. *Kitāb al-Bayzara*, author unknown, ed. Muḥammad Kurd 'Alī (Damascus, 1953); partial French tr. F. Viré, 'Le Traité de l'art de volerie (*kitāb al-bayzara*) rédigé vers 385/995 par le Grand-Fanconnier du calife

fāṭimide al-ʿAzīz bi-llāh', *Arabica*, 12 (1965), pp.1–26; pp.113–39; pp.262–96 and vol.13 (1966), pp.39–76, with index.

19. The *Mukhtār al-ḥikam* was edited by ʿA. Badawī (Madrid, 1958). On its author see the entry 'al-Mubashshir b. Fātik' by F. Rosenthal in the *EI2* and the references given there.

20. Al-Qalqashandī, *Ṣubḥ al-aʿshā fī ṣināʿat al-inshā'* (Cairo, 1912–1938).

21. Portions of the *Mawādd al-bayān* and the whole of the *Qānūn* are extant, the former published in fascimile and in an edition by Ḥusayn ʿAbd al-Laṭīf (Tripoli, 1982) and the latter in editions by, among others, Ayman Fu'ād Sayyid (Cairo, 1990); French tr. by Massé, 'Code de la chancellerie d'état', *BIFAO*, 11 (1914), pp.65–120. There are studies of the *Mawādd* by Bonebakker, 'A Fatimid Manual for Secretaries', pp.295–337, and Abdel Hamid Saleh, 'Une Source de Qalqašandī, Mawādd al-bayān et son auteur, ʿAlī b. Ḫalaf', *Arabica*, 20 (1973), pp.192–200.

22. Published in Cairo, 1961. English tr. Arthur Wormhoudt, *The Revelations of the Plagiarisms of al-Mutanabbi* (Oskaloosa, Iowa, 1974).

23. Al-Zajjājī, the author of the *Jumal*, was a famous grammarian (in Baghdad) from the first half of the 4th/10th century. He died in 338/949.

24. On him see M. Carter, 'Ṭāhir b. Aḥmad b. Bābashadh' in the *EI2* and references given there. Also the *Ittiʿāẓ*, vol. 2, p.318 (notice of his death).

25. On this work see Owen Wright, 'Music at the Fatimid Court: The Evidence of the Ibn al-Ṭaḥḥān Manuscript' in Barrucand, ed., *L'Égypte fatimide*, pp.537–45.

26. See Hanoch Avenary, 'Abu'l-Ṣalt's Treatise on Music', *Musica Disciplina*, 6 (1952), pp.27–32.

27. Published as *Omnia opera Ysaac* (Lyons, 1575).

28. On him see A. Altmann and S. M. Stern, *Isaac Israeli: A Neoplatonic Philosopher of the Early Tenth Century* (Oxford, 1958) and Altmann, 'Isḥāḳ b. Sulaymān al-Isrā'ilī' in the *EI2*.

29. See Michael Dols' introduction to his translation *Medieval Islamic Medicine*, pp.54–66.

30. Dols, *Medieval Islamic Medicine*, pp.67–9.

31. On Ibn Yūnus, see the articles in the *EI2* by B. Goldstein and in the *Dictionary of Scientific Biography* by David King as well as King's 'Aspects of Fatimid Astronomy from Hard-Core Mathematical Astronomy to Architectural Orientations in Cairo', in Barrucand, ed., *L'Égypte fatimide*, pp.497–517 (with a useful bibliography pp.515–17).

32. On this Ibn al-Haytham, who is not to be confused with the North

African Ismaili *dāʿī* of the same name, see the article on him in the *EI2* by J. Vernet; ʿAbd al-Ḥamīd Sabra, 'Ibn al-Haytham and the Visual-Ray Hypothesis', in S. H. Nasr, ed., *Ismāʿīlī Contributions to Islamic Culture* (Tehran, 1977) pp.189–205; Régis Morelon, 'Un Aspect de l'astronomie sous les Fatimides: l'importance d'Ibn al-Haytham dans l'histoire de l'astronomie arabe', in Barrucand, ed., *L'Égypte fatimide*, pp.519–26, and Roshdi Rashed, 'Ibn al-Haytham, mathématicien de l'époque fatimid', in Barrucand, ed., *L'Égypte fatimide*, pp.527–36 (and the works cited in the notes).

33. On this event see Walker, 'Fatimid Institutions of Learning', pp.179–200, and the references given there.

34. The Arabic text has been published many times beginning with a Bulaq edition in the nineteenth century (Alexandria, 1872). A more recent example is that of Muḥammad Fatḥī Abū Bakr (Cairo, 1994). Other editions: London, 1990 and Madrid, 1993.

35. Another date given is 525/1131. See A. Ben Abdesselem, 'al-Ṭurtūshī', in the *EI2*.

36. Al-Silafī took up residence in Alexandria in 511/1117. On him see Cl. Gilliot, 'al-Silafī', in the *EI2*. Al-Silafī composed a work called *al-Faḍā'il al-bāhira fī maḥāsin Miṣr wa'l-Qāhira* which could be of special interest given his attachment to Egypt in this period. Though unpublished, apparently there are MSS. of it in Istanbul and Cambridge.

37. Abū Ḥātim al-Rāzī, *Aʿlām al-nubuwwa*, ed. Salah al-Sawy and Gholam-Reza Aavani (Tehran, 1977); *Kitāb al-Zīna*. fasc. 1 and 2, ed. H. Hamdani (Cairo, 1957 and 1958), fasc. 3, ed. Abdallah Sallum al-Samarra'i in his *al-Ghuluww wa'l-firaq al-ghāliya fi'l-ḥaḍāra al-islāmiyya* (Baghdad, 1972), pp.228–312; and *Kitāb al-Iṣlāḥ*, ed. Ḥasan Mīnūchehr and Mehdī Moḥaghegh (Tehran, 1998).

38. On al-Sijistānī and the question of his support of the Fatimids, see Walker, *Early Philosophical Shiism*, pp.3–24.

39. On this Abū Tammām, see Walker, 'Abū Tammām and His *Kitāb al-shajara*: A New Ismaili Treatise from Tenth Century Khurasan', *JAOS*, 114 (1994) pp.343–52, and *An Ismaili Heresiography: The 'Bāb al-Shayṭān' from Abū Tammām's* Kitāb al-Shajara, critical edition of the Arabic text (with Wilferd Madelung) and English translation and introduction (Leiden, 1998).

40. On the *Īḍāḥ*, see in addition to Poonawala's *Biobibliography*, Madelung, 'The Sources of Ismaʿili Law', *JNES*, 35 (1976) pp.29–40.

41. See the list in Poonawala, *Biobibliography*, pp.78–9.

42. On him see Poonawala, *Biobibliography*, pp.91–2. The *Istitār al-imām*

was edited by W. Ivanow in *Bulletin of the Faculty of Arts, University of Egypt,* 4, part 2 (1936) pp.93–107; English tr. by Ivanow in his *Ismaili Tradition Concerning the Rise of the Fatimids,* pp.157–83.

43. On him see Poonawala, *Biobibliography,* p.99. His treatise, *al-Risāla fi'l-imāma,* was edited and tr. by S. Makarem in *The Political Doctrine of the Ismailis* (Delmar, NY, 1977).

44. On al-Kirmānī see Daniel De Smet, *La Quiétude de l'Intellect: Néoplatonisme et gnose ismaélienne dans l'oeuvre de Ḥamîd ad-Dîn al-Kirmânî (Xe/XIe s.)* (Louvain, 1995), and Walker, *Ḥamīd al-Dīn al-Kirmānī.*

45. D. S. Margoliouth, 'al-Maʿarrī's Correspondence on Vegetarianism', *JRAS* (1902), pp.289–332.

46. This treatise is *Fi'l-radd ʿalā man ankara [yunkiru] al-ʿālam al-rūḥānī,* in *Majmūʿat rasā'il al-Kirmānī,* ed. M. Ghālib (Beirut, 1983).

47. On these two see Poonawala, *Biobibliography,* pp.128 and 129.

Chapter 9: Modern Studies

1. On this document see first Husayn F. Hamdani, *On the Genealogy of Fatimid Caliphs* (Cairo, 1958) and then Hamdani and de Blois, 'A Re-examination of Al-Mahdī's Letter to the Yemenites on the Genealogy of the Fatimid Caliphs', pp.173–207.

2. As an example of new information, see Ibn al-Haytham's account of the divisions of the Shiʿa after Jaʿfar al-Ṣādiq now available in his *Kitāb al-Munāẓarāt* (*Advent of the Fatimids*) text pp.35–7, translation pp.90–2.

3. The original text of this work was later published; see Ismāʿīl b. 'Abd al-Rasūl al-Majdūʿ, *Fahrasat al-kutub wa'l-rasā'il,* ed. 'Alī Naqī Munzavi' (Tehran, 1966).

4. Fortunately, Poonawala is preparing a now badly needed second edition.

5. It is true, however, that the Ṭayyibīs tend to refer to themselves by the term 'Fāṭimī' (i.e. Fatimid).

6. For Egypt the work of Max van Berchem and especially Gaston Wiet his successor in the recording of Arabic inscriptions deserve special mention. Wiet, moreover, made important contributions to several areas other than inscriptions.

7. For a complete list of Canard's writings see 'Marius Canard (1888–1982): A Bio-Bibliographical Notice' by Farhad Daftary in *Arabica,* 33 (1986), pp.251–62.

8. See, for example, his *Makhzūmiyyāt. Études sur l'histoire économique et financière de l'Égypte médiévale* (Leiden, 1977).

9. *Al-Muʿizz li-Dīn Allāh al-fāṭimī: muʾassis al-dawla al-fāṭimiyya fī Miṣr* (Cairo, 1948; Cairo, 1963), and *ʿUbaydallāh al-Mahdī: Imām al-Shīʿa al-ismāʿīliyya wa muʾassis al-dawla al-fāṭimiyya fī bilād al-Maghrib* (Cairo, 1947).

10. 2nd edition ['muzayyada wa munaqqaha jiddan'] (Cairo, 1973 vol.1, 1978 vol.2).

11. This may be an appropriate place to recognise the prolific contributions of the late Syrian Ismaili (Muʾminī, also called Jaʿfarī) writer ʿĀrif Tāmir (Aref Tamer). A complete list of his many books, all in Arabic, is not easily compiled; WorldCat, a prime bibliographical clearing-house, has 105 entries under his name. Even if many are duplicates under slight variations caused by differences in the transcription of titles, and many others seem to be versions of the same or similar work issued by the author himself under different titles, the number remains large indeed. For the Fatimids as such, Tāmir has individual works on each of the first ten caliphs (al-Mahdī through al-Āmir), plus the Qarmatians and the Ṣulayḥid queen Arwa. Unfortunately no single library is likely to acquire more than a few of these, let alone each and every possible variation of them. Thus given that Tāmir's scholarship is often careless and inaccurate, a thorough investigation of all his writings may not be worth the effort.

12. Notably his *Taʾrīkh Fāṭimiyyīn Miṣr* [Urdu] (Hyderabad, 1948) but also his edition of the *Dīwān* of Ibn Hāniʾ (Cairo, 1933).

13. The author of the present work aspires to be included here. For Walker's contributions consult the Bibliography of Modern Studies.

Bibliography I: Medieval Sources

Abu'l-ʿArab, Muḥammad b. Aḥmad b. Tamīm al-Tamīmī. *Kitāb al-Miḥan*, ed. Yaḥyā Wahīb al-Jubūrī. 2nd ed., Beirut, 1988.

——*Kitāb Ṭabaqāt ʿulamāʾ Ifrīqiya*, ed. Mohammed Ben Cheneb in *Classes des savants de l'Ifrīqiya*. Paris, 1915. French tr., Ben Cheneb. Algiers, 1920.

Abu'l-Fawāris. *al-Risāla fi'l-imāma*, ed. and tr. S. Makarem as *The Political Doctrine of the Ismailis*. Delmar, NY, 1977.

Abu'l-Makārim Saʿdallāh Jirjis b. Masʿūd. *Taʾrīkh al-kanāʾis wa'l-adyira*, ed. and tr. B. T. A. Evetts. Oxford, 1895; new ed., Cairo, 1984.

Abū Ṣāliḥ the Armenian, see Abu'l-Makārim Saʿdallāh Jirjis b. Masʿūd.

Abu'l-Ṣalt, see Umayya.

Abū Shāma, Shihāb al-Dīn ʿAbd al-Raḥmān. *Kitāb al-Rawḍatayn fī akhbār al-dawlatayn, al-nūriyya wa'l-ṣalāḥiyya*, ed. Muḥammad Ḥilmī Muḥammad Aḥmad. Cairo, 1956; another ed., Cairo, 1871.

Abū Tammām. *An Ismaili Heresiography: The 'Bāb al-Shayṭān' from Abū Tammām's* Kitāb al-shajara. Ed. and English tr. Wilferd Madelung and Paul E. Walker. Leiden, 1998.

al-ʿAmīdī, Abū Saʿīd Muḥammad. *al-Ibāna ʿan sariqāt al-Mutannabī*. Cairo, 1961. English tr. Arthur Wormhoudt, *The Revelations of the Plagiarisms of al-Mutanabbi*. Oskaloosa, Iowa, 1974.

al-Āmir, see *al-Hidāya* and *Īqāʿ ṣawāʿiq*.

al-Bakrī, Abū ʿUbayd. *al-Masālik wa'l-mamālik*, ed. W. M. de Slane. Algiers, 1857.

Bayzara, see *Kitāb al-Bayzara*.

Benjamin of Tudela. *The Itinerary of Benjamin of Tudela*, English tr. n.p., 1983.

al-Dabbāgh, Abū Zayd. *Maʿālim al-īmān.* See Ibn Nājī.

al-Dhahabī, Muḥammad. *Taʾrīkh al-Islām,* ed. ʿA. Tadmurī. Beirut, 1987–1994.

Kitāb al-Dhakhāʾir wa'l-tuḥaf, ed. Muḥammad Ḥamīd Allāh. Kuwait, 1950. English tr. Ghāda al-Ḥijjāwī al-Qaddūmī, *Book of Gifts and Rarities (Kitāb al-Hadāyā wa'l-Tuḥaf).* Cambridge, MA, 1996.

al-Hidāya al-Āmiriyya, ed. A. A. A. Fyzee. London, etc., 1938.

Ibn ʿAbd al-Ẓāhir. *al-Rawḍa al-bahiyya al-zāhira fī khiṭaṭ al-muʿizziyya al-Qāhira,* ed. Ayman Fu'ād Sayyid. Cairo, 1996.

Ibn Abi'l-Ṣalt, see Umayya.

Ibn Abī Uṣaybiʿa. *ʿUyūn al-anbāʾ fī ṭabaqāt al-aṭibbāʾ.* Beirut, 1965.

Ibn al-ʿAdīm. *Zubdat al-ḥalab min taʾrīkh al-Ḥalab,* ed. Sāmī Dahān. Damascus, 1951–1968, 3 vols; ed. Suḥayl Zakkār. Damascus, 1997, 2 vols.

Ibn al-Athīr, ʿIzz al-Dīn Abu'l-Ḥasan ʿAlī. *al-Kāmil fi'l-taʾrīkh,* ed. C. J. Tornberg. Leiden, 1867; repr. Beirut, 1965–1967.

Ibn Bassām, Muḥammad b. Aḥmad. *Kitāb Anīs fī akhbār Tinnīs,* ed. J. al-Shayyāl in *Majallat al-majmaʿ al-ʿilm al-ʿirāqī,* 14 (1967), pp.151–89.

——*Nihāyat al-ruṭba fī ṭalab al-ḥisba,* ed. Ḥ. al-Dīn al-Samarraie. Baghdad, 1968.

Ibn Buṭlān. *al-Rasāʾil.* Arabic text and tr. Joseph Schacht and Max Meyerhof in *The Medico-Philosophical Controversy Between Ibn Butlan of Baghdad and Ibn Ridwan of Cairo.* Cairo, 1937.

Ibn al-Dawādārī, Abū Bakr b. ʿAbdallāh b. Aybak. *Kanz al-durar wa jāmiʿ al-ghurar,* part 6, *al-Durra al-muḍiyya fī akhbār al-dawla al-fāṭimiyya,* ed. S. al-Munajjid. Cairo, 1961.

Ibn Duqmāq, Ibrāhīm b. Muḥammad. *Kitāb al-Intiṣār li-wāsiṭat ʿiqd al-amṣār.* Cairo, 1894.

Ibn al-Ḥabbāl, Abū Isḥāq Ibrāhīm. *Wafāyat al-miṣriyyīn fī ʿahd al-fāṭimī,* ed. S. al-Munajjid in *Revue de l'Institut des Manuscrits Arabes,* 2 (1956), pp.286–338.

Ibn Ḥajar al-ʿAsqalānī. *Rafʿ al-iṣr ʿan quḍāt Miṣr. al-juzʾ al-awwal fī qismayn,* ed. Ḥāmid ʿAbd al-Majīd, et al. Cairo, 1957–1961. Ms. Istanbul.

Ibn Ḥammād, Abū ʿAbdallāh Muḥammad b. ʿAlī al-Ṣanhājī (also Ibn Ḥamādu). *Histoire des rois ʿobaïdides (Akhbār mulūk banī ʿUbayd wa sīratihum),* ed. and tr. M. Vonderheyden. Algiers and Paris, 1927; ed. ʿAbd al-Ḥalīm ʿUways, Cairo, 1980 [?].

Ibn Hāniʾ al-Andalusī. *Dīwān,* ed. Zāhid ʿAlī. Cairo, 1933; another ed., Beirut, 1964.

Ibn Ḥawqal, Abu'l-Qāsim b. ʿAlī. *Kitāb Ṣūrat al-arḍ,* ed. J. H. Kramers.

Leiden, 1938; French tr. J. H. Kramers and G. Wiet as *Configuration de la terre.* Beirut and Paris, 1964.

Ibn al-Haytham, Abū ʿAbdallāh Jaʿfar. *Kitāb al-Munāẓarāt,* ed. and tr. W. Madelung and P. E. Walker in *The Advent of the Fatimids.* London, 2000.

Ibn ʿIdhārī, Abu'l-ʿAbbās Aḥmad b. Muḥammad al-Marrākushī. *al-Bayān al-mughrib fī akhbār al-Andalus wa'l-Maghrib.* Vol. 1, ed. G. S. Colin and É. Lévi-Provençal. Leiden, 1948.

Ibn Iyās, Muḥammad. *Badā'iʿ al-ẓuhūr fī waqā'iʿ al-duhūr.* Bulaq, 1894.

Ibn al-Jawzī, Abu'l-Faraj ʿAbd al-Raḥmān. *al-Muntaẓam fī ta'rīkh al-mulūk wa'l-umam.* Hyderabad, 1939.

Ibn Khalaf, ʿAlī. *Mawādd al-bayān,* published in fascimile. Frankfurt, 1986; ed. Ḥusayn ʿAbd al-Laṭīf. Tripoli, Libya, 1982.

Ibn Khaldūn. *Kitāb al-ʿIbar wa dīwān al-mubtadā' wa'l-khabar fī ayyām al-ʿarab wa'l-ʿajam wa'l-barbar wa man ʿāṣarahum min dhawi'l-sulṭān al-akbar.* Beirut, 1961. Tr. W. M. de Slane, *Histoire des Berbères et des dynasties musulmanes d'Afrique septentrionale.* Algiers, 1847–1851; Paris, 1978.

Ibn Khallikān, Aḥmad b. Muḥammad. *Wafayāt al-aʿyān,* ed. Iḥsān ʿAbbās. Beirut, 1968. English tr. M. de Slane, *Ibn Khallikān's Biographical Dictionary.* Paris, 1842–1871, 4 vols.

Ibn al-Khaṭīb, Lisān al-Dīn. *Ta'rīkh isbāniyya al-islāmiyya, aw Kitāb Aʿmāl al-aʿlām,* ed. É. Lévi-Provençal. Beirut, 1956.

Ibn Mammātī, Asʿad. *Kitāb Qawānīn al-dawāwīn,* ed. A. S. Atiya. Cairo, 1943. English tr. Richard S. Cooper, *Ibn Mammātī's Rules for the Ministries.* Ph.D. dissertation, University of California, Berkeley, CA, 1973.

Ibn al-Ma'mūn, Jamāl al-Dīn Abū ʿAlī Mūsā. *Nuṣūṣ min Akhbār Miṣr,* ed. Ayman Fu'ād Sayyid. Cairo, 1983.

Ibn Munqidh, Usāma. *Kitāb al-Iʿtibār,* ed. Ph. Hitti. Princeton, NJ, 1930. English tr. Ph. Hitti, *Memoirs of an Arab-Syrian Gentlemen.* New York, 1927; repr. Beirut, 1964.

Ibn Muyassar, Tāj al-Dīn Muḥammad. *al-Muntaqā min Akhbār Miṣr,* ed. Ayman Fu'ād Sayyid. Cairo, 1981.

Ibn Nājī, Abu'l-Qāsim. *Maʿālim al-īmān fī maʿrifat ahl Qayrawān,* ed. Ibrāhīm Shabbūḥ et al. Cairo, 1968–1978.

Ibn Qāḍī Shuhba. *al-Kawākib al-durriyya fi'l-sīra al-nūriyya.* Beirut, 1971.

Ibn al-Qalānisī, Abū Yaʿlā Ḥamza. *Dhayl ta'rīkh Dimashq,* ed. H. F. Amedroz. Leiden and Beirut, 1908; partial English tr. H. A. R. Gibb, *The Damascus Chronicle of the Crusades.* London, 1932.

Ibn al-Qifṭī, Jamāl al-Dīn ʿAlī b. Yūsuf. *Taʾrīkh al-ḥukamāʾ*, ed. J. Lippert. Leipzig, 1903.

Ibn Riḍwān. *al-Rasāʾil*, Arabic text and tr. Joseph Schacht and Max Meyerhof in *The Medico-Philosophical Controversy between Ibn Butlan of Baghdad and Ibn Ridwan of Cairo*. Cairo, 1937.

——*Kitāb Dafʿ muḍarr al-abdān fī Miṣr*, ed. Adil S. Gamal, with English tr. Michael W. Dols in *Medieval Islamic Medicine*. Berkeley, CA, 1984.

Ibn Ruzzīk, Ṭalāʾiʿ. *Dīwān al-wazīr Ṭalāʾiʿ al-Malik al-Ṣāliḥ*, ed. Aḥmad A. Badawī. Cairo, 1958. *Dīwān Ṭalāʾiʿ Ibn Ruzzīk*, ed. Muḥammad Hādī al-Amīnī. al-Najaf, 1964.

Ibn Saʿīd, ʿAlī b. Mūsā al-Maghribī. *al-Nujūm al-zāhira fī ḥulā ḥaḍrat al-Qāhira, al-qism al-khāṣṣ bi'l-Qāhira min Kitāb al-Mughrib fī ḥulā al-Maghrib*, ed. Ḥusayn Naṣṣār. Cairo, 1970.

Ibn al-Ṣayrafī, Abu'l-Qāsim ʿAlī. *al-Ishāra ilā man nāla al-wizāra*, ed. ʿA. Mukhliṣ. Cairo, 1924; ed. Ayman Fuʾād Sayyid. Cairo, 1990.

——*al-Qānūn dīwān al-rasāʾil*, ed. ʿAlī Bahjat, Cairo, 1905; ed. Ayman Fuʾād Sayyid. Cairo, 1990. French tr. Massé, 'Code de la chancellerie d'état', *BIFAO*, 11 (1914), pp.65–120.

Ibn Shaddād, Bahāʾ al-Dīn Yūsuf. *al-Nawādir al-sulṭāniyya wa'l-maḥāsin al-yūsufiyya*, ed. J. al-Shayyāl. Cairo, 1964.

Ibn Taghrī Birdī, Jamāl al-Dīn Abu'l-Maḥāsin Yūsuf. *al-Nujūm al-zāhira fī mulūk Miṣr wa'l-Qāhira*. Cairo, 1929–1949; Cairo, 1963–1971.

Ibn al-Ṭuwayr, Abū Muḥammad ʿAbd al-Salām. *Nuzhat al-muqlatayn fī akhbār al-dawlatayn*, ed. Ayman Fuʾād Sayyid. Beirut, 1992.

Ibn Wāṣil, Jamāl al-Dīn Muḥammad. *Mufarrij al-kurūb fī akhbār banī Ayyūb*. Vols.1–3, ed. J. al-Shayyāl. Cairo, 1953–1960.

Ibn Ẓāfir, Jamāl al-Dīn ʿAlī. *Akhbār al-duwal al-munqaṭiʿa*, ed. André Ferré. Cairo, 1972.

Ibn Zūlāq, Abū Muḥammad al-Ḥasan. *Akhbār Sībawayh al-miṣrī*, ed. Muḥammad Ibrāhīm Saʿd and Ḥusayn al-Dīb. Cairo, 1933.

Idrīs ʿImād al-Dīn. *ʿUyūn al-akhbār*, ed. M. al-Yaʿlāwī as *Taʾrīkh al-khulafāʾ al-fāṭimiyyīn bi'l-Maghrib: al-qism al-khāṣṣ min Kitāb ʿUyūn al-akhbār*. Beirut, 1985.

——*ʿUyūn al-akhbār, al-sabʿ al-sādis*, ed. Muṣṭafā Ghālib. Beirut, 1984.

Īqāʿ ṣawāʿiq al-irghām, ed. A. A. A. Fyzee as an appendix to *al-Hidāya al-āmiriyya*. London, etc., 1938.

al-Iṣfahānī, ʿImād al-Dīn Abū Ḥāmid. *al-Bustān al-jāmiʿ li-jamīʿ tawārīkh ahl al-zamān*, ed. Cl. Cahen, 'Une Chronique syrienne du VIe/XIIe siècle', *BEO*, 7–8 (1837–1838), pp.113–58.

al-Iṣfahānī, al-ʿImād al-Kātib. *Kharīdat al-qaṣr wa jarīdat al-ʿaṣr*. Baghdad, 1955.

ʿIyāḍ b. Mūsā, al-Qāḍī Abu'l-Faḍl. *Tartīb al-madārik wa taqrīb al-masālik li-maʿrifat aʿlām madhhab Malik*, ed. Aḥmad Bakrī Maḥmūd. Beirut, 1968.

——*Tarājim aghlabiyya mustakhraja min Madārik al-Qāḍī ʿIyāḍ*, ed. Muḥammad al-Ṭālibī. Tunis, 1968.

Jaʿfar al-Ḥājib. see al-Yamanī, Muḥammad.

al-Jawdharī, Abū ʿAlī al-Manṣūr. *Sīrat Ustādh Jawdhar*, ed. M. Kāmil Ḥusayn and M. ʿAbd al-Hādī Shaʿīra, Cairo, 1954; French tr. M. Canard, *Vie de l'ustadh Jaudhar*. Algiers, 1958.

al-Karājikī. *Kanz al-fawā'id*. Beirut, 1985.

al-Khushanī, Muḥammad b. al-Ḥārith b. Asad. *Kitāb Ṭabaqāt ʿulamā' Ifrīqiya* in *Classes des savants de l'Ifrīqiya*, ed. Mohammed Ben Cheneb, Paris, 1915; French tr. Ben Cheneb, Algiers, 1920.

al-Kindī. *Kitāb al-Wulāt wa kitāb al-quḍāt*, ed. R. Guest. Leiden, 1912.

al-Kirmānī, Ḥamīd al-Dīn. *Majmūʿat rasā'il al-Kirmānī*, ed. M. Ghālib. Beirut, 1983.

——*Kitāb Rāḥat al-ʿaql*, ed. M. Kāmil Ḥusayn and M. Ḥilmī. Cairo, 1953.

Kitāb al-Bayzara, ed. Muḥammad Kurd ʿAlī. Damascus, 1953; partial French tr. F. Viré, 'Le Traité de l'art de volerie (*kitāb al-bayzara*) rédigé vers 385/995 par le Grand-Falconnier du calife fāṭimide al-ʿAziz billāh', *Arabica*, 12 (1965), pp.1–26; pp.113–39; pp.262–96 and vol.13 (1966), pp.39–76, with index.

al-Majdūʿ, Ismāʿīl b. ʿAbd al-Rasūl. *Fahrasat al-kutub wa'l-rasā'il*, ed. ʿAlī Naqī Munzavī. Tehran, 1966.

al-Makhzūmī. *al-Muntaqā min Kitāb al-Minhāj fī ʿilm kharāj Miṣr*, ed. Claude Cahen and Y. Raghib. Cairo, 1986.

al-Malījī, Abu'l-Qāsim ʿAbd al-Wahb. *al-Majālis al-mustanṣiriyya*, ed. M. Kāmil Ḥusayn. Cairo, n.d. [1947].

al-Mālikī, Abū Bakr. *Kitāb Riyāḍ al-nufūs fī ṭabaqāt ʿulamā' al-Qayrawān wa Ifrīqiya*, ed. Bashīr al-Bakkūsh. Beirut, 1981–1983.

al-Maqrīzī, Tāqī al-Dīn Abu'l-ʿAbbās Aḥmad. *Ighāthat al-umma bi-kashf al-ghumma*, ed. Muḥammad Muṣṭafā Ziyāda and J. al-Shayyāl. Cairo, 1957. French tr. G. Wiet 'Le Traité des famines de Maqrīzī,' *JESHO*, 5 (1961), pp.1–90; English tr. A. Allouche, *Mamlūk Economics: A Study and Translation of al-Maqrīzī's* Ighāthah. Salt Lake City, 1994.

——*Ittiʿāẓ al-ḥunafā' bi-akhbār al-a'imma al-fāṭimiyyīn al-khulafā'*. Vol.1, ed. Jamāl al-Dīn al-Shayyāl, and vols.2–3, ed. Muḥammad Ḥilmī Muḥammad Aḥmad. Cairo, 1967–1973.

——*al-Khiṭaṭ* (*al-maʿrūf bi'l-mawāʿiẓ wa'l-iʿtibār bi'dhikr al-khiṭaṭ wa'l-āthār*), ed. of *musawwada*, Ayman Fu'ād Sayyid. London, 1995. Final complete text, Bulaq, 1853. French tr. of vol.1, pp.2–250, U. Bouriant, 'Description topographique et historique de l'Égypte', *Mémoires publiés par les membres de la Mission Archéologique Française au Caire*, 17 (1895–1900), vols.2–3, pp.250–397 by P. Casanova, 'Description historique et topographique de l'Égypte', *MIFAO*, 3 (1906) and 4 (1920).

——*Kitāb al-Muqaffā al-kabīr*, ed. M. al-Yaʿlāwī. Beirut, 1991.

al-Mu'ayyad fi'l-Dīn al-Shīrāzī, Abū Naṣr. *Dīwān al-Mu'ayyad fi'l-Dīn dāʿī al-duʿāt, ed.* M. Kāmil Ḥusayn. Cairo, 1949.

——*Sīrat al-Mu'ayyad fi'l-Dīn dāʿī al-duʿāt*, ed. M. Kāmil Ḥusayn. Cairo, 1949.

al-Mubashshir b. Fātik. *Mukhtār al-ḥikam wa maḥāsin al-kalim*, ed. 'Abd al-Raḥmān Badawī. Madrid, 1958.

al-Muqaddasī, Shams al-Dīn Abū 'Abdallāh Muḥammad. *Kitāb Aḥsan al-taqāsīm fī maʿrifat al-aqālīm*, ed. M. J. de Goeje. 2nd ed., Leiden, 1906.

al-Musabbiḥī, al-Mukhtār 'Izz al-Mulk Muḥammad. *al-Juz' al-arbaʿūn min Akhbār Miṣr.* Part 1 (historical section), ed. Ayman Fu'ād Sayyid and Th. Bianquis, Cairo, 1978; Part 2 (literary section), ed. Ḥusayn Naṣṣār, Cairo, 1984.

al-Mustanṣir bi'llāh, Abū Tamīm Maʿadd. *al-Sijillāt al-mustanṣiriyya*, ed. 'Abd al-Munʿim Mājid. Cairo, 1954.

Nāṣir-i Khusraw. *Dīwān*, ed. Naṣr Allāh Taqavī, et al. Tehran, 1304–1307/1925–1928); ed. M. Mīnuvī and M. Moḥaghegh, Tehran, 1353/1974. Partial English tr. P. L. Wilson and G. R. Aavani, *Forty Poems from the Divan*, Tehran, 1977 and Annemarie Schimmel, *Make a Shield from Wisdom.* London, 1993.

——*Safarnāma*, ed. with French tr. Charles Schefer, *Sefer nameh: relation du voyage de Nassiri Khosrau*, Paris, 1881. English tr. W. M. Thackston Jr., *Nāṣer-e Khosraw's Book of Travels.* Albany, NY, 1986.

al-Naysābūrī, Aḥmad b. Ibrāhīm. *Istitār al-imām*, ed. W. Ivanow in *Bulletin of the Faculty of Arts, University of Egypt*, vol.4, part 2 (1936), pp.93–107. English tr. Ivanow in his *Ismaili Tradition Concerning the Rise of the Fatimids*, pp.157–83.

al-Nuwayrī, Shihāb al-Dīn Aḥmad. *Nihāyat al-arab fī funūn al-adab: al-juz' al-thāmin wa'l-ʿishrūn*, ed. Muḥammad Muḥammad Amīn and Muḥammad Ḥilmī Muḥammad Aḥmad. Cairo, 1992.

Qāḍī al-Nuʿmān, Abū Ḥanīfa Muḥammad. *Daʿā'im al-Islām*, ed. A. A. A. Fyzee. Cairo, 1951–1961.

——*Iftitāḥ al-daʿwa wa ibtidāʾ al-dawla*, ed. Wadad Kadi. Beirut, 1970; ed. Farhat Dachraoui. Tunis, 1975. (Note that, for convenience, the citations given in this book refer only to the edition of Dachraoui).

——*Kitāb al-Himma fī ādāb atbāʿ al-aʾimma*, ed. M. Kāmil Ḥusayn. Cairo, 1948.

——*Kitāb al-Majālis wa'l-musāyarāt*, ed. al-Ḥabīb al-Faqī, Ibrāhīm Shabbūḥ, and Muḥammad al-Yaʿlāwī. Tunis, 1978.

——*Sharḥ al-akhbār fī faḍāʾil al-aʾimma al-aṭhār.* Beirut, 1994.

al-Qalqashandī, Shihāb al-Dīn Aḥmad. *Ṣubḥ al-aʿshā fī ṣināʿat al-inshāʾ*. Cairo, 1912–1938.

al-Rāzī, Abū Ḥātim. *Aʿlām al-nubuwwa*, ed. Salah al-Sawy and Gholam-Reza Aavani. Tehran, 1977.

——*Kitāb al-Zīna.* Fasc. 1 and 2 ed. H. Hamdani. Cairo, 1957 and 1958, Fasc. 3, ed. ʿAbdallah Sallum al-Samārrāʾī in his *al-Ghuluww wa'l-firaq al-ghāliya fi'l-ḥaḍāra al-islāmiyya.* Baghdad, 1972, pp.228–312.

——*Kitāb al-Iṣlāḥ*, ed. Ḥasan Mīnūchehr and Mehdī Moḥaghegh. Tehran, 1998.

al-Sakhāwī, Shams al-Dīn Abu'l-Khayr Muḥammad. *al-Ḍawʾ al-lāmiʿ li-ahl al-qarn al-tāsiʿ*, ed. Ḥusām al-Dīn al-Qudrī. Cairo, 1934–1936.

——*Kitāb al-Tibr al-masbūk fī dhayl al-sulūk.* Cairo, 1972.

al-Shayzarī, ʿAbd al-Raḥmān b. Naṣr. *Nihāyat al-rutba fī ṭalab al-ḥisba*, ed. al-Sayyid al-Bāz al-ʿArīnī. Cairo, 1946; English tr. R. P. Buckley, *The Book of the Islamic Market Inspector.* Oxford, 1999.

Sibṭ b. al-Jawzī. *Mirʾat al-zamān fī taʾrīkh al-aʿyān.* Years 345–447, ed. J. J. M. al-Hamawundī. Baghdad, 1990. *al-Ḥawādith al-khāṣṣa bi-taʾrīkh al-Salājiqa bayna al-sanawāt 1056 – 1086*, ed. Ali Sevim. Ankara, 1968 (also in *Belgeler: Türk Tarik Belgeri Dergisi*, 14 [1989–1992], pp.1–260). Years 495–654, facsimile ed. J. R. Jewett. Chicago, 1907; printed ed. Hyderabad, 1951–1952.

al-Sijillāt al-mustanṣiriyya, ed. ʿAbd al-Munʿim Mājid. Cairo, 1954.

al-Subkī, Tāj al-Dīn. *Ṭabaqāt al-shāfiʿiyya al-kubrā.* Cairo, 1964– . Beirut, 1999.

al-Suyūtī, Jalāl al-Dīn. *Ḥusn al-muḥāḍara fī akhbār Miṣr wa'l-Qāhira.* Beirut, 1997.

Tamīm b. al-Muʿizz. *Dīwān Tamīm b. al-Muʿizz li-Dīn Allāh al-fāṭimī*, ed. M. Ḥ. al-Aʿẓamī et al. Cairo, 1957.

Taʾrīkh baṭārikat al-kanīsa al-miṣriyya (*History of the Patriarchs of the Coptic Church of Alexandria*, also *Siyar al-bayʿa al-muqaddasa*), ed. Y. ʿAbd al-Masīḥ, A. S. ʿAṭiya, Uswald Burmester and A. Khāṭir. Cairo, 1959–1968.

al-Turtūshī, Abū Bakr Muḥammad b. al-Walīd. *Sirāj al-mulūk*, ed. Muḥammad Fatḥī Abū Bakr. Cairo, 1994; other editions: Alexandria, 1872; London, 1990; Madrid, 1993.

ʿUmāra al-Yamanī, Najm al-Dīn Abū Muḥammad. *ʿOumâra du Yémen: Sa vie et son oeuvre* (*al-Nukat al-ʿaṣriyya fī akhbār al-wuzarāʾ al-miṣriyya, qaṣāʾid min shiʿrihi, wa maqāṭiʿ min nathrihi*), ed. Hartwig Derenbourg. Paris, 1897.

——*Taʾrīkh al-Yaman*, ed. Muḥammad b. ʿAlī al-Akwaʿ. Cairo, 1967.

Umayya b. ʿAbd al-ʿAzīz, Abu'l-Ṣalt al-Dānī. *al-Risāla al-miṣriyya*, ed. ʿAbd al-Salām Hārūn in *Nawādir al-makhṭūṭāt*, vol.1 (Cairo, 1972), pp.5–56.

——*Dīwān*. Collected and ed. Muḥammad al-Marzūqī. Tunis, 1974.

William of Tyre. *A History of Deeds done beyond the Sea*, tr. E. A. Babcock and A. C. Krey. New York, 1943.

Yaḥyā b. Saʿīd al-Anṭākī. *Taʾrīkh*, ed. I. Kratchkovsky with French tr. A. Vasiliev, in *Patrologica Orientalia* 18 (1924), pp.699–833 and 23 (1932), pp.347–520; part 3, ed. Kratchkowsky, French tr. F. Micheau and G. Troupeau, in *Patrologica Orientalia*, 47 (1997), pp.373–559, ed. ʿUmar ʿAbd al-Salām Tadmūrī. Tripoli, Lebanon, 1990.

al-Yamanī, Muḥammad. *Sīrat Jaʿfar al-Ḥājib*, ed. W. Ivanow, in *Bulletin of the Faculty of Arts, University of Egypt*, 4, Part 2 (1936), pp.107–33; English tr. Ivanow in his *Ismaili Tradition Concerning the Rise of the Fatimids*, pp.184–223; French tr. M. Canard, 'L'Autobiographie d'un chambellan du Mahdî ʿObeidallâh le Fâṭimide', *Hespéris*, 39 (1952), pp.279–330; repr. in M. Canard, *Miscellanea Orientalia*. London, 1973, no.5.

Yāqūt b. ʿAbdallāh al-Ḥamawī. *Muʿjam al-udabāʾ*. Beirut, 1993.

Ẓāfir al-Ḥaddād. *Dīwān*, ed. Ḥusayn Nassār. Cairo, 1969.

Bibliography II: Modern Studies

Abu-Izzeddin, Nejla M. *The Druzes: A New Study of Their History, Faith and Society*. Leiden, 1984.

Abu-Lughod, Janet. *Cairo: 1001 Years of the City Victorious*. Princeton, NJ, 1971.

'Alī, Zāhid. *Ta'rīkh Fāṭimiyyīn Miṣr* (Urdu). Hyderabad, 1948.

Al-Imad, Leila S. *The Fatimid Vizierate, 969–1172*. Berlin, 1990.

Allouche, Adel. *Mamlūk Economics: A Study and Translation of al-Maqrīzī's* Ighāthah. Salt Lake City, 1994.

——'The Establishment of Four Chief Judgeships in Fatimid Egypt', *JAOS*, 105 (1985), pp.317–20.

Altmann, A., and S. M. Stern. *Isaac Israeli: A Neoplatonic Philosopher of the Early Tenth Century*. Oxford, 1958.

Amari, Michele, *Storia dei musulmani di Sicilia* (*al-Maktaba al-ʿarabiyya al-ṣiqilliyya: nuṣūṣ fi'l-ta'rīkh wa'l-buldān wa'l-tarājim wa'l-marājiʿ*). Leipzig, 1857.

Assaad, Sadik A. *The Reign of al-Hakim bi Amr Allah (386/996–411/1021): A Political Study*. Beirut, 1974.

Avenary, Hanoch. 'Abu'l-Ṣalt's Treatise on Music', *Musica Disciplina*, 6 (1952), pp.27–32.

Ayalon, David. 'On the Eunuchs in Islam', *Jerusalem Studies in Arabic and Islam*, 1 (1979), pp.67–124.

Bacharach, Jere L. 'African Military Slaves in the Medieval Middle East: The Cases of Iraq (869–955) and Egypt (868–1171)', *IJMES*, 13 (1981), pp.471–95.

Balard, Michel. 'Notes sur le commerce entre l'Italie et l'Égypte sous les Fatimides', in Barrucand, ed., *L'Égypte fatimide*, pp.627–33.

Balog, Paul. 'Fatimid and post-Fatimid Glass Jetons from Sicily', *Studi Magrebini*, 7 (1975), pp.125–48.
——'Fatimid Glass Jetons: Token Currency or Coin-weights?' *JESHO*, 24 (1981), pp.93–109.
——'History of the Dirhem in Egypt from the Fāṭimid Conquest until the Collapse of the Mamlūk Empire', *Revue numismatique*, 3 (1961), pp.109–46.
——'Les Jetons fāṭimites en verre', *Revue belge de numismatique and de sigillographie*, 107 (1961), pp.171–83.
——'Monnaies islamiques rares fatimites et ayoubites', *BIE*, 36 (1953–54), pp.327–45.
——'Note sur quelques monnaies et jetons fatimites de Sicile', *BIE*, 38 (1955), pp.65–72.
——'Notes on some Fāṭimid round-flan dirhems', *Numismatic Chronicle*, ser. 7, 1 (1961), pp.175–9.
——'Poids en plomb du khalife fâṭimide al-Ḥâkim Biamr-illah frappé à Miṣr en l'an 389', *JESHO*, 6 (1963), pp.216–18.
——'Poids forts fatimites en plomb', *Revue belge de numismatique*, 105 (1959), pp.171–88.
——*The Fatimid Glass Jeton*. Naples, 1974–75. [Estratto da *Annali dell'Istituto Italiano di Numismatica*, 18–20 (Rome) 1971–73.]
Bareket, Elinoar. *Fustat on the Nile: The Jewish Elite in Medieval Egypt*. Leiden, 1999.
——'Personal Adversities of Jews during the Period of the Fatimid Wars in Eleventh Century Palestine', in Lev, ed., *War and Society*, pp.153–62.
al-Barrāwī, Rāshid. *Ḥālat Miṣr al-iqtiṣādiyya fī ʿahd al-Fāṭimiyyīn*. Cairo, 1948.
Barrucand, Marianne, ed. *L'Égypte fatimide: son art et son histoire*. Paris, 1999.
Bates, Michael L. 'How Egyptian Glass Coin Weights Were Used', *Rivista Italiana di Numismatica e Scienze Affini*, 95 (1993), pp.539–45.
——'The Chapter on the Fāṭimid *Dāʿīs* in Yemen in the *Ta'rīkh* of ʿUmāra al-Ḥakamī (d. 569/1174): An Interpolation', in *Studies in the History of Arabia, I: Sources for the History of Arabia*, 2 (1979), pp.51–61.
——'The Function of Fatimid and Ayyubid Glass Weights', *JESHO*, 24 (1981), pp.63–92.
Becker, Carl H. *Beiträge zur Geschichte Ägyptens unter dem Islam*. Strassburg, 1902–1903.
Behrens-Abouseif, D. 'The Façade of the Aqmar Mosque in the Context

of Fatimid Ceremonial', *Muqarnas*, 9 (1992), pp.29–38.
Ben-Sasson, Menahem. 'Maimonides in Egypt: the First Stage', in A. Hyman, ed., *Maimonidean Studies*. New York, 1991, vol.2, pp.3–30.
van Berchem, Max. 'La Chaire de la mosquée d'Hébron et le martyrion de la tête de Husain à Ascalon', in *Festschrift Eduard Sachau*. Berlin, 1915, pp.298–310.
——'Matériaux pour un Corpus Inscriptionum Arabicarum, part 1: Égypte', *Mémoires publiés par les membres de la Mission Archéologoque française au Caire*, 19 (1894–1903).
——'Matériaux pour un Corpus Inscriptionum Arabicarum, pt. II: Syrie du Sud, vols.1–3 (Jerusalem)', *MIFAO*, 43–45 (1920–22).
——'Notes d'archéologie arabe: Monuments et inscriptions fatimites', *JA*, 8ème Série, 17 (1891), pp.411–495; 18 (1892), pp.47–86; 19 (1892), pp.377-407.
——'Une Mosqée du temps des Fatimides au Caire: notice sur le Gāmiʿ El Goyû'shi', *Mémoire de l'Institut Égyptien*, 2 (1889), pp.605–19.
Berque, J. 'Du nouveau sur les Banu Hilāl?' *Studia Islamica*, 36 (1972), pp.99–113.
Beshir, B. I. 'The Fatimid Caliphate: 386–487 AH/996–1094 AD', Ph.D. Dissertation, SOAS, University of London, 1970.
——'Fatimid Military Organization', *Der Islam*, 55 (1978), pp.37–56.
——'New Light on Nubian-Fatimid Relations', *Arabica*, 22 (1975), pp.15–24.
Bianquis, Thierry. 'L'Acte de succession de Kāfūr d'après Maqrīzī', *AI*, 12 (1974), pp.263–9.
——*Damas et la Syrie sous la domination fatimide (359–468/969–1076)*. Damascus, 1986–1989.
——'Abd al-Gani ibn Sa'id, un savant sunnite au service des Fatimides', *Actes XXIX C.I.O.*, [Études Arabes et Islamiques I, Histoire et Civilisation I] (1975), pp.39–47.
——'La Prise du pouvoir par les fatimides en Égypte (357–363/968–974)', *AI*, 11 (1972), pp.48–108.
——'Al-Ḥākim bi amr Allāh ou la folie de l'unité chez un souverain fatimide', *Les Africains* (Paris, 1977), vol.11, pp.107–33. (Sous la direction de Charles-André Julien et al., new ed. 1990).
——'Ibn al-Nabulusi, un martyr sunnite au IVe siècle de l'hégire', *AI*, 12 (1974), pp.45–66.
——'L'Espace politique des Fatimides', in Barrucand, ed., *L'Égypte fatimide*, pp.21–8.

——'Le Fonctionnement des dīwān financièrs d'après al-Musabbiḥī', *AI*, 26 (1992), pp.47–61.

——'Notables ou malandrins d'origine rurale à Damas a l'époque fatimide', *BEO*, 25 (1973), pp.185–207.

——'La Transmission du hadith en Syrie a l'époque fatimide', *BEO*, 25 (1972), pp.85–95.

——'Une crise frumentaire dans l'Égypte fatimide', *JESHO*, 23 (1980), pp.67–101.

Bierman, Irene. 'Art and Politics: The Impact of Fatimid Uses of Tiraz Fabrics', Ph.D. dissertation, University of Chicago, 1980.

——*Writing Signs: The Fatimid Public Text*. Berkeley, CA, 1998.

Blachère, R. 'L'Agglomération du Caire vue par quartre voyageurs arabes de moyen-age', *AI*, 8 (1969), pp.1–26.

Blair, Sheila S. *Islamic Inscriptions*. Edinburgh, 1998.

Blake, H., A. Hutt and D. Whitehouse. 'Ajdâbiyah and the Earliest Fâtimid Architecture', *Libya Antiqua*, 8 (1971), pp.105–20.

Bloom, Jonathan M. 'The Early Fatimid Blue Koran Manuscript', *Graeco-Arabica*, 4 (1991), pp.171–7.

——'The Early Fatimid Blue Koran Manuscript', in Francois Deroche, ed., *Les Manuscrits du moyen-orient: essais de codicology et paléographie*. Istanbul and Paris, 1989, pp.95–9.

——'The Fatimids (909–1171), Their Ideology and Their Art', in *Islamische Textilkunst des Mittelalters: Aktuelle Probleme, Riggisberger Berichte*, 5 (1997), pp.15–26.

——'Five Fatimid Minarets in Upper Egypt', *Journal of the Society of Architectural Historians*, 43 (1984), pp.162–7.

——'The Introduction of the Muqarnas into Egypt', *Muqarnas*, 5 (1989), pp.21–8.

——'Al-Ma'mun's Blue Koran?', *REI*, 54 (1986), pp.61–5.

——'Meaning in Early Fatimid Architecture: Islamic Art in North Africa and Egypt in the Fourth Century AH (Tenth Century AD)'. Ph.D. dissertation, Harvard University, 1980.

——*Minaret: Symbol of Islam*. Oxford, 1989.

——'The Mosque of al-Ḥākim in Cairo', *Muqarnas*, 1 (1983), pp.15–36.

——'The Mosque of the Qarāfa in Cairo', *Muqarnas*, 4 (1986), pp.7–20.

——'The Origins of Fatimid Art', *Muqarnas*, 3 (1985), pp.30–8.

——'Paper in Fatimid Egypt', in Barrucand, ed., *L'Égypte fatimide*, pp.395–401.

Bonebakker, S. A. 'A Fatimid Manual for Secretaries', *Annali Istituto Orientale di Napoli*, 37, NS, 27 (1977), pp.295–337.

Bouyahia, Chedly. *La Vie littéraire en Ifriqiya sous les Zirides.* Thèse de doctorates-Lettres, Sorbonne, Tunis, 1972.

Brett, Michael. 'The Battles of Ramla (1099–1105)', in U. Vermeulen and D. De Smet, ed., *Egypt and Syria in the Fatimid, Ayyubid and Mamluk Eras* I, pp.17–38.

——'The Execution of al-Yāzūrī', in U. Vermeulen and D. De Smet, ed., *Egypt and Syria in the Fatimid, Ayyubid and Mamluk Eras* II, pp.15–27.

——'Fatimid Historiography: A Case Study – The Quarrel with the Zīrids, 1048–58', in D. O. Morgan, ed., *Medieval Historical Writing in the Christian and Islamic Worlds.* London, 1982, pp.47–59.

——'The Fatimid Revolution (861–973) and its Aftermath in North Africa', in J. D. Fage, ed., *Cambridge History of Africa.* Cambridge, 1978, vol.2, pp.589–636.

——'Ibn Khaldūn and the Arabisation of North Africa', *The Maghreb Review,* 4 (1979), pp.9–16.

——'Ibn Khaldun and the Invasion of Ifriqiya by the Banu Hilal, 5th century AH/11th century AD', *Actes de colloque international sur Ibn Khaldoun, 1978.* Algiers, 1982.

——'Islam and Trade in the *Bilād al-Sūdān,* Tenth-Eleventh Century AD', *Journal of African History,* 24 (1983), pp.431–40.

——'The Mīm, the ʿAyn and the Making of Ismāʿīlism', *BSOAS,* 57 (1994), pp.25–39

——'The Origins of the Mamluk Military System in the Fatimid Period', in U. Vermeulen and D. De Smet, ed, *Egypt and Syria in the Fatimid, Ayyubid and Mamluk Eras* 1, pp.39–52.

——'The Realm of the Imām: The Fāṭimids in the Tenth Century', *BSOAS,* 59 (1996), pp.431–49.

——*The Rise of the Fatimids: The World of the Mediterranean and the Middle East in the Fourth Century of the Hijra, Tenth Century CE.* Leiden, 2001.

——'The Way of the Peasant', *BSOAS,* 47 (1984), pp.44–56.

——'The Zughba at Tripoli, 429AH/1037–38AD', *The Society for Libyan Studies,* 6 (1974–75), pp.41–7.

Brunschvig, R. 'Argumentation Fatimide contre le raisonnement juridique par analogie (*qiyas*)', in R. Arnaldez and S. van Riet, ed., *Recherches d'Islamologie.* Louvain, 1977, pp.75–84.

——'Fiqh fatimide et l'histoire de l'Ifriqya', in *Mélanges d'histoire et archéologique de l'occident musulmane: Hommage à G. Marçais.* Algiers, 1957, vol.2, pp.13–20.

Bryer, David R. 'The Origins of the Druze Religion', *Der Islam,* 52 (1975), pp.47–84 and pp.239–64; 53 (1976), pp.5–27.

Cahen, Claude. 'L'Administration financière de la armée fatimide d'après al-Makhzūmī', *JESHO*, 15 (1972), pp.163–82, repr. in *Makhzūmiyyāt*, pp.155–74.

——'La Changeant portée sociale de quelques doctrine religieuses', in *L'Elaboration de Islam* (Colloque de Strasbourg, 1959). Paris, 1961, pp.5–22.

——'La Circulation monétaire en Égypte des Fatimides aux Ayyubides', *Revue numismatique*, ser. 6, 26, (1984), pp.208–17.

——'Une Chronique Syrienne du VIe/XIIe siècle', *BEO*, 7–8 (1937–38), pp.113–58.

——'Les Chroniques arabes concernant la Syrie, l'Égypte et la Mésopotamie de la conquête arabe à la conquête ottomane dans les bibliothèques d'Istanbul', *REI*, 10 (1936), pp.333–62.

——'L'Évolution de l'iqṭā' de IXè au XIIIè siècles', *Annales ESC*, 8 (1953), pp.25–52.

——'Histoires coptes d'un cadi médiéval', *BIFAO*, 59 (1960), pp.133–50.

——'Ibn Muyassar', *EI2*.

——'Al-Makhzūmī et Ibn Mammāṭī sur l'agriculture égyptienne médiévale', *AI*, 11 (1972), pp.141–51, repr. in *Makhzūmiyyāt*, pp.179–89.

——*Makhzūmiyyāt: Études sur l'histoire économique et financière de l'Égypte médiévale*. Leiden, 1977.

——'Le Marchands étrangers au Caire sous les Fatimids et les Ayyubides', *Colloque international sur l'histoire du Cairo*, Cairo, 1972, pp.97–101.

——'Note d'historiographie syrienne: La Première partie de l'histoire d'Ibn al-Qalānisī', in George Makdisi, ed., *Arabic and Islamic Studies in honour of Hamilton A. R. Gibb*. Leiden, 1965, pp.156–67.

——'Quelques chroniques anciennes relatives aux derniers Fatimides', *BIFAO*, 37 (1937–1938), pp.1–27.

——'Quelques notes sur les Hilâliens et le nomadisme', *JESHO*, 11 (1968), pp.130–3.

——'Un Récit inédit de vizirat de Dirghām', *AI*, 8 (1969), pp.27–46.

——*La Syrie du nord à l'époque des croisades*. Paris, 1940.

——'Un Texte peu connu relatif au commerce oriental d'Amalfi au Xè siècle', *Achivio Storico per la Province Napolitane*, NS, 34 (1953–1954), pp.1–8.

——'Un Traité financier inédit d'époque fatimide-ayyubide', *JESHO*, 5 (1962), pp.139–59, repr. in *Makhzūmiyyāt*, pp.1–21.

Cahen, Claude, Yusuf Ragheb and M. A. Taher. 'L'Achat et le waqf d'un grand domaine égyptien par le vizir fatimide Tala'i' b. Ruzzik', *AI,* 14 (1978), pp.57–126.

Cahen, Claude, with M. Adda. 'Les Éditions de l'Itti'āẓ al-Ḥunafā' (Histoire fatimide) de Maqrīzī par Aḥmad Hilmy, Sadok Ḥunī (Khouni), Fātiḥa Dib et Peter Kessler', *Arabica,* 22 (1975), pp.302–20.

Canard, Marius. 'L'Autobiographie d'un chambellan du Mahdī 'Obeidallāh le Fāṭimide', *Hespéris* (1952), pp.279–324, repr. in his *Miscellanea Orientalia,* no. 5.

——'al-Basāsīrī', 'al-Djannabi', 'Djarrahids', 'Djawdhar', 'Fāṭimids', 'Hamdanids', 'Ibn Hāni' al-Andalusī', *EI2*.

——*Byzance et les musulmans de Proche Orient.* London, 1973.

——'Le Cérémonial fâtimite et le cérémonial byzantin: Essai de comparaison', *Byzantion,* 21 (1951), pp.355–420, repr. in *Byzance et les musulmans,* item 14.

——'La Destruction de l'Église de la Résurrection par le calife Hâkim et l'histoire de la descente du feu sacré', *Byzantion,* 35(1955), pp.16–43, repr. in *Byzance et les musulmans,* item 20.

——'Deux episodes des relations diplomatiques arabo-byzantines au Xe siècle', *BEO,* 13 (1949–1950), pp.51–69, repr. in *Byzance et les musulmans,* item 12.

——*L'Expansion arabo-islamique et ses répercussions.* London, 1974.

——'Fâtimides et Bûrides à l'époque de calife fâtimite al-Hâfiz li-Dîn-Illâh', *REI* (Paris, 1967), pp.103–17, repr. in *Miscellanea Orientalia,* no. 17.

——*Histoire de la dynastie des Hamdanides de Jazira et de Syrie.* Algiers and Paris, 1951.

——'L'Impérialisme des Fatimides et leur propagande', *Annales de l'Institut d'Études Orientales de la Faculté des Lettres d'Alger,* 6 (1942–47), pp.156–93, repr. in *Miscellanea Orientalia,* no. 2.

——*Miscellanea Orientalia.* London, 1973.

——'Notes sur les Arméniens en Égypte à l'époque fâtimite', *Annales de l'Institut d'Études Orientales de la Faculté des Lettres d'Alger,* 13 (1955), pp.143–157, repr. in *Miscellanea Orientalia,* no. 8.

——'La Procession de Nouvel An chez les Fatimides', *Annales de l'Institut d'Études Orientales de la Faculté des Lettres d'Alger,* 10 (1952), pp.364–98, repr. in *Miscellanea Orientalia,* no. 4.

——'Les Sources arabes de l'histoire byzantine aux confins des Xe et XIe siecles', *Revue des études byzantines,* 19 (1961), pp.284–314, repr. in *Byzance et les musulmans,* item 17.

——'Quelques notes relatives à la Sicile sous les premiers califes fāṭimites', in *Studi medievali in onore di Antonio de Stefano.* Palermo, 1956, pp.569–76, repr. in *L'Expansion arabo-islamique,* item 4.

——'Une Famille de partisans, puis d'adversaires des Fāṭimides en Afrique de Nord', *Mélanges d'histoire et d'archéologie de l'occident musulman.* Algiers, 1958, vol.2 (1957), pp.33–49, repr. in *L'Expansion arabo-islamique,* item 5.

——'Une Lettre de calife fâtimite al-Hâfiz à Roger II', *Atti del Convegno Intern. di Studi Ruggeriani.* Palermo, 1955, pp.125–46, repr. in *Miscellanea Orientalia,* no. 7.

——'Un Vizir chrétien à l'époque fâtimite, l'Arménien Bahrâm', *Annales de l'Institut d'Études Orientales de la Faculté des Lettres d'Alger,* 12 (1954), pp.84–113, repr. in *Miscellanea Orientalia,* no. 6.

Candia, Farrugia de, see Farrugia de Candia.

Cannuyer, Christian. 'L'Intérêt pour l'Égypte pharaonique à l'époque fatimide: Etude sur l'Abrégé des Merveilles (Mukhtaṣar al-ʿajā'ib)', in Barrucand, ed., *L'Égypte fatimide,* pp.483–96.

Casanova, P. 'Les Derniers Fatimides', *MIFAO,* 6 (1897), pp.415–45.

——'La Doctrine secrète des Fatimides d'Égypte', *BIFAO,* 18 (1920), pp.121–65.

Catlos, Brian. 'To Catch a Spy: The Case of Zayn al-Dîn and Ibn Dukhân', *Medieval Encounters,* 2 (1996), pp.99–113.

Chiarelli, Leonard C. 'Sicily During the Fatimid Age'. Ph.D. dissertation, University of Utah, 1986.

Citarella, A. O. 'Patterns in Medieval Trade: The Commerce of Amalfi before the Crusades', *The Journal of Economic History,* 28 (1968), pp.531–55.

——'The Relations of Amalfi with the Arab World before the Crusades', *Speculum,* 42 (1967), pp.299–312.

Cohen, Mark R. 'Administrative Relations between Palestinian and Egyptian Jewry during the Fatimid Period', in Amnon Bohen and Gabriel Baer, ed., *Egypt and Palestine: A Millennium of Association (868–1948).* New York, 1984, pp.113–35.

——*Jewish Self-Government in Medieval Egypt: The Origins of the Office of Head of the Jews, ca. 1065–1126.* Princeton, NJ, 1980.

——*al-Mujtamaʿ al-yahūdī fi Miṣr al-islāmiyya fi'l-ʿuṣūr al-wusṭā.* Tel Aviv, 1987. (Arabic translation of *Jewish Life in Medieval Egypt, 641–1382.*)

Cohen, Mark R., and Sassan Somekh. 'In the Court of Yaʿqūb ibn Killis: A Fragment from the Cairo Genizah', *Jewish Quarterly Review,* NS, 80 (1990), pp.283–314.

Contadini, Anna. *Fatimid Art at the Victoria and Albert Museum.* London, 1998.
Cooper, Richard S. 'The Assessement and Collection of Kharāj Tax in Medieval Egypt', *JAOS*, 96 (1976), pp.365–82.
——'Ibn Mammātī's Rules for the Ministries: Translation with Commentary of the Qawānīn al-Dawānīn', Ph.D. dissertation, University of California, Berkeley, CA, 1973.
Cornu, Georgette. 'Les Tissus d'apparat fatimids, parmi les plus somptueux le «voile de Saint Anne» d'Apt', in Barrucand, ed., *L'Égypte fatimide*, pp.331–7.
Cortese, Delia. *Ismaili and Other Arabic Manuscripts: A Descriptive Catalogue of Manuscripts in the Library of The Institute of Ismaili Studies.* London, 2000.
Cowdrey, H. E. J. 'The Mahdia Campaign of 1087', *English Historical Review*, 42 (1977), pp.1–29.
——*Popes, Monks and Crusade.* London, 1984.
Creswell, K. A. C. *The Muslim Architecture of Egypt.* Vol.1. Oxford, 1952.
Dachraoui, Farhat. *Le Califat fatimide au Maghreb, 296–362/909–973: histoire, politique et institutions.* Tunis, 1981.
——'La Captivité d'Ibn Wâsûl, le rebelle de Sidjilmassa d'après le Qadi An Nu'mân', *CT*, 4 (1956), pp.295–9.
——'Le Crète dans le confit entre Byzance et al-Mu'izz', *CT*, 7 (1959), pp.307–18.
——'Le Commencement de la prédication ismā'īlienne en Ifriqiya', *SI*, 20 (1964), pp.89–102.
——'Contribution à l'histoire des Fatimides en Ifriqiya', *Arabica*, 8 (1961), pp.189–203.
——'Tentative d'infiltration shi'ite en Espagne musulmane sous le règne d'al-Hakim II', *al-Andalus*, 23 (1958), pp.97–106.
Dadoyan, Seta B. *The Fatimid Armenians: Cultural and Political Interaction in the Near East.* Leiden, 1997.
Daftary, Farhad. 'Carmatians', *Encyclopaedia Iranica*, vol.4, pp.823–32
——'The Earliest Ismā'īlīs', *Arabica*, 38 (1991), pp.214–45.
——'Ḥasan-i Ṣabbāḥ and the Origins of the Nizārī Isma'ili Movement', in Daftary, ed., *Mediaeval Isma'ili History and Thought*, pp.181–204.
——'Intellectual Life among the Ismailis: an Overview', in F. Daftary, ed., *Intellectual Traditions in Islam.* London, 2000, pp. 87–111.
——*The Ismā'īlīs: Their History and Doctrines.* Cambridge, 1990.
——'The Ismaili *Da'wa* Outside the Fatimid *Dawla*', in Barrucand, ed., *L'Égypte fatimide*, pp.29–43.

——'Marius Canard (1888–1982): A Bio-bibliographical Notice', *Arabica*, 33 (1986), pp.251–62.

——'A Major Schism in the Early Ismāʿīlī Movement', *SI*, 77 (1993), pp.123–39.

——*A Short History of the Ismailis: Traditions of a Muslim Community*. Edinburgh, 1998.

——'Sayyida Ḥurra: The Ismāʿīlī Ṣulayḥid Queen of Yemen', in G. R. G. Hambly ed., *Women in the Medieval Islamic World: Power, Patronage, and Piety*. New York, 1998, pp.117–30.

——ed. *Mediaeval Ismaʿili History and Thought*. Cambridge, 1996.

Daghfous, Radhi. 'Aspects de la situation economique de l'Égypte au milieu du Vè s/ milieu du XIè s/: Contribution à l'etude des conditions de l'immigrations des tribus arabes (Hilal et Sulaym) en Ifriqiya', *CT*, 25 (1977), pp.23–50.

——'De l'origine des Banu Hilal et des Banu Sulaym', *CT*, 23 (1975), pp.41–68.

Dagorn, René. 'Un Médecin obstétricien et pédiatre à l'époque des premiers Fatimides de Caire', *MIDEO*, 9 (1967), pp.73–119.

Dāwūd, Māysa Maḥmūd (Mayssa Mahmoud Daoud). *al-Maskūkāt al-fāṭimiyya bi-majmūʿat Matḥaf al-Fann al-Islāmī bi'l-Qāhira: dirāsa athariyya wa fanniyya*. Cairo, 1991.

de Goeje, Michael J. 'La Fin de l'empire des Carmathes', *JA*, ser. 9, 5 (1895), pp.5–30.

——*Mémoire sur les Carmathes du Bahraïn et les Fatimides*. 2nd ed., Leiden, 1886.

de Sacy, see Silvestre de Sacy.

De Smet, Daniel. 'Comment déterminer le début et la fin du jeûne de Ramadan? Un Point de discorde entre sunnites et ismaéliens en Égypte fatimide', in U. Vermeulen and D. De Smet, ed., *Egypt and Syria in the Fatimid, Ayyubid and Mamluk Eras* I, pp.71–84.

——'Le Culte du Veau d'Or chez les Druzes', in U. Vermeulen and D. De Smet, ed., *Egypt and Syria in the Fatimid, Ayyubid and Mamluk Eras* II, pp.45–61.

——'Éléments chrétiens dans l'ismaélisme yéménite sous les derniers Fatimides: Le problème de la gnose ṭayyibite', in Barrucand, ed., *L'Égypte fatimide*, pp.45–53.

——'Les Fêtes chiites en Égypte fatimide', *Acta Orientalia Belgica*, 10 (1995), pp.187–196.

——'Les Interdictions alimentaires du calife fatimide al-Ḥākim: marques de folie ou announce d'un règne messianique?' in U. Vermeulen and D. De Smet, ed., *Egypt and Syria in the Fatimid, Ayyubid and Mamluk Eras* I, pp.53–70.

——'Al-Mu'ayyad fi'd-Dīn aš-Šīrāzī et la polémique ismaélienne contre les 'Brahmanes' d'Ibn ar-Rāwandī', in U. Vermeulen and D. De Smet, ed., *Egypt and Syria in the Fatimid, Ayyubid and Mamluk Eras* I, pp.85–98.

——*La Quiétude de l'Intellect: Néoplatonisme et gnose ismaélienne dans l'oeuvre de Ḥamîd ad-Dîn al-Kirmânî (Xe/XIe s.).* Louvain, 1995.

——'La Translation du *ra's al-Ḥusayn* au Caire fatimide', in U. Vermeulen and D. De Smet, ed., *Egypt and Syria in the Fatimid, Ayyubid and Mamluk Eras* II, pp.29–44.

den Heijer, Johannes. 'Apologetic Elements in Coptic-Arabic Historiography: the Life of Afrahām ibn Zur'ah, 62nd Patriarch of Alexandria', in Samir Khalil Samir and J. S. Neilsen, ed., *Christian Arabic Apologetics during the Abbasid Period (750–1258).* Leiden, 1994, pp.192–202.

——'Considérations sur les communautés chrétiennes en Égypte fatimide: l'État et l'Église sous le vizirat de Badr al-Jamālī (1074–1094)', in Barrucand, ed., *L'Égypte fatimide,* pp.569–78.

——'Coptic Historiography in the Fāṭimid, Ayyūbid and Early Mamlūk Periods', *Medieval Encounters,* 2 (1996), pp.67–98.

——'Une Liste d'évêques coptes de l'année 1086', *Itinéraires d'Égypte: Mélanges offerts au père Maurice Martin.* Cairo, 1992, pp.147–65.

——*Mawhūb ibn Manṣūr ibn Mufarrig et l'historiographie copto-arabe: Étude sur la composition de l'Histoire des Patriarches d'Alexandrie.* Louvain, 1989.

Devisee, J. 'Trade and Trade Routes in West Africa', in M. El Fasi, ed., *Africa from the Seventh to the Eleventh Century,* vol.3, *General History of Africa.* Berkeley, CA, 1988, pp.367–435.

Dewhurst, R. P. 'Diwan of Poems in Praise of the Fatimids', *JRAS,* 1926, pp.629–42.

van Doorninck, Jr., Frederick H. 'The Medieval Shipwreck at Serçe Limani: An Early 11th-century Fatimid-Byzantine Commercial Voyage', *Graeco-Arabica,* 4 (1991), pp.45–52.

Eche, Youssef. *Les Bibliothèques arabes.* Damascus, 1967.

Egypt and Syria in the Fatimid, Ayyubid and Mamluk Eras. See Vermeulen, U., ed.

Ehrenkreutz, A. S. 'Arabic Dinars Struck by the Crusaders', *JESHO,* 7 (1964), pp.167–82.

——'The Fatimids in Palestine – The Unwitting Promoters of the Crusades', in Amnon Bohen and Gabriel Baer, ed., *Egypt and Palestine: A Millennium of Association (868–1948).* New York, 1984, pp.66–77.

——*Saladin.* Albany, NY, 1972.

——'Saladin's Coup d'État in Egypt' in *Medieval and Middle Eastern Studies in Honor of Aziz Suryal Atiya.* Leiden, 1972, pp.144–57.

Ehrenkreutz, A. S. and G. W. Heck. 'Additional Evidence of the Fatimid Use of Dinars for Propaganda Purposes', in M. Sharon, ed., *Studies in Islamic History and Civilization in Honor of Professor David Ayalon.* Leiden, 1986, pp.145–51.

Eisenstein, H. 'Die Wezire Ägyptens unter al-Mustanṣir AH452–466', *Wiener Zeitschrift für die Kunde des Morgenlandes,* 77 (1987), pp.37–50.

Elissieff, Nikita, *La Description de Damas d'Ibn ʿAsakir.* Damascus, 1959.

——*Nur ad-Din: Un Grand prince musulman de Syrie au temps des Croisades.* Damascus, 1967.

Elsberg, H. A., and R. Guest. 'The Veil of St. Anne', *The Burlington Magazine,* 68 (1936), pp.140–5.

Encyclopaedia Iranica. London, 1983–

The Encyclopaedia of Islam. 1st ed., Leiden, 1913–36.

The Encylopaedia of Islam. New ed., Leiden, 1960–

Espéroniner, Maryta. 'Les Fêtes civiles et les cérémonies d'origine antique sous les Fatimides d'Égypte', *Der Islam,* 65 (1988), pp.46–59.

van Ess, Josef. 'Biobibliographische Notizen zur islamischen Theologie', *WO,* 9 (1977/78), pp.255–61.

——*Chiliastische Erwartungen und die Versuchung der Göttlichkeit. Der Khalif al-Ḥākim (386–411).* Heidelberg, 1977.

Ettinghausen, Richard. 'Painting in the Fatimid Period: A Reconstruction', *Ars Islamica,* 9 (1942), pp.112–24.

Farrugia de Candia, J. 'Les Monnaies fatimides du Musée de Bardo', *Revue tunisienne* (1936), pp.333–372; (1937), pp.89–136.

——'Monnaies fatimides de Musée du Bardo (Premier supplément)', *Revue tunisienne* (1948), no.15.

Feki, Habib. *Les Idées religieuses et philosophiques de l'ismaelisme fatimide* (thesis, Paris, 1972), Publications de l'Université de Tunis, 1978.

Fierro, Maria Isabel. *La Heterodoxia en al-Andalus durante el periodo omeya.* Madrid, 1987.

Fierro, Maribel. 'On al-Fāṭimī and al-Fāṭimiyyūn', *JSAI,* 20 (1996), pp.130–61.

Forsyth, John Harper. 'The Byzantine-Arab Chronicle (938–1034) of Yaḥyā b. Saʿīd al-Anṭākī', Ph.D. dissertation, University of Michigan, 1977.

Frantz-Murphy, Gladys. *The Agrarian Administration of Egypt from the Arabs to the Ottomans.* Cairo, 1986.
——'A New Interpretation of the Economic History of Medieval Egypt: The Role of the Textile Industry, 245–567/868–1171', *JESHO*, 24 (1981), pp.274–97.
Fu'ād Sayyid, Ayman., see Sayyid, Ayman Fu'ād.
Fyzee, Asaf A. A. 'Aspects of Fatimid Law', *SI*, 31 (1970), pp.81–91.
——*Compendium of Fatimid Law.* Simla, 1969.
——'Qadi an-Nu'man, the Fatimid Jurist and Author', *JRAS* (1934), pp.1–32.
——'The Study of the Literature of the Fatimid Da'wa', in Makdisi, ed., *Arabic and Islamic Studies in Honor of Hamilton A. R. Gibb.* Leiden, 1965, pp.232–49.
Gacek, Adam. *Catalogue of Arabic Manuscripts in the Library of The Institute of Ismaili Studies*, vol.1. London, 1984.
Garcin, J. C. 'Toponymie et topographie urbaines médiévales à Fusṭāṭ et au Caire', *JESHO*, 27 (1984), pp.113–55.
——*Un Centre musulman de la Haute-Égypte médiévale: Qūṣ.* Cairo, 1976.
Gateau, A. 'La Sirat Ja'far al-Hajib: Contribution à l'histoire des Fatimides', *Hespéris*, 34 (1947), pp.375–96.
Gayraud, Roland-Pierre. 'Le Qarāfa al-Kubrā, dernière demeure des Fatimids', in Barrucand, ed., *L'Égypte fatimide*, pp.443–64.
Gellens, Sam Isaac. 'Scholars and Travellers: The Social History of Early Muslim Egypt, 218–487/833–1094', Ph.D. dissertation, Columbia University, 1986.
——'The Search for Knowledge in Medieval Muslim Societies: a Comparative Approach', in D. Eickelman and J. Piscatori, ed., *Muslim Travelers*. New York, 1990, pp.50–65.
Ghālib, Muṣṭafā. *Ta'rīkh al-da'wa al-ismā'īliyya.* 2nd ed., Beirut, 1965.
Gil, Moshe. *Documents of the Jewish Pious Foundation from the Cairo Geniza.* Leiden, 1976.
——*A History of Palestine, 634–1099.* Cambridge, 1992.
——'The Political History of Jerusalem during the Early Muslim Period', in Joshua Prawer, ed., *The History of Jerusalem: The Early Muslim Period, 638–1099* (New York, 1996), pp.1–37.
——*The Tustaries: Family and Sect* [In Hebrew]. Tel Aviv, 1981.
Goitein, Solomon D. 'The Exchange Rate of Gold and Silver Money in Fatimid and Ayyubid Times', *JESHO*, 7 (1965), pp.1–80. Plus additions *JESHO*, 9 (1966), pp.67–8, and errata *JESHO*, 12 (1969), pp.112.

——'From the Mediterranean to India', *Speculum,* 29 (1954), pp.181–97.
——*Letters of Medieval Jewish Traders.* Princeton, NJ, 1973.
——*A Mediterranean Society.* Berkeley, CA, 1967–1993, 6 vols.
——'Medieval Tunisia – The Hub of the Mediterranean', in *Studies in Islamic History and Institutions.* Leiden, 1968, pp.308–28.
——'New Light on the Beginnings of the Kārim Merchants', *JESHO,* 1 (1958), pp.175–84.
——'Petitions to Fatimid Caliphs from the Cairo Geniza', *Jewish Quarterly Review,* 45–46 (1954–56), pp.30–8.
——'Urban Housing in Fatimid and Ayyubid Times (as illustrated by the Cairo Genizah documents)', *SI,* 47 (1975), pp.5–23.
Golvin, Lucien. 'Buluggîn fils de Zîri, prince berbère', *Revue de l'Occident musulman et de la Mediterranée,* 35 (1983), pp.93–113.
——*Le Magrib Central à l'époque des Zirides: recherches d'archeologie et d'histoire.* Paris, 1957.
——'Mahdiya à l'époque fatimide', *Revue de l'Occident musulman et de la Mediterranée,* 27 (1979), pp.75–97.
——*Recherches archéologiques à la Qalʿa des Banû Hammâd.* Paris, 1965.
Goriawala, Muʿizz. *A Descriptive Catalogue of the Fyzee Collection of Ismaili Manuscripts.* Bombay, 1965.
Gottheil, Richard J. H. 'A Distinguished Family of Fatimide Cadis (al-Nuʿman) in the Tenth Century', *JAOS,* 27 (1906), pp.217–96.
——'An Eleventh-century Document Concerning a Cairo Synagogue', *Jewish Quarterly Review* (1907), pp.467–539.
——'Al-Hasan ibn Ibrahim ibn Zulaq', *JAOS,* 28 (1907), pp.217–97.
Griffith, Sidney. 'The *Kitāb Miṣbāḥ al-ʿaql* of Severus ibn al-Muqaffaʿ: A Profile of the Christian Creed in Arabic in Tenth Century Egypt', *Medieval Encounters,* 2 (1996), pp.15–42.
Grohmann, A. 'Tirāẓ', *Encyclopaedia of Islam* (1st ed.).
Guichard, Pierre. 'Omeyyades et Fatimides au Maghreb: Problématique d'un conflit politico-idéologique (vers 929–vers 980)', in Barrucand, ed., *L'Égypte fatimide,* pp.55–67.
Haji, Amin (Hamid). 'Institutions of Justice in Fatimid Egypt (358–567/969–1171)', in A. Al-Azmeh, ed., *Islamic Law: Social and Historical Contexts.* 1988, pp.198–214.
Halm, Heinz. 'Al-Azhar, Dār al-'Ilm, al-Raṣad. Forschungs – und Lehranstalten der Fatimiden in Kairo', in U. Vermeulen and D. De Smet, ed., *Egypt and Syria in the Fatimid, Ayyubid and Mamluk Eras* I, pp.99–110.

——'Le Destin de la Princesse Sitt al-Mulk', in Barrucand, ed., *L'Égypte fatimide*, pp.69–72.

——'Die Fatimiden', in U. Haarmann, ed., *Geschichte de arabischen Welt.* Munich, 1987, pp.166–99.

——'Les Fatimides à Salamya', *REI*, 54 (1986), pp.133–49.

——*The Fatimids and their Traditions of Learning.* London, 1997.

——'The Isma'ili Oath of Allegiance (*'ahd*) and The Session of Wisdom (*majālis al-ḥikma*) in Fatimid Times', in Daftary, ed., *Mediaeval Isma'ili History and Thought*, pp.91–115.

——*Kosmologie und Heilslehre der frühen Ismā'īlīya.* Wiesbaden, 1978.

——'Der Mann auf den Esel: Der Aufstand des Abu Yazid gegen dei Fatimiden nach einem Augenzeugenbericht', *WO*, 15(1984), pp.144–204.

——'Nachrichten zu Bauten der Aglabiden und Fatimiden in Libyen und Tunesien', *WO*, 23 (1992), pp.129–57.

——'Der nubische baqṭ', in U. Vermeulen and D. De Smet, ed., *Egypt and Syria in the Fatimid, Ayyubid and Mamluk Eras* II, pp.63–103.

——'La Refutation d'une note diplomatique du calife 'Abdarraḥmān III par la cour du calife fatimide al-Mu'izz', in *Saber religioso y poder político en el Islam: Actas del Simposio Internacional* (Granada, 15–18 Octobre 1991). Madrid, 1994, pp.117–25.

——*Das Reich des Mahdi: Der Aufstieg der Fatimiden.* Munich, 1991; English tr. M. Bonner, *The Empire of the Mahdi: The Rise of the Fatimids.* Leiden, 1996.

——'Al-Ṣamsa: Hängekronen als Herrschaftszeichen der Abbasiden und Fatimiden', in U. Vermeulen and D. De Smet, ed., *Egypt and Syria in the Fatimid, Ayyubid and Mamluks Eras* I, pp.125–38.

——'Die Sīrat Ibn Ḥaušab: die ismailitischen *da'wa* im Yemen und die Fatimides', *WO*, 12 (1981), pp.107–35.

——'Sitt al-Mulk', *EI2*.

——'Die Söhne Zikrawaihs und des erste fatimidische Kalifat (290/903)', *WO*, 10 (1979), pp.30–53.

——'Der Tod Ḥamzas, des Begründers der drusischen Religion', in U. Vermeulen and D. De Smet, ed., *Egypt and Syria in the Fatimid, Ayyubid and Mamluk Eras* II, pp.105–13.

——'Der Treuhänder Gottes: Die Edikte des Kalifen al-Ḥākim', *Der Islam*, 63 (1986), pp.11–72.

——'Die Zeremonien der Salbung des Nilometers und der Kanalöffnung in fatimidischer Zeit', in U. Vermeulen and D. De Smet, ed., *Egypt and Syria in the Fatimid, Ayyubid and Mamluk Eras* I, pp.111–24.

——'Zwei fatimidische Quellen aus der Zeit des Kalifen al-Mahdi (909–934)', *WO*, 19 (1988), pp.102–17.

Hamblin, William James. 'The Fatimid Army During the Early Crusades.' Ph.D. dissertation, University of Michigan, 1985.

——'The Fatimid Navy during the Early Crusades: 1099–1124', *The American Neptune*, 46 (1986), pp.77–83.

——'To Wage *Jihād* or Not: Fatimid Egypt During the Early Crusades', in Hadia Dajani-Shakeel and Ronald A. Messers, ed., *The* Jihād *and Its Times*. Ann Arbor, Michigan, 1991, pp.31–9.

Hamdani, Abbas. *The Beginnings of Ismāʿīlī Daʿwa in Northern India*. Cairo, 1956.

——'Brethren of Purity, A Secret Society for the Establishment of the Fatimid Caliphate: New Evidence for the Early Dating of their Encyclopaedia', in Barrucand, ed., *L'Égypte fatimide*, pp.73–82.

——'Byzantine-Fatimid Relations before the Battle of Manzikert', *Byzantine Studies*, 3 (1974), pp.169–79.

——'The Dāʿī Ḥātim Ibn Ibrāhīm al-Ḥāmidī (d.596 H/1199 AD) and his Book Tuḥfat al-Qulūb', *Oriens*, 23–24 (1970–1971), pp.258–300.

——'Did the Turkicization of Asia Minor Lead to the Arabization of North Africa?', *The Maghreb Review*, 24 (1999), pp.34–41.

——'Evolution of the Organisational Structure of the Fāṭimī Daʿwah', *Arabian Studies*, 3 (1976), pp.85–114.

——'Examples of Fatimid Realpolitik', *Digest of Middle East Studies*, 7 (1998), pp.1–12.

——'Fatimid History and Historians', in M. J. L. Young et al., ed., *Religion, Learning and Science in the ʿAbbasid Period*. Cambridge, 1990, pp.234–47, pp.535–6.

——*The Fatimids*. Karachi, 1962.

——'Some Aspects of the History of Libya During the Fatimid Period', in Fawzi Gadalla, ed., *Libya in History*. Beirut, 1970, pp.321–48.

——'Some Considerations on the Fatimid Caliphate as a Mediterranean Power', in *Atti Terzo Congresso de Studi Arabi e Islami*. Naples, 1967, pp.385–96.

——'Surt: the City and its History', *The Maghreb Review*, 16 (1991), pp.2–17.

——'The Ṭayyibī-Fāṭimid Community of the Yaman at the Time of the Ayyūbid Conquest of Southern Arabia', *Arabian Studies*, 7 (1985), pp.151–60.

Hamdani, Abbas and F. de Blois. 'A Re-examination of al-Mahdī's Letter to the Yemenites on the Genealogy of the Fatimid Caliphs', *JRAS* (1983), pp.173–207.

Hamdani, Husayn F. 'History of the *Ismāʿīlī Daʿwat* and its Literature during the Last Phase of the Fāṭimid Empire', *JRAS* (1932), pp.126–136, pp.281–300.

——'The Letters of Al-Mustanṣir bi-llah', *BSOAS*, 7 (1933/35), pp.307–24.

——'The Life and Times of Queen Saiyidah Arwā – The Ṣulayḥid of the Yeman', *Journal of the Royal Central Asia Society*, 18 (1931), pp.505–17.

——*On the Genealogy of Fatimid Caliphs.* Cairo, 1958.

——*al-Ṣulayḥiyyūn wa'l-ḥaraka al-fāṭimiyya fi'l-Yaman.* Cairo, 1955.

Hamdani, Sumaiya Abbas. 'From Daʿwa to Dawla: Qadi al-Nuʿman's Ẓāhirī Construction of Fatimid Legitimacy', Ph.D. dissertation, Princeton University, 1995.

——'The Dialectic of Power: Sunni-Shiʿi Debates in Tenth Century North Africa', *SI*, 90 (2000), pp.5–20.

——'The Kitāb al-majalis wa'l-musayarat and Fatimid daʿwa-dawla Relations', *The Maghreb Review*, 19 (1994), pp.266–76.

Hampikian, Nairy, and Monica Cyran. 'Recent Discoveries Concerning the Fatimid Palaces Uncovered During the Conservation Works on Parts of al-Ṣāliḥiyya Complex', in Barrucand, ed., *L'Égypte fatimide*, pp.649–63.

Harīdī, Aḥmad ʿAbd al-Majīd. *Fihris Khiṭaṭ Miṣr.* Cairo, 1983–84.

Ḥasan, ʿAlī Ḥasan. 'al-Ghazw al-hilālī li'l-Maghrib wa natā'ijuhu', *al-Majalla al-ta'rīkhiyya al-miṣriyya*, 24 (1977), pp.103–53.

Ḥasan, ʿAlī Ibrāhīm. *Ta'rīkh Jawhar al-ṣiqillī, qā'id al-Muʿizz li-dīn Allāh al-fāṭimī.* Cairo, 1963.

Ḥasan, Ḥasan Ibrāhīm. *al-Fāṭimiyīn fī Miṣr wa aʿmāluhum al-siyāsiyya wa'l-dīniyya bi'wajh khāṣṣ.* Cairo, 1932.

——'Relations Between the Fatimids in North Africa and Egypt and the Umayyads in Spain during the 4th Century AH (10th Century AD)', *Bulletin of the Faculty of Arts, Fouad I University*, Cairo, 10 (1948), pp.39–73.

——*Ta'rīkh al-dawla al-fāṭimiyya fi'l-Maghrib wa Miṣr wa Suriyā wa bilād al-ʿarab.* 2nd ed., Cairo, 1958; 3rd ed., Cairo, 1964.

Ḥasan, Ḥasan Ibrāhīm and Ṭāhā Aḥmad Sharaf. *al-Muʿizz li-dīn Allāh al-fāṭimī: mu'assis al-dawla al-fāṭimiyya fī Miṣr.* Cairo, 1948; Cairo, 1963.

Ḥasan, Ḥasan Ibrahim and Taha Aḥmad Sharaf. *ʿUbaydallāh al-Mahdī:*

imām al-shīʿa al-ismāʿīliyya wa muʾassis al-dawla al-fāṭimiyya fī bilād al-Maghrib. Cairo, 1947.

Ḥasan, Zaki. *Kunūz al-Fāṭimiyyīn.* Cairo, 1937.

Hirschfeld, Yizhar, Oren Gutfeld, Elias Khamis and Roni Amir. 'A Hoard of Fatimid Bronze Vessels from Tiberias', *al-ʿUṣūr al-Wusṭā,* 12 (2000), pp.1–7, p.27.

Hitti, Philip K. *An Arab-Syrian Gentleman and Warrior in the Period of the Crusades.* New York, 1930.

Hodgson, M. G. S. 'al-Darazi and Hamza in the Origins of the Druze Religion', *JAOS,* 82 (1962), pp.5–20.

——'The Ismāʿīlī State', in *The Cambridge History of Iran:* Volume 5, *The Saljuq and Mongol Periods,* ed. J. A. Boyle. Cambridge, 1968, pp.422–82.

——*The Order of Assassins.* The Hague, 1955.

Hrbek, I. 'Die Slaven im dienste der Fatimiden', *Archiv Orientalny,* 21 (1953), pp.543–81.

Hunsberger, Alice C. *Nasir Khusraw, The Ruby of Badakhshan: A Portrait of the Persian Poet, Traveller and Philosopher.* London, 2000.

——'Nasir Khusraw: Fatimid Intellectual', in F. Daftary, ed., *Intellectual Traditions in Islam.* London, 2000, pp.112–29.

Ḥusayn (Hussein), Muḥammad Kāmil. 'Shiism in Egypt Before the Fatimids', *Islamic Research Association Miscellany,* vol.1, 1948. London, 1949, pp.73–85.

——*Fī adab Miṣr al-fāṭimiyya.* 2nd ed., Cairo, 1963.

——*al-Ḥaya al-fikriyya wa'l-adabiyya bi-Miṣr.* Cairo, 1959.

——*Ṭaʾifat al-ismāʿīliyya, taʾrīkhuhā, nuẓumuhā, ʿaqāʾiduhā.* Cairo, 1959.

Ibn Riḍwān. *Medieval Islamic Medicine: Ibn Riḍwān's Treatise 'On the Prevention of Bodily Ills in Egypt',* tr. Michael W. Dols; Arabic text ed. Adil S. Gamal. Berkeley, CA, 1984.

Idris, Hady Roger. *La Berbérie orientale sous les Zīrīdes, xe-xiie siècles.* Paris, 1962.

——'Buluggīn', *EI2*.

——'Contribution à l'histoire de l'Ifrikiya: Tableau de la vie intellectuelle et administrative a Kairouan sous le Aglabites et les Fa**timides ... d'après le** Riyad En Nufus de Abu Bakr El Maliki', *REI,* 9 (1935), pp.105–78, pp.273–305, p.10 (1936), pp.45–104.

——'Contribution à l'histoire de la vie religieuse en Ifrīqiya zīrīde (Xème – Xième siècles)', in *Mélanges Louis Massignon.* Damascus, 1957, vol.2, pp.327–59.

——'D'al-Dabbag, hagiographe and chroniqueur kairouanais de XIIIe siècle et de son jugement sur les Fatimides', *BEO*, 29 (1977), pp.243–9.

——'Glanes sur les Zirides d'Ifriqiya dans le manuscript d'Istanboul de l'Itti'az al Hunafā'', *Arabica*, 11 (1964), pp.287–305.

——'Hilāl', *EI2*.

——'L'Invasion hilālienne et ses consequences', *Cahier de civilisation médiévale*, 11 (1968), pp.336–69.

——'De la réalité de la catastrophe hilalienne', *AnnalesESC*, 23 (1968), pp.390–6.

——'Problématique de l'épopée ṣanhâdjienne en Berbérie Orientale (X-XIIe siècle)', *Annales de l'Institut d'Études Orientales de la Faculté des Lettres d'Alger*, 17 (1959), pp.243–255.

——'Sur le retour des Zirides a l'obediance fatimide', *Annales de l'Institut d'Études Orientales de la Faculté des Lettres d'Alger*, 2 (1953), pp.25–39.

——'Une des phases de la lutte du Malikisme contre le shi'isme sous les Zirides (XIe S.)', *CT*, 4 (1956), pp.509–17.

——'La Vie intellectualle en Ifrîqiya méridionale sous les Zîrides (XI siècle) d'après Ibn Al-Chabbat', in *Mélanges d'histoire et archéologie de l'occident musulman: Hommage à Georges Marçais*. Algiers, 1957, vol.2, pp.95–106.

al-Imad. See Al-Imad, Leila S.

'Inān, Muḥammad 'Abdallāh. *al-Ḥākim bi-amr Allāh wa asrār al-da'wa al-fāṭimiyya*. Cairo, 1959.

Institut du Monde Arabe. *Trésors fatimides du Caire: Exposition présentée à l'Institut du monde arabe de 28 avril au 30 août 1998*. Paris, 1998.

Irwin, R. 'Factions in Medieval Egypt', *JRAS* (1986), pp.228–46.

Ivanow, Wladimir. *A Creed of the Fatimids*. Bombay, 1936.

——*A Guide to Ismaili Literature*. London, 1933.

——'Ismailis and Qarmatians', *JBBRAS*, NS,16 (1940), pp.43–85.

——*Ismaili Literature: A Bibliographical Survey*. Tehran, 1963.

——*Ismaili Tradition Concerning the Rise of the Fatimids*. London, 1942.

——'The Organization of the Fatimid Propaganda', *JBBRAS*, NS, 15 (1939), pp.1–35.

Jiwa, Shainool. 'Fāṭimid-Būyid Diplomacy During the Reign of al-'Azīz billāh (365/975 - 386/996)', *Journal of Islamic Studies*, 3 (1992), pp.57–71.

——'The Initial Destination of the Fatimid Caliphate: The Yemen or the Maghrib?' *BRISMES Bulletin*, 13 (1986), pp.15–26.

Johns, Jeremy. 'I re normanni e i califfi fatimiti: Nuove prospettive su vecchi materiali', *Del Nuovo sulla Sicilia Musulmana, Gornata de Stu-*

dio, Rome, 1995, pp.9–50.

——'Malik Ifriqiyah: the Norman Kingdom of Africa and the Fatimids', *Libyan Studies*, 18 (1993), pp.89–101.

——'The Norman Kings of Sicily and the Fatimid Caliphate', *Anglo-Norman Studies*, 15 (1993), pp.133–59.

Kessler, Peter Edward. 'The Reign of the Fatimid Caliph al-Mustansir Billah 1027–1094 AD: A Discussion of Maqrizi's Portrayal in the Itti'az al-Ḥunafa'. B.Litt, Oxford, 1971.

Khan, Geoffrey. 'The Arabic Fragments in the Cambridge Genizah Collections', *Manuscripts of the Middle East*, 1 (1986), pp.54–60.

——*Arabic Legal and Administrative Documents in the Cambridge Genizah Collections*. Cambridge, 1993.

——'A Copy of a Decree from the Archives of the Fatimid Chancery in Egypt', *BSOAS*, 49 (1986), pp.439–53.

——'The Historical Development of the Structure of Medieval Arabic Petitions', *BSOAS*, 53 (1990), pp.8–30.

——'A Petition to the Fāṭimid Caliph al-'Āmir', *JRAS* (1990), pp.44–54.

Kheir, H. M. 'A Contribution to a Textual Problem: Ibn Sulaym al-Aswani's Kitab Ahbar al-Nuba wal-Maqurra wal-Bega wal-Nil', *AI*, 21 (1985), pp.9–72.

Khoury, R. G. 'Une Description fantastique des fonds de la Bibliothèque Royale *Ḫizânat al-Kutub* au Caire, sous le règne du calife fatimide al-'Azīz bi-llāh (365–86/975–97)', in Rudolph Peters, ed., *Proceedings of the Ninth Congress of the Union Européene des Arabisants et Islamisants* (Amsterdam, 1–7 September 1978). Leiden, 1981, pp.123–40.

King, David A. 'Aspects of Fatimid Astronomy From Hard-Core Mathematical Astonomy to Architectural Orientations in Cairo', in Barrucand, ed., *L'Égypte fatimide*, pp.497–517.

Klemm, Verena. *Die Mission des fāṭimidischen Agenten al-Mu'ayyad fī'l-Dīn in Širāz*. Frankfurt am Main, 1989.

Köhler, Bärbel. *Die Wissenschaft unter den ägyptischen Fatimiden*. Heldesheim, 1994.

Köhler, M. A. 'Al-Afḍal und Jerusalem – was versprach sich Ägypten vom ersten Kreuzzug', *Saeculum*, 37 (1986), pp.228–39.

Kraemer, Joel. 'A Jewish Cult of the Saints in Fāṭimid Egypt', in Barrucand, ed., *L'Égypte fatimide*, pp.579–601.

Kubiak, Wladyslaw. 'The Burning of Misr al-Fustat in 1168. A Reconsideration of Historical Evidence', *Africana Bulletin* [Warsaw], 25 (1976), pp.51–64.

——*al-Fustat, Its Foundation and Early Urban Development*. Cairo, 1987.

Kühnel, Ernst, and Louisa Bellinger. *Catalogue of Dated Tiraz Fabrics: Umayyad, Abbasid, Fatimid.* Washington, DC, 1952.

Kunitzsch, P. 'Zur Namengebung Kairos (al-Qahir - Mars?)', *Der Islam,* 52 (1975), pp.209–25.

Laqbāl, Mūsā. *Dawr Kutāma fī ta'rīkh al-khilāfa al-fāṭimiyya mundhu ta'sīsihā ilā muntaṣaf al-qarn al-khāmis al-hijrī.* Algiers, 1979.

Launois, Aimée. 'Catalogue des monnaies fatimites entrées au Cabinet des Medailles depuis 1896', *BEO,* 24 (1971), pp.19–53.

Le Tourneau, R. 'La Révolte d'Abu-Yazid au Xme siècle', *CT,* 1 (1953), pp.103–25.

Leiser, Gary. 'The Madrasa and the Islamization of the Middle East: The Case of Egypt', *JARCE,* 22 (1985), pp.29–47.

——'Muslims from al-Andalus in the Madrasas of Late Fāṭimid and Early Aiyūbid Egypt', *al-Qantara,* 20 (1999), pp.137–59.

——'The Restoration of Sunnism in Egypt: Madrasas and Mudarrisūn 495–647/1101–1249', Ph.D. dissertation, University of Pennsylvania, 1976.

Leisten, Thomas. 'Dynastic Tomb or Private Mausolea: Observations on the Concept of Funerary Structures of the Fāṭimid and 'Abbāsid Caliphs', in Barrucand, ed., *L'Égypte fatimide,* pp.465–79.

Lester, Ayala, Yael D. Arnon and Rachel Polak. 'The Fatimid Hoard from Caesarea: A Preliminary Report', in Barrucand, ed., *L'Égypte fatimide,* pp.233–48.

Lev, Yaacov. 'Army, Regime and Society in Fatimid Egypt, 358–487/968–1094', *IJMES,* 19 (1987), pp.337–66.

——'The Fatimid Army, AH 358–427/968–1036 CE: Military and Social Aspects', *Asian and African Studies,* 14 (1980), pp.165–92.

——'The Fatimids and the Aḥdāth of Damascus 386/996–411/1021', *WO,* 13 (1982), pp.98–106.

——'Fatimid Policy Towards Damascus (358/968 -386/996): Military, Political and Social Aspects', *JSAI,* 3 (1981–82), pp.165–83.

——'The Fatimid Conquest of Egypt – Military, Political and Social Aspects', *Israeli Oriental Studies,* 9 (1979), pp.315–328.

——'The Fatimid Imposition of Ismā'īlism on Egypt (358–386/969–996)', *ZDMG,* 138 (1988), pp.313–25.

——'The Fatimid Navy, Byzantium and the Mediterranean Sea, 909–1036 CE/297–427 AH', *Byzantium,* 54 (1984), pp.220–52.

——'The Fatimid Princess Sitt al-Mulk', *Journal of Semitic Studies,* 32 (1987), pp.319–28.

——'The Fatimid Vizier Ya'qūb ibn Killis and the Beginning of the Fa-

timid Administration in Egypt', *Der Islam*, 58 (1981), pp.237–49.
——'The Fatimids and Egypt, 301–358/914–969', *Arabica*, 35 (1988), pp.186–96.
——'Persecutions and Conversion to Islam in Eleventh-Century Egypt', (The Medieval Levant: Studies in Memory of Eliyahu Ashtor) *Asian and African Studies*, 22 (1988), pp.73–91.
——'A Political Study of Egypt and Syria under the Early Fatimids 358/968 – 386/996'. Ph.D. dissertation, University of Manchester, 1978.
——'Regime, Army and Society in Medieval Egypt, 9th–12th Centuries', in Lev, ed., *War and Society in the Eastern Mediterranean*, pp.115–52.
——*Saladin in Egypt*. Leiden, 1999.
——*State and Society in Fatimid Egypt*. Leiden, 1991.
——'The Suppression of Crime, the Supervision of Markets, and Urban Society in the Egyptian Capital during the Tenth and Eleventh Centuries', *Mediterranean Historical Review*, 3 (1988), pp.71–95.
——'Tinnīs: An Industrial Medieval Town', in Barrucand, ed., *L'Égypte fatimide*, pp.83–96.
——ed., *War and Society in the Eastern Mediterranean, 7th-15th Centuries*. Leiden, 1997.
Lewis, A. R. *Naval Power and Trade in the Mediterranean, A.D. 500–1100*. Princeton, NJ, 1951.
Lewis, Bernard. *The Assassins: A Radical Sect in Islam*. London, 1967.
——'Assassins of Syria and Ismāʿīlīs of Persia', in *La Persia nel Medioevo* (Academia Nazionale dei Lincei). Rome, 1971, pp.573–80, repr. in *Studies in Classical and Ottoman Islam*, item 11.
——'An Epistle on Manual Crafts', *IC*, 17 (1943), pp.142–51, repr. in *Studies in Classical and Ottoman Islam*, item 12.
——'Ibn al-ʿAdīm', *EI2*.
——'The Fatimids and the Route to India', *Revue de la faculté des sciences economiques de l'Universite d'Istanbul*, 11 (1949–1950), pp.50–4.
——'Government, Society and Economic Life under the Abbasids and Fatimids', in *The Cambridge Medieval History, The Byzantine Empire*, vol.4, part 1, pp.638–61.
——'An Interpretation of Fatimid History', *Colloque international sur l'histoire du Caire*. Cairo, 1972, pp.287–95.
——'Kamāl al-Dīn's Biography of Rāšid al-Dīn Sinān', *Arabica*, 13 (1966), pp.225–67, repr. in *Classical and Ottoman Islam*, item 10.
——*The Origins of Ismāʿīlism: A Study of the Historical Background of the Fāṭimid Caliphate*. Cambridge, 1940.
——'Palṭiel: A Note', *BSOAS*, 30 (1967), pp.177–81.

——'Saladin and the Assassins', *BSOAS*, 15 (1953), pp.239–45, repr. in *Classical and Ottoman Islam*, item 9.

——'The Sources for the History of the Syrian Assassins', *Speculum*, 27 (1952), pp.475–89, repr. in *Classical and Ottoman Islam*, item 8.

——*Studies in Classical and Ottoman Islam (7th–16th Centuries)*. London, 1976.

Lezine, Alexandre. *Mahdiya: Recherches d'archeologie islamique*. Paris, 1965.

——'Notes d'archéologie ifriqiyenne 4: Mahdiyah, quelques precisions sur la «ville» des premiers fatimides', *REI*, 35 (1967), pp.82–101.

Lindsay, James E. 'Prophetic Parallels in Abu 'Abd Allah al-Shi'i's Mission Among the Kutama Berbers, 893–910', *IJMES*, 24 (1992), pp.39–56.

Lowe, John D. 'A Medieval Instance of Gresham's Law: The Fatimid Monetary System and the Decline of Bimetallism', *Jusur*, 2 (1986), pp.1–24.

Madelung, Wilferd. 'Fatimiden und Baḥrainqarmaṭen', *Der Islam*, 34 (1959), pp.34–88; slightly revised tr., 'The Fatimids and the Qarmaṭīs of Baḥrayn', in F. Daftary, ed., *Mediaeval Isma'ili History and Thought*. Cambridge, 1996, pp.21–73.

——'Ḥamdān Ḳarmaṭ', *EI2*.

——'Ḥamdān Qarmaṭ and the Dā'ī Abū 'Alī', *Proceedings of the 17th Congress of the UEAI* [Union Européenne des arabisants et islamisants], St. Petersburg, 1997, pp.115–24.

——'Das Imamat in der frühen ismailitischen Lehre', *Der Islam*, 37 (1961), pp.43–135.

——'Ḳarmaṭī', *EI2*.

——'Notes on Non-Ismā'īlī Shiism in the Maghrib', *Studia Islamica*, 44 (1976), pp.87–97.

——'The Religious Policy of the Fatimids toward their Sunnī Subjects in the Maghrib', in Barrucand, ed., *L'Égypte fatimide*, pp.97–104.

——'The Sources of Ismā'īlī Law', *JNES*, 35 (1976), pp.29–40.

al-Majdū', Ismā'īl b. 'Abd al-Rasūl. *Fihrist al-Majdū'*, ed. Alinaqi Monzavi. Tehran, 1966.

Mājid (Magued), 'Abd al-Mun'im. 'Aṣl Ḥaflāt al-Fāṭimiyyīn fī Miṣr', *Ṣaḥīfat al-Ma'had al-miṣrī li-l-dirāsāt al-islāmiyya fī Madrīd*, 2 (1954), pp.253–7.

——'La Fonction de juge suprême dans l'état fatimide en Égypte', *L'Égypte contemporaine*, 50 (1960), no. 299, pp.45–56.

——*al-Ḥākim bi-Amr Allāh al-khalīfa al-muftarā 'alayh*. Cairo, 1959, 1982.

——'L'Organisation financière en Égypte sous les Fatimides', *L'Égypte*

contemporaine, 53 (1962), no. 308, pp.47–57.
——'Imra'a miṣriyya, tataza' 'amu muẓāhara fī 'ahd al-Mustanṣir bi'llāh al-fāṭimī', *al-Majalla al-ta'rīkhiyya al-miṣriyya,* 24 (1977), pp.33–8.
——'Mā allafahu al-mu'arrikhūn al-'arab fī mi'at al-sanna al-akhīra min darāsāt fi'l-ta'rīkh al-'arabī: al-fatra al-fāṭimiyya 358–567/696–1171', in *Ḥawlīyāt Kulliyat al-ādāb bi jāmi'at 'Ayn Shams.* Cairo, 1961, pp.11–35.
——*al-Imām al-Mustanṣir bi-Allāh al-fāṭimī.* Cairo, 1961.
——*Nuẓum al-Fāṭimiyyīn wa rusūmuhum fī Miṣr* (*Institutions et cérémonial des Fatimides en Égypte*). 2nd ed., Cairo, 1973 and 1978, 2 vols.
——*Ẓuhūr khilāfat al-Fāṭimiyyīn wa suqūṭuhā fī Miṣr: al-ta'rīkh al-siyāsī.* Alexandria, 1968.
Mamour, P. H. *Polemics on the Origin of the Fatimi Caliphs.* London, 1934.
al-Manāwī, Muḥammad Ḥamdī. *al-Wizāra wa'l-wuzarā' fī'l-'aṣr al-fāṭimī.* Cairo, 1970.
Mann, Jacob. *The Jews in Egypt and Palestine under the Fatimid Caliphs.* Oxford, 1920–22; New York, 1970.
Mansouri, Mohammed-Tahar. 'Juifs et chrétiens dans le Maghreb fatimide (909–969)', in Barrucand, ed., *L'Égypte fatimide,* pp.603–11.
Marçais, Georges. *La Berbérie musulmane et l'orient au moyen age.* Paris, 1946.
——'Les Figures d'hommes et de bêtes dans les bois sculptés d'époque fatimide conservés au Musée du Caire', *Mélanges Maspero,* 3 (Cairo, 1940), pp.241–57.
Marçais, Georges, and Gaston Wiet. 'Le Voile de Sainte Anne d'Apt', *Monuments et Mémoires Fondation Piot,* 34, 1934, pp.177–94.
Margoliouth, D. S. 'al-Ma'arrī's Correspondence on Vegetarianism', *JRAS* (1902), pp.289–332.
Martin, B. G. 'Kanem, Bornu and Fazzān: Notes on the Political History of a Trade Route', *Journal of African History,* 10 (1969), pp.15–27.
Massé, H. 'Ibn al-Cairafi: code de la chancellerie d'État', *BIFAO,* 11 (1914), pp.65–120.
——'Le Poème d'Ibn Hani al-Andalusi sur la conquête de l'Égypte (969)', *Mélanges d'histoire et d'archéologie de l'occident musulman: Hommage à G. Marçais.* Algiers, 1957, pp.121–7.
May, Burkhard. *Die Religionspolitik der Agyptischen Fatimiden 969–1171.* Hamburg, 1975.
Mayerson, P. 'The Role of Flax in Roman and Fatimid Egypt', *JNES,* 56 (1997), pp.201–7.
Meinecke-Berg, Viktoria. 'Fatimid Painting: on Tradition and Style, the

Workshop of Muslim', in Barrucand, ed., *L'Égypte fatimide*, pp.349–58.

——'Materialen zu fatimidischen Holzdekorationen in Kairo I: Holzdecken aus dem fatimidischen Westpalast in Kairo', *Mitteilungen des Deutschen Archäologischen Instituts, Abteilung Kairo*, 47 (1991), pp.227–33.

Mernissi, Fatima. *The Forgotten Queens of Islam*, tr. M. J. Lakeland. Minneapolis, 1993.

Messier, R. Albert. 'Muslim Exploitation of West African Gold during the Period of the Fatimid Caliphate'. Ph.D. dissertation, University of Michigan, 1972.

Meyerhof, Max. 'Über einige privatbibliotheken im fatimidischen Ägypten', *RSO*, 12 (1929–30), pp.286–90.

Miles, George C. *Fatimid Coins in the Collections of the University Museum, Philadelphia, and the American Numismatic Society.* New York, 1951.

Miquel, A. 'L'Égypte vue par un géographe arabe du IVe/Xe siècle: al-Muqaddasi', *AI*, 11 (1972), pp.109–39.

Mones, H. 'Le Malékisme et l'échec des Fatimides en Ifriqiya', in *Études d'orientalisme dédiés à la mémoire de Lévi-Provençal.* Paris, 1962, pp.197–220.

Morelon, Régis. 'Un Aspect de l'astronomie sous les Fatimides: l'importance d'Ibn al-Haytham dans l'histoire de l'astronomie arabe', in Barrucand, ed., *L'Égypte fatimide*, pp.519–26.

Mousa, N. 'Les Études grammaticales en Égypte des origines à la fin des fatimides: Étude bio-bibliographique des grammairiens. Analyse de leurs oeuvres et édition critique d'un traité grammaticale, le Kitab al-Muqaddima fī l-naḥw d'Ibn Bābišādh'. Paris, 1974.

Mouton, Jean-Michel. 'La Présence chrétienne au Sinaï à l'époque fatimide', in Barrucand, ed., *L'Égypte fatimide*, pp.613–24.

Nabarawi, Ra'fat Muḥammad. *al-Sinaj al-zujajiyya li-l-sakka al-fāṭimiyya al-maḥfūẓa bi-Mathaf al-Fann al-Islāmī bi'l-Qāhira.* Cairo, 1997.

Nagel, Tilman. *Frühe Ismailiya und Fatimiden im Lichte der Risālat Iftitāḥ ad-Da'wa: Eine religionsgeschichtliche Studie.* Bonn, 1972.

——'Die 'Urgūza al-Muḫtāra' des Qāḍī an-Nu'mān', *Die Welt des Islams*, 15 (1974), pp.96–128.

Nasr, Seyyed Hossein, ed., *Ismā'īlī Contributions to Islamic Culture.* Tehran, 1977.

Nassār, Ḥusayn. *Ẓāfir al-Haddād.* Cairo, 1975.

Nicol, Norman D. 'Islamic Coinage in Imitation of Fāṭimid Types', *Israel Numismatic Journal*, 10 (1988–89), pp.58–70 + plates.

Oddy, W. A. 'The Gold Content of Fatimid Coins Reconsidered', in *Metallurgy in Numismatics*, 1 (London, 1980), pp.99–118.

O'Kane, Bernard. 'The Ziyāda of the Mosque of al-Ḥākim and the Development of the Ziyāda in Islamic Architecture', in Barrucand, *L'Égypte fatimide*, pp.141–58.

O'Leary, De Lacy. *A Short History of the Fatimid Khalifate*. London, 1923.

Orak, A. 'Les Arméniens en Égypte à l'époque des fatimites', *Cahiers d'histoire égyptienne*, ser. 9, 3 (1958), pp.117–37.

Pauty, Ed. *Bois sculptés d'églises coptes (époque fatimide)*. Cairo, 1930.

——*Les Bois sculptés jusqu'à l'époque ayyoubides*. Cairo, 1931.

Petry, Carl F., ed. *The Cambridge History of Egypt*, volume 1: *Islamic Egypt, 640–1517*. Cambridge, 1998.

Pines, Shlomo. 'Nathanael ben al-Fayyumi et la théologie ismaélienne', *Études historiques juives* (1947), pp.5–22.

——'Shī'ite Terms and Conceptions in Judah Halevi's *Kuzari*', *JSAI*, 2 (1980), pp.165–251.

Poncet, J. 'Encore à propos des Hilaliens: La «Mise au point» de R. Idris', *AnnalesESC*, 23 (1968), pp.660–2.

——'L'Évolution des genres de vie en Tunisie', *CT*, 2 (1954), pp.315–23.

——'Le Mythe de la catastrophe hilalienne', *Annales ESC*, 22 (1967), pp.1099–120.

Poonawala, Ismail K. *Biobibliography of Ismā'īlī Literature*. Malibu, CA, 1977.

——'Ismā'īlī Sources for the History of South-West Arabia', in *Studies in the History of Arabia*, I, *Sources for the History of Arabia*, part 1. Riyadh, 1979, pp.151–9.

——'Al-Qāḍī al-Nu'mān and Isma'ili Jurisprudence', in Daftary, ed., *Mediaeval Isma'ili History and Thought*, pp.117–43.

——'Al-Qāḍī al-Nu'mān's Works and the Sources', *BSOAS*, 36 (1973), pp.109–15.

——'A Reconsideration of al-Qāḍī al-Nu'mān's Madhhab', *BSOAS*, 37 (1974), pp.572–9.

——*al-Sulṭān al-Khaṭṭāb: Ḥayātuhu wa shi'ruhu*. Cairo, 1967; 2nd ed., Beirut, 1999.

al-Qaddūmī, Ghāda al-Ḥijjāwī. *Book of Gifts and Rarities* (Kitāb al-Hadāyā wa al-Tuḥaf): *Selections Compiled in the Fifteenth Century from an Eleventh-Century Manuscript on Gifts and Treasures*. Cambridge, MA, 1996.

al-Qadi, Wadad. 'An Early Fatimid Political Document', *SI*, 48 (1978), pp.71–108.

Quatremère, É. 'Mémoires historiques sur la dynastie des khalifes fatimites', *JA*, ser. 3, 2 (1836), pp.94–142 and 400–59; (1837), pp.45–93 and 165–208.

Qutbuddin, Bazat-Tahera. 'Al-Mu'ayyad fī al-Dīn al-Shīrāzī: Founder of a New Tradition of Fatimid Da'wa Poetry.' Ph.D. dissertation, Harvard University, 1999.

Rabie, H. *The Financial System of Egypt: AH 564–741/AD 1169–1341*. London, 1972.

Rāghib (Ragib, Rājib), Yūsuf. 'Un Contrat de mariage sur soie d'Égypte fatimide', *AI*, 16 (1980), pp.31–7 and plates 3, 14.

——'Deux monuments fatimides au pied du Muqattam', *REI*, 46 (1978), pp.91–155.

——'Un Épisode obscur d'histoire fatimide', *SI*, 48 (1978), pp.125–32.

——'Les Mausolées fatimides du quartier d'al-Mashāhid', *AI*, 17 (1981), pp.1–30.

——'Un Oratoire fatimide au sommet du Muqattam', *SI*, 65 (1987), pp.51–69.

——'Les Sanctuaires du gens de la famille dans la cité des morts au Caire', *RSO*, 51 (1977), pp.41–132.

——'al-Sayyida Nafisa, sa légende, son culte et son cimetière', *SI*, 44 (1976), pp.61–86, p.45; (1977), pp.27–55.

——'Sur un groupe de mausolées du cimetière du Caire', *REI*, 40 (1972), pp.189–95.

——'Sur deux monuments funéraires du cimetière d'al-Qarafa al-Kubra au Caire', *AI*, 12 (1974), pp.67–83.

Rashed, Roshdi. 'Ibn al-Haytham, mathématicien de l'époque fatimide', in Barrucand, ed., *L'Égypte fatimide*, pp.527–36.

van Reeth, J. '*Al-Qumāma* et le *Qā'im* de 400 AH: le trucage de la lampe sur le tombeau du Christ', in U. Vermeulen and D. De Smet, ed., *Egypt and Syria in the Fatimid, Ayyubid and Mamluk Eras* II, pp.171–90.

Répertoire chronologique d'épigraphie arabe, ed. Ét. Combe, J. Sauvaget, G. Wiet, et al. Cairo, 1933– .

Richard, J. 'Les Bases maritimes des fatimides, leurs corsaires et l'occupation franque en Syrie', in U. Vermeulen and D. De Smet, ed., *Egypt and Syria in the Fatimid, Ayyubid and Mamluk Eras* II, pp.115–29.

Richards, D. S. 'A Fatimid Petition and "Small Decree" from Sinai', *Israel Oriental Studies*, 3 (1973), pp.140–58.

——'Fragments of a Slave Dealer's Day-book From Fusṭāṭ', in Yūsuf Rāghib, ed., *Documents de l'Islam Médiéval: Nouvelles perspectives de re-*

cherche. Cairo 1991, pp.89–96.
——'Shāwar', *EI2.*
Rosenthal, Franz. 'Al-Mubashshir ibn Fātik', *Oriens,* 13–14 (1961), pp.133–58.
——'al-Makrīzī, Takī al-Dīn Abū'l-'Abbās Aḥmad b. 'Alī b. 'Abd al-Ḳādir (766–845/1364–1442)', *EI2.*
Rousset, Marie-Odile. 'La Céramique des XIe et XIIe siècle en Égypte et au Bilād al-Shām: État de la question', in Barrucand, ed., *L'Égypte fatimide,* pp.249–64.
Russel, D. 'Are There any Remains of the Fatimid Palaces of Cairo?', *JARCE,* 3 (1964), pp.115–21.
Sabra, Abd al-Hamid. 'Ibn al Haytham and the Visual-Ray Hypothesis', in Nasr, ed., *Ismaili Contributions to Islamic Culture,* pp.187–216.
Saifuddin, Ja'far us Sadiq M. al-Aqmar. *A Living Testimony to the Fatemiyeen.* Croydon, Surrey, 2000.
Saleh, Abdel Hamid. 'Le Rôle des bédouins d'Égypte à l'époque fatimide', *RSO,* 54 (1980), pp.51–65.
——'Une Source de Qalqašandī, Mawādd al-bayān et son auteur, 'Alī b. Ḫalaf', *Arabica,* 20 (1973), pp.192–200.
Saleh, Marlis Joan. 'Government Relations with the Coptic Community in Egypt during the Fāṭimid Period (358–567AH/ 969–1171CE)'. Ph.D. dissertation, University of Chicago, 1995.
Salinger, Gerard. 'A Muslim Mirror for Princes', *Muslim World,* 46 (1956), pp.24–39.
Samir, Samir Khalil. 'The Role of the Christians in the Fāṭimid Government Services of Egypt to the Reign of al-Ḥāfiẓ', *Medieval Encounters,* 2 (1996), pp.177–92.
Sanders, Paula. 'Claiming the Past: Ghadîr Khumm and the Rise of Ḥâfiẓî Historiography in Late Fâṭimid Egypt', *SI,* 75 (1992), pp.81–104.
——'The Court Ceremonial of the Fatimid Caliphate in Egypt', Ph.D. dissertation, Princeton University, 1984.
——'From Court Ceremony to Urban Language: Ceremonial in Fatimid Cairo and Fustat', in C. E. Bosworth et al., ed., *The Islamic World from Classical to Modern Times: Essays in Honor of Bernard Lewis.* Princeton, NJ, 1989, pp.311–21.
——'The Fāṭimid State, 969–1171', in Petry, ed., *The Cambridge History of Egypt,* vol.1, pp.151–74.
——'A New Source for the History of Fāṭimid Ceremonial: The *Rasā'il al-'Amīdī*', *AI,* 25 (1991), pp.127–31.
——*Ritual, Politics and the City in Fatimid Cairo.* Albany, NY, 1994.

Sayyid, Ayman Fu'ād. 'L'Art du livre', in *Dossiers d'Archéologie,* 233 (May 1998): *Égypte, L'Âge d'or des Fatimides,* pp.80–3.

——*La Capitale de l'Égypte jusqu'à l'époque fatimide (al-Qâhira et al-Fustât) : essai de reconstitution topographique.* Beirut and Stuttgart, 1998.

——*al-Dawla al-fāṭimiyya fī Miṣr: tafsīr jadīd.* Cairo, 1992; 2nd ed., Cairo, 2000.

——'Dirāsa naqdiyya li-maṣādir ta'rīkh al-Fāṭimiyyīn fī Miṣr', in *Dirāsāt ʿarabiyya wa islāmiyya muhdā ilā Maḥmūd Muḥammad Shākir.* Cairo, 1982, pp.129–79.

——'Early Methods of Book Composition: al-Maqrīzī's Draft of the Kitāb al-Khiṭaṭ' in *The Codicology of Islamic Manuscripts, Proceedings of the Second Conference of Al-Furqān Islamic Heritage Foundation, 1993* (London, 1995), pp.93–101.

——'Le Grand Palais fatimide au Caire', in Barrucand, ed., *L'Égypte fatimide,* pp.117–25.

——'Khizānat kutub al-Fāṭimiyyīn, hal baqiya minhā shay'?' in *Majallat Maʿhad al-makhṭūṭāt al-ʿarabiyya,* 42 (1998), pp.7–32.

——'Lumières nouvelles sur quelques sources de l'histoire fatimide en Égypte', *AI,* 13 (1977), pp.1–41.

——'al-Madāris fī Miṣr qabla al-ʿaṣr al-ayyūbī', in ʿAbd al-ʿAẓīm Ramaḍān, ed., *Ta'rīkh al-madāris fī Miṣr al-islāmiyya,* Cairo, 1992, pp.87–136.

——'Nuṣūṣ ḍā'iʿa min Akhbār Miṣr li-l-Musabbiḥī', *AI,* 17 (1981), pp.1–54.

——'Remarques sur la composition des Ḫiṭaṭ de Maqrīzī d'après un manuscrit autographe', in *Hommages à la mémoire de Serge Sauneron, II, Égypte post-pharaonique,* IFAO (1979), pp.231–58 + plates.

——'Tanẓīm al-ʿaṣīma al-fāṭimiyya wa idāratuhā fī zaman al-Fāṭimiyyīn', *AI,* 24 (1988): Arabic pp.1–14.

——*Ta'rīkh al-madhāhib al-dīniyya fī bilād al-Yaman ḥattā nihāyat al-qarn al-sādis al-hijrī.* Cairo, 1988.

Sayili, Aydin. *The Observatory in Islam.* Ankara, 1960.

Scanlon, George T. 'Fāṭimid Filters: Archaeology and Olmer's Typology', *AI,* 9 (1970), pp.37–51.

——'Fustat and the Islamic Art of Egypt', *Archeology,* 21 (1968), pp.188–195.

——'Leadership in the Qarmatian Sect', *BIFAO,* 59 (1960), pp.29–48.

——'A Note on Fatimid-Saljuq Trade', in D. S. Richards, ed., *Islamic Civilization.* Oxford, 1973, pp.265–74.

Schacht, Joseph, and Max Meyerhof. *The Medico-Philosophical Controversy between Ibn Butlan of Baghdad and Ibn Ridwan of Cairo: A Contribution to the History of Greek Learning Among the Arabs.* Cairo, 1937.

Schätze der Kalifen. See Seipel, Wilfried, ed.

Schlumberger, Gutave. *Campagnes du Roi Amaury 1 er de Jérusalem en Égypte au XIIe siècle.* Paris, 1906.

Seipel, Wilfried, ed. *Schätze der Kalifen: Islamische Kunst zur Fatimidenzeit: eine Ausstellung des Kunsthistorischen Museums Wien.* Vienna, 1998.

Setton, Kenneth M., ed. *A History of the Crusades:* Vol.1, *The First Hundred Years,* ed. M. W. Baldwin. 2nd ed., Philadelphia, 1955.

Shaked, Shaul. *A Tentative Bibliography of Geniza Documents.* Paris, 1964.

Sharon, Moshe. 'A New Fâṭimid Inscription from Ascalon and its Historical Setting', *'Atiqot,* 26 (1995), pp.61–86.

——*Corpus Inscriptionum Arabicarum Palestinae.* Leiden, 1997, vol.1 (A); Leiden, 1999, vol.2 (B–C).

al-Shayyāl, Jamāl al-Dīn. 'The Fatimid Documents as a Source for the History of the Fatimids and Their Institutions', *Bulletin of the Faculty of Arts, Alexandria University,* 8 (1954), pp.3–12.

——'Kitāb Anīs fī akhbār Tinnīs', *Majallat al-majmaʿ al-ʿilm al-ʿirāqī,* 14 (1967), pp.151–89.

——*Majmūʿat al-wathāʾiq al-fāṭimiyya.* Cairo, 1958.

——'Awwal ustādh li-awwal madrasa fi'l-Iskandariyya al-islāmiyya', *Majallat Kulliyyat al-Adāb, Alexandria University,* 11 (1957), pp.3–29.

Shoshan, Boaz. 'Fatimid Grain Policy and the Post of the Muḥtasib', *IJMES,* 13 (1981), pp.181–9.

Silvestre de Sacy, Antoine I. *Exposé de la religion des Druzes.* Paris, 1838; repr., Paris, 1964.

Smoor, Pieter. 'Fāṭimid Poets and the 'Takhalluṣ' that Bridges the Nights of Time to the Imām of Time', *Der Islam,* 68 (1991), pp.232–62.

——'Al-Mahdī's Tears: Impressions of Fāṭimid Court Poetry', in U. Vermeulen and D. De Smet, ed., *Egypt and Syria in the Fatimid, Ayyubid and Mamluk Eras* II, pp.131–70.

——'"The Master of the Century": Fāṭimid Poets in Cairo', in U. Vermeulen and D. De Smet, ed., *Egypt and Syria in the Fatimid, Ayyubid and Mamluk Eras* I, pp.139–63.

——'Palace and Ruin, a Theme for Fāṭimid Poets?' *WO,* 22 (1991), pp.94–104.

——'The Poet's House: Fiction and Reality in the Works of the "Fāṭimid" Poets', *Quaderni di Studi Arabi,* 10/1992 (1993), pp.45–62.

——'Wine, Love, and Praise for the Fāṭimid Imāms, The Enlightened of God', *ZDMG,* 142 (1992), pp.90–104.

Sourdel, D. 'Biens fonciers constitués en waqf en Syrie fatimide pour

une famille de Sarifs damascains', *JESHO*, 15 (1972), pp.269–96.
Staffa, Susan Jane. *Conquest and Fusion: The Social Evolution of Cairo, AD 642–1850*. Leiden, 1977.
Stern, Samuel M. 'Cairo as the Centre of the Ismāʿīlī Movement', *Colloque international sur l'histoire du Caire*. Cairo, 1972, pp.437–50, repr. in *Studies in Early Ismāʿīlism*, pp.234–56.
——*Coins and Documents from the Medieval Middle East*. London, 1986.
——'The Early Ismāʿīlī Missionaries in North-West Persia and in Khurāsān and Transoxania', *BSOAS*, 23 (1960), pp.56–90, repr. in *Studies in Early Ismāʿīlism*, pp.189–233.
——'An Embassy of the Byzantine Emperor to the Fatimid Caliph al-Muʿizz', *Byzantion*, 20 (1950), pp.239–58, repr. in *History and Culture*, item 9.
——'The Epistle of the Fatimid Caliph al-Āmir (al-Hidāya al-Āmiriyya)—Its Date and Its Purpose', *JRAS* (1950), pp.20–31, repr. in *History and Culture*, item 10.
——'A Fatimid Decree of the Year 524AH/1130AD', *BSOAS*, 23 (1960), pp.439–55.
——*Fatimid Decrees: Original Documents from the Fatimid Chancery*. London, 1964.
——'Heterodox Ismāʿīlism at the Time of Al-Muʿizz', *BSOAS*, 17 (1955), pp.10–33, repr. in *Studies in Early Ismāʿīlism*, pp.257–88.
——*History and Culture in the Medieval Muslim World*. London, 1984.
——'Ismāʿīlīs and Qarmaṭians', in *L'Élaboration de l'Islam*. Paris, 1961, pp.99–108, repr. in *Studies in Early Ismāʿīlism*, pp.289–98.
——'Ismaʿili Propaganda and Fatimid Rule in Sind', *Islamic Culture*, 23 (1949), pp.298–307, repr. in *Studies in Early Ismāʿīlism*, pp.177–88.
——'Al-Mahdī's Reign According to the 'Uyūn al-Akhbār', in *Studies in Early Ismāʿīlism*, pp.96–145.
——'An Original Document from the Fatimid Chancery Concerning Italian Merchants', *Studi orientalistici in onore di Giorgio Levi Della Vida*, Rome, 1956, vol.2, pp.529–38, repr. in *Coins and Documents*, item 5.
——'A Petition to the Fāṭimid Caliph al-Mustanṣir Concerning a Conflict within the Jewish Community', *Revue des études juives*, 127 (1969), pp.203–22, repr. in *Coins and Documents*, item 7.
——*Studies in Early Ismāʿīlism*. Jerusalem and Leiden, 1983.
——'The Succession to the Fatimid Imam al-Āmir, the Claims of the later Fatimids to the Imamate, and the Rise of Ṭayyibī Ismailism', *Oriens*, 4 (1951), pp.193–255, repr. in *History and Culture*, item 11.
——'Three Petitions of the Fāṭimid Period', *Oriens*, 15 (1962), pp.172–

209, repr. in *Coins and Documents*, item 6.

Stillman, Yedida, and Paula Sanders. 'Ṭirāz', *EI2*.

Stillman, N. A. 'A Case of Labor Problems in Medieval Egypt', *IJMES*, 5 (1974), pp.194–201.

——'The Eleventh-century Merchant House of Ibn 'Awkal (a Geniza Study)', *JESHO*, 16 (1973), pp.15–88.

Surūr, Muḥammad Jamāl al-Dīn. *al-Dawla al-fāṭimiyya fī Miṣr: siyāsatuhā al-dākhiliyya wa maẓāhir al-ḥaḍāra fī 'adhihā*. Cairo, 1965–1966, 1974, 1979.

——*al-Dawla al-fāṭimiyya fī Miṣr fī al-qarnayn al-rābi' wa al-khāmis min al-hijra*. Cairo, 1957, 1970.

——*Miṣr fī 'aṣr al-dawla al-fāṭimiyya*. Cairo, 1960.

——*al-Nufūdh al-fāṭimī fī bilād al-Shām wa'l-'Irāq fī'l-qarnayn al-rābi' wa'l-khāmis ba'd al-hijra*. Cairo, 1964.

——*al-Nufūdh al-fāṭimī fī jazīrat al-'arab*. Cairo, 1950, 1957, 1959, 1964.

——*Siyāsat al-Fāṭimiyīn al-khārijiyya*. Cairo, 1967 and 1976.

——*Ta'rīkh al-dawla al-fāṭimiyya*. Cairo, 1994.

Tabbaa, Yasser. 'The Transformation of Arabic Writing: Part 1, Qur'ānic Calligraphy', *Ars Orientalis*, 21, pp.119–48.

——'The Transformation of Arabic Writing: Part 2, The Public Text', *Ars Orientalis*, 24, pp.119–47.

Talbi, Mohamed. *L'Emirat aghlabide*. Paris, 1966.

Tāmir, 'Ārif. *Arwā, bint al-Yaman*. Cairo, 1970.

——*al-Ḥākim bi-amr Allāh: khalīfa, wa imām, wa muṣliḥ*. Beirut, 1982.

——*al-Khalīfa al-fāṭimī al-khāmis al-'Azīz bi-Allāh, qāhir al-Qarāmiṭa wa Aftikīn*. Beirut, 1982.

——*Malikat al-Yaman*. Latakia, Syria, 1986.

——*al-Mu'izz li-dīn Allāh al-fāṭimī, wāḍi' usus al-waḥda al-'arabiyya al-kubra*. Beirut, 1982.

——*al-Mustanṣir bi-llāh al-fāṭimī*. Beirut, 1990.

——*al-Qā'im wa al-Manṣūr al-fāṭimiyyān: amāma thawrat al-khawārij*. Beirut, 1982.

——*al-Qarāmiṭa bayna al-iltizām wa'l-inkār*. Damascus, 1996.

——*al-Qarāmiṭa: aṣluhum, nash'atuhum, ta'rīkhuhum, Ḥurūuhum*. Beirut, 1960.

——*'Ubayd Allāh al-Mahdī*. Beirut, 1990.

Taylor, Christopher. 'Reevaluating the Shi'i Role in the Development of Monumental Islamic Funerary Architecture: the Case of Egypt', *Muqarnas*, 9 (1992), pp.1–10.

Thiry, J. 'L'Égypte et le déclin de l'Afrique du Nord (XIe – XIIe siècle)', in Vermeulen and De Smet, ed., *Egypt and Syria in the Fatimid, Ayyubid and Mamluk Eras* II, pp.237–48.

Tibi, Amin. 'Byzantine-Fatimid Relations in the Reign of Al-Muʿizz Li-Din Allah (r.953–975AD) as Reflected in Primary Arabic Sources', *Graeco-Arabica* 4 (1991).

Traboulsi, Samer F. 'Gender, Authority and Legitimacy in Medieval Yemen: The Case of Arwa Bint Ahmad', MA thesis, American University of Beirut, 1998.

Troupeau, G. 'La Description de la Nubie d'al-Uswani', *Arabica*, 1 (1954), pp.276–88.

——'Un Traité de christologie attribute au Calife fatimide al-Muʿizz', *AI*, 15 (1979), pp.11–24.

Tyan, Emile. *Histoire de l'organisation judiciaire en pays d'Islam.* 2nd ed., Leiden, 1960.

Udovitch, Abraham L. 'Fatimid Cairo: Crossroads of World Trade – from Spain to India', in Barrucand, ed., *L'Égypte fatimide*, pp.681–91.

——'A Tale of Two Cities; Commercial Relations between Cairo and Alexandria', in Miskimin et al. ed., *The Medieval City.* New Haven, 1978, pp.143–62.

——'Merchants and *Amīrs*: Government and Trade in Eleventh-Century Egypt', (The Medieval Levant: Studies in Memory of Eliyahu Ashtor) *Asian and African Studies*, 22 (1988), pp.53–72.

Vajda, G. 'L'Aventure tragique d'un Qadi maghrébien en Égypte fatimide', *Arabica*, 15 (1968), pp.1–15.

——'La Masyaha d'Ibn al-Hattāb al-Rāzī: Contribution à l'histoire du sunnisme en Égypte fatimide', *BEO*, 23 (1970), pp.21–99.

van Berchem, van Doorninck, van Ess and van Reeth, see under Berchem, Doorninck, Ess and Reeth.

Vatikiotis, P. J. *The Fatimid Theory of State.* Lahore, 1957; 2nd rev. ed., Lahore, 1981.

——'The Rise of Extremist Sects and the Dissolution of the Fatimid Empire in Egypt', *IC*, 31 (1957), pp.17–25.

Vermeulen, U. and D. De Smet, ed., *Egypt and Syria in the Fatimid, Ayyubid and Mamluk Eras* I*: Proceedings of the 1st, 2nd and 3rd International Colloquium organized at the Katholieke Univeriteit Leuven in May 1992, 1993 and 1994.* Louvain, 1995.

Vermeulen, U. and D. De Smet, ed., *Egypt and Syria in the Fatimid, Ayyubid and Mamluk Eras* II*: Proceedings of the 4th and 5th International Colloquium organized at the Katholieke Univeriteit Leuven in May 1995 and 1996.* Louvain, 1998.

Viré, François. 'Le Traité de l'art de volerie (*kitāb al-bayzara*) rédigé vers 385/995 par le Grand-Fanconnier du calife fāṭimide al-'Azīz bi-llāh', *Arabica*, 12 (1965), pp.1–26; 113–39; 262–96 and 13 (1966), pp.39–76.

von Grunebaum, G. E. 'The Nature of the Fatimid Achievement', *Colloque international sur l'histoire du Caire*. Cairo, 1972, pp.199–215.

Walker, Paul E. *Abū Ya'qūb al-Sijistānī: Intellectual Missionary*. London, 1996.

——'Abū Tammām and his *Kitāb al-shajara*: A New Ismaili Treatise from Tenth-Century Khurasan', *JAOS*, 114 (1994), pp.343–52.

——*The Advent of the Fatimids,* see Ibn al-Haytham.

——'Another Family of Fatimid Chief Qadis: The al-Fariqis', *Journal of Druze Studies*, 1 (2000), pp. 49–69.

——'A Byzantine Victory Over the Fatimids at Alexandretta (971)', *Byzantion*, 42 (1972), pp.431–40.

——'The "Crusade" of John Tzimisces in the Light of New Arabic Evidence', *Byzantion*, 47 (1977), pp.301–27.

——*Early Philosophical Shiism: The Ismaili Neoplatonism of Abū Ya'qūb al-Sijistānī*. Cambridge, 1993.

——'Fatimid Institutions of Learning', *JARCE*, 34 (1997), pp.179–200.

——*Ḥamīd al-Dīn al-Kirmānī: Ismaili Thought in the Age of al-Ḥākim*. London, 1999.

——'The Ismaili Da'wa and the Fatimid Caliphate', in C. Petry, ed., *Cambridge History of Egypt*, vol.1, pp.120–50.

——'The Ismaili Da'wa in the Reign of the Fatimid Caliph al-Ḥākim', *JARCE*, 30 (1993), pp.160–82.

——'An Isma'ili Version of the Heresiography of the Seventy-two Erring Sects' in Daftary, ed., *Mediaeval Isma'ili History and Thought*, pp.161–77.

——'Succession to Rule in the Shiite Caliphate', *JARCE*, 32 (1995), pp.239–64.

——*The Wellsprings of Wisdom*. Salt Lake City, 1994.

Walker, Paul E. and W. Madelung. *An Ismaili Heresiography: The 'Bāb al-Shayṭān' from Abū Tammām's* Kitāb al-Shajara, ed. and English tr. Leiden, 1998.

Wiet, Gaston. *Les Marchés du Caire*. Cairo, 1979.

——'Matériaux pour un corpus inscriptionum arabicarum, part 1: Égypte, vol.2', *MIFAO*, 52 (1929–30).

——'Une Nouvelle inscription fatimide au Caire', *JA* (1961), pp.13–20.

——'Nouvelles Inscriptions fatimides', *BIE*, 24 (1941–42), pp.145–58.

——'Un Proconsul fatimide de Syrie: Anushtakin Dizbiri (mort en 433/1042)', *Mélanges de l'Université Saint-Joseph,* 46 (1970–1), pp.383–407.

——'[Review of] Ibn Muyassar, *Annales d'Égypte,* ed. H. Massé', *JA,* 18 (1921), pp.65–125.

——'Le Traité des famines de Maqrizi', *JESHO,* 5 (1962), pp.1–90.

Williams, Caroline. 'The Cult of Alid Saints in the Fatimid Monuments of Cairo, Part I: The Mosque of al-Aqmar', *Muqarnas,* 1 (1983), pp.37–52.

——'The Cult of Alid Saints in the Fatimid Monuments of Cairo, Part 2: The Mausolea', *Muqarnas,* 3 (1985), pp.39–60.

——'The Qur'anic Inscriptions on the *Tabut* of al-Husayn', *Islamic Art,* 2 (1987), pp.3–14.

Wright, Owen. 'Music at the Fatimid Court: The Evidence of the Ibn al-Ṭaḥḥān Mansucript', in Barrucand, ed., *L'Égypte fatimide,* pp.537–45.

Wüstenfeld, Ferdinand. *Geschichte des Fatimiden-Chalifen.* Göttingen, 1881; repr. Hildesheim, 1976.

al-Ya'lāwī (Yalaoui), Muḥammad. *al-Adab bi-Ifrīqiya fi'l-'ahd al-fāṭimī.* Beirut, 1986.

——'Controverse entre le Fatimide Al-Mu'izz et l'Omeyyade Al-Nasir, d'après le *Kitab al-majālis wa-l-musāyarāt* du cadi Nu'mān', *CT,* 26 (1978), pp.7–33.

——'Ibn Hani, poète chi'ite et chantre des Fatimides au Maghreb', in Julien, ed., *Les Africains.* vol.6, pp.97–125.

——'Les Relations entre Fatimides d'Ifriqiya et Omeyyades d'Espagne à travers le *Diwan* d'Ibn Hani', in *Acta 2 Coloquio Hispano-tunecino* (1972) pp.13–30.

——'Sur une possible régence du prince fatimide Abdallah b. Mu'izz en Ifriqiya au IV/Xe siècle', *CT,* 22 (1974), pp.7–22.

——*Un Poète chiite d'occident au IV/Xè siècle: Ibn Hani' al-Andalousi.* Tunis, 1976. Arabic tr. by author, *Ibn Hānī' al-Maghribī al-Andalusī shā'ir al-dawla al-fāṭimiyya.* Beirut, 1985.

Zakkar, Suhayl. *Akhbār al-Qarāmiṭa fi'l-Aḥsā', al-Shām, al-'Irāq, al-Yaman.* Beirut, 1980.

——*The Emirate of Aleppo 1004–1094.* Beirut, 1971.

——*Madkhal ilā ta'rīkh al-ḥurūb al-ṣalībiyya.* Beirut, 1973.

Index